T0306074

# Transnational Law and State Transformation

This book contributes new theoretical insight and in-depth empirical analysis about the relationship between transnational legality, state change and the globalisation of markets.

The role of transnational economic law in influencing and reorganising national systems of governance evidences the constitutional dimensions of global capitalism: the power to institute new rules and limits for national states. This form of new constitutionalism does not undermine the state but transforms it by eroding national capacities and implanting global alternatives. While leading scholars in the field have emphasised the much-needed value of case studies, there are no studies available which consider the cumulative impact of multiple axes of transnational legal ordering on the national state or its constitution. The monograph addresses this empirical gap, whilst expanding the theoretical scope of the field.

Mongolia's recent transformation as a mineral-exporting country provides a rare opportunity to witness economic and legal globalisation in process. Based on a careful empirical analysis of national law and policy-making, the book traces the way distinctive processes of transnational legal ordering have reorganised and reframed the governance of Mongolia's mining sector, specifically by redistributing state power in relation to the market, sub-national administrations and civil society. The book investigates the role of international financial institutions, multinational corporations and non-governmental organisations in normative transmission, as well as the critical role of national actors in embedding transnational investment norms within the domestic legal and policy environment. As the book demonstrates, however, the constitutional ramifications of transnational legal ordering extend beyond the mining regime itself into more fundamental questions of the trajectory of state transformation, institutionally and ideologically.

The book will be of interest to scholars of international law, global governance and the political economy of development.

**Dr Jennifer Lander** is Lecturer in Law at De Montfort University in Leicester (UK). She received her PhD in Law from the University of Warwick, where she consequently held an Early Career Fellowship at the Institute of Advanced Study prior to taking up her post at De Montfort University.

## Part of the Law, Development and Globalization series

*Julio Faundez*, University of Warwick, UK
*Adriaan Bedner*, University of Leiden, The Netherlands

The Art of Building Fences: Constructing New Patterns of Enclosure and Openness on the "Final Frontier"
Source: Photo taken by the author on the Orkhon River in Selenge *aimag*.

For information about the series and details of previous and forthcoming titles, seehttps://www.routledge.com/law/series/CAV30

# Transnational Law and State Transformation

The Case of Extractive Development in Mongolia

Jennifer Lander

Routledge
Taylor & Francis Group
a GlassHouse Book

First published 2020
by Routledge
2 Park Square, Milton Park, Abingdon, Oxon OX14 4RN

and by Routledge
52 Vanderbilt Avenue, New York, NY 10017

*Routledge is an imprint of the Taylor & Francis Group, an informa business*

*A Glasshouse book*

First issued in paperback 2021

*British Library Cataloguing-in-Publication Data*
A catalogue record for this book is available from the British Library

*Library of Congress Cataloging-in-Publication Data*
Names: Lander, Jennifer, author.
Title: Transnational law and state transformation : the case of extractive development in Mongolia / Jenny Lander.
Description: Abingdon, Oxon ; New York, NY : Routledge, 2020. | Series: Law, development and globalization | Based on author's thesis (doctoral -University of Warwick, 2017) issued under title: The law and politics of foreign direct investment, democracy and extractive development in Mongolia : a case study of new constitutionalism on the 'final frontier'. | Includes bibliographical references and index.
Identifiers: LCCN 2019033610 (print) | LCCN 2019033611 (ebook) | ISBN 9780367076641 (hardback) | ISBN 9780429021954 (ebook)
Subjects: LCSH: Mining law—Mongolia. | Investments, Foreign—Law and legislation—Mongolia. | Law and economic development—Mongolia. | Law—Mongolia—Foreign influences. | Mongolia—Politics and government—1992–
Classification: LCC KPJ334.4 .L36 2020 (print) | LCC KPJ334.4 (ebook) | DDC 343.517/3077—dc23
LC record available at https://lccn.loc.gov/2019033610
LC ebook record available at https://lccn.loc.gov/2019033611

ISBN: 978-0-367-07664-1 (hbk)
ISBN: 978-1-03-208606-4 (pbk)
ISBN: 978-0-429-02195-4 (ebk)

Typeset in Galliard
by codeMantra

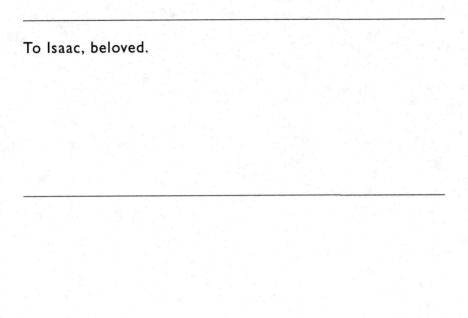

To Isaac, beloved.

# Contents

# Tables and Maps

## Tables

## Maps

# Preface
## The state has forgotten its reason for being?

"Yet the critique of capitalism is out fashion"
Ellen Meiksins Wood (1995: 1)

In 2014, I interviewed a leader of an environmental movement which had been turning up the heat on the Mongolian government since 2005 for failing to effectively regulate the mining sector. A soft-spoken man, he said simply, 'the State has forgotten its reason for being.' Five years later, his words ring in my ears as I put the finishing touches on this manuscript.

There are many complex reasons why the Mongolian state may be suffering from amnesia about its *raison d'etre*, and, of course, the assessment of such a condition fundamentally depends upon one's vantage point. For instance, perceptions will diverge as to the nature and purpose of the state depending on whether you are an environmental activist or a foreign investor in Mongolia, and whether you are negatively impacted by the effects of mineral extraction or someone who wants to expand such activity. This book cannot pretend to definitively resolve the question of state change satisfactorily for all parties to the claim. What the book does try to achieve is a deeper understanding of the *process* of state transformation in the pursuit of global economic competitiveness, and offer some explanation as to why this process is fraught with legitimacy crises as national publics and global economic constituencies seek to influence its trajectory.

Since starting this research project in 2012, I have been consistently struck by the correlation between mining, markets and the recurring question about the role – and identity – of the state. Twenty years ago, the discovery of vast riches in the South Gobi and across Mongolia sparked a mining boom, as foreign investors, multinational and domestic companies and "ninja" artisanal miners scrambled for the good stuff buried beneath the Mongolian steppe. Hopes were high for development as the country's mineral wealth was subjected to exploration and extraction – and yet, twenty years later, it is hard to be optimistic about Mongolia's current socio-economic and political trajectory.

Central Ulaanbaatar has grown into a shiny, expensive and relatively cosmopolitan capital, boasting luxury brands like Gucci and Louis Vuitton, proliferating coffee shops where you can get as fine an espresso as anywhere and a growing number of global fast-food chain restaurants. Middle- and upper-class Mongolians of the younger generation are increasingly learning English as the second language of choice and seeking education abroad to increase their chances of competitive earnings in top jobs in the public and private sectors. Fashionable, entrepreneurial and talented, this generation of young Mongolians appears to be embracing the "good life" of market capitalism: choice, opportunity, individuality and global exposure.

But there is a long way to fall from the top, and the gap widens between those on the ladder and those waiting to get on the first rung. The *ger* districts which ring Ulaanbaatar grow deeper and wider, as rural migrants abandon the increasing poverty associated with the herding economy for the lotto ticket to The City. For residents on the periphery of Ulaanbaatar, there is no guaranteed access to electricity, running water, education, healthcare, waste disposal services, heating and public transport. During the minus 40-degree Celsius winters, the lethal combination of burning wood, coal, plastic – anything flammable – spreads thick pollution into every corner of the river valley. Cancers of all kinds are on the rise. Meat prices are at their highest ever, as Mongolia begins to export more and more of its livestock to China. Anxiety hums beneath the heaving traffic.

Outside of Ulaanbaatar, the air is cleaner but livelihoods are vulnerable. The approximate 20 to 30% of the Mongolian population that continues to practise semi-nomadic pastoralism faces an unprecedented degree of change in their natural environment. Pasture quality and water access have diminished since the withdrawal of state support for the herding economy following the collapse of the socialist regime in the early 1990s. The dramatic increase in the number of goats on the Mongolian steppe – largely in response to the liberalisation of cashmere prices – has led to systematic soil erosion, speeding up already rapid processes of desertification. Dust storms, infused with coal dust from the South Gobi, blow across the country, reaching as far as the West Coast of the United States.

It boggles the mind as to why a country with only three million people and vast mineral riches should be in a position of *growing* economic insecurity, socio-environmental vulnerability and rapidly reducing public morale. And most Mongolians I have spoken to blame the government. Allegations of corruption, misuse of public funds, nepotism and elitism infuse everyday conversation. Politics and, increasingly, democracy are blamed for Mongolia's development woes. If only a strong leader would rise up.

Equally, when speaking with the foreign minority working in corporate, investment and international development sectors, the story shows remarkable parallels. It is the government's fault that it failed to take advantage of the boom in global commodity prices. The government overspent during good times and now the country is suffering, due to a lack of "fiscal discipline." Parliament kept trying to change laws rather than promoting a stable investment environment. Investment and mining policies and legislative frameworks have been too inconsistent and unstable in the past, and now Mongolia is paying the price. Less cynical narratives suggest that the relatively young market democracy is simply "learning from mistakes"; others darkly surmise that the state has been captured by political elites with no interests apart from their own advancement.

Missing from these common narratives where disappointment in the state is the common denominator is any systematic understanding of the inter-dependencies between market-led development and a changing role for the state. The hapless or malevolent depictions of the state do not have much explanatory value as to why successive governments seem unable to satisfy the demands of domestic publics and foreign investors, for example. The emphasis on personal abuses of power and individual case studies of corruption in the government – which I do not dispute – hides the reality of deeper structural shifts in the overall pattern of national governance when it comes to Mongolia's natural resource wealth. While these patterns are not deterministic, it is important to identify the grain which incentivises state power in particular directions and which shapes the policy options on the table at any given time. I hope that this book will illuminate some of the grain against which social, economic, political and legal relations are being shaped in the pursuit of market-led "development," in Mongolia and beyond.

*Ulaanbaatar, Mongolia*
*June 2019*

# Acknowledgements

I write these acknowledgements as I fly from Ulaanbaatar back to the United Kingdom. Right before I left for Chinggis Khan International Airport, I asked my friend if we could stop by the old Soviet apartment block where I spent almost five of the happiest years of my life as a teenager, near the Jukov Museum. The park in front of the building is mostly a car park now. The hill just beyond the building which used to be the outskirt of the city – usually featuring just a *ger* or two – is now covered in new apartment blocks, a hotel and a high-end supermarket. My old grey block of apartments – five stories high, eight stairwells long – looks faded and nostalgic next to these new developments. But this place must be acknowledged as the origin story of the book. Here, I first learned of the mining boom in the late 1990s and early 2000s, heard tales of artisanal "ninja" mining and the rising interest of China, Canada, Australia and many others in Mongolian mineral wealth. This was the place where, as a ten-year old, I first asked my dad what a "market economy" was and what made it different to other kinds of economy, and where I learned first-hand about public disillusionment with social, political and economic changes in the name of development. I was yet to learn the role of law in all of it, which would come some years later.

Consequently, I want to acknowledge the people who took me to Mongolia in the first place. My parents – Alastair and Rebecca Lander – responded to the public health crisis gripping Mongolia in the wake of the post-Soviet "transition" in the 1990s, when levels of child malnutrition and undiagnosed infectious diseases dramatically increased with the collapse of the national health system. Equally, I want to acknowledge my sister Rachael, who has been a true friend – across continents and back – throughout the years. Fieldwork would also have been much less enjoyable without my dear extended "family" in Mongolia who welcomed me back as a twenty-something PhD student eager to learn more about the mining economy. In particular, I want to thank Oyuna and Uyanga, Rob and Marlene, Saikhnaa, Tseren, Suzi, Gabi, and Sam and Anne for their friendship and hospitality

This book would never have emerged without the support of colleagues and professors at Warwick Law School, where I did my graduate work (2012–2017). George Meszaros, my PhD supervisor, provided steadying guidance and constructive critical feedback at each stage of the PhD process, when much of the research which informs this book was conducted. I am also very thankful to Ann Stewart for her support through my PhD studies and beyond; she deserves special mention for her (gentle) prods to just get on with the book. I also want to gratefully acknowledge other faculty members at Warwick for their kindness and support at various phases of the thesis/book projects: Sam Adelman, Abdul Paliwala, Julio Faundez, Illan rua Wall, Sharifah Sekalala, Celine Tan, Kirsten McConnachie (now at the University of East Anglia), Dora Kostakopoulou, Andrew Williams, Stephen Connelly and James Harrison. A generous departmental scholarship from Warwick Law School enabled me to do the majority of the research for this book in the first place, for which I am grateful. I completed the manuscript at De Montfort Law School in Leicester in the company of new colleagues, to whom I am grateful for their warm welcome.

Many thanks to Nicola Sharpe and Colin Perrin at Routledge for their forbearance and guidance, as well as the series editors – Julio Faundez and Adriaan Bedner – who have provided helpful guidance and comments on the manuscript. Many thanks also to the long-enduring friends and colleagues, as well as anonymous reviewers, who provided feedback on draft chapters and the book proposal. Particular thanks to Pascale Hatcher for her encouragement and feedback. All input was gratefully received, and all errors and omissions are my own. While substantially revised, some of the data and arguments in Chapter 3 and 4 was published previously in the *Law, Social Justice and Global Development Journal* and part of Chapter 5 appears in *The Limits of Law and Development: Neoliberalism, Governance and Social Justice*, edited by Sam Adelman and Abdul Paliwala.

Along the way, there have been a number of friends who have spoken necessary words of both consolation and challenge in the process of completing this work. Rose, Shang-Chin, Rhiannon, Natalie, David, Rebekah, Alix, Sofia and Euge – thank you. Big thanks especially to Lisa, who travelled with me to Mongolia in 2014 and left me with a postcard saying "You can do it!!" scrawled almost illegibly on the back (I still have that postcard). Finally, I am very thankful to Revds. Mark Stafford and George Westhaver at Pusey House in Oxford, and Revds. Alastair Kirk and Kate Pearson at Warwick Chaplaincy for being tangible signs of God's love and presence over the years.

Finally, this book is dedicated to my husband Isaac, who has faithfully entertained my exhilarations and anxieties in the course of writing this book, and in the end wouldn't let me give up.

All glory be to the God who falls with every sparrow,
the One understands the complexity of power struggles and political economy,
Who is in the business of making all things new.

# Mongolian words and acronyms

*Please note that with regard to Mongolian names, the "surname" (patronymic) is indicated as an initial before the personal name, as is customary for formal reference in Mongolia (e.g. D. Batbold).

## Glossary of Mongolian words

| | |
|---|---|
| *Aimag* | – Province (territorial and administrative unit) |
| Soum | – District within a province |
| *Bagh* | – Sub-district within a district |
| *Khural* | – Council |
| *Khoshuun* | – Pre-socialist territorial and administrative unit |
| *Nutag* | – Pastoral district (customary) |
| *Negdel* | – Soviet agricultural cooperative |
| *Khot ail* | – Group of nomadic families who move together (customary) |
| *Tugrik* | – Mongolian currency |
| Deel | – Traditional Mongolian clothing |

## Acronyms

| | |
|---|---|
| ADB | – Asian Development Bank |
| BIT | – Bilateral Investment Treaty |
| BMZ | – Federal Ministry for Economic Cooperation and Development (Germany) |
| CAO | – Compliance Advisor Ombudsmen |
| CMEA | – (Soviet) Council for Mutual Economic Assistance |
| CRIRSCO | – Committee for Mineral Reserves International Reporting Standards |
| EBRD | – European Bank for Reconstruction and Development |
| EITI | – Extractive Industries Transparency Initiative |
| FDI | – Foreign Direct Investment |
| GDP | – Gross Domestic Product |

| | | |
|---|---|---|
| GIZ | – | Deutsche Gesellschaft für Internationale Zusammenarbeit (German Development Corporation) |
| GMI | – | Global Mining Initiative |
| HDF | – | Human Development Fund |
| IFC | – | International Finance Corporation (World Bank Group) |
| IIED | – | International Institute for Environment and Development |
| IMA | – | Invest Mongolia Agency |
| IMRI | – | Integrated Mineral Resource Initiative |
| IPC | – | Investment Protection Council |
| LDA | – | Local Development Agreement |
| MCC | – | Mongolian Copper Corporation |
| MIGA | – | Multilateral Investment Guarantee Agency (World Bank Group) |
| MNT | – | Mongolian currency code |
| MP | – | Member of Parliament |
| MPC | – | Minerals Policy Council |
| MPP | – | Mongolian People's Party (name of the MPRP after 2010) |
| MPR | – | Mongolian People's Republic |
| MPRP | – | Mongolian People's Revolutionary Party |
| NDA | – | National Development Agency |
| NGO | – | Non-governmental organisation |
| OTIA | – | Oyu Tolgoi Investment Agreement |
| PS | – | Performance Standards |
| SEFIL | – | Strategic Entities Foreign Investment Law |
| SGWMIR | – | South Gobi Water and Mining Industry Roundtable |
| SOE | – | State-Owned Enterprise |
| TPC | – | Tripartite Council |
| UMMRL | – | United Movement for Mongolian Rivers and Lakes |
| UNCTAD | – | United Nations Committee on Trade and Development |
| UNDP | – | United Nations Development Programme |
| UNIDO | – | United Nations Industrial Development Organisation |
| USD | – | U.S. Dollars |
| VAT | – | Value-Added Tax |
| VCP | – | Voluntary Code of Practice |

# Map of Mongolia

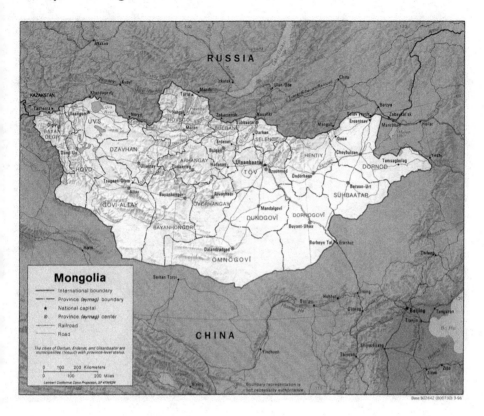

*Map 1* Administrative map of Mongolia.

# Part I

# Theory and summary of the book

# Chapter 1

# Transnational law, state transformation and global markets

## Economic development and material constitutional change

### Decoding "development": a socio-legal approach

> Whatever the response, the claim to expertise in optimising the lives of others is a claim to power, one that merits careful scrutiny.
>
> Tania Murray Li, *The Will to Improve* (2007: 5)

> Is law, for example, relatively autonomous, and if so, autonomous of what, and how relatively?
>
> E. P. Thompson, *The Poverty of Theory* (1978: 288)

The concept of development may be commonplace, but its meaning has proven elusive. Thousands of pages have been written by scholars from different disciplines to define the term in relationship to a particular goal or desired quality: sustainability, freedom, economic growth, human, green. These terms, however well intended, create a mirage over the complex policies and power struggles which imbue any so-called "development" strategy. If we are to get a conceptual grip on its material and normative implications, we must decode the mirage.

This book explores *the constitutional significance of extractive development through a socio-legal analysis of Mongolia's mining regime.* Recognising that readers may be coming to this book from a variety of disciplinary backgrounds, a few definitions are in order. Firstly, *extractive* development refers to an economic model that depends upon the exploration, extraction and export of non-renewable resources, usually with little or very limited processing (Acosta, 2013: 62). These resources are commonly understood to include minerals, oil and gas reserves, and water (i.e. hydropower), which form the raw material base of modern energy systems. The *development* side of the term refers to the contemporary concept of social progress which has dominated discourses of societal improvement since the end of the Second World War. The concept of "development" is a distinctly modern 'collective improvement strategy' (see Li, 2007; Lander, 2019) based upon the normative standards and experiences of industrialised consumer societies in the West (Ferguson, 1990; Craig and Porter, 2006; Li, 2007; Carroll, 2012b). When the terms "developing" and "developed" may be used from time to time in this book, they refer to the mainstream construction of a distinction between countries on the basis of this industrialised concept of development. Recognising the significant debates about the use of these terms, it is important to note that their use in this book refers to a mainstream discursive construction which this book hopes to unpick. The terms Global North and Global South are used to refer to the unequal distribution of resources and power which correlates with the division between countries on the developing/developed continuum.

There are many studies which focus on how countries in the Global South can effectively use natural resources to 'develop' (see Auty, 2001; Humphreys et al., 2007). Extractive development *strategies* are precisely the conglomeration of laws, policies and social institutions which organise extractive production in a manner intended to produce collective improvement along modern sensibilities of *progress*. This type of scholarship seeks primarily to produce policy prescriptions to improve a country's developmental trajectory (e.g. to increase economic growth or value in the production process). In contrast, this book takes a broadly sociological approach to extractive development. Instead of the question "how should extractive industries be organised to produce development?" it asks, "what kind of social change is produced in the pursuit of this goal?" Development itself is such a fickle and flimsy concept that starting with the substance of the social change it requires, authorises and justifies seems a good a place as any to start if we are to really get a grip on what it *means* in reality.

The reorganisation of economies in the name of development since the end of the Second World War has consistently engaged with broad-based processes of *institutional* change both within national states and at the international scale. While the precise focus of reform has altered and shifted with the re-articulation of the concept of development, a sociological analysis of development cannot escape from the effervescent presence of law. The reorganisation of economies is a distinctly socio-legal task, involving a fairly wholesale transformation of the political and regulatory relations of production (Cox, 1987; Wood, 1995). All organised forms of production, accumulation and redistribution have historically depended upon political-juridical institutions and relations, whether in the family, tribe, federation, empire or national state (ibid.: 251; Polanyi, 1944/2001: 59–70). Consequently, an economy is a distinctively social *institution*, thoroughly 'embedded and enmeshed' (ibid.: 250) within political and juridical relations. The creation of a new economic *order* in the pursuit of development relies upon the renegotiation of the authoritative rules and relations which governed the pre-existing system.

Socio-legal analysis views law as constitutive of social reality (including the economy). From a socio-legal methodological perspective, the relatively submerged nature of law does not render it any less central to the analysis, because the *context* and *sub-text* of law may be given as much if not more analytical emphasis as the legal texts themselves (Frerichs, 2012; Perry-Kessaris, 2013). This is the central distinction between a "socio-legal" and "legal" approach, the latter reading law from the standpoint of doctrinal coherency. As Amanda Perry-Kessaris writes in *Approaches to the Study of International Economic Law*, 'socio-legal approaches consider not only legal texts, but also the contexts in which they are created, destroyed, abused, avoided, and so on; and sometimes their sub-texts' (2013: 6). Citing Sabine Frerichs (2012: 9), Perry-Kessaris (ibid.) goes on to explain what these terms mean:

> By text I mean the legal text, that is, the written rules and doctrines, or what can be considered black letter law. By subtext I refer to the moral subtext of a legal text, that is, its implied or deeper meaning. This includes the different notions of justice underlying a legal argument which make it necessary also to read between the lines. By context I refer to the social context of a legal text, that is, its forceful link with reality. In this perspective, law is not a self-contained discourse but a powerful social institution.

This book adopts a socio-legal perspective by seeking to understand how contemporary extractive development strategies necessitate – and are enabled by – transformations in legal and political institutions and relationships. The scale of analysis is simultaneously national and transnational. Through the case study analysis of Mongolia, the book focuses on the national state as the mediating locus of transformation, although it brings a transnational perspective on legal ordering associated with global market-led development to bear on the question of state transformation. Virtually, all "national" economic strategies now revolve around becoming *globally* competitive, whether in relation to financial services, agriculture and manufacturing, extractive and energy industries, technology and telecommunication, health and education (see Braithwaite and Drahos, 2000). All of these economic sectors are governed by legal rules and norms that are increasingly *trans*national in their scope, meaning that a body of legality has achieved regulatory resonance and effectiveness across scales of jurisdiction (international, regional, national, sub-national) (ibid.).

It is safe to say that, in general, development strategies premised on finding a competitive niche in the global economy trigger a juggernaut of socio-legal change within national states to mitigate investment risk and effectively build markets (Carroll, 2012a). However, the normative drivers behind domestic governance reform to enable global economic integration have a distinctively *transnational* flavour. While rules and norms governing aspects of investment protection (e.g. non-discrimination, fair and equitable treatment, protections from expropriation, corporate liability, access to dispute resolution) may originally have their origins in Anglo-American legal systems (Schneiderman, 2008), these "local" norms have become effectively globalised through the multilateral and bilateral regimes governing trade and investment, global governance frameworks, alongside the evolving 'running code' (Calliess and Zumbansen, 2010) of private commercial legal practice. To be able to conceptualise the legal complexity associated with market-led development strategies, the traditional distinctions between domestic and international law offer little assistance (Berman, 2005). While national and international laws clearly still exist, the global economy is, in practice, regulated by a much more complex range of legal processes and norms which break down traditional binaries between national/ international, public/private and hard law/soft law (Zumbansen, 2012). Soft law norms like "good governance" or benchmarking ratings, for example, as well as private legal mechanisms (e.g. contract law and project finance structures) can have a very concrete regulatory effects within national states, particularly because they tangibly influence perceptions of investment risk (see Perry-Kessaris, 2011; Bhatt, forthcoming)

The concept of transnational law helps to identify the complex ways in which 'border-crossing regulatory regimes' (ibid.: 312) operate simultaneously *beyond* and *through* national jurisdictions. As Gregory Shaffer (2014: 3) proposes, transnational law refers quite simply to 'legal norms that apply across borders to parties located in more than one jurisdiction.' This definition helpfully includes not only public and private international law as separate categories, but also the '*interaction* of publicly and privately made law' (ibid., emphasis added). A complex array of legal norms regulates the global economy, some public, some private, some binding, some non-binding. According to Shaffer (ibid.: 1–2), viewing global economic integration as a transnational legal *process* recognises the way that 'these norms are constructed, carried and conveyed, always confronting national and local processes, which may block, adapt, translate or appropriate a transnational legal norm.' The emphasis on *ordering* focuses energy on tracing legal normative diffusion through stages of 'construction, flow and settlement' rather than primarily seeking to establish a new category or scale of law (see Shaffer, 2016). This is where the emphasis of transnational and global law scholarship diverges. Global law scholarship tends to focus on explaining the life of law "beyond" the state, often without reckoning with the ongoing significance of national jurisdictions as sources, targets and transit sites for transnational legal processes. The more limited focus of the transnational law concept on normative diffusion across borders is conceptually beneficial given the diversity of legal phenomena that exist beyond the exclusive control of the national state, yet in reality 'operate at more limited sub-global levels' (Twining, 2009: 24). "Global law" semantically suggests a higher order of denationalised (i.e. not national or international) law that exists *above* and *beyond* national states, whereas a transnational law perspective seeks to map the multidirectional flow of legal norms *across* and *within* legal borderlands (Shaffer, 2014: 214).

When it comes to the regulation of global markets, transnational legal norms have achieved a remarkable degree of consolidation (Braithwaite and Drahos, 2000). In contrast to norms that might require market competitiveness to be tamed for some other moral or social good (e.g. human rights or protection of environmental commons), the transnational mobility of market-facilitating legal norms is naturally reinforced by the accumulation incentives states have to participate in global markets, as well as the mechanisms which protect private capital and investment (see Bhatt, forthcoming). No state can be described as autonomous from the universal reach of global capitalism, which has achieved an unprecedented degree of hegemony in terms of economic organisation vis-à-vis the particular "legal structure" associated with processes of commodification (Cutler, 2005: 532, citing Kennedy, 1985: 976–977). As Cutler (ibid.) puts it, 'the commodity system presupposes laws of contract and property that legitimate and enforce private ownership of the means of production and exchange.' While capitalist economic systems originated within and expanded from particular *national* jurisdictions in Europe, 'each state itself experiences competitive imperatives to accumulate' within the global economy (Dunn, 2014: 84). Transnational legal norms are consequently mobilised through multilateral and bilateral investment and trade frameworks which facilitate capital mobility,[1] as well as the legal relations and economic power disparities that structure negotiations between agents and recipients of capital investment and states (Sassen, 2007: 12). All states negotiate new norms and relations in the context of 'common capitalist imperatives' (Dunn, 2014: 80) 'common capitalist imperatives' (Dunn, 2014: 80). Quite simply, 'capitalist imperatives' (ibid.) are those which incentivise states to facilitate the constantly expanding creation of market "value" (i.e. through the commodification of material and immaterial things), the extraction and maximisation of profit ("surplus value"), and the consequent reinvestment of profit to produce even higher returns. As Brian Tamanaha (2008: 406) puts it, the global capitalist economy should be credited with 'the most powerful contemporary impetus, momentum and penetration of new [legal] norms.' And nowhere is transnational legality becoming more consolidated than in the context of "risky" extractive industries and their volatile global markets.

Transnational legal norms associated with the 'commodity form' (see Cutler, 2005) are transmitted across borders via the legal infrastructure of the global economy, but are also diffused through the agency of supra- and sub-national actors and networks (Garth and Dezalay, 1996; Zumbansen, 2013; Bhatt, forthcoming; Shaffer, 2014: 1). The intrinsic ordering impetus of global capitalism, supported as it is by particular legal forms and norms, is also reinforced by the most powerful agents and institutions of the global economic system. International and regional development financing institutions, commercial law firms, private banks, credit ratings agencies and influencing organisations (e.g. World Economic Forum) almost universally buy into the market logic of risk mitigation and investment promotion. Thus, taking a bird's-eye view of the socio-legal "web" of transnational market-facilitating rules, norms and networks, a distinctive set of "stability norms" designed to facilitate and secure global markets (e.g. non-discrimination, anti-expropriation, political risk mitigation, contract enforcement and competitiveness) has achieved an unprecedented degree of hegemony across the global economic order.[2]

The key question this book explores is how this increasingly consolidated body of norms becomes authoritative *within* states seeking global economic integration – and pursue "development" – vis-à-vis competitiveness in natural resource markets. While much transnational legal scholarship focuses on the identification of bodies of 'transnational law applying to transnational situations' (Shaffer, 2014: 5), this book takes a road slightly less travelled by problematising the implications as well as the means by which transnational legal norms infuse a domestic governance system, and become institutionally protected and promoted by the national state. While many scholars at the law and globalisation nexus would object to any exclusive focus on national jurisdictions, I argue that the resistance to some degree of methodological nationalism overreacts to the claim of globalisation "beyond" the state. If globalisation is a process, not a thing in itself, then it inevitably transforms the material "stuff" of the social world, and we cannot escape the national state if this is so. The compelling evidence of economic history points to the powerful mediation of social relations by the national state to produce the conditions through which "global" capitalist expansion becomes possible, and the national state – through its territorial jurisdiction – remains the authoritative locus through which transnational legal, economic, political and social processes must pass to become material (i.e. affecting lived reality). The universal reality of the territorial nation-state cannot be ignored unless we are content to play with abstractions. Consequently, the concern with transnational law in this book falls within what Gregory Shaffer describes as the "socio-legal" study of transnational law, which seeks to understand how transnational norms effect practical and symbolic changes within a national jurisdiction (ibid.; see also Halliday and Shaffer, 2015).

The socio-legal approach focuses on transnational legal *ordering*, as opposed to the mere identification of transnational legal processes. A transnational legal *order* (TLO) can be defined as 'a collection of formalized legal norms and associated organizations and actors that authoritatively order the understanding and practice of law *across* national jurisdictions' (ibid.: 475, emphasis added). As a methodological concept (Shaffer, 2014: 213), TLO provides a useful lens to unpick the increasingly complex and coordinated relationship between transnational legality and global economic change, and the role of the state in mediating and negotiating transnational legal and economic flows. The methodological emphasis of transnational legal ordering helps to contextualise and historicise the legal and political dimensions associated with market-based strategies of economic development. Viewing global economic integration as a transnational legal ordering *process* enables recognition of the ways in which '[legal] norms are constructed, carried and conveyed, always confronting national and local processes, which may block, adapt, translate or appropriate a transnational legal norm' (1–2). This approach emphasises the role of social conflict in determining the depth and veracity of change, as well as the role of national institutions in embracing, resisting or undermining the ordering effects of transnational law. This is also where the study of transnational law in relation to the global economy connects powerfully with questions of state transformation.

## Development code-cracking: the conceptual origin story of the book

There are three distinctive interdisciplinary traditions of development "code cracking" to which this book owes a serious intellectual debt: (a) critical socio-legal approaches to law *in* development, (b) political anthropologies of the relationship between development and the state and (c) critical political economy and international law approaches to global constitutionalism. The following discussion seeks to remedy the fact that these threads of scholarship are rarely all brought together in the same place as intellectual interlocutors, despite the rich theoretical tapestry they weave.

The research underpinning this book was largely conducted over the course of my PhD when I was based at Warwick Law School in the UK (2013–2017). Since the 1970s, Warwick Law School has pioneered a critical and contextual approach to the role of law in development, with close links to the Third World Approaches to International Law (TWAIL) movement. Initially established in the 1970s by a group of decolonial scholars formerly based at the University of Dar es Salaam, a distinctive law *in* development cohort of academics at Warwick deconstructed the dominant vision of law as an instrumental technology of industrial capitalism in the Global South (see Lander, 2019). Led in the early years by Abdul Paliwala, William Twining, Issa Shivji, Yash Ghai and Upendra Baxi, amongst others, the Warwick School is well known for interrogating the ambivalent role of law in constructing broad-based social change in the name of development, with emancipatory and oppressive potential (see Adelman and Paliwala, 1993). The constitutive role of law in building global markets, legitimising multilateral organisations (see Tan, 2011), shaping the norms and patterns of contemporary legal development assistance (Faundez, 1997), constructing gender relationships (Stewart, 2011) and supporting the diffusion of new technologies (Paliwala, 2007) gives legal norms and relations an active role in the production of dominant and resistant conceptions of developmental social change. The recognition of the pluralistic possibilities of law, both in form and in terms of facilitating alternative socio-political pathways (see Meszaros, 2013), has consequently generated a different kind of socio-legal conversation about law and development which keeps 'power at the heart of the study of law and legal institutions' (Tan, 2013: 29). The influence of the Warwick School approach to law as constitutive of the hegemonic social reality produced in the pursuit of development – as well as being a means to challenge it – links clearly with the approach to transnational legality adopted in this book. Transnational law is not analysed as a legal field in itself, but in relation to the institutions and relations that perform development governance.

This approach dovetails with the ground-breaking work of political anthropologists like James Ferguson and Tania Murray Li regarding the construction of governance relations through development programmes, initiatives and strategies. The pioneering scholarship of James Ferguson in *The Anti-Politics*

*Machine* (1990) unpicked the primary *function* of development programmes and policies in inculcating bureaucratic and anti-political modes of governance rationality within public sector institutions in Lesotho. Ferguson's anthropological approach to the study of the 'international "development" apparatus' (ibid.: 17) in the context of Lesotho pushed beyond formal accounts of the intention or purpose of the development strategy. As he put it (ibid.), 'the anthropologist cannot take "planning" at its word.' In this way, Ferguson was able to take account of how the concrete *effects* of development planning – regardless of willed purpose by any particular group of political elites or international development agencies – were to produce what he called 'the anti-politics machine' (ibid.: 21). The anti-politics machine, in Ferguson's terms, refers to the political effects of economic change in the name of development:

> ...outcomes that at first appear as mere "side effects" of an unsuccessful attempt to engineer an economic transformation become legible in another perspective as unintended yet instrumental elements in a resultant constellation that has the effect of expanding the exercise of a particular sort of state power while simultaneously exerting a powerful depoliticising effect.
>
> (Ibid.)

While Ferguson was observing a period when the "international development apparatus" was largely focused on state-led development planning, rather than the type of market-led development as we shall see in the case in Mongolia, his approach has important resonance with the one taken in this book. The process of pursuing natural resource-based development has created ample opportunities for international financial institutions, foreign investors and multinational companies to construct a consistent discourse of the state's failure, ineptitude and instability, which in turn drives and legitimises legal and institutional reform initiatives at the national and sub-national levels.

In a similar vein, albeit a different context, Tania Murray Li's monograph *The Will to Improve* (2007) examines the role of World Bank-sponsored programmes in Indonesia in constructing new authoritative social norms to condition local communities to the paradigm of "development," recast in Li's terms as *improvement*. Like Ferguson, Li draws attention to the 'inevitable gap between what is attempted and what is accomplished' (ibid.: 1) which reinforces the effort made by international development agencies and national bureaucrats to "overcome" the gap. Where Ferguson focuses on the institutional apparatus of development, rather than 'the people to be developed' (Ferguson, 1990: 17), Li develops a rich ethnography that examines the relationship between new technologies of governance and rural populations in the Indonesian highlands, and how resistance both shapes and is shaped by claims to authority (Li, 2007: 282). While Ferguson and Li do not engage explicitly with law or *legal* norms per se, their studies particularly highlight the role of international organisations engaged in border-crossing norm diffusion in the name of development, and the role of national and sub-national institutions in mediating such "development." Both of these scholarly works evidence the deep political and social transformations at stake in these strategies for collective improvement, mediated through state–society relations. They consistently raise the issue of political *closure* as the institutional and normative repertoire of development governance privileges expertise, technique and bureaucracy. The anthropological tradition from which both scholars work assists them in rendering "development" as 'strange... to explore its peculiarities and its effects' (Li, 2007: 3).

The approach to state transformation in this book has also been heavily influenced by the critical perspectives of political economists of development and global governance loosely associated with the Murdoch School of International Relations. The Murdoch School approach emerged in the 1980s with a group of scholars at the Asia Research Centre at Murdoch University critical of the modernisation blueprints underpinning dominant development thinking and practice at the time (see Robison, 1986; Rodan, 1989). Against the backdrop of the fall of the Soviet Union and the unprecedented expansion of global markets in the late 1980s and early 1990s, the Murdoch School largely focused on contextualising global and international dynamics in terms of the way they are 'filtered through domestic socio-political relations' (Hameiri and Jones, 2014: 4). By focusing on the state as a filter or mediating locus for social conflicts, these critical political economy perspectives brought national and sub-national power relations to the fore, arguing that intra-state relations were key to understanding the empirical reality and implications of development strategies (see Robison and Hadiz, 2004). This emphasis contrasted with mainstream international relations scholarship at the time, which had become increasingly enchanted with the claims that an international sphere of institutions and ideology was effectively "hollowing out" or reducing the sovereignty of national states (see Strange, 1988; Scholte, 1997; Jarvis, 2012: 467).

In more recent years, the relatively exclusive focus on domestic power struggles within national states has expanded, under the pioneering influence of Kanishka Jayasuriya, Toby Carroll, Shahar Hameiri, Darryl Jarvis and others, to take account more coherently of the state's transnational encounters with an increasingly coherent and coordinated global economic – and legal – system, as well as the constitutive role of states in constructing it in the first place. Against the growing trend in both international relations and international legal scholarship in the 1990s and early 2000s to 'cast [the debate] in terms of the decline of sovereignty in the face of deep structural changes in the world economy,' Jayasuriya (2001a: 442) argued that such a "simplistic" interpretation reified the idea of static 'settled boundaries between domestic and international domains.' Instead, he argued for a state *transformation* perspective to grasp how the state's governing apparatus is re-constituted (i.e. quite literally remaking the whole from smaller parts) in the context of globalisation. State *transformation* – rather than erosion – focuses on the relationship between intrinsic and extrinsic dimensions of state change, recognising 'the way in which the changing architecture of power both globally and within the states serves to rupture and fragment the institutions and processes of governance' (ibid.).

Following Jayasuriya's lead, a growing number of scholars both within and beyond the Murdoch School began to interrogate the ways in which economic globalisation is predicated upon the simultaneous "internationalisation" of aspects
of the state apparatus alongside the domestication of transnational norms, rules
and institutions within the state. Rather than introducing or over-emphasising a
new global scale of political and legal order to which state sovereignty has been
delegated (ibid.), the focus lies on the way that previous configurations of state
power become unsettled, get shaken up and are resettled into new patterns of
political authority through negotiations with *transnational* dynamics of capital accumulation and geo-political competitiveness (see Scholte, 1997; Hall and
Biersteker, 2002; Robison, 2006). As Hameiri and Jones (2014: 15) argue, 'the
trajectory of any given country's politics is always articulated within broader patterns of geopolitics and capitalist economic development and can never be fully
understood in isolation' (see also Woodley, 2015).

Notably, Jayasuriya's pioneering exploration of state transformation in the
context of transnational economic and political dynamics has explicitly engaged
the distinctive role of transnational *legality* in changing 'the internal architecture of the State' (Jayasuriya, 1999: 454). Drawing on an emerging body of literature seeking to reimagine questions of both state and law *together* in the global
economy in the 1990s (see Picciotto, 1997; Slaughter, 1997), Jayasuriya pos-
ited in the late 1990s and early 2000s that new forms of governance associated
with the global economy 'challenge the Westphalian framework of sovereignty
that has underpinned dominant models of international relations and law' (ibid.:
430). However, he argued that 'changes in the nature of sovereignty' (Jayasuriya,
2001a: 442) more importantly shift the *form* of governance, than the *scale* of it.
The 'dispersion and dissolution of powers of governance' (ibid.: 443) towards
civil society and market actors alongside the internalisation of international regulatory norms within state institutions and agencies characterises a basic 'move
away from government to governance' (ibid.). This shift can be understood in
terms of the widespread move away from the "command and control" and inter-
ventionist models of national government characteristic of Soviet and Western
welfarist states towards an increasingly internationalised *regulatory* state model.
The regulatory state enables market formation and legal transnationalisation –
and is, in turn, shaped by these forces – through the re-articulation of government as management of (primarily) market social relations, imbued with notions
of supply, demand, consumption, liability and contract. Jarvis (2012: 465) sums
up the shift in national state modality that is co-constitutive of the globalisation
of economic and legal relations:

> Unlike its predecessor, the regulatory state is a more circumspect one, fo-
> cused on the efficient management of regulatory policy, the stabilisation of
> inflation and interest rates, balancing national fiscal accounts, and setting
> in place the parameters for market expansion through private sector capital
> formation and efficient market operation. The discourses of national politics

reflect this change with political elites judged on the basis of their abilities to "manage" the economy, create optimal investment conditions, attract investment capital, secure the blessings of ratings agencies, and make markets work by sustaining private sector interest. As much as anything, the age of the regulatory state is an age of managerialism.

Jarvis' account of the regulatory state dovetails with the critique offered by Jayasuriya, Slaughter and others. It is the 'disaggregation' (Slaughter, 2004: 12) and 'internationalisation' of aspects of the *national* state that has facilitated the degree of economic and normative interconnectedness characteristic of "globalisation." In Slaughter's terms, the increasingly disaggregated nature of the state in its international as well as domestic relations reflects 'simply the rising need for and capacity of different domestic government institutions to engage in activities beyond their borders' (ibid.). Institutional disaggregation at both the domestic and international levels (ibid.: 13), varying degrees of internationalisation across these institutions and a general shift towards the regulation of market economy as the telos of governance characterises the dynamics of contemporary state transformation (see Harrison, 2004). As this book will argue, the seeds of the regulatory state were planted in Mongolia's post-socialist transition and brought to fruition through the country's consequent integration into the global minerals economy.

Transnational legal norms often influence internal processes of state formation through sector-specific entrance points vis-a-vis multilateral organisations. Consequently, critical – or 'heterodox' (Campbell and Hatcher, 2019) – political economy approaches tracing transnational influence on national mining regimes offer a particularly important literature informing this book. Pioneered by Bonnie Campbell and other scholars from the Research Group on Mining Activities in Africa (GRAMA) (see Gagné-Ouellet, 2013; Hatcher, 2014) at the University of Quebec in Montreal, national mining regimes are analysed as spaces of state transformation because of the intensified degree of transnational norm diffusion in extractive industries. In general, regulatory regimes can be defined as 'sets of implicit or explicit principles, norms, rules and decision-making procedures around which actors' expectations converge in a given area of international relations' (Krasner, 1983: 2). Krasner's definition has been usefully applied by the GRAMA school (Campbell, 2009; Gagné-Ouellet, 2013; Hatcher, 2014) to understand how the transnational regulatory complex of 'rules, norms and decision-making procedures can influence a government's political decision-making space' (Gagné-Ouellet, 2013: 50). These critical approaches situate mining regimes as part of the 'structure of power that condition(s) relations among the actors involved' (Campbell, 2010: 198). The study of a *mining regime*, therefore, includes but is not limited to the study of mining codes or legislation. To understand the operation of a mining regime, one must also pay attention to relevant investment rules, environmental regulation and administrative responsibility, as well as the norms and values which these structures both produce and represent, in addition to the distinctive role of international agencies in seeking to influence the substance of the regime. Thus, mining regimes become a crucial locus whereby the internationalisation of the state can be witnessed (see Chapter 4). The particular 'politics of mining' (Campbell and Hatcher, 2019: 643) – and, I argue, its associated legality – is constructed around norms which privilege the private sector through export-oriented mineral extraction and large-scale-mining, where the national economic contribution of mining to the national economy is cast primarily through the regulatory mode of taxation rather than state ownership (see Gagné-Oullet, 2013: 52).

The way of thinking about state change in relation to globalisation just described has arisen partly in critical dialogue with the growing claims of supranational constitutionalism "beyond" the state in the wider international relations/law literatures. In the 1990s, methodological nationalism which prioritised the national state as a key locus of agency quickly fell out fashion within dominant international relations and international law debates about law and globalisation (see Berman, 2005). Foreshadowed by Philip Jessup's early recognition of legal transnationalisation in the post-war period (1956), a new wave of socio-legal scholarship in the 1990s questioned whether the former anchoring of law and regulation within the national state was becoming permanently untethered with the rapid expansion of markets. Formerly in the national state/domestic law paradigm, the principles of subsidiarity and legal hierarchy were relatively clear, with associated institutions to resolve disputes when these boundary lines were in question. In the West, the liberal model of constitutionalism had thoroughly associated legal systems with the state apparatus, and many scholars within both international relations and international law disciplines began to believe that the 'state/law nexus' (Zumbansen, 2013: 31) was rapidly becoming disassociated in a global legal environment characterised by plurality, hybridity and increasing specialisation. Apart from its ongoing reliance on dependable national jurisdictions, the world of trade, finance and investment appeared to be increasingly governed by a hybrid, semi-autonomous legal order derived in part from formal legal rules, and in part by customary commercial practice, internal corporate governance and voluntary standard-setting procedures (see Calliess and Zumbansen, 2010). The formation of *global* governance regimes where the authorising role of the state was indirect or only one piece amongst a much larger puzzle of actors and norms suggests to many scholars that the nation-state is in decline. International relations scholarship widely embraced new topics of scholarship beyond the formal national/international paradigm, focusing on the production of global governance regimes and particularly the influence of non-state actors within them.

Made anxious by the fragmentation of the (inter)national legal system (Koskenniemi and Leino, 2002; Zumbansen, 2012) and a perception of growing disorder as the scale of transactions, complexity and impact of the world economy has expanded, a growing number of legal scholars have sought a solution to "order issues" vis-à-vis the concept of global constitutionalism. This body of literature emphasises that a coherent system of *global* law can and should be formally created to govern the gaps in the international system, by extending, reinforcing and creating new legal infrastructures similar to state-centric models to administrate the global economic system. Constitutionalism in this literature is a normative and formalist project which seeks to supplement the international legal order with stronger judicial, deliberative and executive functions. It subscribes generally to the traditional positivist concept of the constitutional, as a unitive legal and political system which reflects the collective will of its subjects to pursue particular rational ends. Consequently, global constitutionalists want to extend the antidote of constitutional rights, processes and values to the "global" scale to cover the glaring "governance gaps" generated by the patchwork of legality which governs cross-border transactions and interactions. Constitutional democracy is seen as a normative good because of the way it creates order and legitimate authority out of the messy world of power politics. Rules are needed to turn the Leviathan into a lapdog, to make the jungle of international relations into a law-abiding sphere.

This normative approach is represented well in the work of Anne Peters (2009: 400), for whom the concept of constitutionalism offers a much-needed antidote to the sense of unfairness, injustice and ineffectiveness of international law in relation to global problems. As she puts it:

> Globalization puts the state and state constitutions under strain. Global problems compel states to cooperate within international organizations and through bilateral and multilateral treaties. What were typically governmental functions, such as guaranteeing human security, freedom, and equality, are in part transferred to "higher" levels. Moreover, non-state actors, acting within states or even in a transboundary fashion, are increasingly entrusted with the exercise of traditional state functions, even with core tasks such as military and police activity. All this has led to "governance" which is exercised *beyond* the states' constitutional confines. This means that state constitutions can no longer regulate the totality of governance in a comprehensive way. Thus, the original claim of state constitutions to form a complete basic order is defeated. National constitutions are, so to speak, hollowed out and traditional constitutional principles become dysfunctional or empty. This affects not only the constitutional principle of democracy, but also the rule of law, the principle of social security, and the organization of territory. Therefore, if we wish to preserve the basic principles of constitutionalism, we must ask for compensatory constitutionalization on the international plane.

In contrast, the other dominant strand of global constitutionalism argues that constitutionalism already exists as a social fact "beyond" the national state. The argument goes that the 'organisational revolution' (Teubner, 2011: 314) within modern societies spurred the creation of 'large-scale autonomous non-state institutions... [which] have raised distinctive constitutional problems of their own' as intermediaries between the citizen and the state. With the advent of renewed and heightened globalisation since the end of the Second World War, these non-state constitutions have become increasingly complex, by adding a strong transnational dimension to whichever system we may investigate. The idea is that functionally differentiated regulatory systems may communicate with one another but they are all structured according to their own internal norms, with a unique communication "code" and processes of legitimisation. Constitution-alism is thus based upon a systems view of the social: it provides a way to speak and think of the internal coherence of social relations in various transnational sectors, akin to biological and ecological "systems." Constitutionalisation from this perspective is a reflexive social process achieved by the agency of the subjects of that constitutional system, rather than achieved through the political and le-gal apparatus of the state and backed by force. The constitutional is conceived in functional terms as the 'coherent arrangement of rules, reflecting specific struc-tures of expectations...linked to the deployment of legal sanctions as a means of establishing compliance' (Kjaer, 2014: 65).

Under the influence of sociologists like Niklas Luhmann, the constitutional is conceived through its function as a legitimation structure for societal integra-tion, rather than as a normative ideal type or simply a reflection of power inter-ests (Thornill, 2017: 495). Prominent scholars such as Gunther Teubner, Chris Thornhill and Peer Zumbansen have sought to explain the radically "autopoie-tic" nature of global law in general, as a social system which no longer requires being coupled with the political authority of the national state to reproduce itself. For example, Gunther Teubner (2012) argues that we must move beyond traditional constitutional thinking to capture the irrevocably fragmented nature of law in its global iteration, which is no longer sutured to a particular way of organising "government." The constitution of governments, while relevant, is made relative by the presence of other constitutions of different social forms of organisation, such as multinational corporations, education services, suprana-tional organisations like the EU and international organisations like the WTO. Teubner's theory of societal constitutionalism seeks to move us out beyond the shadow of the nation-state to recognise the multiple "sub-constitutions" of global society. He recognises constitutions which govern, for example, the World Trade Organisation, multinational enterprises, non-governmental certifi-cation programmes, environmental protection, intellectual property and global value chains.

This distinctly sociological approach has been described as a *'counter-thesis to the doctrine of the constitution which claims that the constitution must categori-cally be related to the state'* (Thornhill, 2011: 212). From Thornhill's point of view, 'transnational constitutional pluralism' should supplant the methodolog-ical nationalism of traditional constitutional scholarship. As he goes on to say:

> From this perspective, all communication systems are de-coupled from legal/ political centres of control, and they produce, more or less spontaneously,

an internally self-regulatory micro-structure, reaching beyond geographical borders. Regional borders or the borders of nation states are replaced by functional borders as points of reference for constitutional foundation and constitutional validity.

One of the unifying features of this diverse range of scholarship – despite intense debates between scholars on some of the finer detail – is its highly pluralistic understanding of constitutionalism. Pluralist global/transnational constitutionalists are united in favour of frameworks which emphasise the 'layered and complex nature of constitutionalism' (Zumbansen, 2012b: 20) under conditions of globalisation. The phenomenon of legal transnationalisation itself suggests to these constitutional sociologists the emergence of 'a multilevel constitutional universe' (ibid.: 4).

From both normative and functional perspectives on global constitutionalism, scholars have latched onto the "constitutional" to give weight to the forms of legal ordering that appear to be occurring beyond the national state as a result of legal and economic globalisation. Whether coming from a normative perspective where global constitutions produce order beyond the state or a systems theory perspective which sees constitutional norms as a type of communication (Blokker and Thornhill, 2017: 9), global and transnational constitutionalism varieties are concerned with the way in which legal norms regulate, stabilise and symbolise emergent forms of global social ordering. It is interesting that both of the main strands – normative and functional – reach towards the language of the constitutional to describe the effects of global economic integration on law, yet do not – by and large – retain the connection between the constitutional and the state. The constitutional provides a common language to continue to be able to speak of legal ordering *despite* the declining centrality of the state. Both of these broad approaches – despite important differences within and between them – can be aptly described as "multi-constitutionalist" as they emphasise the radical break of legal authority from the state and the proliferation of transnational/global constitutional "systems" which regulate different aspects of social life. They seek to move away from so-called "methodological nationalism" and engage with the state as one of many "sites" of institutional power. While the normative global constitutionalists want to create an overarching order out of the milieu of global governance and the pluralists see a future of increasing fragmentation, these two broad camps generally accept the inevitability, if not the desirability, of the state being decentred by legal and economic globalisation.

Drawing on a small but influential body of scholarship within international relations and law associated with literature on "new constitutionalism", this book takes issue with the marginalisation of the state from the majority of new literature on transnational and global law. While this book does seek to reckon with new transnational 'regimes of norm creation' and the 'contextual' nature of constitutional law (Zumbansen and Bhatt, 2018: 5), it resists the common tendency among transnational constitutionalists to deterritorialise these processes or, in other words, to speak of them without maintaining the linkage with the territo-rial state. Drawing on critical political economy perspectives as described in the work of Jayasuriya and the 'Murdoch International' School (Hameiri and Jones, 2014), as well as neo-historical materialists like Robert Cox and Ellen Meik-sins Wood, the "new constitutionalists" have offered a critique of constitutional change in the global economy through analyses of the impact of global eco-nomic processes upon the political and institutional capacities of states. Led by prominent international relations and international economic law scholars such as Stephen Gill, Claire Cutler and David Schneiderman, this branch of schol-arship understands the constitutional primarily in an informal *de facto* sense, rather than a formal process of revising a written national constitution. Rather than trying to formalise or create a 'supra-national' liberal constitutional order at the global level (Peters, 2009), scholars argue that emerging global governance regimes *already* penetrate national governing spaces, impacting the constitution of national states in legal, sociological and economic terms () as well as produc-ing rules which enforce new public/private, political/economic boundaries to sustain the artifice of the neutrality and necessity of the global market economy (see Gill and Cutler, 2014). Thus, *new constitutionalism* refers 'to the uneven emergence of a *de facto*[3] constitutional governance structure for the world mar-ket (one that is intended to operate regionally, nationally and globally)' (Cutler, 2015: 89; see also Gill, 1995).

Critical constitutionalists point to the 'constitution-like' (Schneiderman, 2008: 4) features of transnational legal rules and norms, particularly in terms of embedding the preferences of investors within national regulatory regimes. Investors in a global market economy typically look for stable currency com-mitments from central banks (i.e. deflationary monetary policy), flexible taxa-tion rates that respond to declines in commodity prices and policy stability to not only predict but maximise returns on investments (Polanyi, 1944/2001; Stanford, 2008; Streeck, 2014). The market principles of macroeconomic stabil-ity, competition and the legal protection of private property rights are thereby adopted and institutionalised by national states in order to expand their own ac-cess to global capital and to open up new frontiers of investment in return. This particular form of institutionalisation typically involves domestic legal reform (i.e. introducing a flexible rate of exchange, removing state controls from capi-tal markets, allowing exceptions to national taxation rates for large-scale inves-tors, introducing international accounting standards and reforming competition policy – see UNCTAD, 2009: 7), but also the entry into a complex 'interlocking web of rules and rule-enforcing structures' (Schneiderman, 2008: 25) that exist beyond the scope of national political life and, once ratified, 'place significant limits on state action' (ibid., Sassen, 2007; Tan 2013).

Generally sceptical of legal formalism, the new constitutionalists eschew the projects of the "multi-constitutionalists." In particular, they are critical of the goal of global constitutionalism to architect a "global" legal order based on cos-mopolitan, liberal or pragmatic values (Gill, 2015: 4). Equally, they implicitly, if not explicitly, resist the fragmented notion of law's autopoietic character because of its radical disconnection of law from structures of power. As Schneiderman (2016: 26) puts it:

> In a critical constitutional account, power and political economy are prominently brought back into the fold of international economic law.

In contrast to the "multi-constitutionalism" literature, the new – or critical – constitutionalists emphasise the *disciplinary* power of legal and economic globalisation upon the national state as a 'constitution-like' (Schneiderman, 2008) force (regulating national political life) which limits the public power of the state. The key to the constitutional lies in the *de facto* reproduction of the characteristics of (national) liberal constitutionalism (e.g. a public–private divide) to facilitate global market expansion. While the multi-constitutionalists perceive plural and fragmented forms of legal and political ordering, the new constitutionalists observe the production of a new global unity which cuts across national state systems, undermining and eroding democratic state capacities in favour of markets.

In contrast to transnational constitutional pluralists, new constitutionalists like David Schneiderman make no apology for what might be called "methodological nationalism" in Chris Thornhill's terms. He argues that national states continue to be the most privileged site of political-juridical power, both in terms of their capacity to close off alternative social futures and their ongoing relevance as a site of contestation and resistance (Schneiderman, 2013: 93, 164). The rules of the global economy privilege particular state and corporate interests and exert constitution-like force insofar as they create binding constraints on political processes which might threaten or challenge market function, trade relationships and investment capital. Furthermore, they have argued that focusing on transnational legal processes without reference to the way that these are grounded and differentiated in specific jurisdictions obscures the state's role in "global" reconfigurations of power (Sassen, 2007: 14–15; Schneiderman, 2013: 12, 33), and the way that the national and the local are strategically incorporated into new "globally-oriented" state formations, as Saskia Sassen suggests (Sassen, 2007). Critical constitutionalists are particularly concerned that democratic state capacities and options are limited by global economic integration – the subordination of national democracy to transnational or supranational norms and rules. They are particularly animated by the role of power, interests and new class formations in shaping the transnational rules which appear to constrain or destructively pluralise the function of national constitutions.

## Parts of a whole: state, law and market from material constitutional perspective

What these critical literatures have in common – spanning anthropology, political economy and law – is a sustained awareness that the history of development cannot be delinked with the rise of industrial capitalism and the global expansion of markets. Throughout history, the powerful interdependencies of political authority, regulation and systems of production and accumulation challenge the commonplace view that the spheres of "state," "economy" and "law" can be conceptualised as separate phenomena. Social orders of every kind – tribal, feudal, empire and nation-state – have evolved out of the interaction of three pressing tendencies in human beingness, namely our dependence on norms and sanctions, durable social structures and the satisfaction of material needs and wants. All known human societies have been organised by relative degrees of hierarchy, and that organisational structure has been reinforced and regulated by ordering norms and rules, enforced through sanctions. Equally, the sustenance of the social group as a whole as well as the legitimacy (and expansion) of the organisation-ordering system has required the accessibility and consumption of material goods. The systematic production and accumulation of 'want satisfying material means' can be understood as the 'empirical economy' of human social orders (Polanyi, 1957: 248). As noted earlier, all organised forms of production, accumulation and redistribution rely upon political-juridical institutions and relations (ibid.: 251; Polanyi, 1944: 59–70).[4] These organisational structures and ordering norms create the grid of power relations and rules (formal or informal) that provides a social framework for the production, consumption, distribution and trade of material and immaterial goods and services, as well as social reproduction.

In capitalist economic systems, the creation of "markets" as a distinct economic sphere away from direct state control reflects a unique historical process of "disembedding" from their imbricated status within the social fabric, a process with which the national state form is deeply implicated. Prior to the centralisation of the state, the fragmentation of power held by diverse poles of political authority (e.g. aristocrats, religious institutions and the military) correlated with fragmented systems of production and accumulation, with highly localised and regionalised forms of trade and markets which were embedded within the social order (Wood, 2002: 20–21). Social expectations of reciprocity and redistribution existed alongside market exchange as the basis of the economic system (Polanyi, 1957: 250). Markets, both local and regional, may have been structured by profit maximisation and price mechanisms, but even when these were not highly localised, they formed only one part of the "patchwork" of economic systems which sustained feudal polities and empires. The fact that 'a market is a meeting place for the purpose of barter or buying and selling' (ibid.: 59) did not historically correlate with a whole economy being dominated by market principles of exchange or acquisition as we find today. Historically, market principles associated with exchange were limited by the presence of other social values, such as reciprocity, redistribution and the welfare of a community, as well as the technological barriers to forming competitive market systems beyond creating linkages between 'separate, distinct, and discrete markets' (Wood, 2002: 20, citing Kerridge, 1988: 6). The fragmentation of political authority simultaneously *enabled* markets to function (i.e. by authorising social space for barter and exchange) whilst also *restricting* the scope of market expansion (Polanyi, 1944/2001: 65). However, as the next section will discuss in more detail, the contemporary dominance of market economy has relied upon distinct two processes of state formation and associated legal change: nationalisation with a central judicial infrastructure to enforce property rights, followed by *selective* globalisation of national state functions and deregulation.

The history of market formation, as we will soon see, shows us a socio-legal pattern of the deeply intertwined relationship between political institutions, legal forms and market expansion. If we scratch the surface of contemporary market-led development, I argue that we can see these three constitutive elements continuing to interact as the national state enables and adapts to global market capitalism. Against the tide of socio-legal scholarship focused on global legal and economic processes, the evidence of this book suggests that we ignore processes of state and legal transformation at great cost to our understanding of global capitalism.

The book's focus on the transformation of power relations, patterns of governance and institutional arrangements reflects a broadly *materialist* theoretical standpoint (see Rupert and Smith, 2002). A materialist mode of inquiry pays attention to the *active construction* of the social world, particularly the interdependencies between "economic" systems of accumulation and "political-legal" systems of authority. As Ellen Meiksins Wood (2002: 18) puts it:

> The 'historical' in historical materialism allows us to explore the conditions and implications of this historically specific separation [between the political and economic spheres]. Its 'materialism' focuses our attention not on some transhistorical economic sphere, but on historically specific material conditions of social reproduction, which not only affect all social spheres but constitute them as distinct spheres in the first place. From that perspective, we can explore a development like globalisation not as some ahistorical natural process but as a truly historical one.

The commitment to de-naturalise the commonplace assumption that the political sphere of authority is conceptually separable from the economic sphere of production and accumulation opens our eyes to the thoroughly interdependent relationship between state, markets and law. Consequently, the broadly materialist approach of this book draws appreciatively on Bob Jessop's conception of the state as a 'site of strategic action' (1990: 10), which emphasises the role of *authoritative* action in relation to processes of accumulation. While Jessop acknowledges that the state does not "exist" as an object/subject to which one could point and say 'there is the state' (Jessop, 2008: 3), the state is distinguishable from other types of social formations even though it is a 'social relation' (ibid.: 1 citing Poulantzas). It includes a concrete 'juridico-political apparatus' (ibid.: 6) and more immaterial 'capacities-liabilities and forces' (ibid.) that shape the *potential* of the state. In that sense, it is both abstract and concrete. As Jessop (ibid.: 7) puts it:

> For the state involves a paradox. On the one hand, it is just one institutional ensemble among others within a social formation; on the other, it is

peculiarly charged with overall responsibility for maintaining the cohesion of the social formation of which it is merely a part.

Methodologically, a materialist approach to state transformation as well as constitutionalism is best served through a spatial conception of the state. As "a site of strategic action" defined by relational coordinates, a spatial approach helpfully illuminates the material complexity of state power. A state can thus be defined as 'an ensemble of juridical-political institutions and regulatory capacities grounded in the territorialisation of political power' (Brenner et al., 2003: 7), infused with an ideological *raison d'être* which reflects and constructs its social legitimation processes. The concept of the state as an "ensemble" helpfully breaks down the concept of the state as a monolithic entity stripped of history and process. This definition expresses the idea that "states" are – empirically – institutionally consolidated relations of *governance* which are expressed territorially. The spatial approach to the state is reflected in the book's adoption of language of *architecture, apparatus, infrastructure* and *axes* to illuminate how the material institutions and relations of state power are re-articulated and re-coordinated around new normative principles (see Jayasuriya, 2001b; Brenner et al., 2003).

The territoriality of state power is intimately related to control over the *places of the governed,* wherein relations of legitimation emerge, as well as access to, if not control over, the means of accumulation. Political authority depends upon a process of mutual recognition between the governed and the governing – a relationship of legitimation – as well as resources to continually maintain these relations, as well as territorial control. These two sets of relations – of legitimation and accumulation – characterise social relations of political authority across history, whether based on kinship, feudalism, empire or "national sovereignty." Jessop's recognition of the 'relational orientation' of the state (1982: 253) suggests that the state, a specific social formation, is constituted by interactions with other social processes of production, accumulation and normative ordering. Consequently, throughout this book, shifting intra-state and state–society relations are the lens through which state transformation is conceived, contextualised within shifting geo-political and geo-economic relations with other states.

By focusing on the construction of foundational patterns of governance produced in the pursuit of particular development strategies, the hope is that the mutually constitutive relationship between state formation, legal change and market expansion can be brought into the light. While trying not to elide relevant distinctions between these institutions, the purpose of the book is to highlight their active interdependency and interaction, including moments of crisis and resolution, which produce the possibility for a given trajectory of "development." Global markets have not emerged as an organic 'catallaxy' (Hayek, 1988), but depend upon legal forms and norms which construct, protect and promote market price mechanisms. Equally, these legal forms and norms do not emerge from the ether, but are produced, legitimised, internalised and enforced through the legal and judicial systems of national states. Transnational legal norms do not exist or originate in an ether, but are produced through concrete social conflicts about the terms and parameters of governance. This is particularly evident in terms of the changing legal and institutional implications of development, as described earlier. The question of *which* norms become transnationally dominant depends upon the framing and assessment of the regulatory problem, as well as the barriers to cross-border transmission and institutionalisation (see Shaffer, 2014: 214–215; Shaffer and Coye, 2017: 3).

I argue that any meaningful encounter with processes of economic – and legal – globalisation provokes *constitutional* questions for national states. The approach to constitutionalism here seeks to think prior to the establishment of basic rules for governance, and to understand how these rules, structures and relations (a) construct new patterns of political economy and (b) perform 'a crucial "framing function," setting the parameters not just for how politics is contested, but what is deemed politically contestable' (Anderson, 2014: 283, citing Christodoulidis, 2011: 209). I argue that the relationship between global market economy, market legality and the competitive state is co-*constitutive* in the sense of creating conditions for the possibility of each other, but also in the literal sense of the verb "to constitute": to form part of a *whole*. As a verb, rather than a noun, the term is inherently productive and relational. Inherent in the verb lies the crucial question: how is the "whole" made? What is the lynchpin of the particular patterns of social, legal, political and economic relations within which we find ourselves? Out of the plurality of social relations, how do some patterns become authoritative? I argue, following Goldoni (2019: 86), that a *constitutional* perspective should illuminate the baseline patterns and processes of 'rule, redistribution and recognition' which underpin relations between 'those that are governed and those who govern.'

Material constitutionalism does not negate or oppose the formal constitution of a state. Formal constitutions reflect and institute important configurations of social relations through, for example, the "separation" of state power into different horizontal domains (e.g. legislative, judicial and executive), as well as "vertical" institutions (e.g. national/sub-national layers of administration). Rather, material constitutionalism seeks to understand why the formal order has developed in the way that it has, as well as to highlight any disjuncture between the theory and practice of government. Material constitutional approaches are primarily concerned with the question of 'why has this social order given to itself these forms of law and not others?' (Goldoni, 2019: 85). The material constitution thus takes account of a wider range of factors than a doctrinal approach to constitutionalism, and yet importantly includes the formal constitution in its assessment of constitutional reality. As Goldoni (2019: 85) argues, 'the material constitution provides the key for understanding why the constitutional order has taken up certain forms.' It also provides a way of recognising how constitutional conflicts unfold at multiple institutional locations, including but not limited to constitutional courts.[5]

In contrast to traditional Marxist approaches which reduce constitutions to a superstructure determined by the mode of production (ibid.:72–74; Wood, 1995: 49–75), a materialist approach seeks to understand constitutions as a form of social relation. As Wood cogently argues (ibid.:27–28):

> Relations of production themselves take the form of particular juridical and political relations – modes of domination and coercion, forms of property and social organization – which are not mere secondary reflexes, nor even just external supports, but *constituents* of these production relations... political organization plays a significant part in *constructing* relations of production.

Thus, the materialist approach to constitutional analysis in this book asserts that 'the economic sphere rests firmly on the political' (ibid.: 30). I would add to Wood's insights a crucial hyphen: political-*legal* or juristic infrastructures are fundamental to a proper understanding of material constitutional reality.

Thus material constitutionalism seeks to contextualise how both *de jure* and *de facto* rubrics of social relations we commonly take for granted (e.g. the formal separation of powers or practical institutional distinctions between state, market and civil society) exist in reality as a spectrum – or 'condominium' (Levi-Faur, 2005: 14) – of social relations folded in particular patterns (Frerichs, 2011). As Levi-Faur (2005: 14) puts it, 'the state is embedded in the social and economic order; any change in the state is expected to be reflected in the economy and the society, and vice versa.' The material constitution is the political and legal lynch-pin of these overarching social patterns, shaping manifestations of both state and economy, underpinned by particular forms of law. Importantly, this political and juridical scaffolding shapes the available means and processes by which 'want satisfying material means' (i.e. the economy) may be produced and accumulated (Polanyi, 1957: 248).

The value of a constitutional perspective that takes into account the material "stuff" of our social world lies partly in its open-ended curiosity about the interaction of the plural micro, meso and macro elements which create the "structural metadata" of social order. A pre-conceived idea or historical instance of a constitutional order that is not receptive to new empirical information turns the concept of constitutionalism into a static and nostalgic shell. However, in equal measure, the purpose of asking the constitutional question cannot simply be to identify plurality; constitutionalism speaks to the *whole*, even if formed through many parts. Constitutional law is particularly intertwined with the production of hegemonic social relationships in that by its very nature 'it induces people to comply with a dominant set of practices and institutions' (Litowitz, 2000). Thus, there is something distinctively monist about the language of constitutionalism (Loughlin, 2014). It speaks to the higher level of authoritative ordering which frames the breadth and width of claims for recognition and redistribution within the jurisdiction of the state, as well as the extent to which resistance to rule can be tolerated. Obviously, these boundaries may be situated differently within different societies: the constitutional from a material point of view does not refer to the ideal placement of boundaries but to the fact of their existence. However, if there is too much focus on constitutive elements without seeking to understand how these produce a change in the overarching social order, I would argue that we are no longer engaging in constitutional analysis.

The reader may wonder how this exclusivity can be justified when there appear to be clear forms of legal ordering that exist "beyond" the national state. This book does not dispute the empirical realities of legal pluralism at all, engaged as it is in analysing the effects of legal ordering as a result of global economic integration. However, unless legal plurality can be shown to have supplanted or become embedded within national constitutional forms, it cannot be said to be constitutional per se. Legal ordering beyond the state may be a constitutional element, but in and of *itself* legal orders beyond the state are not constitutional unless they clearly become authoritative over or within national constitutional settlements at least in practice, if not on paper. The national state apparatus remains one of the 'key enablers and enactors of the global scale' (Sassen, 2006: 3), with its unique mediating position in relation to transnational legal and economic norms and processes.[6] Whether through weakness, ignorance or its own deliberate fault, the state provides the boundaries of *jurisdiction*, 'the legally fixed boundaries of competence, power and authority' (Zumbansen, 2013: 473). Even where there seem to be gaps in the governance capacity of the state, it is still through these neglected or created "holes" in the institutional fabric that transnational processes must pass to actively construct *globalised* national and local social realities.

## Seeking reward and mitigating risk: the changing dynamics of "development" in the global economy

> The identification of a problem is intimately linked to the availability of a solution.
>
> (Li, 2007: 7)

The history of modern capitalism, characterised by the relentless pursuit of accumulation and commodification to create new markets, is a story shaped by the struggle to insulate and protect markets from socio-political controls. Simultaneously, the expansion of capitalism into new frontiers of accumulation has historically *depended* upon territorial and jurisdictional access granted by state institutions. Mindful of the dangers of abstract definitions of state, economy and law, there are strong *historical* reasons to take questions of state formation and legal form seriously in relation to market capitalism. Contemporary capitalism arose in the unique, historical conditions of late medieval and early modern constitutional conflicts and commercial relations. The national state and capitalism emerged together, as distinct but complementary systems of authority and accumulation. Crucially, this complementary system of national state and market capitalism was enabled by a constitutional configuration which made the segmentation of power into political/economic, public/private divisions possible (Schneiderman, 2008). Consequently, this introductory chapter makes reference to particular historical episodes of market capitalism, as this specific history has much to tell us about contemporary patterns of state, law and economy in a global context.

The origin story of our current global economic system and its associated development strategies is distinctively capitalist. Quite simply, capitalism is an economic system premised upon the constantly expanding creation of market "value" (i.e. through the commodification of material and immaterial things), the extraction and maximisation of profit ("surplus value") and the consequent reinvestment of profit to produce even higher returns. Capitalist economic systems are inexorably expansive and prone to crisis as they confront market and non-market barriers to further expansion (e.g. finite resource bases, withdrawal of regulatory support, market saturation). From the origins of market capitalism in England, we can see the central role of the nationalisation of state institutions and legal systems in enabling market capitalism to take off. In England, the tensions between market expansion and the medieval system of political authority were reconciled within a *national* constitutional settlement which centralised political power to enable a private economic sphere for market relations to flourish. Market capitalism in England began to thrive under the conditions of the constitutional settlement achieved through the Glorious Revolution and the 1689 Bill of Rights. While agitations for greater protection of private property rights had risen to boiling point in the earlier part of the seventeenth century, the separation of powers between the Crown, Parliament and the courts created an institutional environment of distributed sovereignty, where the state as a whole could less easily expropriate at its pleasure. The institutional protection of a distinct juridical sphere set apart from the power of the Crown and obedient to statute was central to the marketisation of England's economy, in addition to the creation of an independent national bank in 1694 (Polanyi, 1944/2001: 233). Thus, whilst the development of capitalism did not directly "cause" the national state in England, their emergence and maturation were co-eval (Wood, 2002: 19).[7] Furthermore, to create stable social environments for markets to emerge, consolidate and expand (i.e. based on market prices, demand and supply), legal relations needed to be distinguished from political relations. Patronage could only take the market so far; what was needed for capitalist markets to really expand beyond parochial and political borders was certain, anonymous and inalienable legal rights which could be defended in any court of law in the land.

Uniquely in the rise of modern capitalism, law as well as markets have become systematically disembedded from the direct coercive control of the state, although crucially oxygenated by the powerful protection provided by its jurisdiction. As Frerichs (ibid.: citing Polanyi, 1957: 250) argues, 'even though law is not particularly mentioned [by Polanyi], it can easily be identified as one of the institutions providing the economic process with "unity and stability, structure and function, history and policy."' The expansion of capitalism beyond England and the increasing hegemony of "self-regulating" market mechanisms in the sphere of international trade in the nineteenth century mutually reinforced the internationalisation of regulatory mechanisms (e.g. international price-setting mechanisms), legal forms (e.g. contracts) and norms (e.g. the public/private distinction). These characteristics of a "private" sphere of international law became increasingly institutionalised as the "public" inter-state political system was consolidated in the seventeenth, eighteenth and nineteenth centuries (O'Rourke and Williamson, 1999; Cutler, 2003: 46). Analysis of the rise of the modern *lex mercatoria* ("law merchant") as a regime of private commercial norms operating across domestic and international jurisdictions has been cogently addressed elsewhere (Wood, 1981; Cutler, 1999, 2003) but a few key points can be distilled here.[8] At the most basic level, capitalist market expansion beyond the national sphere depended on the parallel expansion of its constitutive norms, notably market mechanisms for price-setting and contractual protections for property rights (Cutler, 1999: 59–60). As Cutler (ibid.) argues, legal rules which created shared expectations for bargaining, contract enforcement, competition and access to markets became a 'common language and normative framework, enabling merchants from diverse legal and political systems to speak to one another and to transact in a relatively stable, predictable, and secure environment.' Some of these rules were enforced within the "public" inter-state system, through treaties, as well as arising from the customary "private" practice of commercial agents.

Our contemporary period of economic globalisation since the end of the Second World War has only heightened the co-constitutive dynamic between state, market and law evident from previous centuries of market capitalism. As soon as the protectionist interruption to the international trading system subsided with the end of the Second World War, Western states sought to revive the inter-state economic system and integrate newly independent post-colonial states by promoting capitalist industrialisation through development financing and law and development programmes in the 1950s and 1960s. The post-war period invited renewed processes of state and market formation, as well as the promotion of a particular set of legal institutions in the so-called Third World, notably independent judiciary, the rule of law and the recognition and protection of private property rights. Development financing was never simply focused on economic stimulus, but rather embodied a package of social change through the promotion of bureaucratic state institutions and independent judicial systems which would enforce the rule of law. Former colonial powers could no longer simply extend markets through imperialism; so, the challenge in the post-war environment was to create, at the very least, persuasive conditions for newly independent states to "align" with the Western capitalist consensus about how economies, states and judicial institutions should be organised.

### Development as state modernisation

In the 1950s, a great deal of Western scholarly attention in political science, law and economics began to focus on the means by which *political, economic and legal modernisation* occurred. Well-represented in the work of Walt Rostow (1959), the modernisation paradigm was premised upon a linear plan for subsistence societies to "progress" towards consumer societies characterised by surplus generation, in order to increase wealth, production and consumption levels, technology and overall standards of living. Following the apparent success of US-driven "foreign assistance" packages to rebuild industries and restore markets in Germany and other Western European states through the Marshall Plan, foreign assistance agencies in the U.S. as well as the newly formed Bretton Woods Institutions began to export the model internationally (see Chwieroth, 2008). The Marshall Plan blueprint had three distinctive economic ingredients: 'raw materials, industrial equipment, and international liquidity' (Packenham, 1973: 34). The injection of capital stimulus was intended to catalyse national industry. Crucially, technical assistance programmes accompanied these economic ingredients to enable 'integrated development of the economic resources and productive capacities of economically underdeveloped areas' (Act for International Development, 1950, Section 418(a); see also Lander, 2019).

Newly independent post-colonial states and those which were non-aligned to the Soviet Union were required to adopt a blueprint of reforms understood to have led to successful industrialisation and modernisation in the West: 'bureaucratic governmental apparatus, capitalist market systems, "generalised universalistic legal system" and democratic political systems' (Tamanaha, 2011: 209). The nationalisation of the state and law was recognised as a critical variable in the development of industry and markets in Western European and North American contexts (Jayasuriya, 2001a: 443). Consequently, the 1950s and 1960s saw the emergence of a new "field" of scholarly and practitioner activity under the banner of Law and Development (see Lander, 2019). Foreign assistance agencies in the United States began to make connections with prominent law schools to support legal interventions in the so-called Third World to support economic and political modernisation processes. As Trubek and Galanter (1974: 1066) argued at the height of the first Law and Development movement, 'action agencies became interested in attracting legal scholars into assistance work.' As collaborations grew between "action agencies" and scholars, universities like Yale and Chicago began to develop specific programmes and centres to harness these initially disparate collaborations into a more definable "field" (e.g. the Yale Programme in Law and Modernisation).

In addition to achieving the geo-political objectives of the United States (i.e. to prevent Third World state alignment with the Soviet Union), law and development interventions in the 1960s were premised on the idea that British and American legal systems could – and should – be "transplanted" into post-colonial contexts (Tamanaha, 2011: 211). This assumption of the legitimacy and feasibility of legal transplants led to an almost missionary zeal by the American Bar Association, university law programmes and agencies like the Peace Corps (Gardner, 1980). As the then director of the Peace Corps, Robert Sargent Shriver (1963: 459), put it:

> The Peace Corps is conducting a talent hunt through major U.S. law schools. Using the facilities of the American Bar Association and the American Bar Foundation, Peace Corps officials are combing student bodies around the nation, looking for resourceful, mature, imaginative young men who would like to teach others and learn from others... Volunteer lawyers, answering the challenge of public service, will share in an experience that will enrich their entire lives. They will have learned that liberty under the law, be it the civil or the common law, and the equal rights of individuals to live a life of freedom, limited only be respect for the similar rights of others, are the needs of all peoples.

The title of Shriver's article – *Peace Corps Lawyers: Building Emerging African Societies* – sums up the missionary spirit of law as a development project. The idea that individual liberty, protected by law, should constitute the bedrock of all independent states as a universal foundation was the telos of the post-war vision of what it meant to modernise:

> Newly emerging nations in today's world, particularly in Africa, stand upon the frontiers of constitutional government. Free of colonial administration, they are preparing to solidify their independence through the establishment of modern legal systems. But they have far to go, as our forefathers did.
>
> (Shriver, 1963: 456)

As Shriver's quote indicates, liberal constitutional systems were understood by law and development scholars and policy promoters to be foundational to the logical and proper development of societies. Recalling the discussion in the previous section, establishing a constitutional system to support a public–private divide was essential for capitalist industrialisation in England. The law and development reformers in the 1960s sought to recreate similar institutional conditions for industrial "take-off" (Rostow, 1959) to occur in the so-called Third World, although maintaining unequal trade and investment relations for the benefit of capital-exporting states in the West. "Third World" states were attenuated to the neo-colonial overtones of "development" and sought to protect their sovereignty and economic prospects through coalition-building and radicalisation of the international legal system. In 1955 in Bandung, Indonesia, states from Asia and Africa, many newly independent, met to discuss their priorities for self-determination, economic development and peace. During the 1970s, coalition-building between states in the Third World led to the delivery of a set of proposals to the United Nations demanding the establishment of a New

International Economic Order (NIEO), which favoured sovereignty, economic justice and greater control over the terms of trade and investment. However, the radical agenda emanating from scholars and political leaders from "Third World" states to use international law to promote development on equal, sovereign terms was ultimately stymied by the intensification of pressure to become competitive in *global* markets since the 1980s. State formation within post-colonial states was already being shaped by pressures from Western capital-exporting states to follow constitutional patterns which would facilitate market development and expansion, although the focus on the time was that the national state should be the driver of development. The recommitment amongst Western powers and "aligned" states to the institutions of liberal political and economic systems based on the limitation of the state and the promotion of capitalist markets, as well as the re-creation of an international banking and monetary regime, set the scene for an unprecedented level of global economic and legal integration in the decades to follow.

## Development as marketisation

The initial post-war period was characterised by increasing levels of *inter*national cooperation between capitalist-aligned states, reflected in the active resuscitation of the world economy by Western states through the Bretton Woods Institutions and bilateral economic assistance packages. The national state had been promoted in both development financing and within Western economies as the major player in domestic market formation and growth, through nationalised industries, services and provision of subsidies. The state was not only a domestic *regulator* of private market capitalism but a crucial agent of capital investment and expansion in its own right. This reflected the post-war consensus in contexts like Britain, where the state sought to stimulate growth for economic recovery as well as welfare through high levels of national investment in health, education, transport and infrastructure. However, the late 1970s marked an important shift towards the market as the driver of development rather than the state, characterised by the privatisation of national industries, the deregulation of domestic markets and the liberalisation of trade, investment and finance.

The 1970s was a contradictory decade in terms of the world economy, with significant degrees of American unilateralism and the global deregulation of currency with the 'abandonment of the convertibility of money into gold' (Gold, 2008: 187). In 1971, U.S. President Richard Nixon singlehandedly dismantled the Bretton Woods system of fixed exchange rates based on the valuation of the U.S. dollar against the price of gold. The intensification of foreign investment, international currency speculation and increasing volumes of trade through the 1960s had led to a situation where capital expansion pushed against fixed exchange rates. U.S. gold reserves could no longer provide the backing for the amount of U.S. dollars in circulation, which led to the devaluation of the dollar and undermined U.S. trade power. Consequently, President Nixon and his economic advisers suspended the convertibility of dollars to gold which had been the financial basis for valuation in the international economy. After some initial attempts to maintain a fixed exchange rate under the 1971 Smithsonian Agreement, the Western powers adopted a system of floating exchange rates. The shift to floating exchange rates had an astronomical impact upon state capacity to protect domestic markets from the impact of global price fluctuations, a point that was brought home sharply after the Organisation of Arab Petroleum Exporting Countries (OPEC) unilaterally introduced a price hike on oil exports in 1973 (Venn, 2002). The removal of fixed exchange rates signalled an important move towards the intensification of *global* market effects, beyond a regulated international system.

The mixed economy model in Western states, characterised by significant state ownership and regulation of domestic markets, came under pressure in the 1980s with claims of inefficiency and profitability of state-led industry. Led politically by the likes of Ronald Reagan in the U.S. and Margaret Thatcher in the UK and ideologically by a renewed commitment to economic liberalism, a new division of labour between the state and the market was articulated through extensive privatisation of national industries. The substantial "withdrawal" of the state from the economy across sectors entailed a shift in its role from capital owner and controller of market forces to that of regulator, manager and enforcer of the legal framework for private transactions. Private market forces were given pride of place in terms of domestic resource allocation and production across a variety of industrial sectors and financial services (i.e. banking and investment) were significantly deregulated.

The 1990s intensified and accelerated the global reach of ideologies of privatisation, deregulation and liberalisation of trade and finance with the fall of the Soviet Union at the beginning of the decade (Trubek and Santos, 2006). The new liberal consensus amongst Western states asserted that economic development occurred best in systems characterised by regulatory – as opposed to developmental – states, market economies and a strong procedural approach to the rule of law. This revised development blueprint was exported to post-Soviet states through "structural adjustment" packages offered through the International Monetary Fund (IMF) and the World Bank (Biersteker, 1990), in a similar way to those development assistance packages offered by the U.S. government in the 1950s and 1960s. These structural adjustment packages required the adoption of liberal political and economic institutions to promote marketisation of formerly state-controlled economies, as well as the opening of these markets to foreign investment and trade.

In exchange for economic stimulus packages in the wake of a collapsing Soviet Union, post-socialist states were required to privatise national assets, create independent central banks and remove national currency controls and tariff barriers to trade and investment, as well as constitutional systems premised upon electoral democracy and the institutional separation of legislative, judicial and executive powers. The zeal of Western powers and international financial institutions to promote liberal constitutions and market economies through economic assistance to the new post-Soviet states was accompanied by the resurgence of law and development initiatives. These initiatives went beyond the construction of a domestic public–private divide and the transplanting of Western institutions into "developing" state systems to facilitate national industry and growth. The purpose of the neoliberal rule of law projects was to create juridical conditions for national states to "participate" in the *global* economy through rendering domestic–international borders porous and penetrable for private and international capital investment. The other aspect of law and development efforts focused on assisting developing countries – both post-Soviet and others – to participate in the increasingly coordinated multilateral trading system.

The establishment of the World Trade Organisation (WTO) in 1995 marked an important milestone in terms of the consolidation of multilateral trade rules which sought to achieve non-discrimination for all member states, guarantees for competition and commercial policy and 'progressive liberalisation' of trade (i.e. anti-protectionism). Here again, we can see the role of national states in constructing international regimes to provide certainty and security for markets. Since 1947, the General Agreement on Tariffs and Trade (GATT) had transformed from a relatively small-scale multilateral agreement between twenty-three member states focusing on the removal of tariff barriers to a comprehensive, binding system governing tariffs as well as standards for trade in goods, covering agriculture, textiles, animal products, machinery and natural resources. The Uruguay Round of negotiations culminated in 1995 with the General Agreement on Trade in Services which extended WTO rules to trade in services, as well as Trade Related Aspects of International Property Rights (TRIPS). The TRIPS regime seeks to account for and regulate the increasing level of commercial value derived from the branding of goods and services. Finally, 1995 marked the creation of the World Trade Organisation, a new multilateral organisation to regulate trade alongside the former Bretton Woods institutions – the IMF and the World Bank. The formation of the WTO was the fulfilment of the original intention of GATT, to create a robust, institutionalised multilateral trading system with its own judicial appellate committee to enforce breaches of the rules. Within this wider context, further multilateral and bilateral investment agreements proliferated to create even more open trade and investment relations between countries, according preferential rights to investors.

The collapse of the Soviet Union and the consequent consolidation of a strong rules-based multilateral trading system under the WTO prompted a radical increase of alignment between domestic regulatory environments and international 'regulatory infrastructures' (Picciotto, 2016: 5) to enable competitive participation in global markets (Schneiderman, 2008: 62). At the international level, these regulatory infrastructures include bilateral investment treaties (BITs), regional trade agreements and multilateral treaties to enable or enhance their status as capital-friendly jurisdictions (Gill, 1998; Schneiderman, 2008, 2013; Tan, 2013; Cutler, 2014). Multilateral and bilateral frameworks impose limits on taxation levels as well as national expropriation of private profits, reduce or eliminate tariffs on exports and imports, and establish market price-setting mechanisms across economic sectors. These agreements also give parties access to international arbitration tribunals to settle disputes, rather than domestic courts, whose resolutions are binding (Schneiderman, 2008: 46). International regulatory instruments like multilateral trade agreements have played a crucial role in terms of enforcing economic marketisation by prohibiting state actions which interrupt, distort or threaten market price mechanisms through discrimination against foreign capital investment, expropriation of private assets and other assertions of distinctively "national" interests.

The rapid disembedding of markets from national political controls since the 1980s and 1990s has led to intensified integration in economic and regulatory terms, where barriers to the movement of capital, goods, services, technology, labour and information have been removed or reduced (Drezner, 2007: 10). Thus, one of the key features of our current epoch of globalisation which distinguishes it from past instances of 'partial globalisation' (ibid.) is its scope. As Drezner (ibid.) puts it, 'the current era of globalisation encompasses most of the world's nations and all the great powers.' All nation-states have high stakes in their position within global markets (Held and McGrew, 2003), seeking to be rule-makers rather than rule-takers within the transnational regulatory and governance regimes that shape global trade, investment and finance (Braithwaite and Drahos, 2000).

## Building markets, building states: understanding the contemporary paradigm

In the 1980s and early 1990s, the general faith in the free market to automatically produce development was at an all-time high, reflected in what is commonly known as the Washington Consensus policies which promoted de-regulation, privatisation and liberalisation of centralised, planned economies in the so-called Third World (Williamson, 2005).[9] The Soviet Union had collapsed, and multilateral financial institutions, backed by Western powers, were actively constructing deregulated markets in tandem with national governments in post-socialist states. However, by the early 2000s, the disastrous social impacts of structural adjustment and widespread criticism of the Washington Consensus led to a re-evaluation of the role of the state by international development policy-makers. Consequently, the "post-Washington Consensus" maintained the centrality of the market for development, but recognised the importance of the *regulatory* function of the state to maintain a basic social security net and provide reliable rules 'that define the allocative and settlement mechanisms of markets and the requirements for market participation' (Jarvis, 2012: 468; Carroll, 2012a;).

The regulatory capacity of states to *manage* market-led development strategies has since become a key target for multilateral and bilateral development support. While in the 1980s and 1990s the focus of development assistance was to create legislative frameworks which legally opened the economy to private capital investment with a minimal role for the state, the focus since the late 1990s has shifted definitively towards the role of an "effective state" to harness the potential and regulate the risks of globalised markets without protectionist distortions to price-setting mechanisms or the legal protections upon which capital investment relies. As this chapter will discuss, the scope of governance reform to promote development on these terms has steadily expanded to encompass both "hard" and "soft"[10] spheres of domestic regulation, as well as broader institutional and social dimensions which affect investment. As the International Finance Corporation (IFC) of the World Bank Group put it in a recent 'Investment Reform Map' report for Mongolia (IFC, 2018: 2):

> Experience shows that to attract FDI, statutory (*or de jure*) openness is not sufficient because other constraints in the overall investment climate can easily deter investment in an economy.

The opening of the regulatory capacity of states in the Global South to *qualitative* scrutiny by multilateral financial institutions, global benchmarking organisations (e.g. *Doing Business* standards) and credit ratings agencies, as well as state departments in the Global North (e.g. U.S. Department of State's Investment Climate reports) introduces a new dimension to any market-based development strategy. Transnational scrutiny of state regulatory capacity is particularly heightened in relation to *extractive* development due to the volatility of global commodity markets. Led by the World Bank, the language of 'investment climate' has become part of transnational legal parlance since 2002 (see Perry-Kessaris, 2008: 3). Since then, 'investment climate assessments... have become hard political currency within client states [of the World Bank]' (ibid.). In the context of this type of environmental activism, states in the Global South must show themselves to be worthy of investment confidence, by resisting the temptations offered by boom and bust cycles of mineral rents to increase state control of markets, spend beyond their means and make political promises to their national constituencies that would require any significant increase in the redistributive role of the state (i.e. to increase tax and spending levels) (Jarvis, 2012: 468). Beyond market-promoting legislative frameworks, the state is particularly charged under the contemporary development consensus to harmonise legal frameworks and soft regulatory incentives in a way that cultivates investor confidence in a country's *'general investment climate'* (IFC, 2018: 2). To prevent "pollution" of the investment atmosphere upon which their development strategy depends, states have to firstly become sensitive to (i.e. recognise) and consequently mitigate sources of risk which threaten investment flows. The intangibility and virtually limitless potential of such "environmental" reform draws a radical breadth of social relations and issues into its remit.

Since Douglass North's pioneering work on the role of institutions in economic development (North, 1991), comparative and longitudinal studies in the field of new institutional economics have demonstrated a positive correlation between foreign direct investment[11] (FDI) flows and a number of key institutional variables. Specifically, the stability of government, a secure and reliable legal system, and efficient bureaucracy are known to be 'closely associated' (Busse and Hefeker, 2007: 412) with FDI. In the early 1990s, as suggested earlier, the focus of institutional reform was on introducing basic prerequisites within domestic legal and political systems for market creation and expansion, such as the formal recognition and protection of private property rights. In more recent years, however, studies have begun to proliferate to understand the complex interaction between investor perceptions, institutions and FDI flows through the concept of political risk and investment profiling.

In particular, the *quality* of government stability, bureaucracy and 'law and order' systems (Busse and Hefeker, 2007: 400) has come under significant scrutiny by investors and multinational corporations as well as "development professionals" from international institutions like the World Bank. While the economics literature can agree on only a limited set of 'closely associated' variables as noted earlier, this seemingly narrow consensus hides a whole world of associated governance profiling in relation to the concept of political risk. Take the "stability" of government, for instance. What does this term really mean? Does it mean, at a basic level, that the government is not vulnerable to a coup? Or, less clearly, does it mean that the government is not prone to instigating swift changes to legislation? Similarly, how far does the concept of an "effective" legal system stretch? Are we referring to the independence of the judiciary and the availability of a domestic dispute resolution system, or investor access to international arbitration? Do we mean that legal rights are protected in general, or that *property* rights are specifically privileged? Equally, when determining the quality of bureaucracy, are we simply concerned that there is a basic *system* in place for gaining access to a new market (e.g. securing permits to mine)? More often than not, the sub-text of "quality bureaucracy" engages a new range of standard-setting relating to efficiency, ethics (e.g. anti-corruption) and institutional design.

These institutional variables form a critical component of the overall investment profile of a given state, alongside "regulatory indicators" of economic profitability. In addition to demonstrating that domestic political and legal institutions do not pose a risk to FDI, investors look for legislative and regulatory measures which ease or expedite the process of business registration, prevent national expropriation of foreign assets and maximise profits through tax stabilisation incentives and asset repatriation rights. The attractiveness of the investment environment goes beyond the regulations, laws, codes and repatriation rules governing investment to include wider policies and processes, such as accounting standards, competition policy and environmental management systems (UNCTAD, 2009: 7). Thus, becoming an attractive destination for FDI implies a significant domestic legal reform, as well as general recalibration of the wider policy and political environment that may indirectly affect perceptions of investment-worthiness.

It is very important to emphasise, however, that these domestic reforms are indissolubly linked with rule-making and norm-generating structures and processes beyond the state. Unlike the modernisation theories and initiatives of the 1960s and 1970s, which focused on *state*-led industrial development, domestic reform in the name of global market-based development over the past thirty years has sought to render the territorial borders of the national state porous and penetrable for private and international capital investment. Since the 1980s and early 1990s, Western powers and international financial institutions have zealously promoted domestic reform to dovetail with participation in the increasingly dense rule-making structures of the global economy. Through development-lending conditionalities, states in the Global South were incentivised if not compelled by international financial institutions to enter into multilateral and bilateral treaties to signal their openness for trade and investment in the global marketplace, as well as commitment to the principles of non-discrimination, the rule of law and foreign investment protection (Tan, 2011). For example, the elimination and reduction of domestic tariff barriers to trade in goods and services is a baseline requirement for states to access preferential trading relationships and markets through the WTO. Similarly, domestic adoption of anti-discrimination rules (i.e. between domestic and foreign investment) is a prerequisite for participation in multilateral and bilateral investment treaties which create the legal framework for further investment agreements.

Between the hard lines of the international trade and investment rules regimes, states also adopt and inculcate an increasing range of soft "global governance" benchmarking norms and international standards within their national development policies. International financial institutions and economic organisations like the World Bank and the World Economic Forum have introduced prominent good governance indicators and competitiveness benchmarks,[12] which include a range of social, environmental, political and legal measures of state effectiveness. However, "non-governmental" organisations like the International Organisation for Standardisation (ISO) have also contributed hugely to developing a global 'audit culture' (Shore and Wright, 2015) through the creation of well over 20,000 standards covering virtually every economic sector. ISO prides itself on the production of 'voluntary, consensus-based, market relevant International Standards that support innovation and provide solutions to global challenges' (ISO, 2019). Many of these standards are now widely adopted by states, particularly to address specific regulatory gaps or enhance reputation through association with a recognised standard.

Managing reputational risk is particularly acute for governments in the extractives sector, where economic returns on investments can be notoriously unpredictable given the volatility of market prices in the sector, alongside heightened conflict over socio-environmental impacts. Global anti-corruption and transparency initiatives (e.g. Extractive Industries Transparency Initiative) have become particularly prominent metrics of political risk and certainty in a given country's investment environment, as a result of the widely recognised association between natural resource extraction and corrupt behaviour by political elites. States increasingly use global governance norms as standards of accountability within their own social and environmental regulations and policies on impact assessment, environmental and social responsibility, and community participation. Even while states may not explicitly implement international standards into domestic regulatory frameworks, they can still become paradigmatic for national and local socio-environmental governance (Szablowski, 2007). As will be explored in Chapter 6 of this book, voluntary codes of conduct, investment performance standards and alternative dispute resolution mechanisms have been steadily introduced into Mongolia's mining governance framework through the activities of multinational corporations, transnational NGOs and international financial institutions. Through adoption of international standards and participation in global governance initiatives, states seek to build an attractive image of broad-based governance effectiveness.

The psychosocial dimension of attracting investment is increasingly recognised as an important part of global marketing strategies for states, reflected in the growing discourse of 'nation branding' (Dinnie, 2008). Around the world, teams of marketing experts develop and promote positive images of national jurisdictions to enhance the state's global competitiveness as a destination for FDI. For example, South Africa has an International Marketing Council (IMC) with a mandate 'to establish a compelling brand image for South Africa, which correctly positions the country in terms of its investment potential, credit worthiness, export opportunities, tourism potential and international relations' (Johnston, 2008: 5). In Mongolia's case, a nation-branding strategy was introduced by President Elbegdorj at the Mongolian Economic Forum in 2013. Its aim was to counteract the reputation Mongolia was quickly gaining at the time as a risky destination for investment due to the re-regulation of the mining sector. The President stated that 'the State itself has become the biggest risk,' noting that this perspective has been routinely reinforced by international standards agencies such as Ernst and Young (quoted in the UB Post, Khash-Erdene, 2013). The Minister for Economic Development at the time – N. Batbayer – stated at the same forum that:

> I believe Mongolia can not only brand its products, but become a global brand nation. We have vast lands, rich with mineral wealth. Some countries have already drained their natural resources but we are just beginning to explore them. Last year Mongolia successfully released its first government bonds, named after our Great Chinggis Khaan, worth 1.5 billion USD.

When we ventured to promote our bonds to other nations, we told them that Mongolia has the eighteenth largest land size – land that is full of mineral wealth; our two great neighbours are up to 500 times larger in population so we are well-positioned for trade; we are the descendants of the great Chinggis Khan; we are citizens of a democratic Mongolia; we value human rights; and we protect private property through the rule of law. And we asked them to work with us and they agreed. When we offered to sell 1.5 billion USD of bonds, they proposed to buy 15 billion USD of bonds. This indicates rising global interest and the enormous potential Mongolia has. We promised those that purchased our bonds that we would use this money for great development... The time of Mongolia to establish its name and brand has come.

For capital-importing states, whose "global" future is reliant on sustaining foreign investment interest (Schneiderman, 2013: 12), successful (i.e. "competitive" in market terms) integration into the global economy depends upon the authorisation of a complex and undetermined set of institutional prerequisites for transnational capital investment, as it is unlikely that without these legal guarantees investors will take the risk of investing (Stanford, 2008: 145). As Harvey (2005: 89–90) puts it:

> Capital accumulation through price-fixing market exchange flourishes best in the midst of certain institutional structures of law, private property, contract and security of the money form... Capitalists do not absolutely require such a framework to function, but without it they do face greater risks...

The adoption of particular legal rules and norms in the pursuit of market-led development cannot be explained in purely instrumental terms, however. Legal rules practically enable capital flows by easing or removing barriers, but they also construct *perceptions* of risk. State participation in the rule-making structures of the global economy alone does not necessarily guarantee investment, as indicated by the varied impact of different legal instruments on improving investment levels. For example, a 2009 United Nations Committee on Trade and Development (UNCTAD, 2009) report found that BITs had a negligible impact on improving FDI flows by themselves, whereas other instruments of economic cooperation –'Preferential Trade and Investment Agreements' – improved investment flows from developed to developing countries (ibid.: xii). In fact, there is some evidence that BITs 'do not attract the most development-enhancing FDI' (Colen and Guariso, 2013: 156). However, the UNCTAD report noted that regardless of actual direct impact from participation in global economic instruments, there was usually an indirect benefit of 'enhancing the attractiveness of countries' by adding 'policy and institutional determinants for FDI,' such as 'improv[ing] investment protection and add[ing] to the security, transparency, stability and predictability of the investment framework' (UNCTAD, 2009: xii).

## Contextualising extractive development

> There's always huge specific risks when you're looking at a hole in the
> ground.
>
> (Foreign investor in Mongolia[13])

In this wider context of global economic integration and market-based development, *extractive* development strategies are particularly charged with the perception of investment risk (see Tan, 2015). While all accumulation strategies premised upon competitiveness in global markets lead to new encounters and negotiations between the national state and the web of transnational legal norms described earlier, natural resource extraction is particularly "loaded" in terms of the scrutiny applied to state institutions (Hatcher, 2014: 17). For foreign investors, the reward potential may be high, but it requires close encounters with national bureaucracy as well as 'intensely local' (Bebbington et al., 2018: 218) negotiations to access the actual sites of extraction and sustain production in the face of conflict and interruptions. The transnational governance of extractive development expansively sweeps diverse aspects of economic, environmental, political and social relations into its remit. It is consequently a paradigmatic development strategy through which to understand the implications of transnational legal ordering, as it encapsulates the 'whole of society approach' (Carroll, 2012a: 351) characteristic of contemporary development governance.

Mining is particularly associated with concepts of risk from an investor perspective. A naïve company may assume that once a mining licence is issued, they will have uninhibited access to begin exploring and exploiting a mineral site. However, depending on the scale of the deposit, the state's interest may suddenly increase, particularly during global commodity price booms. Consequently, shareholder and corporate anxiety looms large that the original terms of agreement may be subject to change. In many jurisdictions, states have constitutional rights to the sub-soil, which are then "leased" through licences to private or foreign enterprises. The permanent sovereign ownership rights of states in relation to mineral deposits thus present a distinctive threat of expropriation, as compared to manufacturing, agricultural or technology sectors. Perceptions of risk based on anxieties about expropriation and nationalisation are also augmented by the tendency of national governments to heighten redistributive commitments based on anticipated mineral rents. When those rents do not materialise in a way that meets public expectations, states can be galvanised by, or even intentionally foment, domestic legitimacy crises to regain control of natural resources. Relatedly, foreign investors as well as companies fear that nationalisation may lead to the reintroduction of "discriminatory" measures which privilege domestic capital access to resource frontiers above foreign capital. There are also concerns that significant mineral exporters will use the fact that natural resources are unevenly distributed globally to increase export prices and create unpredictable supply markets for non-producers (Bellmann, 2016). Consequently, investors seek to build stability into the terms of their agreements with states, through legal stabilisation agreements (effectively "freezing" the applicable law or tax rates at the time the agreement is signed), concession agreements and careful construction of project financing contracts (see Bhatt, forthcoming: Chapter Four).

In addition to investor concerns about *national* sources of political and economic risk to an investment in mineral extraction, *local* or sub-national administrations are also perceived as a distinctive source of risk to projects. Sub-national administrations invariably seek to increase local benefits based on the proximity to the site of extraction, introducing another dimension of risk to an extractive project. In part, this is often because local communities suffer the brunt of extractive activities, through physical displacement, environmental degradation, infrastructure development and the significant social upheaval associated with mining. Mines, usually in rural areas, often require external sources of labour power, which introduce new social dynamics in relation to the preexisting communities. Equally, the development of urban housing, amenities and infrastructure can challenge traditional livelihoods and ways of life. While some of these changes may be welcomed, more often than not, new faultlines of social conflict emerge around extractive zones. Facing their own legitimacy crises at a local level, sub-national administrations may put pressure on developers to make contributions to ameliorate local discontent and concern, as well as to enhance personal and public wealth.

Growing concern over multiple and intersecting sources of risk in extractive industries has led to sector-specific binding and non-binding governance frameworks governing trade and investment relations (i.e. Energy Charter Treaty), anti-corruption and transparency (i.e. Extractive Industries Transparency Initiative), socio-environmental impacts (e.g. IFC Performance Standards, Equator Principles) and corporate social responsibility (e.g. Responsible Mining Index). Notably, it is the construction of a discourse of risk to *capital* investment which imbues global governance initiatives and motivates the introduction of new forms of legality into national and local jurisdictions. As Hatcher (2014: 33 citing Emel and Huber, 2008: 1398) suggests, 'capital has come to claim a monopoly over the idea of risk.' Even corporate social responsibility initiatives to gain a 'social license to operate' are primarily premised on securing stable local conditions for ongoing extraction of resources (Harvey and Bice, 2014).

The construction of a discourse of risk imbues transnational influence on mining regimes across the Global South. This risk-imbued approach to mining governance is exemplified in the lending safeguards, political risk insurance products and policy emphases of the World Bank Group (Hatcher, 2014; Tan, 2015), as well as other international financial institutions, credit ratings agencies and multinational corporations. This focus on risk has increased as the World Bank Group and other development finance institutions have come under systematic fire from transnational advocacy groups and mining-impacted communities for their promotion of deregulated, market-led extractivism since the 1980s. Drawing on the ground-breaking work of Bonnie Campbell (2004), the first and second generations of mining codes promoted by the World Bank Group through structural adjustment policies in the 1980s and 1990s focused on reducing the role of the state, opening national mining sectors to FDI and entrusting poverty reduction and development to the mechanism of the "invisible hand" of the market (see also Hatcher, 2014: 20). This approach to mining regulation in Africa, which is increasingly promoted in post-socialist countries in the 1990s, aligns closely with the broader development rationality of marketisation as described earlier. As Hatcher (ibid.: 21) puts it, 'by the end of the 1990s, countries were actively competing to have the most deregulated and liberalised mining regime,' based on the consistent advice from international financial institutions that such openness would incentivise FDI.

Notably, this approach failed abysmally to produce the kind of development anticipated by national governments and their publics across the Global South. The increasing pressure on the development financial institutions as well as multinational corporations to redeem themselves from the failure of the pure marketisation model in the late 1990s and early 2000s led to a renewed focus on the role of the state in terms of playing a socially necessary function as a regulator and manager of market dynamics in the pursuit of development. The practical outworking of this renewed focus on the role of the state and the market as the "dynamic duo" of development has led to a *positive* emphasis on the role of the state. Consequently, the extent to which the state *effectively* supports a market-led development strategy has become a new focus for international development institutions (both multilateral and bilateral). The 'third generation' of mining regimes (Campbell, 2004) since the early 2000s reflects this shifting paradigm where extractive development is coterminous with transformation – rather than negation – of the role of the state in the value-laden framework of effective market management. The substance of state transformation in these terms can really only be determined by looking at a case study in detail, as the rest of this book proposes to do. However, it is safe to say that despite variations over time, transnational influence on mining regime formation has consistently transmitted a 'particular politics' (Hatcher, 2014: 12) about the role of the state.

## Conclusion

This chapter has mapped out the framing theory for this book. It has argued for an interdisciplinary conceptualisation of the constitutional in terms of the reproduction of foundational patterns of governance, where relations of state, market and law are conceptualised as distinctive elements of a whole. The first part of the chapter introduced key concepts which will be deployed throughout the book and provided an intellectual genealogy of the author's approach to state transformation in relation to key debates in the international relations and international law literatures. The second part of the chapter contextualised the co-constitutive dynamics of state, market and law within changing conceptions of economic development and globalisation generally, and then in relation to extractive development more specifically. The following chapter will introduce the case study of Mongolia and provide a short discussion of the research process and roadmap of the book, moving on to the substantive empirical contribution in Part II.

## Notes

1 Capital mobility is 'the ability to move funds and assets across borders unrestricted by policies or legislation' (Gill and Cutler, 2014: 313).
2 Hegemony contrasts with 'supremacy' or outright domination in that sense that it 'combines coercion and consent, force and persuasion in an ethical, cultural and political process whereby the principal ideals, institutions and material potentials of the leading social forces are legitimised' (Gill and Cutler, 2014: 317; see Gramsci, 1971).
3 *De facto* and *de jure* are used in this book to designate a 'situation or condition that exists in reality' (*de facto*) and 'a situation, entitlement or claim that exists by right or law' (*de jure*) (Gill and Cutler, 2014: 315).
4 For example, Western feudalism was organised on the basis of 'parcellised sovereignty' (Wood, 2002: 19), whereby the 'extra-economic' (ibid) power of the feudal lords to extract surplus from serfs was crucial to systematising processes of accumulation, as well as guaranteeing further production. Equally, albeit differently, the empires of East Asia (e.g. that of Chinggis Khan in the thirteenth century and the Manchu/Qing Empire which followed) were organised according to the political logic of suzerainty, whereby the Emperor exacted tribute from its regions whilst giving the nobles and princes governing them a relatively high degree of control and autonomy (see Chapter 3).
5 Many thanks to Dr Johanna Cortés Nieto (Rosario University, Colombia) for her insight on this subject. See Cortés Nieto, 2019.
6 Critics of such a claim might point to examples where we can see transnational law appear to elide the national level and penetrate local spaces with global legal norms. David Szablowski's study of the role of transnational law in local struggles about mining in the Peruvian Andes is very insightful on this point. He points to the strategic "selective absence" of the state in making these "global-local" encounters a realistic possibility.
7 However, Polanyi credits the self-regulating market with the creation of the 'liberal state' form, upon 'non-interference in the formation and functioning of markets and, namely, the price mechanisms' (Frerichs, 2017: 255, citing Polanyi, 1944/1957: 3, 69).
8 While a system of *lex mercatoria* also existed during the medieval period, the differentiations from its modern capitalist counterpart are significant. The modern (capitalist) *lex mercatoria* relied on the production of a public–private division, and the securing of conditions for the consolidation of *corporate* power alongside the national state.
9 The Washington Consensus focused on ten aspects of economic reform, covering fiscal discipline, reducing public expenditure, reforming taxation framework, liberalising the financial sector and exchange rates (i.e. adopting floating rather than fixed exchange rates), liberalising trade regimes to promote and protect foreign investment,

privatisation of national industries and assets, economic deregulation (i.e. the removal of exit and entry constraints for capital investors), and the recognition and judicial protection of private property rights ( Williamson, 2005).

10 Hard law refers to legislation or statutes which can be legally enforced in a court of law. Soft law or mechanisms are 'rules that do not have the binding force of legislation, but that are nevertheless influential in shaping behaviour' (Gill and Cutler, 2014: 323).

11 Foreign Direct Investment 'refers to the investment outside the home country of the investing company in which control over the resources transferred remains with the investor' (O'Brien and Williams, 2010: 186). It can also be understood as 'transnational production' (ibid., 188), carried out by a range of firms designated by their status of working beyond national jurisdictions. Transnational producers may go by different names (i.e. international firms, multinational/transnational/ global corporations) but they are essentially engaged in the same form of economic activity.

12 The World Bank's good governance indicators include (1) voice and accountability, (2) political stability and the absence of violence, (3) government effectiveness, (4) regulatory quality, (5) rule of law and (6) control of corruption. The World Economic Forum's Global Competitiveness Report is based on a complex benchmarking standard which assesses the aggregate impact of twelve "pillars" of competitiveness clustered under four headings: enabling environment, markets, human capital and innovative eco-system (see Schwab, 2018).

13 Author interview, 15th July 2019.

# References

Acosta, A. 2013. "Extractivism and Neo-Extractivism: Two Sides of the Same Coin." In M. Lang and D. Mokrani (eds.) *Beyond Development: Alternative Visions from Latin America*. Amsterdam/Quito: Transnational Institute/Rosa Luxemburg Foundation, pp. 61–86.

Adelman, S. and Paliwala, A. 1993. *Law and Crisis in the Third World*. London: Hans Zell.

Anderson, G. 2014. "Constitutionalism as a Critical Project: The Epistemological Challenge to Politics." In S. Gill and C. Cutler (eds.) *New Constitutionalism and World Order*. Cambridge: Cambridge University Press, pp. 281–294.

Auty, R. M. (ed.) 2001. *Resource Abundance and Economic Development*. Oxford: Oxford University Press.

Bebbington, A., Abdulai, A. G., Humphreys Bebbington, D., Hinfelaar, M., and Sanborn, C. 2018. *Governing Extractive Industries: Politics, History, Ideas*. Oxford: Oxford University Press.

Bellmann, C. 2016. "Trade and Investment Frameworks in Extractive Industries: Challenges and Options." E15 Expert Group on Trade and Investment in Extractive Industries – Policy Options Paper. Geneva: International Centre for Trade and Sustainable Development (ICTSD) and World Economic Forum. Available at http:// e15initiative.org/wp-content/uploads/2015/09/E15_ICTSD_Trade_Investment_ Frameworks_Extractive_Industries_report_2015.pdf

Berman, P. 2005. "From International Law to Law and Globalisation." *Columbia Journal of Transnational Law* 43: 485–556.

Bhatt, K. Forthcoming. *Concessionaires, Financiers and Communities: Implementing In-digenous Peoples' Rights to Land in Transnational Development Projects*. Cambridge: Cambridge University Press.

Biersteker, T. J. 1990. "Reducing the Role of the State in the Economy: A Conceptual Exploration of World Bank and IMF Prescriptions." *International Studies Quarterly* 34(4): 477–492.

Blokker, P. and Thornhill. C. (eds.) 2017. *Sociological Constitutionalism*. Cambridge: Cambridge University Press.

Braithwaite, J. and Drahos, P. 2000. *Global Business Regulation*. Cambridge: Cambridge University Press.

Brenner, N., Jessop, B., Jones, M., and Macleod, G. (eds.) 2003. *State/Space: A Reader*. Oxford: John Wiley and Sons.

Busse, M. and Hefeker, C. 2007. "Political Risk, Institutions and Foreign Direct Invest-ment." *European Journal of Political Economy* 23(2): 397–415.

Calliess, G. P. and Zumbansen, P. 2010. *Rough Consensus and Running Code: A Theory of Transnational Private Law*. Oxford: Hart Publishing.

Campbell, B. (ed.). 2004. "Regulating Mining in Africa: For Whose Benefit?" Discussion Paper 26. Uppsala: Nordica Africa Institute.

———— (ed.). 2009. *Mining in Africa: Regulation and Development*. London, Ottawa and Uppsala: Pluto, IDRC and Nordica Africa Institute.

————. 2010. "Revisiting the Reform Process of African Mining Regimes." *Canadian Journal of Development Studies* 30(1–2): 197–217.

Campbell, B. and Hatcher, P. 2019. Neoliberal Reform, Contestation and Relations of Power in Mining: Observations from Guinea and Mongolia. *The Extractive Industries and Society* 6: 642–653.

Carroll, T. 2012a. "Introduction: Neo-Liberal Development Policy in Asia beyond the Post-Washington Consensus." *Journal of Contemporary Asia* 42(3): 350–358.

————. 2012b. "Working on, through and around the State: The Deep Marketisation of Development in the Asia Pacific." *Journal of Contemporary Asia* 42(3): 378–404.

Chwieroth, J. M. 2008. "International Liquidity Provision: The IMF and the World Bank in the Treasury and Marshall Systems." In Andrews, D. M. (ed.) *Orderly Change: International Monetary Relations since Bretton Woods*. Ithaca, NY and London: Cornell University Press, pp. 52–77.

Colen, L. and Guariso, A. 2013. "What Type of Foreign Direct Investment Is At-tracted by Bilateral Investment Treaties?" In O. De Schutter, J. Swinnen, and J. Wouters (eds.) *Foreign Direct Investment and Human Development: The Law and Economics of International Investment Agreements*. Abingdon/New York: Routledge, pp. 138–156.

Cortés Nieto, J. 2019. "Governing the Poor in Contemporary Colombia." University of Warwick, PhD Thesis.

Cox, R. 1987. *Power, Production and World Order: Social Forces in the Making of History*. New York: Columbia University Press.

Craig, D. and Porter, D. 2006. *Development beyond Neoliberalism? Governance, Poverty Reduction and Political Economy*. New York: Routledge.

Cutler, C. 1999. "Locating 'Authority' in the Global Political Economy." *International Studies Quarterly* 43: 59–81.

————. 2003. *Private Power and Global Authority: Transnational Merchant Law in the Global Political Economy*. Cambridge: Cambridge University Press.

———. 2005. "Gramsci, Law and the Culture of Global Capitalism." *Critical Review of International Social and Political Philosophy* 8(4): 527–542.

———. 2014. "New Constitutionalism and the Commodity Form of Global Capitalism." In Gill, S. and Cutler, C. (eds.) *New Constitutionalism and World Order.* Cambridge: Cambridge University Press, pp. 45–62.

———. 2015. "New Constitutionalism, Democracy and the Future of Global Governance." In S. Gill (ed.) *Critical Perspectives on the Crisis of Global Governance.* Basingstoke, Hampshire/New York: Palgrave Macmillan, pp. 89–104.

Dinnie, K. 2008. *Nation Branding: Concepts, Issues, Practice.* Abingdon: Routledge.

Drezner, D. W. 2007. *All Politics Is Global.* Princeton, NJ: Princeton University Press.

Dunn, B. 2014. *The Political Economy of Global Capitalism and Crisis.* Abingdon: Routledge.

Faundez, J. (ed.) 1997. *Good Government and Law: Legal and Institutional Reform in Developing Countries.* Basingstoke: Macmillan Press Ltd.

Ferguson, J. 1990. *The Anti-Politics Machine: Development, Depoliticisation and Bureaucratic Power in Lesotho.* Minneapolis: University of Minnesota Press.

Frerichs, S. 2011. "Re-embedding Neoliberal Constitutionalism: A Polanyian Case for the Economic Sociology of Law." In C. Joerges and J. Falke (eds.) *Karl Polanyi, Globalisation and the Potential of Law in Transnational Markets.* Oxford/Portland, OR: Hart Publishing, pp. 65–84.

———. 2012. "Studying Law, Economy and Society: A Short History of Socio-Legal Thinking." Helsinki Legal Studies Research Paper No. 19 (University of Helsinki). Online. Available at: https://papers.ssrn.com/sol3/papers.cfm?abstract_id=2022891. Accessed 1st June 2019.

———. 2017. "The Rule of the Market." In Blokker, P. and Thornhill, C. (eds.) *Sociological Constitutionalism.* Cambridge: Cambridge University Press, pp. 241–264.

Gagné-Ouellet, S. 2013. "Regulatory Framework Review and Mining Regime Reform in Mali: Degrees of Rupture and Continuity." In Campbell, B. (ed.) *Modes of Governance and Revenue Flows in African Mining.* London: Palgrave Macmillan.

Gardner, J. A. 1980. *Legal Imperialism: American Lawyers and Foreign Aid in Latin America.* Madison: University of Wisconsin Press.

Garth, B. and Dezalay, Y. 1996. *Dealing in Virtue: International Commercial Arbitration and the Construction of a Transnational Legal Order.* Chicago, IL: University of Chicago Press.

Gill, S. 1995. "Globalisation, Market Civilisation, and Disciplinary Neoliberalism." *Millennium Journal of International Studies* 23(3): 399–423.

———. 1998. "New Constitutionalism, Democratisation and Global Political Economy." *Pacifica Review: Peace, Security and Global Change* 10(1): 23–38.

———. (ed.) 2015. *Critical Perspectives on the Crisis of Global Governance.* Basingstoke, Hampshire/New York: Palgrave Macmillan.

Gill, S. and Cutler, C. 2014. *New Constitutionalism and World Order.* Cambridge: Cambridge University Press.

Gold, E. R. 2008. "Legal Foundations of the U.S. Dollar, 1933–1934 and 1971–1978." In Andrews, D. M. (ed.) *Orderly Change: International Monetary Relations since Bretton Woods.* Ithaca, NY and London: Cornell University Press, pp. 177–188.

Goldoni, M. 2019. "Introduction to the Material Study of Global Constitutional Law." *Global Constitutionalism* 8(1): 71–93.

Gramsci, A. 1971. *Selections from the Prison Notebooks.* New York: International Publishers.

Hall, B. R. and Biersteker, T. J. (eds.) 2007. *The Emergence of Private Authority in Global Governance*. Cambridge: Cambridge University Press.

Halliday, T. C. and Shaffer, G. 2015. *Transnational Legal Orders*. Cambridge: Cambridge University Press.

Hameiri, S. and Jones, L. 2014. "Murdoch International: The "Murdoch School" in International Relations." Murdoch University Asia Research Centre Working Paper No. 178. Available at: www.murdoch.edu.au/Research-capabilities/Asia-Research-Centre/_document/WP178.pdf

Harrison, G. 2004. *The World Bank and Africa: The Construction of Governance States*. Abingdon: Routledge.

Harvey, B. and Bice, S. 2014. "Social Impact Assessment, Social Development Programmes and Social Licence to Operate: Tensions and Contradictions in Intent and Practice in the Extractive Sector." *Impact Assessment and Project Appraisal* 32(4): 327–355.

Harvey, D. 2005. *A Brief History of Neoliberalism*. Oxford: Oxford University Press.

Hatcher, P. 2014. *Regimes of Risk: The World Bank and the Transformation of Mining in Asia*. New York/London: Palgrave Macmillan.

Hayek, F. A. 1988. *The Fatal Conceit: The Errors of Socialism*. Chicago, IL: University of Chicago Press.

Held, D. and McGrew, A. 2003. *The Global Transformations Reader: An Introduction to the Globalisation Debate*, 2nd Edition. Cambridge: Polity Press.

Humphreys, M., Sachs, J. D., and Stiglitz, J. E. 2007. *Escaping the Resource Curse*. New York: Columbia University Press.

IFC. 2018. "Investment Reform Map for Mongolia: A Foundation for a New Investment Policy and Promotion Strategy." Ulaanbaatar: IFC. Available at http://documents.worldbank.org/curated/en/158851537431181525/Investment-Reform-Map-for-Mongolia-A-Foundation-for-a-new-Investment-Policy-and-Promotion-Strategy

ISO. 2019. "About Us." www.iso.org/about-us.html. Accessed 30th May 2019.

Jarvis, D. S. L. 2012. "The Regulatory State in Developing Countries: Can It Exist and Do We Want It? The Case of the Indonesian Power Sector." *Journal of Contemporary Asia* 42(3): 464–492.

Jayasuriya, K. 1999. "Globalisation, Law and the Transformation of Sovereignty: The Emergence of Global Regulatory Governance." *Indiana Journal of Global Legal Studies* 6: 425–455.

———. 2001a. "Globalisation, Sovereignty, and the Rule of Law: From Political to Economic Constitutionalism?" *Constellations* 8(4): 442–460.

———. 2001b. "Globalisation and the Changing Architecture of the State: The Regulatory State and the Politics of Negative Coordination." *Journal of European Public Policy* 8(1): 101–123.

Jessop, B. 1982. *The Capitalist State*. Oxford: Martin Robertson & Company Ltd.

———. 1990. *State Theory: Putting Capitalist States in Their Place*. Cambridge: Polity Press.

———. 2008. *State Power: A Strategic-Relational Approach*. Cambridge: Polity Press.

Jessup, P. 1956. *Transnational Law*. New Haven, CT: Yale University Press.

Johnston, Y. 2008. "Country Case Insight – South Africa: Developing Brand South Africa." In K. Dinnie (ed.) *Nation Branding: concepts, Issues, Practice*. Abingdon: Routledge, pp. 5–13.

Khash-Erdene, B. 2013. "Economic Forum 2013 Aims to Establish Mongolian Brand" 7th March *UB Post* http://ubpost.mongolnews.mn/?p=3235 Accessed 1st March 2019.

Kjaer, P. 2014. *Constitutionalism in the Global Realm: A Sociological Approach.* London: Routledge.

Koskenniemi, M. and Leino, P. 2002. "Fragmentation of International Law? Postmodern Anxieties." *Leiden Journal of International Law* 15: 553–579.

Krasner, S.D. (ed.). 1983. *International Regimes.* Ithaca: Cornell University Press.

Lander, J. 2019. "Doing 'Law in/and Development': Theoretical, Methodological and Ethical Reflections." In N. Creutzfeldt, M. Mason and K. Mcconnachie (eds.) *Routledge Handbook on Socio-Legal Theory and Methods.* Abingdon: Routledge.

Levi-Faur, D. 2005. "The Global Diffusion of Regulatory Capitalism." *The Annals of the American Academy of Political and Social Science* 598: 12–32.

Li, T. M. 2007. *The Will to Improve: Governmentality, Development and the Practice of Politics.* Durham, NC and London: Duke University Press.

Litowitz, D. 2000. "Gramsci, Hegemony, and the Law." *Brigham Young University Law Review* 2: 515–551.

Loughlin, M. 2014. "Constitutional Pluralism: An Oxymoron?" *Global Constitutionalism* 3(1): 9–30.

Meszaros, G. 2013. *Social Movements, Law and the Politics of Land Reform: Lessons from Brazil.* Abingdon: Routledge.

North, D. C. 1991. 'Institutions.' *The Journal of Economic Perspectives* (5)1: 97–112.

O'Brien, R. & Williams, M. 2010. *Global Political Economy 3rd Edition.* Basingstoke, Hampshire/New York: Palgrave Macmillan.

O'Rourke, K. and Williamson, J. 1999. *Globalisation and History.* Cambridge, MA: MIT Press.

Packenham, R. A. 1973. *Liberal America and the Third World: Political Development Ideas in Foreign Aid and Social Science.* Princeton: Princeton University Press.

Paliwala, A. 2007. "Free Culture, Global Commons and Social Justice in Information Technology Diffusion." *Law, Social Justice & Global Development Journal* 1: 1–21. Available at https://warwick.ac.uk/fac/soc/law/elj/lgd/2007_1/paliwala/paliwala.pdf

Perry-Kessaris, A. 2008. *Global Business, Local Law: The Indian Legal System as a Communal Resource in Foreign Investment Relations.* Aldershot, Hampshire and Burlington, VT: Ashgate Publishing Company.

———. 2011. Prepare Your Indicators: Economics Imperialism on the Shores of Law and Development. *International Journal of Law in Context* 7(4): 401–421.

———. (ed.) 2013. *Socio-Legal Approaches to International Economic Law: Text, Context, Subtext.* Abingdon: Routledge.

Peters, A. 2009. "The Merits of Global Constitutionalism." *Indiana Journal of Global Legal Studies* 16: 397–411.

Picciotto, S. 1997. "The Regulatory Criss-Cross: Interaction between Jurisdictions and the Construction of Global Regulatory Networks." In W. Bratton, J. McCahery, S. Picciotto and C. Scott (eds.) *International Regulatory Competition and Coordination: Perspectives on Economic Regulation in Europe and the United States.* Oxford: Clarendon Press.

———. 2016. "Critical Theory and Practice in International Economic Law and the New Global Governance." In M. Bungenberg, C. Herrmann, M. Krajewski and J. P. Terhechte (eds.) *European Yearbook of International Economic Law Volume 7 2016.* Published online www.springer.com/gb/book/9783319292144. Accessed 2nd December 2016.

Polanyi, K. 1944/1957. *The Great Transformation: The Political and Economic Origins of Our Time*. Boston, MA: Beacon Press.

———. 1944/2001. *The Great Transformation: The Political and Economic Origins of Our Time*. 2nd Edition. Boston, MA: Beacon Press.

———. 1957. "The Economy as Instituted Process." In K. Polanyi, C. M. Arensberg, H. W. Pearson (eds.) *Trade and Market in the Early Empires*. Chicago, IL: Henry Regnery Company.

Robison, R. 1986. *Indonesia: The Rise of Capital*. Sydney: Allen and Unwin. (ed). 2006. *The Neoliberal Revolution: Forging the Market State*. Hampshire: Palgrave.

Robison, R. and Hadiz, V. R. 2004. *Reorganising Power in Indonesia: The Politics of Oligarchy in an Age of Markets*. New York: RoutledgeCurzon.

Rodan, G. 1989. *The Political Economy of Singapore's Industrialization: National State and International Capital*. London: Macmillan.

Rostow, W. W. 1959. "The Stages of Economic Growth." *The Economic History Review* 12(1): 1–16.

Rupert, M. and Smith, H. (eds.). 2002. *Historical Materialism and Globalisation*. London: Routledge.

Sassen, S. 2006. *Territory, Authority, Rights: From Medieval to Global Assemblages*. Princeton, NJ: Princeton University Press.

———. 2007. *The Sociology of Globalisation*. London/New York: W. W. Norton & Co.

Schneiderman, D. 2008. *Constitutionalising Economic Globalisation: Investment Rules and Democracy's Promise*. Cambridge: Cambridge University Press.

———. 2013. *Resisting Economic Globalisation: Critical Theory and International Investment Law*. Basingstoke, Hampshire/New York: Palgrave Macmillan.

———. 2016. "Global Constitutionalism and International Economic Law: The Case of International Investment Law." In M. Bungenburg, C. Herrmann, M. Krajewski, and J. P. Terhechte (eds.) *European Yearbook of International Economic Law*. New York: Springer Publishing.

Scholte, J. A. 1997. "Global Capitalism and the State." *International Affairs* 73(3): 427–452.

Schwab, K. (ed.) 2018. "Global Competitiveness Report." Geneva: World Economic Forum.

Shaffer, G. 2014. *Transnational Legal Ordering and State Change*. Cambridge: Cambridge University Press.

———. 2016. "Theorising Transnational Legal Ordering." *Annual Review of Law and Social Science* 12: 231–253.

Shaffer, G. and Coye, C. 2017. "From International Law to Jessup's Transnational Law, from Transnational Law to Transnational Legal Orders." UC Irvine School of Law Research Paper No. 2017–02. Available at SSRN: https://ssrn.com/abstract=2895159

Shore, C. and Wright, S. 2015. "Governing by Numbers: Audit Culture, Rankings and the New World Order." *Social Anthropology* 23(1): 22–28.

Shriver, R. S. Jr. 1963. "Peace Corps Lawyers: Building Emerging African Societies." *American Bar Association Journal* 49(5): 456–459.

Slaughter, A. M. 1997. "The Real World Order." *Foreign Affairs* 76(5): 183–197.

———. 2004. *A New World Order*. Princeton, NJ: Princeton University Press.

Stanford, J. 2008. *Economics for Everyone: A Short Guide to the Economics of Capitalism*. London: Pluto Press.

Stewart, A. 2011. *Gender, Law and Justice in a Global Market*. Cambridge: Cambridge University Press.

Strange, S. 1988. *States and Markets.* London: Pinter.

Streeck, W. 2014. *Buying Time: The Delayed Crisis of Democratic Capitalism.* London/ New York: Verso Books.

Szablowski, D. 2007. *Transnational Law and Local Struggles: Mining, Communities and the World Bank.* Bloomsbury: Hart Publishing.

Tamanaha, B. Z. 2008. "Understanding Legal Pluralism: Past to Present, Local to Global." *Sydney Law Review* 30: 375–411.

———. 2011. "The Primacy of Society and the Failures of Law and Development." *Cornell International Law Journal* 44: 209–247.

Tan, C. 2011. *Governance through Development: Poverty Reduction Strategies, International Law and the Disciplining of Third World States.* Abingdon: Routledge.

———. 2013. "Navigating New Landscapes: Socio-legal Mapping of Plurality and Power in International Economic Law." In A. Perry-Kessaris (ed.) *Socio-Legal Approaches to International Economic Law: Text, Context, Subtext.* Abingdon: Routledge, pp. 19–35.

———. 2015. Risky Business: Political Risk Insurance and the Law and Governance of Natural Resources. *International Journal of Law in Context* 11(2): 174–194.

Teubner, G. 2011. (translated by Michelle Everson) *Networks as Connected Contracts.* Oxford and Portland, OR: Hart Publishing.

———. 2012. *Constitutional Fragments: Societal Constitutionalism and Globalisation.* Oxford: Oxford University Press.

Thompson, E. P. 1978. *The Poverty of Theory and Other Essays.* London: The Merlin Press Ltd.

Thornhill, C. 2011. *A Sociology of Constitutions: Constitutions and State Legitimacy in Historical-Sociological Perspective.* Cambridge: Cambridge University Press.

Trubek, D. and Galanter, M. 1974. "Scholars in Self-Estrangement: Some Reflections on the Crisis in Law and Development Studies in the United States." *Wisconsin Law Review* 4: 1062–1102.

Trubek, D. and Santos, A. (eds.) 2006. *The New Law and Economic Development: A Critical Appraisal.* Cambridge: Cambridge University Press.

Twining, 2009. *General Jurisprudence: Understanding Law from a Global Perspective.* Cambridge: Cambridge University Press.

United Nations Conference on Trade and Development (UNCTAD). 2009. The Role of International Investment Agreements in Attracting Foreign Direct Investment to Developing Countries. *UNCTAD Series on International Investment Policies for Development.* London/Geneva: United Nations. Published online http://unctad.org/en/ docs/diaeia20095_en.pdf Accessed 1st March 2019.

Venn, F. 2002. *The Oil Crisis.* London: Longman.

Williamson, J. 2005. "The Washington Consensus as Policy Prescription for Development." In T. Besley and R. Zagha (eds.) *Development Challenges in the 1990s: Leading Policy-Makers Speak from Experience.* Washington D.C. /New York: World Bank and Oxford University Press, pp. 31–60.

Wood, E. M. 1981. The Separation of the Economic and the Political in Capitalism. *New Left Review* 127: 66–95.

———. 1995. *Democracy against Capitalism: Renewing Historical Materialism.* London/New York: Verso Books.

———. 2002. "Global Capital, National States." In Rupert, M. and Smith, H. (eds.) *Historical Materialism and Globalisation.* London: Routledge, pp. 17–39.

Woodley, D. 2015. *Globalisation and Capitalist Geopolitics: Sovereignty and State Power in a Multi-Polar World*. London/New York: Routledge.

Zumbansen, P. 2012a. "Defining the Space of Transnational Law: Legal Theory, Global Governance, and Legal Pluralism." *Transnational Law and Contemporary Problems* 21(2): 305–336.

———. 2012b. "Comparative, Global and Transnational Constitutionalism: The Emergence of a Transnational Legal-Pluralist Order." *Global Constitutionalism* 1(1): 16–52.

———. 2013. "*Lochner* Disembedded: The Anxieties of Law in a Global Context." *Indiana Journal of Global Legal Studies* 20(1): 29–69.

Zumbansen, P. and Bhatt, K. 2018. "Transnational Constitutional Law." TLI Think! Paper 6/2018; King's College London Dickson Poon School of Law Legal Studies Research Paper No. 2018–05. Available at SSRN: https://ssrn.com/abstract=3117352 or doi:10.2139/ssrn.3117352

# Chapter 2

# Introduction to the case study

## Constituting a resource frontier in Outer Mongolia

> You are all invited to Mongolia. Come take a look at this and try to understand the difference between developing a mineral province and a mere promotion on an individual mineral occurrence.
>
> Robert Friedland, CEO of Ivanhoe Mines addressing an investor conference in Tampa, Florida in 2005 (Friedland, 2005)

In terms of political and economic status, Mongolia has existed on the margins of global power since the fall of Chinggis Khan's empire in the fourteenth century. A land-locked desert steppe sandwiched between the territorial boundaries of Russia and China, Mongolia has a rich but largely hidden history, overshadowed by the prominence of its neighbours in the international sphere. However, since the late 1990s, Mongolia has risen to international prominence as the "final frontier" of untapped mineral wealth, boasting some of the world's largest reserves of high-quality coking coal, copper, gold, fluorspar and iron ore, in addition to recent discoveries of extensive natural gas and petroleum resources. Some of the world's largest deposits of copper, high-quality gold, iron, coking coal and fluorspar lie within its territory, estimated to be worth approximately 1.3 trillion U.S. dollars and constituting almost 17% of the world's mineral reserves (National Development Agency, 2019: 14).

Perceived widely as one of the few "success stories" of post-socialist transition (Fish, 2001), Mongolia's stable democratic political system and market-friendly economy have made this new resource frontier all the more tempting for foreign investment. Even the lack of infrastructure has not proven to be a major barrier for foreign mining companies to take the risk of a frontier investment. With Mongolia's two most significant mineral deposits located in the South Gobi, only 100 kilometres from the Chinese border, and China throwing capital and manpower at roads and railways, Mongolia seems to have everything needful to successfully harness foreign capital flows and find a competitive niche in the global economy. Referring to mega-mines Oyu Tolgoi (copper and gold) and

Tavan Tolgoi (coking coal), Robert Friedland (2005), CEO of Ivanhoe mines, candidly put it at an investor conference:

> You load [copper and coal ore] into trucks and they go across the Gobi Desert... heading for China. And you trade it for money. This is what mining is supposed to be.

Mongolia joined the ranks of other post-socialist and post-colonial states seeking to attract foreign investment in natural resources in the late 1990s. Mongolia in particular gained an international reputation in the early years of the new millennium as a vast frontier, full of mining potential, with only 25% of its minerals base having been explored by 2013 (International Business Publications, 2013: 145). In its national development strategy, the Mongolian state also recognised mineral extraction and export as the main driver of economic development, at least in the short to medium term (Government of Mongolia, 2007; see also Lander, 2014). However, to enable much-needed foreign investment in its formerly state-owned minerals sector, the Mongolian state needed to demonstrate – legally, not just rhetorically – that the sector was *open* for investment. Like other post-socialist countries that were desperate to attract foreign direct investment (FDI) in the 1990s and early 2000s (Knottnerus and Olivet, 2016: 2), successive governments sought to elevate national competitiveness in the sphere of investment and trade through natural resource extraction. A pro-market, democratised state governing a country with vast mineral potential sparked strong investment interest, as it offered a largely unexplored frontier of accumulation at a time with few horizons of new extractive possibilities.

In the early 1990s, the groundwork had already been laid for Mongolia to pursue its comparative advantage in minerals in the global economy. Mongolia was one of many countries which received assistance from multilateral financial institutions to promote market-driven development strategies. In the wake of a collapsing Soviet Union, Mongolia had embarked on a major project of political and economic liberalisation (Pomfret, 2000; Reinert, 2000: 16; Rossabi, 2005: 43–114). Determined to avoid economic and political dependence on either of its "superpower" neighbours, Mongolia looked to Western powers and multilateral assistance. In exchange for aid and loans from international financial institutions (i.e. the IMF and the World Bank), Mongolia underwent a "structural adjustment" process which unified distinct programmes of political and economic reforms regarded at the time as a development blueprint for post-socialist states (Sachs, 1994). Mongolia was praised by Western democracies, international development institutions and academics as a 'model pupil' (Reinert, 2000: 17) of post-socialist transition (Munkh-Erdene, 2011: 61), as the state simultaneously adopted programmes of political liberalisation and economic deregulation to constitute a liberal democratic state and a free market economy (Fish, 2001; Fritz, 2002). This broad-based liberalisation of the political and economic spheres and the limitation of state power were two parts of the same picture of constitutional reform of the Mongolian state, by establishing a constitutional democracy based on the separation of powers and the election of political representatives, with private capital favoured as the driver of economic development (Munkh-Erdene, 2011). Endowed with incredible mineral wealth and a small population, Mongolia seemed to have everything going for it when it emerged on the global minerals market in 1997: a major market for its minerals to the south (China) and the interest of the Western investment establishment, relative to its Central Asian neighbours. In the mid-1990s, the World Bank recognised Mongolia's potential to become competitive in the global minerals economy and supported the Mongolian government to create one of the most open, investor-friendly mining regimes in Asia (Hatcher, 2014).

However, behind the formal appearance of readiness for global economic integration, elements of potential conflict with market-led development lay dormant in Mongolia's national institutions. For example, Mongolia's 1992 democratic constitution embodies the political tension over the country's developmental trajectory between the former communist and the new capitalist regime. Article 5.2 recognises 'all forms of private and public property' (Article 5.2) as a means to promote economic development 'based on different forms of property which takes into account universal trends of world economic development and national specifics' (Article 5.1). The pluralistic conception of property rights enshrined in Mongolia's democratic constitution partly reflected the state's new commitment to a market economy based on transferable property rights and market price mechanisms. The recognition and protection of private property were critical to Mongolia's adherence to 'universal trends of world economic development' (ibid.) and integration within the global capitalist economic system which now had a hegemonic status after the fall of the Soviet Union (Korsun and Murrell, 1995; Harvey, 2005; Munkh-Erdene, 2011: 62). At the same time, Mongolia's long history of pastoral production necessitated state protection of public forms of property, such as customary use-rights in state-owned land. The resistant attitude of Mongolians, particularly in rural areas, to land privatisation (Tumenbayer, 2002; Endicott, 2012) meant that the state had to balance its new recognition of private property with an ongoing commitment to protecting public property forms. In developmental terms, this constitutional "compromise" legally reflects the ideological tension between the socialist–nationalist legacy of the state and its new capitalist commitment to global market-led economic development.

This constitutional ambiguity was essentially untested until 1997, when the liberal 1997 Minerals Law was introduced. The 1997 Minerals Law marked a radical departure from previous mineral codes, by simultaneously enabling an unprecedented level of foreign private investment into Mongolia's natural resource sector and restricting the ownership rights of the state. Like other historical mining booms around the world, some domestic and mostly foreign extractors arrived on this new mineral frontier, and scrambled for access to geological maps and licences from the Mineral Resources Authority of Mongolia (MRAM). Around the same time, in the early 2000s, in an unprecedented rural mobilisation, Mongolian citizens began to organise themselves into movements to protest private extractive access to land and water resources which had previously been held in public trust by the state. What had seemed like a constitutional compromise between the state's support for public and private forms of property – or "national specifics" and "universal trends" in developmental terms – turned into a major political and legal conflict about the terms of access for mining companies to Mongolia's minerals.

Between 1997 and 2014, a multi-dimensional social conflict unfolded in back-and-forth processes of legal reform as well as political bargaining within the state and beyond it, with pressure from both global and national pro-extractive and environmental lobbies. Investor associations, civic environmental movements, international development and financial institutions, Western embassies, global credit rating agencies, government ministries and political parties all entered the fray. In response to shifting public sentiment as well as the discovery of extensive high-grade mineral deposits in the South Gobi (i.e. Oyu Tolgoi and Tavan Tolgoi), national legislators and policy-makers sought to adjust the mining regime to better suit national interests in 2006.

The combination of growing public concern about foreign ownership of Mongolian minerals, as well as environmental impacts, and the instability of the legislative and policy framework heightened the perception of *risk* for foreign investment. In particular, investors' ire was provoked by new legislative measures between 2006 and 2012 which (a) designated some mineral deposits as "nationally strategic" (thereby permitting direct state participation as a shareholder), (b) introduced new screening requirements for investment, (c) limited further mining licences and (d) increased taxation and royalty levies. The attempted renegotiation of a major investment agreement and the cancellation or freezing of many mining licences under new anti-corruption and environmental measures in 2011 further frustrated the mining sector as signs of 'creeping expropriation' (Schneiderman, 2005: 847) and nationalism. These measures reflected shifting domestic public sentiment about mining, particularly concerning foreign control of national resources, the environmental and social impacts of mining on rural communities, and heightened expectations for redistribution from the state.

However, a vocal transnational network of market-promoting actors instigated a 'counter-reform' movement (Campbell and Hatcher, 2019: 648–649) by framing these changes as illegitimate "nationalist" moves by the government and claiming that Mongolia was departing from the transnational legal and political consensus about the role of the state in market-led economies. By 2013, almost every international business or financial analysis of Mongolia's mining economy was saturated with investor woes, predictions of economic failure and threats of investment withdrawal unless the state curbed its new preference for "nationalist" legal reforms and policy-making. Consequently, many who had been willing to risk a frontier investment became wary in this allegedly "unstable" legal and political environment. The combination of a downturn in global commodity prices and alleged loss of confidence in the regulatory function of the state led to a cataclysmic drop in investment flows, spurring a debt crisis. FDI in Mongolia's mining sector dropped from an all-time high at 44% of Gross Domestic Product (GDP) in 2011 to 0.8% in 2015 (Erdenebileg, 2017).

In 2014, the Mongolian government published a new state policy committed to 'strengthen private sector development and establish a stable investment environment' (Otgochuluu, 2016: 68) and made a series of political and legal reforms that sought to eviscerate political and legal risks to investment in the mining economy. The new policy and practices of governance associated with the State Policy on the Minerals Sector 2014–2025 both established and reflected new cross-party consensus within the state that extractive development should be *market-led* and the state's role should be to *stabilise the investment environment* (ibid.). By establishing a new regulatory regime to structure the mining sector, the pro-investment State Policy and its accompanying institutional reforms clearly reflect the way that pro-extractive interests eventually became hegemonic within the apparatus of the state, at the expense of alternative socio-political paths. The emergence of a globally oriented political and legal regime for Mongolia's mining industry one-sidedly resolved the tension articulated in the 1992 Constitution in favour of the protection of private property rights and integration into the "world economy," at the expense of a mixed economic system based on forms of public property and 'national specifics' (Constitution of Mongolia, 1992, Article 5.1). The question is, how did such an important material constitutional development come to pass? While the following four chapters of this book are dedicated to unpacking this question, I will now provide some reflections on the methodological choices which informed the way I approached the case study.

## A note on research methods

The Mongolian case study does not squeeze easily into a disciplinary narrative. The political, economic and legal dimensions of broad-based social change catalysed by the pursuit of global competitiveness in minerals extraction mean that – in reality – these conceptual spheres are blurred in practice. Even interdisciplinary perspectives which seek to catch the overflow of meaning would likely focus on the particular dyad associated with their field. A Law and Economics scholar, for instance, would be particularly interested in the relationship between legal reforms and market revitalisation after 2014, whereas a sociologist might focus on shifting patterns of social conflict about the mining sector, focusing on civil society movements. Equally, a political scientist might focus on the relationship between the mining economy and institution-building. All of these approaches would bring degrees of illumination to a very complex picture of socio-legal change reverberating across economic, political and institutional domains and through national and local scales of governance in Mongolia. This book takes a different approach. Instead of adopting a particular conceptual lens, it seeks to construct a kaleidoscopic imaginary of how different elements produce an overarching *pattern* of norms and relations.

The methodology of this book is premised on the basic idea that more knowledge about relatively abstract ideas like "economic globalization" and "transnational law" needs to be developed through the close study of concrete social contexts and institutional environments.

As Schneiderman (2013: 6) argues, the value of case studies in the wider field of "new constitutionalism" is their capacity to 'illuminate precisely the circumstances and the means by which transnational legality operates' (see also Zumbansen, 2012 regarding the need for more case studies). This emphasis on developed a detailed empirical picture is particularly important when it comes to building theory about contemporary processes of state formation. The legal web and negotiating framework which facilitates the mobility of capital transnationally is produced by states in the first instance, but also *produces* different kinds of states; when 'securing[s] these rights, options and powers entail[s] even a partial relinquishing of components of state authority, then we can posit that this process sets up the conditions for a transformation in the role of the state' (Sassen, 2007: 34). In this sense, Mongolia was not a "test-case" for a preconceived hypothesis about the effect of global economic integration on the state. My preliminary instinct based on the review of critical literature about economic globalisation and the state (Harvey, 2005; Sassen, 2007; Schneiderman, 2008, 2013) was that aspects of the state could be strengthened and weakened simultaneously, and that a means of exploring these dynamics was to situate them within a longer time frame. Methodologically, this entailed the development of a *historical* perspective about the Mongolian state and economic change (see Chapter 3). The purpose was to understand more fully the significance of the current political, legal and economic "moment" for the state, which entailed the analysis of 'subtle interplays continuity and change' in Mongolian state formation (Scholte, 1997: 428). Yet, *how* does one analyse continuity and change? Which facts provide the material of analysis, and against which values should the material be evaluated?

What I mainly wanted to comprehend historically was the mutual constitution of state, economic and legal systems over time. The primacy of the historical and, consequently, the emphasis on the *process* of institutional transformation entailed an integrated approach to data collection, analysis and theory-building, where the purpose of explicating a seemingly singular issue (e.g. the construction of Mongolia's mining regime) was located 'in a relation of mutual determination with an external field of social forces' (Burawoy, 1998: 20). This sounds nice and straightforward, as if a straight line could be drawn from the particular to the general, but in my experience, there was much to-ing and fro-ing between the poles, in a 'dialogue of conceptualisation and empirical engagement' (Thompson, 1978: 359).

Tracking the trajectory of Mongolia's mining regime through the lens of legal developments provides a crucial insight into the social struggle for power over the process of extractive development. The law has played an ambivalent role in the sense that its conflicts reveal the balance of power between competing interests in the bid to develop an export-oriented extractive development strategy driven by foreign capital. The law also empirically attests to the state's negotiation with global capital(ists), and simultaneous struggle to maintain political legitimacy with its national constituency (Streeck, 2014). As the case of Mongolia demonstrates, these battles for hegemony within the state are fought out over time. Consequently, examining the historical development of law from a socio-legal perspective was an appropriate and illuminating methodological choice to understand the framing dynamics of conflict over Mongolia's resource wealth.

Probing deeper into the conflicts within Mongolia's mining industry, I began to notice new patterns of governance within state–society, intra-state and inter-state relations. Firstly, new conflicts were clearly emerging which impacted the governance relationship between the state and the citizen regarding socio-environmental issues. New non-state actors – mining companies and NGOs – have taken on direct roles in governance, as the state's power to regulate socio-environmental conflict has become diffused through a complex, hybrid regime of actors and legal norms. Furthermore, contestations between state and market actors over royalty and taxation rates, the terms and conditions of investment contracts and the revision of investment legislation led to the incorporation of market actors and norms *within* the regulatory apparatus of the state. Secondly, intra-state conflicts within central state institutions and between central and sub-national administrations have led to new balances of power which enhance the power of executive ministries and technical agencies over the power of elected actors and institutions. Fiscal decentralisation belied a deeper process of political recentralisation about the terms of Mongolia's engagement with foreign investment, led by powerful financial and mining ministries at the central level working in conjunction with the World Bank Group. Finally, Mongolia's pursuit of extractive development has led to the renegotiation of its relationship with global powers in the region, particularly China. Notably, these different – apparently disparate – dimensions of state transformation were facilitated by the same thread of transnational legal norms premised on political risk mitigation and stability within the national investment environment. Understanding how all of these different axes worked together to form a bigger picture of state transformation, transnational legality and market-building were vital to conceive of the breadth of material constitutional change precipitated through extractive development. The combination of economic crisis and the strategic agency of actors operating within, around and beyond the state promoting legal and political order for the market has produced a new degree of synergy and institutional harmonisation between market forces, governance relations and legal norms in Mongolia.

Methodologically, this bigger picture of material constitutional change was pieced together through closely analysing the legal, policy and political changes in Mongolia's mining regime (1997–2017), with two field trips in 2014 and 2015. As the reader will notice in the consequent substantive chapters, there are regular references to primary interview data. In 2014 and 2015, I spent four months carrying out qualitative fieldwork in Mongolia with elite state and non-state actors seeking to influence the mining regime. I conducted approximately forty semi-structured interviews with influential representatives from key government ministries, agencies and sub-national administrations, civil society organisations, international financial institutions, mining companies and investor associations and lobby groups. The interviews typically lasted between one and two hours. I also observed three NGO-led forums about the social and environmental impacts of mining and one government-sponsored forum about Community Development Agreements, as well as three forums (two national level, one regional level) which focused upon different aspects of mining governance (transparency, corporate social responsibility and local economic impacts, respectively). After the main periods of fieldwork (2014–2015), I maintained contact over email with some of the research participants and conducted a few follow-up interviews.

These interviews and forums gave invaluable insight about the context and sub-text of the 2014 reforms to Mongolia's mining regime, as well as dominant discourses that were rising to prominence at the time – both within and outside of state institutions – about the role of national law and governance in the globalising mining economy. In terms of referencing the interviews, names have been removed but positions have largely been included, depending on the terms of consent, in order to contextualise the significance of the interview for the reader. The significance of the interviews is not so much *who* said what, but rather *what* was said *where* (i.e. the institutional location – and seniority – of the perspective). I have used endnotes to reference the date of the interview. I may be critical overall of the trajectory of state change in Mongolia, but I am very grateful for the generosity of the research participants in giving their time and perspective to informing this case study. While some may disagree with my conclusions, I hope that the book may still provide valuable food for thought and a broader historical perspective to inform ongoing policy, advocacy and academic responses.

Finally, it should be acknowledged that the book's empirical material has been inevitably shaped by the particular juncture when the fieldwork was conducted (2014–2015), which was a period of intensive change in terms of legal developments. During this time, the Democratic Party was at the helm and consequently my interviews with central government personnel occurred in this particular political landscape as the Mongolian economy was quickly moving to the brink of a debt crisis. However, follow-up communications with key actors as well as analysis of further developments under the Mongolian People's Party (MPP), elected in 2016, suggest that core elements of the "stability reforms" pursued since 2014 have become institutionalised within Mongolia's mining regime, despite electoral turnover. While the MPP may be critiqued by foreign investors and international institutions for resuscitating populist discourse as the Mongolian economy has begun to pick up since 2017 (IFC, 2018), the actual policy and legislative measures taken by the MPP suggest that there is no significant difference between the parties in terms of foreign investment protection. In fact, as discussed in Chapter 7, the trajectory of change in terms of constructing a state apparatus to support private investment appears to be moving from strength to strength when one looks at the substantive commitments of the mining regime.

## Chapter outline

This chapter concludes Part I of the book, which has provided a theoretical framework (Chapter 1) and an introduction to the case study (Chapter 2). I argue in the following substantive chapters of this book (Part II) that recent economic crises associated with the collapse of investment in mining provided an opportunity for Mongolian law, institutions and governance frameworks to be reoriented around stability-enhancing transnational legal norms to create the support structures for a globally competitive minerals market. In conjunction with international and corporate actors, pro-extractive actors and institutions *within* the state facilitated the integration of transnational legal norms into the mining regime through a series of deft institutional, legal and financial manoeuvres designed to address the perception of risk to foreign investment. These reforms and institutional measures are the subject of Chapters 4–6, which follows the purging of "nationalist" law and politics from Mongolia's mining regime to assuage the effects of economic crisis by restoring market confidence. To set the scene, Chapter 3 historicises Mongolia's contemporary development strategy through an analysis of state, economic and legal change in the twentieth century. Deep socio-legal change associated with modern "collective improvement" strategies is nothing new, although the means and the ends of development have changed from national industrialism towards global market competitiveness.

Chapter 4 picks up from the discussion of Mongolia's transition to a market democracy in the 1990s through a chronological discussion of the key legal developments in the country's mining regime. Tracking the trajectory of Mongolia's mining regime through the lens of legal developments provides a crucial insight into the social struggle for power over the process of extractive development. The law has played an ambivalent role in the sense that its conflicts reveal the balance of power between competing interests in the bid to develop an export-oriented extractive development strategy. Chapters 4 and 5 trace the role of internal change agents within the national state operating in conjunction with transnational investment networks and financial institutions to effectively address sources of political instability within the apparatus of the state through legal and financial mechanisms of incentive and constraint.

Chapter 5 analyses the post-2014 reforms to reinvigorate failing market confidence in Mongolia's extractive sector, entailing selective (dis)empowerment of executive, legislative and technical institutions. Two "axes of reordering" within the apparatus of the state are observed, notably the redistribution of decision-making power between the executive and the legislative within the central state, and the restriction of self-government in favour of central state management at the sub-national level of government. In Chapter 6, I shift focus away from central and local state institutions towards the relationship between the state and organised civil society, highlighting a third axis of reordering as a result of the emerging stability consensus: the exclusion of conflictual social movements from formal mining governance processes and debates and the introduction of consensus-based mechanisms of participation and multi-stakeholder governance. The reordering processes described were largely achieved through legal mechanisms, constraining the kind of political and social power that had been perceived as disruptive to investor confidence. I also discuss new alternative modes of governance which incorporate civil society and impacted communities as collaborators and stakeholders in devising multi-stakeholder governance solutions.

Overall, Chapters 3–6 provide detailed analyses of the political, legal and economic means by which transnational norms achieve an ordering effect within the Mongolian state's jurisdiction. The chapters trace the articulation and institutionalisation of transnational norms premised on the stability for the investment environment to govern institutional and political relations (a) within central state institutions, (b) between central and sub-national administrations and (c) within state–society relations. In relation to the first two axes of reordering, the conditioning of national and local governance to mitigate perceptions of nationalism and corruption has recalibrated the relationship between the state and the market. This recalibration has occurred vis-à-vis institutional designs which seek to exclude or limit role of political representatives and enhance the role of executive administration in relation to decision-making processes about the conditions of mining, investment and socio-environmental regulation. The third axis of reordering analysed in Chapter 6 focuses on the 'redrawing of the relationship between state and citizen' (Carroll, 2012: 351) that has further insulated the market – and the state – from the practically disruptive and politically de-legitimising "risks" associated with protest, civil disobedience and ongoing disputes with local communities impacted by mining. The taming of environmental civil society's 'unruly politics' (Hatcher, forthcoming) was largely achieved through legal and institutional mechanisms, constraining the kind of political and social power that had been perceived as disruptive to investor confidence. At the local level, where residents are directly impacted by mining activities, new alternative modes of social development governance have been nationally legislated to ameliorate social discontent, alongside new multi-stakeholder governance mechanisms initiated by international organisations and multilateral financial institutions, in conjunction with multinational mining companies. Notably, these alternative governance mechanisms incorporate civil society and impacted communities as stakeholders to collaboratively devise multi-stakeholder governance solutions.

Part III of the book transitions from case study analysis into political and theoretical reflections upon processes of material constitutionalism in Mongolia, and the wider insights that the case study generates. Chapter 7 summarises and critically reflects upon the practical and normative implications of transnational legal ordering for the Mongolian state, bringing together the intra-state and state–society dimensions analysed in Chapters 4–6. Chapter 8 concludes the book by returning to some of the big ideas that have animated this work as explored in Chapter 1. The concluding chapter offers a broader theoretical reflection on the lessons we can learn from the Mongolian case study about the constitutional implications of legal transnationalisation and economic globalisation.

## References

Burawoy, M. 1998. "The Extended Case Method." *Sociological Theory* 16(1): 4–33.

Campbell, B. and Hatcher, P. 2019. "Neoliberal Reform, Contestation and Relations of Power in Mining: Observations from Guinea and Mongolia." *The Extractive Industries and Society* 6: 642–653.

Carroll, T. 2012. "Introduction: Neo-Liberal Development Policy in Asia beyond the Post-Washington Consensus." *Journal of Contemporary Asia* 42(3): 350–358.

Constitution of Mongolia. 1992. Official English translation. Available at https://www.conscourt.gov.mn/?page_id=842&lang=en. Accessed 2nd June 2019.

Endicott, E. 2012. *A History of Land Use in Mongolia: The Thirteenth Century to the Present*. New York: Palgrave Macmillan.

Erdenebileg, Z. 2017. "China-Mongolia Relations: Challenges and Opportunities." 6th January *China Briefing* www.china-briefing.com/news/2017/01/06/china-mongolia-relations.html. Accessed 23rd April 2019.

Fish, M. S. 2001. "The Inner Asian Anomaly: Mongolia's Democratisation in Comparative Perspective." *Communist and Post-Communist Studies* 34: 323–338.

Friedland, R. 2005. "Nothing Like It on Planet Earth – Robert Friedland's Tour d'Tolgoi". Address delivered at the BMO Nesbitt Burns Global Resources Conference, Tampa, Florida, 24th April 2005. Published online by *Resource Investor*. www.resourceinvestor.com/pebble.asp?relid=9010. Accessed 26th April 2019.

Fritz, V. 2002. "Mongolia: Dependent Democratisation." *Journal of Communist Studies and Transition Politics* 18(4): 75–100.

Government of Mongolia. 2007. "Millennium-Development Goals-Based Comprehensive National Development Strategy 2007–2021." Annex to State Great Khural Resolution 12th February 2008. Available online: www.adb.org/sites/default/files/linked-documents/cps-mon-2012-2016-oth-01.pdf. Accessed 23rd April 2019.

Harvey, D. 2005. *A Brief History of Neoliberalism*. Oxford: Oxford University Press.

Hatcher, P. 2014. *Regimes of Risk: The World Bank and the Transformation of Mining in Asia*. New York/London: Palgrave Macmillan.

IFC. 2018. "Investment Reform Map for Mongolia." Washington, DC: World Bank Group.

International Business Publications. 2013. *Mongolia Mining Laws and Regulations Handbook: Vol. 1 Strategic Information and Regulations*. Washington, DC: Global Investment Centre.

Knottnerus, R. and Olivet, C. 2016. "Mongolia's Experience with Investment Treaties and Arbitration Cases." [Report] Transnational Institute: Online www.tni.org/en/publication/mongolias-experience-with-investment-treaties-and-arbitration-cases. Accessed 23rd April 2019.

Korsun, G. and Murrell, P. 1995. "The Politics and Economics of Mongolia's Privatisation Programme." *Asian Survey* 35(5): 472–486.

Lander, J. 2014. "A Critical Reflection on Oyu Tolgoi and the Risk of a Resource Trap in Mongolia: Troubling the Resource Nationalism Frame." *Law, Social Justice and Global Development Journal* (2): 1–28. Available at https://warwick.ac.uk/fac/soc/law/elj/lgd/2013_2/2013_2_lander/lander_lgd_2013_2_pub02_2014-.pdf

Munkh-Erdene, L. 2011. "Mongolia's Post-Socialist Transition: A Great Neoliberal Transformation." A paper presented at the Conference on *Mongolians after Socialism: Economic Aspiration, Political Development, and Cultural and Spiritual Identity*, Ulaanbaatar, Mongolia, June 27th–29th. www.sarr.emory.edu/MAS/MAS_Chap4_Munkh-Erdene.pdf. Accessed 23rd April 2019.

National Development Agency. 2019. "Your Guide to Invest in Mongolia 2019." Ulaanbaatar: National Development Agency/Invest in Mongolia.

Otgochuluu, C. 2016. "Mongolia's State Policy on the Minerals Sector and Its Application in the Promotion of Sustainable Development." *Law in Transition Journal* 2016: 66–75.

Pomfret, R. 2000. "Transition and Democracy in Mongolia." *Europe-Asia Studies* 52(1): 149–160.

Reinert, E. S. 2000. "Globalisation in the Periphery as a Morgenthau Plan; The Underdevelopment of Mongolia in the 1990s: Why Globalisation Is One Man's Food and Another Man's Poison." In S. Lhagva (ed.) *Mongolian Development Strategy: Capacity Building*. Ulaanbaatar: Mongolian Development Research Centre.

Rossabi, M. 2005. *Mongolia: From Khans to Commissars to Capitalists*. Berkeley: University of California Press.

Sachs, J. 1994. "Understanding Shock Therapy," Occasional Paper No. 7. London: The Social Market Foundation.

Sassen, S. 2007. *The Sociology of Globalisation*. London/New York: W. W. Norton & Co.

Schneiderman, D. 2005. "Banging Constitutional Bibles: Observing Constitutional Culture in Transition." *University of Toronto Law Journal* 55: 833–852.

———. 2008. *Constitutionalising Economic Globalisation: Investment Rules and Democracy's Promise*. Cambridge: Cambridge University Press.

———. 2013. *Resisting Economic Globalisation: Critical Theory and International Investment Law*. Basingstoke, Hampshire/New York: Palgrave Macmillan.

Scholte, J. A. 1997. "Global Capitalism and the State." *International Affairs* 73(3): 427–452.

Streeck, W. 2014. *Buying Time: The Delayed Crisis of Democratic Capitalism*. London/New York: Verso Books.

Thompson, E. P. 1978. *The Poverty of Theory and Other Essays*. London: The Merlin Press Ltd.

Tumenbayer, N. 2002. "Herders' Property Rights vs. Mining in Mongolia." Paper prepared for Conference on Environmental Conflict Resolution, Watson Institute for International Studies, Brown University, Providence, RI, Spring 2002 (University of Vermont: Online): 1–15. www.uvm.edu/~shali/Mining%20Mongolia%20paper.pdf. Accessed 23rd April 2019.

Zumbansen, P. 2012. "Defining the Space of Transnational Law: Legal Theory, Global Governance, and Legal Pluralism." *Transnational Law and Contemporary Problems* 21(2): 305–336.

# Part II

# The case study

# Chapter 3

# State, law and economy in Mongolia

## A historical overview

## Introduction: tracing material constitutional change over time

In this book, the recurring question underlying its methodology relates to the way that state-economic orders are instituted politically and legally. The "instituted" nature of economic systems in general (Polanyi, 1957: 248) makes a historical analysis of power and production not only interesting, but a vital component to understanding the constitutional significance and implications of fundamental changes in the process of producing and accumulating 'want satisfying material means' (ibid.). When it comes to Mongolia's extractive economy, *how* has it been instituted in terms of political and legal action? Who or what *facilitates* the reorganisation of productive forces, or *fails* to prevent it? As a site of dominant political-juridical power, the state is a fundamental reference point in order to understand the process and implications of economic change. More specifically, conceiving of the state as a 'site of strategic action' (Jessop, 1990: 10) is useful as a means of exploring various social conditions (political, legal, ideological) that shape the reorganisation of production because it emphasises the role of *authoritative* action. The focus on the state as the most privileged site of political-juridical power further emphasises the way in which alternative social futures are being actively closed off and 'forgotten' (Schneiderman, 2013: 35, 18). This is an important sub-text of this chapter and the two following, which seek to explain the manner in which particular state forms and economic organisation have come to dominate *over alternatives*.

The contemporary literature on constitutional or 'constitution-like' (Schneiderman, 2008: 8, 2015: 67) processes and transnational forms of ordering within the global political economy has proliferated within the context of a "Polanyian turn" in the study of law, institutions and 'transnational markets' (Joerges and Falke, 2011: 1). As Joerges and Falke (ibid.: 2) put it, Karl Polanyi's 'notion of embeddedness' critiques the understanding

> of any organic, let alone harmonious, evolution of modern economies and societies... The capitalist economy is, instead, characterised as a product of deliberate, inherently contradictory, political action, with movement

promoting a disembedding of the economy from social institutions, on the one hand, and counter-movements striving for protection against the destructive implications of such dis-embedment, on the other.

As discussed in Chapter 1, Karl Polanyi critiqued the abstract conceptualisation of the market economy in neoclassical economics. Polanyi's account of English industrialisation in *The Great Transformation* (1944/2001) provides ample and definitive evidence of the way that the state actively constructs and maintains the domain of the market economy through legal and political institutions, such as guaranteeing the 'continuity of titles to property' upon which the market system depends (ibid.: 243). Polanyi emphasised the historically constructed nature of the 'institutional separation of society into an economic and political sphere' (ibid.: 74) in order to proactively denaturalise its assumed position in liberal economic theory.

Crucially, Polanyi recognised the role of the state in the formation of a sphere of economic exchange based on price mechanisms, economic value and the law of contract, as well as the state's potential to help ameliorate the social "dislocations" associated with the commodification[1] of labour, the environment and money within the market framework of exchange (Polanyi, 1944/2001: 59–60, 71–80; Ebner, 2011: 21). Markets presume certain types of social relations, notably characterised by commercial motivations and contractual relationships (Ebner, 2011: 30). As Polanyi (1944/2001: 71) puts it, 'a market economy is an economic system controlled, regulated and directed by market prices.' He adds that:

> A further group of assumptions follows in respect to the state and its policy. Nothing must be allowed to inhibit the formation of markets... Neither price, nor supply, nor demand must be fixed or regulated; only such policies and measures are in order which help to ensure the self-regulation of the market by creating conditions which make the market the only organising power in the economic sphere.
>
> (Ibid.)

In this sense, 'markets are never fully disembedded, for they always require some institutional scaffold to sustain their operation' (Ebner, 2011: 27; Polanyi, 1944/2001: 71). However, the social basis of that 'institutional scaffold' (Ebner, 2011: 27) is crucial in terms of distinguishing what type of social relations the market is embedded in. For instance, while markets can be said to always be 'politically embedded in distinct legal rules and institutions' (ibid.), these legal rules and institutions, depending on their location and motives, might reinforce rather the idea that the economy should be 'organised in separate [economic] institutions, based on specific [economic] motives and conferring a special status' (Polanyi,1944/2001: 60). This type of "embeddedness," referring to the institutional architecture that supports the functioning of a market economy, is essentially a form of social ordering based on the market (ibid.), where 'rules and norms institutionalise the competitive order of market exchange' (Ebner, 2011: 28).

Embeddedness, in the normative sense in which Polanyi uses the term, refers to the economy being embedded in *non-economic* social relations, which effectively disrupts the commodification of people, land and money. Thus, while markets do involve a particular kind of sociality, Polanyi's understanding of the "social" is a specifically *de-commodified* notion, where relations are regulated by non-economic institutions and norms. As Ebner argues (2011: 33), Polanyi's connection between embeddedness and decommodification is a "crucial" dimension of Polanyi's normative contribution to the study of the 'formation of transnational markets': the description of the political-legal coordination of markets is part of a critique of the particular *kind* of social relations involved. In fact, as Schneiderman points out (2008: 4), Polanyi was one of the first to link the idea of liberal constitutionalism with its function as a 'device for securing uniformity and homogeneity in state practices' for the purposes of instituting a *separate* economic sphere.

The historical rendering of the instituted nature of the economy, inspired by Polanyi's approach, dovetails neatly with the working definition of the state given in the first chapter, described as 'an ensemble of juridical-political institutions and regulatory capacities grounded in the territorialisation of political power' (Brenner et al., 2003: 7). The idea of state power as an "ensemble" helpfully breaks down the concept of the state as a unitary institution. For example, the power of the state is constituted by diverse *forms* of power (e.g. administrative, legislative, bureaucratic, authoritarian, democratic), political and economic constituents (e.g. voters, financiers) and mediated by different institutions. The following exposition of Mongolian history will examine the role of the state in relation to the organisation of the economy during three distinct periods (aristocratic pastoralist, communist-industrialist, democratic-market) in order to illuminate the way in which state-economic relations have shifted over time, with reference to geopolitical context, socio-political constitution and normative-juridical structure. I argue that, prior to state socialism in the twentieth century, the economic sphere was firmly entangled within political relations, but became gradually "disembedded" from that position. The industrialising impetus of the socialist state gradually distinguished the economy from the state, as will be demonstrated in due course, but it was only in the context of the post-socialist transition that the creation of a "free" market economy (i.e. outside of the state's direct control) was attempted. This historical background lays the foundation for the development of my argument that Mongolia's extractive transformation since the late 1990s represents a material process of constitutional change, as legal, political and economic relations have been gradually reoriented to adapt conditions of globalisation.

It must be stated at the outset of the substantive portion of this chapter that I am heavily indebted to the work of David Sneath and other political anthropologists for the analysis of early (pre-socialist) Mongolian statecraft. Favouring methods that examine the complexity of historical social relations, anthropological sources have been invaluable for deconstructing the developmentalist assumptions that have characterised both Western (capitalist) and Soviet (technological

Marxist) renderings of Mongolian history in the twentieth century. This chapter is a re-reading of mostly secondary historical sources with regard to pre-socialist state forms, although I do work with primary legal and policy texts from the socialist and democratic periods in the latter part of the chapter. Aware of the limitation of my Mongolian language ability, I only attempt a modest overview of the state-economic nexus in order to show systemic trends.

## State-economic relations prior to the national state: an overview of the Mongol aristocratic-pastoral order (twelfth–twentieth centuries)

> Without the a priori separation of the social forms into tribe or state by their presumed essences, we can see state and state-conditioned processes distributed through the lifeworlds of those subject to all manner of political authorities. This appears to have been as true of pastoral aristocratic orders as it is of the industrial "governmental" state.
>
> (David Sneath, 2007: 4)

There has been a strong tendency in Western anthropological and political theory, as well as popular culture, to idealise the nomadic culture of the steppe as egalitarian and opposed to the hierarchical, bureaucratic structures of sedentary states (Sneath, 2007). Through the lenses of evolutionary political theory, nomadic societies have typically been cast within the framework of tribalism. In the Mongolian case, this is particularly so: Mongol society has regularly been designated as "tribal" (ibid.: 53–54), characterised by an egalitarian political culture and simple modes of production (pastoral nomadism), or as a form of feudalism (Bold, 2001; Sneath, 2007: 125–131). As will be discussed later in the chapter, the feudalist frame served a critical narrative purpose for the communist revolutionaries in the early twentieth century, who portrayed the political and religious nobility as feudal overlords to be overthrown. In the anthropological literature, Mongols have also been regularly portrayed as fiercely independent, horizontally organised social groups lacking centralised authority or the type of stratification needed for class formation (Sneath, 2007: 2–5). The presumed lack of hierarchy was based on an assumption that nomadic, mobile societies were a pre-political form of social organisation, having not acquired the complex political structures found in sedentary societies, such as stratification, centralisation and class formation (ibid.: 53, citing Burnham, 1979: 349–360; Dahl, 1979: 261–280; Bold, 2001). In many ways, these perceptions have informed contemporary popular representations of Mongolia, both Western and Mongolian. The image of independent nomads with complete freedom of movement has powerful "pre-political" (i.e. pre-territorial) connotations, feeding modern national pride about Mongolians as "close to nature" and independent (Orhon, 2011), as well as reinforcing more negative tropes (i.e. "lazy," "disorganised," "distrustful").

Notably, this "ideal-type" perspective about the nomad as wandering boundless and free (Sneath and Humphrey, 1999) is linked with the treatment of pastoralism as a simple subsistence mode of production, portrayed as both pre-political and pre-economic. However, this simplistic understanding of early Mongol society simply lacks evidence after a closer analysis of primary historical texts and critical anthropological engagements with Mongol political and economic history. The movements of Mongol nomads have always been embedded within not only relations but institutions of rule (Sneath and Humphrey, 1999; Sneath, 2010). While the establishment of the first Mongol nation-state in 1921 – the Mongolian People's Republic (MPR) – manifested particularly modern territorial and national state characteristics, it was not the first instance of statecraft on the steppes of Inner Asia (Sneath, 2007). As far as we know, ethno-linguistic 'house societies' (Sneath, 2007: 111) have inhabited the region of Inner Asia from at least 200 B.C. with the Xiongnu Empire (ibid.: 114; di Cosmo, 1994). Furthermore, as Sneath (2007: 16) emphasises, mobile pastoralism should be understood 'as a political economy,' in contrast to the tribal narrative that frames it 'as a simple subsistence economy unable to support great complexity or hierarchy' (ibid.: 20). He argues that (ibid.: 17):

Mobile pastoralism is framed and transformed by political power just as sedentary agriculture is, and, while clearly different, it allows just as many possibilities for the accumulation of wealth and the construction of large-scale systems as agricultural techniques do. In both cases, the economic possibilities depend upon the nature of the property regimes that exist for resources and products and the wider political systems that frame them.

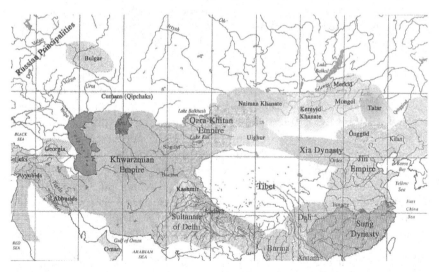

*Map 3.1* Map of Mongol Territories in the Twelfth Century prior to Chinggis Khan's Empire.
(Source: Sneath, 2007: x – used with permission)

## Socio-political constitution of the early Mongol state

David Sneath (2006a, 2007) argues that the pre-socialist Mongol state was distinguished by its complex aristocratic political formation. Against the tribal construction of early Mongol society, he argues that Levi-Strauss' idea of the "house society" is more appropriate for understanding political forms in the Inner Asian region: tribal terminology inaccurately perpetuates the "mythical" imagination of early Mongol society as 'the ideal-typical pastoral nomadic society, composed of egalitarian clans of fierce and free tribesmen' (Sneath, 2007: 156). Similarly, he uses the notion of "ruling houses" to counteract the simplistic frame of feudalism that characterises much of the literature about Mongol statecraft during the Chinggisid and Qing Empires. The feudal bias in the literature is argued both by Sneath and Skrynnikova to reflect a simplistic interpretation of Mongol 'vocabularies of power' (Sneath, 2006: 11; Skrynnikova, 2006: 85–115), by primarily understanding the early Mongol state in kinship/tribal or feudal terms. A primary example of this oversimplification can be seen in the treatment of the terms *qarachu* and *bo'ol* which are commonly translated, respectively, as "commoner" and "slave" (Skrynnikova, 2006: 87–115). When translated, these terms fit neatly into a feudal imagination, close as they are to the notion of a vassal. However, a feudal order based on lord–vassal relations obscures the particular 'institutions of submission-dominance' (Sneath, 2006a: 12) that actually characterised political relations at the time. In contrast to the absolute nature of the lord–vassal relationship, the Mongol aristocratic order was based on relative and multiple layers of hierarchy:

> '"Submission" as "slaves" did not mean the total deprivation of rights... the term bo'ol, then, does not mark a unit of the class structure [but] it models relations inside the unfolding political organisation... the terms bo'ol as well as qarachu ('commoner') mark hierarchy inside the political community and form part of the mechanism for socio-political integration. Bo'ol status gives both material benefit (transfer of allegiance to a stronger suzerain provides, correspondingly, a higher level of protection and patronage) and social status in a prestigious community. In no way did the term bo'ol mark a certain type of dependence. Dependence supposes an indispensable non-equality of the sides: the subordinated side receives partial compensation in the form of patronage, protection and help because it is not in a state to secure its existence independently; while the senior side demands recognition of dependence in some form (social and material). This is what we see in Mongolian society of pre-empire and empire periods.
>
> (Skrynnikova, 2006: 101)

This is important because it demonstrates that 'pre-eminently political formations' (Sneath, 2007) existed prior to the socialist nation-state, supported by a unique mode of production: pastoral nomadism. To belong in the early Mongol polities was neither based purely on familial association or feudal domination, but reflected a complex "social contract" characterised by a distinctive form of statecraft itself, not simply a *developmental step* towards the formation of a "real" state (Sneath, 2007). Kinship relations were certainly a historical part of the social order of Inner Asia, but like class and ethnicity, not its principal basis (Sneath and Humphrey, 1999: 15). For example, even prior to the Mongol Empire in what is typically referred to as the "tribal era" of Mongolian history, 'ruling houses or lineages were not related by descent to the people they ruled' (Sneath, 2006a: 14), thus undermining the notion that kinship relations were primary in early political formations. As Sneath argues, Mongol aristocratic statecraft included a variety of 'power technologies' that we associate with states in political theory, such as stratification, forms of territorialisation, taxation and military service (Sneath, 2006a: 16, 2007: 5).

It is vital to note the centrality of the pastoral economy within this aristocratic system of rule; relations of production were thoroughly embedded *within* the socio-political relations of the state. The political and economic viability of both the aristocratic houses and, later, the monasteries depended upon the control of nomadic subjects and the productivity of livestock raising. Pastoral production was thus absolutely embedded within this political formation. This was partly due to the way that the control of nomadic subjects was critical to the legitimacy of the early Mongol state. Despite changes in the wider geopolitical environment in which Mongol ruling houses existed, the fundamental intertwining of the aristocracy and pastoral production meant that mobile pastoralism continued as a politically embedded economy up until the socialist period. The symbiosis of the political and economic during this period meant that it is not possible to draw a distinct line between state and the pastoral economy, in the sense that the 'property regime' (Sneath, 2007: 17) was fixed firmly within aristocratic power relations.

Thus, the 'allocation of subjects to domains of power was a key feature of aristocratic power' (Sneath, 2006a: 17). Against feudal forms of rule, however, this allocation occurred in a context where the nobility did not *own* land but exercised 'collective sovereignty' (ibid.: 7) in the administration of pastoral production. According to Sneath (ibid.), collective sovereignty conceptualises the way in which Mongol aristocracies treated the rule as a 'common project of the ruling house' and consequently entailed a strong sense of loyalty amongst their nomadic subjects, who were integrated into the aristocratic order through the relative hierarchies of *bo'ol* and *qarachu*. "Economic" production was thus thoroughly embedded and difficult to differentiate within the socio-political hierarchy.

Chinggis Khan's conquest of Eastern and Central Asia in the thirteenth century, through the Middle East to the border of Western Europe, continues to be the most significant era of Mongolian history in terms of consolidating a strong sense of Mongol identity and territory. There are a number of reasons for this. Chinggis Khan united the fragmented 'khanates' (Sneath, 2010: 110) into what we know of now as the 'Chinggisid polity' through military coercion, but also through the introduction of a written *Mongolian* script and the promulgation of a politico-religious myth on his divine 'right to rule' (Rachewiltz, 1973/2010: 167) based on the commonly held shamanist worldview of Inner Asian pastoralists. Rachewiltz (ibid.: 168) argues that this politico-religious myth was a critical ideological tool to the formation of a territorial Empire. Confounding expectations of the "boundless, wandering nomad," the Mongolian identity that was forged through the Mongol Empire was both mobile and territorial, with 'intertwined' (Munkh-Erdene, 2006: 57) ethno-linguistic and politico-religious discourses that imply a strong sense of political unity between the Mongol people and the early Mongol statecraft (see Rachewiltz, 1973/2010: 168). According to Munkh-Erdene (2006: 60–61), the coincidence of these two discourses existed throughout the era of the Chinggisid polity through the Qing Empire up until the socialist revolution of 1921. This strong sense of Mongol identity preceding the development of a national state explains the initial popular resistance to the secularisation and socialisation policies and purges of the socialist Party in the late 1920s and 1930s (Bawden, 1989: Chapters 7 and 8), as will be discussed in a later section.

Following the reign of Kubilai Khan,[2] whose rule of the Mongol Empire has been characterised as a time of peace, disputes between the Mongol nobility destabilised the Empire as a whole. The Inner Asian region was fragmented into princedoms under the various Mongol nobles who had been given authority over portions of land by the Khan. In the second half of the sixteenth century, the adoption of Buddhism as the official religion of the Empire, following the conversion of Altan Khan, added the power of Buddhist religious establishments to the interlocking milieu of political authority of the period (ibid.: 28). In particular, the monasteries functioned in similar ways to the aristocratic ruling houses, imposing taxes upon the subjects of their domains and perpetuating a similar form of political relations based upon relative hierarchy and collective sovereignty. However, the rise of Buddhism also added strength to the growing sense of boundaries around what legitimately constituted Mongol identity.[3] Integrated as it was into the political ideology of the state, the rise of Buddhist institutions was achieved not only through missionary activity by Tibetan Buddhist lamas but also through anti-shamanist violence, which forced the majority of Mongols to abandon their traditional beliefs (ibid.: 32–33). As Bawden (ibid.: 33) notes:

> While missionizing against the shamans, the lamas took care to identify themselves with the ruling class, with the result that while Buddhism thoroughly penetrated all levels of Mongol society in the coming centuries, organisationally it developed almost as a state within a state. It was a body distributing high titles, owning enormous wealth in flocks and herds and in serfs, and enjoying such political prestige that the Manchu emperors tacitly recognised the supreme head of the faith... the "Living Buddha" of Urga, as a quasi-ruler over the people... From very early on the nobility and the higher clergy saw in mutual identification of interests the way to continuing power.
> (see also ibid.: 69)

When the Mongol nobles submitted to Manchu rule in 1691, Mongol territories were overlaid with a "colonial" administrative structure based on the

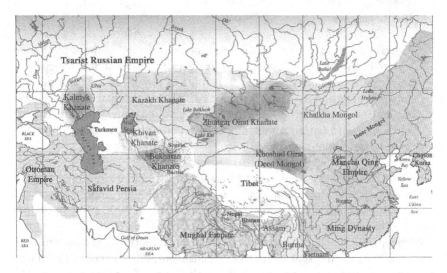

*Map 3.2* Map of Mongol Territory in the Manchu Qing Empire.
(Source: Sneath, 2007: xi)

boundaries – "banners" – of the nobles' land (Kaplonski, 2010: 639) and expanded the imperial architecture of statecraft again where it had contracted into smaller units with the demise of the Mongol Empire. Under Manchu authority, the boundaries of the *khoshuun* were reformulated into tighter 'territorial-administrative units' (Fernandez-Gimenez, 1999: 320; Sneath, 2001: 44). The administrative framework of *khoshuun* was incorporated by Manchu imperialists as a critical mechanism of local governance that enabled the ongoing functioning of the pastoral economy, reflective of the way that 'pastoralism and the political hierarchy were inextricably combined' (Sneath, 2001: 47). Critically, Kaplonski (2010: 639; Sneath, 2001: 44) notes that these areas were divided into units and sub-units – *soums* and *baghs* – wherein the people were 'divided into commoners and "personal retainers of the nobility."'[4] While the *khoshuun* reflected formalised boundaries by the Qing administration, customary flexibility was retained in the sense that the boundaries of the *baghs* (sub-districts) were more blurred, depending on the varying pasture needs of the small herding groups of around two to twelve families – *khot ail* – who moved together within the area (Fernandez-Gimenez, 1999: 320; Upton, 2009: 1401).

### Sustaining the aristocratic state: embedded economy and customary norms

The imposition of Manchu authority was colonial in the sense that it was a foreign power, but the aristocratic 'sub-strata of power' (Sneath, 2007: 4) remained fundamentally undisturbed, particularly in Outer Mongol lands.[5] As Sneath (2006a: 17) argues:

> Certainly since the time of the Mongol Empire, and perhaps from long before it, the steppe aristocracy and its distinctive form of military-civil administration can be seen as the 'sub-strata of power' upon which grander imperial designs were based... the broader picture that emerges is of power structures more centralised... or less centralised, interacting in various modes of articulation, competition and superimposition as part of contingent historical processes.

Under the Manchu rule, customary Mongol law was codified, meaning that the regulation of pastureland and water was gradually brought under the auspices of the Qing Empire's legal system (Kaplonski, 2010: 639). The law of custom and empire allegedly operated side by side under the Qing Dynasty (Fernandez-Gimenez, 1999: 231); it appears that the Manchu authorities had final authority and installed formal dispute settlement mechanisms, but generally allowed pastoralists to maintain customary practice within those formal boundaries. The 'administrative division' (Sneath, 2001: 44) between the Inner and Outer Mongol lands established by the Manchu meant that the Qing Dynasty exercised less direct control over the latter. While each *bagh* (sub-district) had a tax-collector and an administrative office to resolve disputes, it appears that few formal disputes were recorded as the customary 'first-come-first-served law of the steppe' (Fernandez-Gimenez, 1999: 321) continued to prevail regarding campsites (Sneath, 2001: 44).

This is an important observation because it demonstrates the way in which access to institutions of state entailed access to the mode of production: land, animals and pastoral labour. It reflects the way in which the control of state institutions – through the nobility – was central to accessing productive processes, to the extent that there was no significant differentiation between the "political" and the "economic." This is evident in the Mongolian term for government –*zasagiingazar* –which can be understood as the *place* (*gazar*) from where pastoral land is administered (Sneath, 2001: 47). Additionally, it affirms the continuity of adaptive statecraft on the Mongol steppe, even in periods of conquest by foreign powers. The addition of layers of imperialism did not undermine the power per se of Mongol nobles but resituated it within further layers of governance: the aristocracy was the 'raw material for empire builders' (Sneath, 2006a: 18).[6] This points to the tenacity of Mongol institutions in the context of changing political milieus, and the importance of local institutions in a pastoral society. As the following sections will demonstrate, we can see the ways in which Mongolian state institutions have continued to adapt under new political and economic conditions, despite expressing varying degrees of centralised and decentralised political authority (Sneath, 2007: 4). The significant axis of change relates to the state's relationship to the economy, which became increasingly developed as a distinct area of state management following the 1921 socialist revolution. The industrialisation of Mongolia's economy during the period of state socialism laid the foundation for the "liberation" of the market from the direct control of the state during the transition to a market economy in the early 1990s.

However, the fact that herders themselves had 'personal' (if not private) property rights in the livestock (Sneath, 2001) prevented relations of total domination between the nobility and the "common" herder, as the latter were key to wealth creation. In this sense, the labour of herders was not fully alienated from the means of production. The inter-dependency of noble and commoner, reflected in property relations (Sneath, 2007: 17), entailed a position of significance for the nomadic subject. For example, it is debated as to whether princes had the right to alienate land or control land *exclusively* (Fernandez-Gimenez, 1999: 321), as the rights to winter camps and pastures tended to be allocated based on customary use (ibid.: 323). Even where princes were granted formal rights to pasture, Sneath (2001: 45; Bawden, 1968/1989: 90–91) notes that customary norms of land use by "commoners" often overrode the Emperor's law in practice as some herders were known to physically resist the arrival of princes claiming their pasture, suggesting that property was viewed as commonly held rather than exclusively held by the nobility (Fernandez-Gimenez, 1999: 323). While the territorial boundaries of *nutag* ("homeland")were enforced by the nobility, the *nutag* itself as a geographical concept was based on the four customary seasonal pastures required in Mongol pastoral practice (ibid.: 321).

In this sense, then, the basic needs of the pastoral economy informed state governance and vice versa. The fact that the governance of pastureland and the mobility of pastoralists were central to the economic viability of early expressions of the Mongol state is an important insight into state-economy relations prior to the formation of the MPR in 1921. The economy was thoroughly integrated into the political system and sustained the aristocratic hierarchy. The economy did not exist in its own right as a "sphere" separate to the state.

While it is not the purpose of this chapter to develop this era of Mongolian history in great detail, it is accurate to say that the pastoral mode of production was intertwined with state formation as opposed to existing prior to it. Customary norms were reinforced by Empire's power, suggesting that at that time the political, juridical-normative and economic were part of the same social whole. The subject-state dynamic was not The Nomad vs. The Noble, but rather both were imbricated within the aristocratic-pastoral political economy. As Endicott (2012: 44) argues regarding early Mongol history (thirteenth century), responsibility for the nobility, or the Khan, was directly linked to his capacity to ensure 'that pastureland and water [were] at least sufficient, if not abundant, for his own people.' Authority to administrate land, water and mobility did not reflect the *ownership* of land (ibid.), and the exercise of political authority appears to have been complementary with the requirements of pastoral nomadism. The governance of land, herds and pastoral labour thus perpetuated pastoralism as an embedded economy within Mongol social and state structures, as pastoralism sustained early Mongol polities.

## Distinguishing the economic from the political: state socialism, national industrialisation and regional integration in the Soviet Union (1924–1990)

Considering Mongolia's history until the beginning of the twentieth century, the conceptual separation of political and economic life under the post-1990 market-democracy model reflects a rapid pace of social change. In the literature on Mongolia's post-socialist transition, scholars emphasise the contrast between the socialist and democratic eras, especially highlighting the shift from a command economy to a deregulated market economy (Orhon, 2003; Rossabi, 2005). The latter binary view creates a false antagonism between the two, obscuring the way in which the socialist state prepared the foundation for market-based capitalist economic development by introducing the concept of labour, currency, surplus value extraction, investment, basic finance (i.e. banks and monetary policy) and industrial production. Rather than a radical break with the past, the marketisation of the Mongolian economy since 1990 represents a transformation *within* an industrial model of development, in which the state-economy distinction had already been firmly established.

The socialist period was fundamental in terms of establishing the "economy" as a distinct institution from the political sphere to be governed by the state, a barely recognised legacy of that time. Despite being heavily regulated and under the command of the state, the creation of a separate economic sphere, in which the state acted with increasing displays of a distinctly *economic* rationality (efficiency, competition, profit maximisation), is significant in terms of breaking the pre-socialist conceptual unity between productive and political power. This section will outline the way in which an agrarian-industrial economy was established in outer Mongolia under the tutelage of the Soviet Union and how the country was integrated into a regional market. The creation of a distinct economic sphere and limited market integration were essential stepping stones for Mongolia's post-1990 economic integration into the global minerals sector.

### A shifting situation: new geopolitical challenges in the early twentieth century

The beginning of the twentieth century intensified the triangular competition for control over and access to Mongol resources and territory between Russia, China and Japan with the rise of nationalist statecraft (Kotkin, 1999: 3).[7] Mongol territory had been shaped by Qing-Russian border disputes as early as 1727, when the Qing-Russian Treaty of Khiatka established the outer boundary of Mongol territory within the Qing Empire. The Qing Empire and Tsarist Russia began to disintegrate in the early years of the twentieth century with the rise of Han nationalism against the authority of the Manchu and the agitation of communist movements in Russia. Sino-Russian rivalry over Mongol territory intensified, as the Chinese began to pursue a policy of sovereign land acquisition and cultural assimilation in this region that had been historically governed under conditions of suzerainty (i.e. tributary relations).

With the decline of the Qing Empire, the policy of the new Chinese authorities shifted from prohibition to promotion of land appropriation (Sneath, 2001: 54) particularly in Inner Mongolia where land was increasingly alienated for permanent agricultural settlements. Under Manchu leadership of the Qing Dynasty, customary Mongol practices of land use required by mobile pastoralism had been generally respected. As Sneath notes (ibid.: 51), 'Mongolians had occupied a relatively privileged place in the social order.' However, the emergence of Han Chinese nationalism changed this "soft" approach to the governance of territory. In particular, the scale of land appropriation – 'land booms' (ibid.: 52) – by the Han-Manchu elites sparked a *revolutionary* reaction from Mongols. Lan (1999: 50) notes that 'the Mongols demonstrated their opposition openly and repeatedly against the New Administration': 'creating Chinese administrative units, reducing the power of banner *jasags* (i.e., the power of the Mongol nobility and monasteries), and replacing Mongolian garrisons with Chinese troops' along the border with Russia. Despite intense resistance and armed revolts in Inner Mongolia,[8] the enclosure of land for cultivation was carried out under Manchu military coercion. In part, according to Lan (ibid.: 53), the inefficacy of resistance in Inner Mongol territory was due to the lack of unity between the Mongol aristocracy:

> Most of their ruling princes were already partly sinicised and some of the Inner Mongolian princes approved the New Administration.

Observing the loss of relative autonomy and the violent disruption of the pastoral economy in Inner Mongolia, a more coordinated and unified group in Outer Mongolia sought to cut off their 'alliance' (ibid.: 52) with the Qing Empire by seeking Russian support.

Owen Lattimore (1934: 126 quoted in Sneath, 2001: 51) observed that 'the futility of mere resistance as a method of preserving the integrity of Mongol territory and Mongol people' led to the formation of an armed separatist movement in the Outer Mongol lands. For Mongols in the Inner Mongol area of the old Qing Dynasty, the new Han authorities 'standardized' (Sneath, 2001: 52) what was once a semi-autonomous region (*amban*) of the Empire into a closely administered province of the Chinese state. The 'assimilationist' (ibid.) approach of the new Chinese state was instrumental in the development of a Mongol nation-state in the Outer Mongol lands and the claiming of *Mongolian* national identity. Lattimore (ibid.) poignantly remarks that it was at this point in history that Mongol leaders recognised 'the fact that independence cannot be maintained without the creation of social forms adequate to the life of a modern nation in a modern world.' Thus, while mobile pastoralism has been shown to be 'inextricably combined' (Sneath, 2001: 47) with the constitution of political authority and economy in Inner Asia, the establishment of a national, territorial state in response to the imperial expansionism of the Chinese state implied significant discontinuities in the administration of nomadic pastoralism. Specifically, the 'broad strata of authority' (Nisbet, 1974: 612) typifying the space between the nomadic subject and the sovereign which had enabled far more fluid boundaries collapsed as the state became defined by *national* borders.

As the Qing Dynasty was steadily transformed into a Han nationalist state (Sneath, 2001: 49–53), the Mongol separatists faced the dilemma of safeguarding the Outer Mongol region from Chinese acquisition, as well as preventing Japanese economic interests and Russian warlords from threatening new forms of colonisation (ibid.: 53). The Chinese threat at that time was the most pressing.[9] A group of Mongol princes and senior Buddhist lamas organised a secret delegation to Russia to ask for protection and assistance in July 1911 (Tatsuo, 1999: 71–72). There appears to have been no clear consensus about which form this assistance was to take, as some of the princes wanted independence from the Chinese and others wanted a restoration of their previous position within the Qing Empire. Fundamentally, Russian assistance was invited to prevent the New Administration but did not necessarily entail becoming a protectorate of Russia nor achieving full national independence in the minds of the Mongol drafters (ibid.). In the letter delivered by the delegation to the Russian government, the perspective of the Mongol delegation was that they were no longer able to submit to the Manchu Emperor as they had peacefully done for 200 years, because of the new Qing policies of land appropriation, blaming the 'Han Chinese bureaucrats' for taking political power and bringing 'confusion and discord to the affairs of the state' (Khalka Delegation Letter, 1911 quoted in ibid.: 72). According to Tatsuo's translation (ibid.: 73),

> the letter pointed out, "we cannot bear" the new policy of government, which was designed to "search out ways to turn Mongol land into farmland, which, if accomplished, will inevitably destroy our traditional way of life."

The emphasis of the delegation was upon preserving 'peace and tranquillity' and, above all, 'our traditional way of life' (ibid.); it appears to have been more of a request for guaranteeing political space and the boundaries of a place in which the Mongol state (aristocratic and religious institutions) and society (nomadic) could continue. Between 1912 and 1921, a bargain was struck between Russia, Outer Mongolia and China whereby Russia would support the establishment of an autonomous Outer Mongolian region under Chinese suzerainty, led by the Mongol religious and political leader known as the Bogd Khan (ibid.: 75; Bawden, 1968/1989). However, this set-up proved to be too weak to protect Mongolia from its southern neighbour. In 1918, the Chinese army returned 'to prevent Soviet aggression feared from the north' (Bawden, 1968/1989: 202), which led to the complete reinstatement of Chinese authority in 1920 in what Bawden (ibid.) has described as 'humiliating circumstances' for the Mongols.

While there is neither space nor necessity to cover this period of Mongolian state history in more detail, it must be said that this was a complex political moment for the Mongols. While Russia was clearly the preferred option to China, it is not equally clear that the Mongol revolutionaries were particularly inspired by Leninist-Marxism, apart from a few notable leaders such as Sukhbaatar and Choibalsen who have, in hindsight, been credited as the most influential actors on the revolutionary process. The narrative that emphasises these individuals' commitment to socialist ideology obscures the lack of unity within the revolutionary leadership, between "rightist" nationalists who prioritised Mongolian independence and "leftist" revolutionaries who allegedly prioritised the wholesale "emancipation" of Mongolia from not only China but aristocratic-religious 'feudalism' (see ibid.: 277).

Between 1921 and 1923, the Red Army drove out the Chinese and "White" Russians, and established sufficient territoriality to declare Mongolia an independent state. Rather than immediately socialising Mongolia's only means of production – livestock – the new Mongolian state initially encouraged a form of managed capitalism in line with Lenin's New Economic Policy to boost economic recovery. In 1924, the Mongol State Bank was established, with the *tugrig* as the national currency. Interestingly, some currency speculation was permitted at this time and commercial transactions were taking place without significant interference from the state (ibid.: 274). Mongolia's limited industry (a handful of factories) and services sector was primarily driven by foreign companies; Mongols themselves were primarily occupied in the pastoral sector. While Mongolia's socialist transition was narrated later by socialist historians – Mongolian and Russian – as a triumph of the peasant over the feudal lord, the historical reality suggests a much more complex and violent picture, driven by geopolitical necessity.

### Socialist constitutionalism: new institutions and revolutionary legality for the Mongol People's Republic

In 1920, D. Sukhbaatar and a small group of revolutionary Mongol leaders sought the assistance of the Red Army in securing the borders of the Outer Mongol territories and established a revolutionary government that operated through a compact with the Bogd Khan, the presiding Buddhist suzerain (Butler and Nathanson, 1982: 174). After the Bogd Khan's death in 1924, the new Mongolian Peoples' Republic no longer required a compromise with the religious establishment and declared its independence as an aligned state of the Soviet Union, following the successful demarcation of its southern border with China. While the MPR maintained its formal independence from the Soviet Union, the group of revolutionary leaders adopted Leninist socialism as the governing ideology of the new Mongolian nation-state. Caroline Humphrey (1978: 139), an eminent Mongolist, explains that it is essential to 'take into consideration the political position of Mongolia as a nation-state' following the declaration of its "independence" in 1921:

Neither China nor the Soviet Union were going to follow a Mongolian policy. The Mongols had to decide which of their two neighbours offered the best prospects as protector and they then had no option but to act as an ally, loyal not only in foreign affairs but also as a true follower of the ideology and social reconstruction.

The introduction of Buddhism as an imperial religion had ultimately reinforced the cohesiveness of aristocratic socio-political order by perpetuating the "intertwined" ethno-linguistic and political-religious discourses that had come to define the 'conception of political unity' between Mongol people and early Mongol statecraft (Munkh-Erdene, 2006: 55–57). Consequently, for the purposes of the more radical socialist revolutionaries, the destruction of the Buddhist church was seen as the key to the establishment of the socialist state. This was not only because Buddhism challenged socialism as a competing ideology, despite initial attempts to accommodate both (Bawden, 1968/1989: 264–273), but because of the economic power vested in the lamaseries. While the new established Mongolian People's Revolutionary Party (MPRP) had Soviet backing, the clergy outflanked the new political leadership both in terms of numbers and distribution throughout the country. According to Kaplonski (2011: 434), there were initially only 100–150 party members against 80,000–100,000 lamas, and the party members were mostly based in the capital city. Furthermore, the indigenisation of Buddhism amongst Mongols and the entrenched nature of the aristocratic-clerical order meant that ordinary Mongols, particularly outside of Ulaanbaatar, were deeply resistant to the destruction of clerical institutions.

The death of the Bogd Khan provided a political opening for the adoption of socialist institutions (1924 Constitution of the Mongolian People's Republic, Annex 1). In 1924, Mongolia adopted its first socialist constitution that called for the reorganisation of political and economic power in the name of the 'labouring people' (ibid.). Compared to later constitutions, this initial constitution bears limited resemblance to its Soviet counterpart and is more nationalist in its language than socialist: 'the unified economic policy is in the hand of the Government' (Article 3d). While the Constitution contextualises its 'Declaration of the Rights of Labouring People' with the acknowledgement that 'the labouring masses of the whole world are striving to uproot capitalism and to attain socialism' (Article 3n), this internationalist statement is immediately followed by a nationalist "Note":

> Nevertheless, as circumstances may demand, the possibility of entering into friendly relations with diverse foreign Powers is not excluded, provided, however, that any attempt against the independence of the Mongolian People's Republic shall meet with decisive resistance in all circumstances.

In fact, the text of the 1924 Constitution clearly reflects a Mongolian *national* adaptation of socialism. Private property in livestock was still permitted, while property in land, minerals, forests and waters were common property (Article 3a). The role of the state in relation to the economy had more of a regulatory character than a completely socialised one,[10] based on the fact that the basis of the new national economy – livestock – was personally owned. There was little surplus value to extract from herding, given that it had not been organised in a way to generate economic growth or maximise surplus value. Thus, while the 'first real object of the Mongol Republic consists in the abolition of the remains of the feudal theocratic order' (Article 2), consensus was initially absent as to the precise manner in which the new notion of a national economy should be governed, although that quickly changed.

Developing a socialist legal system and institutional base was a critical step in consolidating the new state. Within the first ten years of the MPR's formation, 'revolutionary-democratic law and its system were fundamentally formed and established' (Dashniam, 1974 in Butler and Nathanson, 1982: 167). Statutes mandating and governing the establishment of state agencies, judicial institutions, central and local *khurals* (parliaments) were enforced, and legislation passed in the areas of labour, family, criminal and civil law. Similar to the 1924 Constitution, 'revolutionary-democratic law' (ibid.) has been portrayed by Mongol socialist legal scholars as an intermediary between the rejection of 'feudal and capitalist law' and 'socialist law' (ibid.: 168). It was rationalised as an 'embodiment in law of the aspirations of socially progressive and revolutionary classes' (ibid.: 168) and to make socialist social relations normative:

> Revolutionary-democratic law played a vital role in developing the forces of production, in providing citizens' needs, in educating workers with revolutionary ideology, in the struggle by people against remnants of the past, in respecting and observing revolutionary legality, and in strengthening new labour discipline.
>
> (Ibid.: 169)

However, as noted previously, the critical part of establishing the MPR as a socialist, Soviet Union-aligned state was to be the dissolution of the monasteries and the purging of political dissent from the clerical class (Kaplonski, 2012). As Kaplonski argues, the 'question of the lamas' (ibid.: 72–73) reflected a fundamentally political, as opposed to religious, conflict between the new socialist government and the Buddhist establishment. The Buddhist church not only had a strong legitimacy in Mongol society based on the fervent religiosity of the population, but through their central role in 'economics, livestock, education and healthcare' (ibid.: 73). Consequently, the lamaseries posed a fundamental threat and roadblock to the strategic interests of the new socialist state. Supported by Moscow and the Red Army, the socialist political leadership took a drastic action to dissolve clerical power and institutions in the late 1930s, following a decade of efforts to undermine them through taxation, incentives, prohibitions and prosecutions (ibid.: 74). Significantly, Kaplonski argues that the failure of these methods in the 1920s and early 1930s created the conditions for the use of brutal force by the state, which would have been delegitimised if exercised earlier by a 'contingent'[11] (ibid.) state which had yet to consolidate its sovereignty over the Mongolian population. Between 1937 and 1939, approximately 18,000 lamas were purged by national and Soviet armed forces, and virtually all of the lamaseries (700) were destroyed (ibid.: 73).

The destruction of the Buddhist establishment enabled the MPR to consolidate its modernist and secular programme of development. Productivity, modernisation and nationalism were the core impetus of the new state ideology. Notably, there was, despite this rhetoric, some overlap between "feudal" and "revolutionary" legal norms in the early period of the socialist state, which arguably reflects the new state's need to borrow legitimacy from the previous order. However, the inclusion of some norms from 'feudal legislation' (ibid.) was justified in hindsight by socialist legal scholars: 'the utilisation of old legal norms meant putting new meanings into old forms of law, and... destroying these laws from within' (ibid.).

The MPR's trajectory of constitutional development was to become consistently more aligned with that of the Soviet Union. Following the disastrous first attempts at collectivisation, as will be discussed later, it was not until 1940 that Mongolia was 'formally committed' to a 'non-capitalist development path' (Butler and Nathanson, 1982: 176) when the 1940 Constitution made an explicit commitment to state planning (ibid.).[12] By 1960, Mongolia was fully committed to socialist state forms and Marxist–Leninist ideology; the latter was described as 'all triumphant' in the preamble of the 1960 Constitution (reproduced in Butler and Nathanson, 1982: 179–193), with Labour Power as the driving force of its self-proclaimed socialist accumulation strategy.

Institutions of "democratic centralism" were established, with clear distributions of administrative responsibility and subsidiarity between central and provincial administrations. In particular, the provincial, district and sub-district *khurals* and executive offices were charged with specific responsibilities in political and economic management. Article 55 obligated these sub-central administrations to:

> Direct economic and cultural political construction on [its] territory;
>> Direct and control the work of economic and cooperative organisations;
>> Confirm the economic plan and local budget; take measures to fulfil them;
>> Direct the activity of agencies of administration subordinate to them;
>> Ensure observance of the rule of socialist community life, protect the rights and interests of state enterprises and institutions, agricultural associations, and other cooperatives, and also protect the rights of citizens;
>> Ensure the precise observance of laws, and also the strict fulfilment of decisions of superior agencies;
>> Ensure the extensive and active participation of the working people in all domains of state, economic and cultural construction.

Clearly, the state had formed the institutions and legal-normative framework to execute and legitimise a specifically socialist regime of accumulation. However,

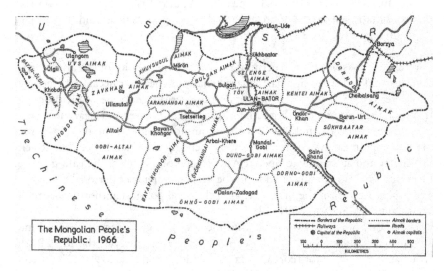

*Map 3.3* The Mongol People's Republic in 1966.
(Source: Bawden, 1968: 449)

how was an "economy" to be actually formed out of the aristocratic-pastoralist entanglement? How were herders to be made into a "productive" labour force? These questions, crucial to understanding the socialist political economy and the role of the state therein, will be examined in the following section.

## Introducing "economic development" into Mongol steppe society

Unlike other polities where pastoralism was practised alongside other forms of production, pastoralism *was* the only basis of what could be described as a "national economy" in the MPR, as most Mongols within the newly established borders were herders (Humphrey, 1978: 139). According to Humphrey (ibid.), this unique position 'leant distinction to the Mongolian socialist revolution.' It also generated conflict between the revolutionaries about the new Republic's pathway towards economic development, as there was no prior state of capitalism for the "proletariat" to rise up against. In fact, as Bawden (1968/1989: 244) puts it:

> There was no working class, and no native capitalist class either, for though there were recognisable groups within the populations these did not coincide with social classes in the Marxist sense. Divisions were vertical rather than horizontal. It was the work of years to engineer class consciousness and a class struggle. Delegates to the important Third Party Congress in 1924 to lay down the lines on which the new republic was to develop, were

confused by talk of classes. As one of them put it: "Whom are we to consider as capitalists, as middle herdsmen and as poor herdsmen? And how are we to distinguish them?"'

The vertical divisions that structured the relative hierarchies of the aristocratic-clerical social order gave it a particularly tenacious character because its inequalities were so layered that they did not produce resistance to the whole order per se. While there were inequalities in decision-making power and clear hierarchies of status between the nobility and the "common" people, the dependency of the whole political system upon livestock herding gave herders economic self-sufficiency and autonomy to operate within the boundaries of the ruling house. Livestock was also not alienated from the herder; systems of personal ownership were operative within the 'jurisdiction of the local political authority that regulated their use' (Sneath, 2001: 43).

The MPRP was faced with the unforeseen challenge of turning herders into an industrial labour force. By the end of the 1920s, however, the MPRP had articulated a strategy for reorganising production (Boikova, 1999: 107) in conjunction with the Soviet Union. The 1929 Soviet-Mongolian Agreement

> stated that the working people of Mongolia had made a decision on the non-capitalist development of their country by promoting their own industry, enlarging and further developing their own cattle-breeding and agriculture, collectivising agriculture, developing cooperative and state trade,[13] and having the government regulate the economy.
>
> (Ibid.: 108)

Part of the legitimising narrative of the socialist reformers was a critique of pre-socialist "feudalism" where nobles and clerics were framed as holders of private property at the expense of the 'exploited class' of *arat* (commoner) (Dashniam, 1974 in Butler and Nathanson, 1977: 168; Mönkhjargal, 1977 in Butler and Nathanson, 1982: 499). In the words of a socialist Mongol legal scholar, T. Monkhjargal (ibid.), 'an important factor in developing a non-capitalist path was liquidating the economic power of the feudal class and forcing foreign exploitative capital out of the nation's economy.'

In reality, the "working people of Mongolia" were uninformed about the intention to "socialise" the means of production (i.e. livestock), as the MPRP in Ulaanbaatar operated apart from the majority of the rural Mongol population. Consequently, the first phase of collectivisation of the herds (1929–1932) was a complete disaster. As Lattimore (1949: xxxvi–xxxvii) observed:

> The attempted forced march toward socialisation and collectivisation frightened and antagonised the herdsmen who formed the main bulk of the population and who owned its chief economic resource, the flocks and herds.

They regarded collectivisation not as a new form of ownership but as depri-
vation of ownership, and in resistance to it they slaughtered their cattle by
the thousand. The whole attempt had to be abandoned, and the country
returned to private ownership of livestock, modified by a strong emphasis on
cooperative enterprises of all kinds as a means of turning the minds of the
people toward the potential advantages of group enterprise in contrast with
sole reliance on the enterprise of the individual or the household.

Initial collectivisation was a failure because the anti-feudal premise of the en-
deavour was miscalculated: the aristocratic-clerical order was hierarchical but
property was not fundamentally alienated from the "commoner." Land was
organised on the basis of personal use-rights within a custodial framework
(Sneath, 2001: 43) rather than *private* property rights, and herders owned their
own livestock. Thus, given that they were owners of Mongolia's sole "means of
production," herders were able to resist collectivisation unlike other pastoralists
in the Soviet Union. The Party soon realised that by sending herds over the
border into China or slaughtering them, herders had the power to 'deplete the
country's productive capital' (Dupuy and Blanchard, 1970: 299). Many animals
also died due to a lack of a sense of ownership and responsibility in the newly
formed collectives. Between 1930 and 1932, the number of livestock dropped
dramatically from 24 million to 16.2 million (Endicott, 2012: 68). Following
this initial failure to immediately collectivise the herders, it was acknowledged
that completely skipping the capitalist phase of development had been idealistic.
The New Turn Policy, instigated to repair the political and economic fall-out
from forced collectivisation, can be understood as an

> ideological retreat from socialism in that it was publicly admitted that only
> by fostering private enterprise could prosperity and confidence be restored.
> The new motto was "raise high private initiative, and bring the private
> cattle-herding economy to a new level."
>
> (Bawden, 1968/1989: 352)

Specific steps were taken in order to transform the herding population into an
organised force of labour and to 'rationalise' (ibid.: 310) production so that surplus value could be generated and extracted to increase the yield of the economy
and sustain the new nation-state. Industrial development was now dependent
upon diverse capital inputs, whereas previously 'livestock represented both capital and income as well as a measure of wealth, a medium of exchange, and almost
the only source of food, clothing and shelter' (Dupuy and Blanchard, 1970:
297). In a limited sense, the socialist period introduced a capitalistic economy
by organising production in a way intended to 'generate the expansion of capital'
(Cox, 1987: 57) albeit for the purposes of the state. This was a gradual process
of incorporating herders into the logic of industrial production. Until the 1950s,

herders were simply encouraged to pool their labour and increasing levels of support were granted to herders to incentivise them to work together and increase their "industrial" outputs of wool, meat and dairy products. The state enabled this process by providing tax incentives and tangible support to herders, such as repairing winter sheds and providing Soviet-purchase machines to assist with haymaking. A compromise was also struck by granting nomads permission to have some private livestock in the context of the *negdel*. By the early 1960s, the majority of herders had been incorporated into *negdels*, reflecting both a change in social mind-set and the reality of 'propaganda and economic compulsion' (Bawden, 1968/1989: 399).

The modernising impetus of the socialist state cannot be understated. Writing in 1970, Dupuy and Blanchard (1970:v) explained that 'one goal constantly preached is the conversion 'from an agricultural-industrial society to an industrial-agricultural state' – by which is meant the eventual dominance of industry over stockraising.' The desire to collectivise the herds and "rationalise" pastoral production was part of a broader vision of gradually creating a sedentary "modern" workforce primarily engaged in factory production. In the 1960s and 1970s, the livestock collectives (*negdels*) modelled an almost Fordist division of labour, with specialised tasks assigned to different groups of herders, who had formerly attended to all aspects of the production process prior to collectivisation. In a similar way, herds were also "specialised" into one type of livestock rather than the customary five-animal herds (i.e. sheep, goats, camels, horses and cows) (Endicott, 2012: 73). As Endicott (ibid.) notes, the *negdels* were given specific "production goals" under the Five-Year Development Plans, adding that 'this external source of authority reduced herders to state employees without much scope for independent decision-making vis-à-vis pasture use.' Land, however, remained public: unfenced and uncommodified, as the *negdels* still depended on nomadism, although now under bureaucratic supervision (ibid.: 78–79). Humphreys (1978: 156) also observed that the herding collectives tended to reflect the pre-socialist territories of the *khoshuun*, as 'many *negdel* centres were on the sites of disbanded lamaseries.' Thus, despite huge change, there were elements of continuity with aristocratic forms of statecraft in the governance of pastoralism and territory in the socialist period.

The state also introduced specific legal forms to enhance productivity as national development accelerated, which reinforced the formation of an economic sphere distinguished from but governed explicitly by the state. A good example of introducing distinctly *economic* legality was the case of economic contracts, which were 'especially influential and significant in perfecting economic relations' (Mönkhjargal, 1977 in Butler and Nathanson, 1982: 499), according to a socialist jurist of the time. In 1961, the General Conditions for Economic Contracts were introduced by the Council of Ministers. Economic contracts had a 'planned character' (Aiuush, 1976a in Butler and Nathanson, 1982: 498) in the sense that 'the money-commodity relationship' (ibid.: 497) was planned, but they created the possibility of private (i.e. non-state) economic exchanges and added another layer of distance between the direct state control and the productive sphere. As Aiuush (ibid.: 498) puts it:

> Capitalist theorists consider that contracts during the period of socialism are the technical instrument of planning. This denies the independent and increasing role of contracts... Planning is one way to provide the national economy with unified guidance by the state, and economic contracts are one way to develop the initiative of economic organisations.

This quote from Aiuush, a Mongol socialist jurist, reflects a blurred boundary between socialist and capitalist economic governance in the late socialist period. From Aiuush's perspective, contracts enable some *private freedom* in the economic sphere and have efficiency-enhancing utility, which runs counter to classical socialist economic theory. Although the adoption of a (private) legal form to enhance productivity and initiative is intuitively *capitalist*, it was in fact planted firmly within socialist rationality: 'In order to perfect socialist economic relations the role of legal coordination must constantly increase' (Aiuush, 1976b: 501). Within the first five years of planning, the number of economic contracts increased by fifteen times (ibid.), demonstrating the incorporation of capitalist legality within a socialist framework to enhance accumulation.

By 1970, approximately 60% of the population were still employed in livestock herding (Dupuy and Blanchard, 1970: 308). However, by the end of the 1980s, that number had declined to under 20% (Fratkin and Mearns, 2003: 117), following heightened industrial development of the 1960s and 1970s (Bumaa, 2001: 54). This remarkable social shift from a "simple" pastoralist mode of production in the 1920s to a mixed economy controlled by the state (manufacturing, agriculture and mining) was a product of the centralisation of state power. After 1948, following the disastrous first effort at collectivisation, the purges of "dissidents" and clerics, and the Second World War, the MPRP began to produce Five-Year Plans, following Soviet development models. This heightened developmentalism was enabled by a deepening aid and trade relationship with the Soviet Union in the 1950s (ibid.: 293), with large-scale exports of manufacturing equipment and personnel to the MPR. The Soviets had an interest in maintaining Mongolia as an effective buffer state, and therefore were willing to invest in the country's self-sufficiency.

The Soviet Union was also the primary beneficiary of Mongolian industrial development, having a monopoly on its foreign trade. Mongolia exported mostly raw commodities to the Soviet Union (i.e. copper, coal, meat, dairy products and wool) in exchange for processed imports. In terms of economic and social outcomes, the Soviet era of Mongolian history caused a remarkable shift in Mongolian society. In 1978, Humphreys (1978: 158) wrote that Mongolia had one of the highest standards of living in Asia, as the country was virtually self-sufficient in terms of food production. Pastoral products such as meat and wool were exported to market on the Soviet trading bloc – the Council for

Mutual Economic Assistance (CMEA) – and the discovery of copper deposits near Erdenet led to the establishment of a state-owned copper mine. Mass education was enforced and widespread literacy was achieved; the children of herders were sent to boarding schools in the urban centres of *aimags* to learn new herding techniques or other skills (ibid.: 145). According to Humphreys (ibid.: 149), the dominant perception of nomadic pastoralists under Soviet socialism was that they were "unsystematic," "inefficient" and "idle." The explicit intent of collectivisation and mass education was to instil an industrial work ethic into Mongolians (ibid.).

Mining minerals to export to Russia became a significant portion of industrial production in the late socialist period. In 1978, a Russian–Mongolian joint venture in copper extraction began operations in Erdenet, a small urban centre north of Ulaanbaatar. The Nailaikh coal mine on the outskirts of Ulaanbaatar was similarly a stalwart of coal production at the time. The industry was tightly controlled, mainly exploited by joint venture projects with Russia, and served domestic consumption and Soviet demand. Prices were fixed by the state, with preferential purchasing rates for the Soviet Union. While this might have changed if the Soviet Union had not collapsed, mining remained a relatively small focus in Mongolia, although geological mapping was undertaken for future exploitation and was part of an overall evaluation of Mongolia's productive assets. Notably, these maps provided the basis for the "minerals rush" in the mid-late 1990s in the wake of the liberalisation of the economy. The introduction of private property interests in land through extractive industries was thus avoided at this time, as the state alone had the right to explore and extract minerals. Copper ore became Mongolia's most lucrative export from the 1970s onwards (Goyal, 1999: 634).

As indicated in the section on socialist constitutionalism, the ability of the state to effectively extract surplus value and "develop" the economy was critically enabled by local government branches, which were key loci to teach 'Communist industrial discipline' to former nomads (Dupuy and Blanchard, 1970: 294). The sheer scale of Mongolian territory and the challenge of governing a remote population required the systematic diffusion of central authority through administrative sub-divisions. Just as the Qing rulers had overlaid customary boundaries established within the Mongol Empire with the *khoshuun*, the socialist political engineers in Ulaanbaatar and Moscow also chose an adaptive governing strategy, to some extent a 'new formulation of earlier political relations' (Sneath, 2001:47). While they reconfigured the boundaries of the provinces (*aimags*) and established new districts (*soums*) in line with the administrative requirements of new industry (i.e. the *negdels*) (Endicott, 2012: 74), they capitalised on the cultural inheritance of Mongolian familiarity with local institutions as a means of achieving state national goals. While the socialist state was unitary, elections were held at district and provincial levels, although in reality, these "elections" were political appointments.

To conclude this section, the period of socialist state formation evidences significant continuities and discontinuities with the pre-socialist era of Mongol statecraft. The central aspect of socialist statecraft in Mongolia in political-economic terms was related to the governance of labour and livestock; similarly, pastoralism was at the heart of pre-socialist state forms. However, the governance of pastoralism in the socialist period was no longer an end in itself, but a means to industrial development. Livestock was commodified as a capital asset for the state in the name of the "people," and the work of the new socialist subjects was converted into a pool of *labour*, organised to enable industrial production (although it was not subordinated to a free market system of price-based supply and demand). However, despite the introduction of a distinctively *economic* rationality within the state, it was contained within the political discourse of Soviet socialism. While we could describe the pre-socialist era as a completely politicised economy – with production and statecraft 'intertwined' to use Munkh-Erdene's phrase (2006: 56) – the socialist state was a loosened braid, in the sense that the political-institutional and economic production became two distinctive fields of social life. However, economic production was still embedded *within* the political sphere, as the government actively organised trade, exchange and price values.

## Democratising the government, depoliticising the economy? The post-socialist Mongolian state

Perhaps surprisingly for some, Mongolia's democratic revolution in 1990 has many parallels with its socialist counterpart. Just as the socialist revolution began in Ulaanbaatar in the wake of the collapsing Qing Empire, Mongolia's democratic revolution was initiated by young, urban and predominantly male Mongolians as the Soviet Union crumbled at the end of the 1980s. The democratisation of the Mongolian state occurred in similar conditions of emergency,[14] where the 'rules of the game' (Swyngedouw, 2005: 1991) fundamentally shifted with the hegemonic rise of self-regulating market capitalism and the demise of alternatives (i.e. the Soviet Union). Once again, Mongolia needed to politically reorient itself to survive economically without Soviet assistance or access to its regional market, as well as to maintain its independence, thereby facing the same geopolitical predicament of asymmetrical relationships with its neighbours (Wachman, 2010). The social violence accompanying this period of revolution, however, was economic rather than military. While the revolution was peaceful in the sense that there were no outbreaks of physical violence, the majority of the Mongolian population endured a seismic shift in their social environment, as the economy was forcibly rent from direct state control.

### (Re)constitutionalisation part I: a new blueprint for accumulation

> The measures that constitute shock therapy do not by themselves create 'agonizing pain' in the body politic. The image of plummeting living standards as a result of rapid economic reforms is completely wrong-headed...
> Jeffrey Sachs in 'Understanding Shock Therapy' (1994: 25)

Mongolia's path to nation-state status had depended in large degree upon the Soviet Union. When the latter began to crumble in the late 1980s, so did the bulwark of aid, trade support and investment that had enabled the Mongolian economy to industrialise. Similar to the early 1920s, maintaining Mongolian independence required a new orientation to prevent re-colonisation by China, with which Mongolia had maintained a tense and fragile relationship. The demise of the Soviet Union ushered in an era of Western hegemony, laden with "End of History" optimism about the future of market democracy. Mongolia was one of many post-socialist states in Central Asia and Eastern Europe caught up in waves of local and global optimism about the transformative power of liberal institutions to effectively mediate the political and economic spheres: separation of powers doctrine, constitutional democracy, private enterprise and (the liberal version of) the rule of law.[15]

Mongolia's democratic revolution was driven by both pragmatic necessity and ideological fervour, similar to its socialist predecessor. Led politically by young idealists caught up in the narrative of *openness* in the late 1980s (following the movements for *perestroika* and *glasnost* in the Soviet Union) (Sanders, 1988), the post-socialist transition was also pushed hastily along by forces of economic crisis. Educated in Russian and Eastern European universities, the young, urban and elite leaders of the reform movement had been exposed in varying degrees to the principles of multi-party elections, democracy and the market economy (Rossabi, 2005: 4–5). The young Mongolians who lead the democratic revolution did not topple socialist party rule, but managed to erode its monopoly on power through the introduction of multi-party elections and the removal of hard-line members of the MPRP. The MPRP won the first democratic election in 1990 because of the failure of the democratic reform movement to adequately reach out to the rural electorate. However, the MPRP tactically offered some leadership positions to the democratic reformers, allowing a peaceful transition to multi-party elections. A strong contingent of the reform group, led by D. Ganbold and others known as the 'Club of Young Economists' (Fritz, 2008: 771), was inspired by the 'creative destruction' (Harvey, 2005: 23) model of the neoliberal Washington Consensus (ibid.: 27; Klein, 2007: 155–170), where a minimally involved government facilitates a rapid transition to a market economy through privatisation and economic liberalisation. The new leaders of the MPRP following the July 1990 elections were more moderate and somewhat conciliatory towards the reformers; the first democratically elected Prime Minister offered Ganbold the influential cabinet role as the First Deputy Premier (Rossabi, 2005: 28).

The "new" government of the democratic Mongolia that emerged in the wake of a crumbling Soviet Union was a genuine ideological hybrid, which comprised both the MPRP and the new democratic parties, the more powerful of which advocated a hasty transition to a market economy in line with the advice of International Financial Institutions (IFIs). The political leadership of Mongolia did not have much time to work through their differences or come to a compromise as the collapse of the Soviet Union precipitated an economic crisis that required hasty political realignment. The sudden removal of all Soviet financing – 30%–35% of Mongolia's Gross Domestic Product (GDP) – by the beginning of 1991 (Goyal, 1999: 644) and the dissolution of the CMEA meant that Mongolia's economy not only contracted suddenly but lost most of its export markets within the space of two years. Exports declined from USD 832 million in 1989 to USD 370 million in 1991 (Sneath, 2006b: 150). The government introduced rationing for basic foodstuffs in 1991 and began printing *tugriks* to make up for its sudden shortfall in budget (Goyal, 1999: 643). Inflation skyrocketed from virtually nil in 1989 to 121.2% in 1991 and 321% in 1992 (ibid.). With little credit, high levels of debt obligation to the Soviet Union (Heaton, 1992: 53), rapidly declining revenues and its northern neighbour demanding hard currency for fuel and other vital materials (Rossabi, 2005: 35), Mongolia was on the brink of an economic and social disaster. Despite improved relations with China since the 1980s, Mongolia was reticent to seek Chinese assistance due to the long history of colonisation and geopolitical tension between the two states; the government looked towards the West for new sources of assistance and trade (ibid.: 36).

One of the main goals of post-socialist Mongolian foreign policy was to steer a path clear of its two neighbours – Russia and China – through alignment with Western powers. Mongolia's "Third Neighbour Policy" struck a delicate 'balance between its two neighbours... by declaring itself neutral as between Moscow and Beijing' (Wachman, 2010: 589), while reaching out to new allies. The negotiation of this balancing and distancing strategy was to 'avoid being subordinated to either of the two, whilst benefiting from the munificence and commercial opportunities each might provide' (ibid.). While not *overcoming* its asymmetrical position in relation to its neighbours, Mongolia carefully achieved relative autonomy in the 1990s and early 2000s. During this time, Mongolia was primarily indebted to IFIs, such as the World Bank, the International Monetary Fund (IMF) and the Asian Development Bank (ADB) (Rossabi, 2005), and was a beneficiary of significant Euro-American aid, particularly from the U.S. and Germany.

In early 1991, Mongolia was admitted to the IMF, the ADB and the World Bank, following a visit from the U.S. Secretary of State in 1990 (ibid.: 37). From 1990 to 1992, a series of economic reforms were undertaken by the government of Mongolia to fulfil the conditions placed on its receipt of assistance from international donor agencies. These conditionalities followed the six tenets of shock therapy by requiring price liberalisation, linking the Mongolian *tugrik* to international currency, eliminating government subsidies, privatising state assets and banking, selling most SOEs and liberalising tariffs on trade (ibid.). According to Sachs in 'Understanding Shock Therapy,' the triad of crises – state bankruptcy, system collapse and structural transformation – were to be addressed through 'the rapid introduction of the six core institutions of capitalism' (Sachs, 1994: 29):

1.) A monetary system based on a stable, convertible currency; 2.) Freedom of international trade and foreign investment; 3.) Private property rights...; 4.)

Private ownership of a high proportion of national assets; 5.) Corporate control of large enterprises…; and 6.) A social safety net.

Other reforms undertaken by the government included introducing a floating exchange rate and setting up a Stock Exchange, as well as a commercialised banking system (IMF, 2003: 1). The optimism of the Mongolian reformers and the goals of international financial advisers converged at least on practical aspects of institutional transformation, which satisfied the aims of both: the continued survival of an independent nation-state and the incorporation of post-socialist states into the capitalist market economy. The role of IFIs, particularly the IMF, the World Bank and the ADB in this process was marked. As Fenwick (2007: 182) puts it:

> In supporting the new 'rules of the game' in Mongolia, the ADB alone supported the development of several major pieces of legislation in the early-to-mid 1990s, including a Bank Law and a Central Bank Law… and the review of laws relating to business entities, contracts, secured transactions, bankruptcy, and foreign investment. In total, more than 25 pieces of legislation were passed in Mongolia in the four years from 1991 that related in some way to transition. This included a new Civil Code (of approximately 400 articles) incorporating the important underpinnings of commercial life – contractual and property rights.

In terms of economic reforms, Mongolia was a model student of the Washington Consensus, instituting the privatisation, liberalisation and deregulation of its economy without delay (Munkh-Erdene, 2011; Sukhbaatar, 2012). Mongolia initiated its privatisation programme in the first year of its post-socialist transition (Korsun and Murrell, 1995: 473), starting with public assets, state-subsidised industries, welfare systems and importantly, the rural herding collectives – *negdels* (Sneath, 2003: 441–442). While requiring a huge amount of effort to legislate and implement this marketisation mandate, it also marked a shift in Mongolia's political and economic history because the public administration of pastoral land use was no longer a central governance concern. The economic vision of the new democratic Mongolia was a continuation of the industrial development narrative of Soviet socialism, where "traditional" economic modes were to be bypassed to make way for more "developed" forms of economy.

Privatisation played a critical role in Mongolia's post-socialist transition, 'leading as it did to an irreversible shift in productive assets from the state to the private sector, with the intention of creating a pluralist, liberal, capitalist market economy' (Nixson and Walters, 2006: 1558). Mongolia's national development strategy in these early days of reform was focused on enabling the 'active participation' (Goyal, 1999: 641) of the private sector to stimulate efficient economic growth and to create self-reliant citizens 'who had the mentality of private property owners' (Korsun and Murrell, 1995: 474). Mongolia's extensive privatisation programme embodied these aspirations, making it the most critical feature of all the market reforms undertaken (ibid.: 472–474). The "new" democratic government systematically privatised 470 state-owned enterprises including the *negdels*; 55% of this privatisation occurred in 1992 alone (Anderson et al., 2000: 530). By 1995, 95% of livestock, trade and services had been privatised (Goyal, 1999: 636). The dividends derived from the privatisation of SOEs were supposed to be divided amongst the public equally in the form of vouchers that could be exchanged on the Stock Exchange or at auctions for shares in the new private company (Korsun and Murrell, 1995: 475–476). The voucher system was promulgated on the basis of an inclusive approach to Mongolia's national assets in addition to 'providing the laboratory in which the Mongolian people would learn the psychology of capitalism' (ibid.: 476). While egalitarian in theory, the shares were concentrated in the hands of a few and had the effect of *increasing* inequality; Rossabi points out that 'many citizens who were not conversant with a market economy sold their vouchers at depressed prices and thus gained very little from the redistribution of public assets' (Rossabi, 2005: 51).[16]

The privatisation of SOEs and the *negdels* shrunk Mongolia's industrial base by exposing inefficient industries to free market mechanisms, causing most of them to collapse (UNIDO, 2011: 51). While some commentators saw this as inevitable, others perceived active *underdevelopment* of post-socialist states as a result of "shock therapy" and privatisation (Reinert, 2000). As Reinert (ibid.: 3) forcefully puts it, 'fifty years of industry-building was virtually annihilated over a period of only four years, from 1991 to 1995.' While Mongolia did not inherit a particularly *wide* industrial base from the Soviet era, it had 'slowly, but successfully, built a diversified industrial sector' (ibid.; Honeychurch, 2010: 410). Critically, the *negdels* had functioned as agricultural industries during the Soviet era, producing meat and dairy products for export as well as subsistence. Declining demand for Mongolian meat products as a result of the collapsed CMEA and the privatisation of the *negdels* transformed pastoralism into a predominantly subsistence economy (Sneath, 2003: 448). The impact of privatisation displaced agricultural products as Mongolia's largest export (Worden and Savada, 1989), given the emphasis of Mongolia's reformers, both domestic and international, on developing Mongolia's global comparative advantage: minerals (Honeychurch, 2010: 409–410).

Following widespread privatisation measures in the 1990s, the deregulated pastoral economy became both a form of subsistence and a social safety net for the thousands of Mongolians facing unemployment as it provided at least subsistence and the possibility of some cash by selling meat, dairy and wool products (Pomfret, 2000: 154). The number of semi-nomadic herders swelled to over 30% of the total population and 50% of the working population (Mearns, 2004: 108), undoing all the "progress" made to gradually urbanise and settle Mongolia's nomadic population in the socialist period. This was the first time that herding operated outside of an intricate system of administration, either under customary law (which had been eroded in the twentieth century) or state law (ibid.: 139).

In contrast to previous eras where political authority over the Mongolian population was inevitably related to the governance of pastoral land use, the democratic state of Mongolia can almost be defined by its *devolving* relationship with pastoralism as an economic system; as Mearns put it in 2004 (ibid.):

> Institutional arrangements governing pasture-land management have undergone profound transformation over the past decade in ways that reflect a virtual abdication of public administration rather than decentralisation or purposive intervention.

The deregulation of the pastoral economy goes hand-in-hand with the intent of Mongolia's democratic reformers to change the collectivised mentality of Mongolians to that of 'private property owners' (Korsun and Murrell, 1995: 474). This intent to develop the 'psychology of capitalism' (ibid.: 476) in Mongolians was embodied in the process of privatisation of the *negdels* and state farms, where herders were given shares in the form of vouchers in these SOEs to be traded on the new Stock Exchange. Where the Socialist period had initially tried to force the "psychology" of communalisation upon herders in the 1920s and 1930s to no avail, the capitalist ambitions of the democratic reformers for herders also produced disappointing and mixed results (Rossabi, 2005: 51). The lack of practical state support combined with the influx of new herders on the land has led to a remarkable disintegration of 'established co-ordination norms' (Mearns, 2004: 139) rising inequality between wealthy and poor herders, and pastureland degradation (Fernandez-Gimenez, 2000: 1320).

### (Re)constitutionalisation part II: a new political-legal regime

The economic reforms that have been described would not have been possible without a liberal democratic constitution recognising private property rights and mandating institutional reform for the rule of law to protect them. The drafting of the 1992 constitution was the first necessary inroad into the 'monolithic' (Bedeski, 2006: 82) centralised socialist state by abolishing one-party rule, establishing the separation of executive, judicial and legislative powers, installing a semi-presidential system and creating a basic framework for electoral democracy (Fritz, 2008.: 771; see also Sanders, 1992). These basic liberal constitutional structures were arguably necessary for Mongolia to undertake a national privatisation programme by introducing the formal rights of contract and ownership of private property (Korsun and Murrell, 1995: 473). The constitution, however, was a highly contested document; it was drafted in a series of 'marathon sessions' (Fish, 1998: 129) over a period of 71 days by a constitutional committee appointed by the democratically elected interim government. While Fish argues that its emergence out of a 'process of genuine deliberation and struggle within the national legislature' (ibid.) is a sign of its legitimacy, the deliberation was arguably under the duress of an extreme recession.[17] This secondary argument could explain why some of the more contentious points that the drafters faced were not resolved, particularly relating to land use and property rights (Fritz, 2008: 775).

For example, in paragraph two of Article Six of the constitution, the state remains vested with the ownership of all land as in the socialist era, '*except* that given to the citizens of Mongolia for private ownership' (Constitution of Mongolia, 1992, Article Six, emphasis added). Yet, paragraph three, which describes the ownership entitlements of Mongolian citizens, maintains state ownership of "public" pastureland and subsoil. Thus, citizens' land possession rights are thereby limited to rights of *usus* and *fructus* – to use and collect the fruits of the land. This is consistent with customary legal norms of pastoral land entitlements based on use rather than exclusive ownership. The preceding Article (Five) of the Constitution, however, affirms that Mongolia shall develop its economy 'based on all forms of property' – both private and public – and uphold the rule of law to protect the owner's rights. Articles Five and Six of the Constitution contain deeply incompatible ideological clauses regarding property rights; the Constitution is supposed to facilitate 'different forms of property consistent to universal trends of world economic development *and* country specifics' (Article 5:1, emphasis added). The contradiction and limitation of this pluralistic recognition in a capitalist market economy will be explored in the following chapter when we turn to Mongolia's mining economy.

## Mongolia as a model market democracy?

In sum, Mongolia's democratisation and incorporation into the global capitalist order were accompanied by a radical break between the political and economic spheres. In particular, this break was characterised by the introduction of institutions to both legitimise and execute this unprecedented diremption in the organisation of political and economic power. While the socialist state had created some basic institutions of capitalist production but set them within a specifically socialised framework, the 'emancipation of the economy from the political structure' (Sneath, 2003: 441–442) became a goal in its own right for the post-socialist state. This reflected the assumption of the international development consensus at the time (i.e. the Washington Consensus) that the market would naturally produce positive outcomes for society. The political sphere was not simply restricted from controlling the economy, but its very fabric was forcefully reorganised so that any prospect of regaining economic control would not only be "unconstitutional" but unthinkable within the terms of liberal democracy. The scope of Mongolian democracy has consequently been limited by the fact that 'the people were only granted rights when the awful adjustment had been made' (Polanyi, 1944/2001: 234); the democratisation of the Mongolian state under liberal democratic terms did not include the democratisation of economic power since it had been transferred to a separate "private" sphere.

## Conclusion

The purpose of this chapter has been to establish a historical narrative of the co-constitutive relationship between the state and the economy in Mongolia. Using Karl Polanyi's idea that all economies are "instituted" but some are "disembedded" (i.e. self-regulating market economies), I have attempted to outline some of the key continuities and changes in the state-economy relationship. The aristocratic-pastoralist period was characterised by a general integrity of production *within* the fabric of the political system, imbued with customary legal norms overlaid by the more bureaucratic laws of Empire. A strong ethno-linguistic and religious narrative reinforced the political authority of the aristocracy and, later, the Buddhist monasteries, although this authority was tempered by the latter's reliance on common herders to sustain pastoral accumulation. In the early twentieth century, the Mongol state primarily responded to regional geopolitical forces, leading to an independence movement and the formation of an independent nation-state. The unity of the aristocratic-pastoral social order was at times violently and at other times gradually dismantled during the socialist period, where the economy was formed as a separate sphere to the state, although governed within an explicitly political framework. Collectivisation and the making of a labour force out of the predominantly pastoralist population was a feat of long-term social planning and coercion by the state. Somewhat ironically, the socialist period introduced the basic mechanics for a market economy, including the (regulated) principles of 'truck, barter and exchange' (Polanyi, 1944/2001: 59), labour, currency, surplus value extraction and, in later years, economic contracts. Despite this period of state-economic formation being described in its constitutions as "non-capitalist," it actually provided the material market basis to establish an economy outside of the direct control of the state after the fall of the Soviet Union. However, as Polanyi (ibid.: 60) puts it, 'the step which makes regulated markets into a self-regulating market, is indeed crucial.'

In contrast to the two previous eras, Mongolia's democratic/market transformation did not push it towards one of its neighbours but to the West. Rather than Soviet advisors, Mongolia sought out the advice of IFIs. While this involved a political realignment with the "global" values of human rights, the rule of law and a (liberal) democratic political system, it is significant that Mongolia's main sources of support at the beginning of the 1990s were *economic* organisations. For example, the United States, Germany and other Western countries became part of Mongolia's geopolitical reorientation through its "Third Neighbour Policy,"[18] but their role was usually mediated under the aegis of economic development institutions, such as the IMF, the World Bank and USAID. The institutionalisation of a boundary between the political and economic spheres – mediated by the rule of law – within the liberal constitutional framework neatly matched Mongolia's new imperative to adjust to a global market economy, with few viable alternatives.

In terms of its national norms, Mongolia was in a great deal of flux in the early 1990s, lacking a concrete narrative for itself apart from the international (Western) applause at its "remarkable" adoption of liberal political and economic institutions (Fish, 1998, 2001). The reality in Mongolia was much more chaotic, and most Mongolians remember it as a time of disarray and economic devastation. At the same time, it is also remembered as a time of optimism for the possibilities of a democratic future, capitalist economic development and the rule of law, in contrast to the growing disillusionment of the present era. Drawing on this context, the following two chapters will engage with the institutionalisation of an extractive economy in Mongolia (1994–2014) and the way that state power has been systematically reorganised to facilitate foreign direct investment in the mining sector.

## Notes

1 Commodification can be defined as 'the process of transforming social relations and processes, things (e.g. life-forms, land, natural resources) or ideas into commodities or good that can be bought and sold in capitalist markets' (Gill and Cutler, 2014: 314).
2 Chinggis Khan's grandson, who ruled the Mongol Empire at its height (1260–1294).
3 The rise of Buddhism in Mongolia occurred at the expense of shamanism, which was gradually forced 'underground' or synthesised within a Buddhist framework (Bawden, 1968/1989: 32–33).
4 The institutionalisation of hierarchy within the *baghs* is similar to a governance strategy practised during the Mongol Empire in conquered Chinese regions where an 'intermediary structure composed of both Mongols and Chinese' was established to maintain control over peasants and those most likely to escape the rule of the administration (Kaplonski, 2010: 639).
5 In Inner Mongolia, leagues were established in addition to the *khoshuun* ruled by the princes, which enabled the top-down rotation of authority designated by the Emperor.
6 For example, Sneath and Boldbaatar (2006: 298–299) point out that Mongol princes were treated with exemplary regard by the Manchu administration and continued their aristocratic modes of governance despite becoming an auxiliary aspect of the overarching governance strategy of the Qing Empire.
7 This geopolitical dynamic has ongoing relevance for Mongolian state formation, in relation to China and Russia's competition over access to Mongolian mineral resources in the early twenty-first century. One historian, Stephen Kotkin (1999: 17), emphasises that, 'Mongol history, for better or worse, is Russian history and it is Chinese history.' At the same time, he argues that such a recognition 'must not degenerate into a one-way search for the influence of outsiders on the Mongols.' As B. Baabar (1988/2010: 1037), arguably Mongolia's most famous living historian, stated vehemently in *Buu Mart*: 'Whether in Moscow or Beijing, let there never be a fashion to share jokes about a dying tribe called the Mongols!'
8 Strategies deployed included both indirect and direct forms of resistance: signing petitions, impeding land surveys, refusing to pay contract fees and land taxes, armed attacks on Chinese officials and the raiding of Chinese local governments (Lan, 1999: 49).
9 In 1907, a Department of Colonisation was established in Beijing to enable the export of Han Chinese to Mongol territories and permit the acquisition of land (Kotkin and

Elleman, 1999: 30). In 1911, the level of threat was heightened with the establishment of a 'colonisation bureau' (ibid.) in Ulaanbaatar.

10  In Article 5 of the 1924 Constitution, the attributes of the 'supreme organs of the Mongol People's Republic' included raising foreign and domestic loans (5a), to regulate foreign and domestic trade (5d), public economic planning (5e), to approve the Republic's budget and establish taxes and revenues (5h), to organise currency and credit (5i), and to 'establish the general principles of the use of land,' define provincial boundaries and 'regulate the exploitation of mineral wealth, forests,' etc. (5j).

11  Kaplonski (2012: 74) describes the MPR in the 1920s and 1930s as a 'contingent state, a phrase he argues is a useful shorthand to argue that socialist Mongolia was not a well-established, uncontested state widely recognised as legitimate by the majority of the population.'

12  The MPR continued to adapt some aspects of Soviet constitutionalism in ways that indicate a "softer" mode of authoritarianism. For example, the Soviet provision "he who does not work, neither does he eat" (Article 12) was interpreted more positively in the Mongolian constitution mas 'honest and conscientious labour is the basis of the development of the national economy' (Hazard, 1948: 164).

13  As Boikova (1999: 109) accurately points out, the Agreement also essentially gave the Soviet Union monopoly access to economic relationships with Mongolia by granting the Soviet Union Most-Favoured Nation status, reinforced by the clause stating that 'the exceptional privileges which the USSR and Mongolia granted to each other should not be applied to other countries.'

14  From 1990 to 1992, the purchasing power of consumers diminished severely with annual inflation rates leaping to 325.2% in 1992. Unemployment compounded the capacity of most Mongolians to afford basic provisions as it rose from 1.3% in 1989 to around 20% by 1994 (World Bank, 1996: v). Government spending on social welfare declined rapidly during Mongolia's transition to a market democracy, from 40% of government expenditure before the transition to 11.1% of GDP in 1993 (ADB, 2008: 1–2). Under the Soviet-style command economy, Mongolians had enjoyed universal healthcare, employment, education and pension schemes, in addition to the provision of benefits to vulnerable groups (ibid.). Following the market transition, real expenditure on health was reduced 46% from 1990 to 1992 and the education budget was reduced by 56% (Sneath, 2006b: 149–150). The sudden decline in living standards combined with the cash poverty of most Mongolians resulted in rising levels of inequality: the earliest Gini coefficient data shows an increase from 0.31 in 1995 to 0.35 in 1998 (ibid.). The lack of available data from the Soviet era and the early years of the transition makes the original levels of pre-transition inequality levels difficult to determine in terms of the Gini coefficient, but they were generally considered to be low (see Rossabi, 2005: 35).

15  The rule of law is a contested concept, but at its most basic refers to the universal application of fairly drafted and defined laws, as opposed to arbitrary exercises of power. In liberal legal theory, which plays the strongest role in terms of affecting global rule of law norms (Jayasuriya, 2001), the rule of law is explicitly associated with the protection of private property rights (May, 2014a: 68, 2014b).

16  Rossabi also notes that by 2003, 0.5% of the population owned over 70% of the shares of the privatised companies.

17  Some scholars argue that the recession Mongolia faced in the collapse of the Soviet Union was more severe than that faced by any country in the Great Depression – see Korsun and Murrell (1995: 473–474), and Boone (1994: 314–328).

18  Mongolia's "Third Neighbour Policy" is the foundational approach of the state's post-socialist foreign policy to seek political and economic allies beyond Russia and China.

# References

Aiuush, D. 1976a. "The Plan and Economic Contracts." *AT* 2: 16–17. Republished in Butler, W. E. and Nathanson, A. J. 1982. *The Mongolian Legal System, Contemporary Legislation and Documentation*. The Hague: Martinus Nijhoff, 497–498.

———. 1976b. "Economic Contract Discipline." *AT* 5: 43–48. Republished in Butler, W. E. and Nathanson, A. J. 1982. *The Mongolian Legal System, Contemporary Legislation and Documentation*. The Hague: Martinus Nijhoff, 501–504.

Anderson, J. H., Young, L. & Murrell, P. 2000. 'Competition and Privatisation Amidst Weak Institutions: Evidence from Mongolia.' *Economic Inquiry* 38(4): 527–549.

Asian Development Bank (ADB). 2008. "Mongolia: Health and Social Protection – Rapid Sector Assessment." ADB: Online www.oecd.org/countries/mongolia/42227662.pdf. Accessed 23rd April 2019.

Baabar, B. E. 1988. "Buu Mart!" Translated by Sukhjargalmaa. Republished in D. Sneath and C. Kaplonski (eds.) 2010. *The History of Mongolia Volume III*. Boston: Brill, pp. 1028–1037.

Bawden, C. R. 1968/1989. *The Modern History of Mongolia*. 2nd Edition. London/New York: Kegan Paul International Ltd.

Bedeski, R. E. 2006. "Mongolia as a Modern Sovereign Nation-State." *The Mongolian Journal of International Affairs* 13: 77–87.

Boikova, E. 1999. "Aspects of Soviet-Mongolian Relations." In Kotkin, S. and Elleman, B. (eds.) *Mongolia in the Twentieth Century: Landlocked Cosmopolitan*. Abingdon: Routledge, pp. 107–122.

Bold, Bat-Ochir. 2001. *Mongolian Nomadic Society: A Reconstruction of the "Medieval" History of Mongolia*. Richmond, Surrey: Curzon.

Boone, P. 1994. "Grassroots Macroeconomic Reform in Mongolia." *Journal of Comparative Economics* 18(3): 314–328.

Brenner, N., Jessop, B., Jones, M. and Macleod, G. (eds.) 2003. *State/Space: A Reader*. Oxford: John Wiley and Sons.

Bumaa, N. D. 2001. "The Twentieth Century: From Domination to Democracy." In P. Sabloff (ed.) *Modern Mongolia: Reclaiming Genghis Khan*. Philadelphia, PA: University of Pennsylvania Museum of Archaeology and Anthropology, Chapter Two.

Burnham, P. 1979. "Spatial Mobility and Political Centralisation in Pastoral Societies." In L'Equipe Ecologieet Anthropologie des Societies Pastorales (ed.) *Pastoral Production and Society*. Cambridge: Cambridge University Press, pp. 349–360.

Butler, W. E. and Nathanson, A. J. 1982. *The Mongolian Legal System, Contemporary Legislation and Documentation*. The Hague: Martinus Nijhoff.

Constitution of Mongolia. 1992. Official English translation. Available at https://www.conscourt.gov.mn/?page_id=842&lang=en. Accessed 2nd June 2019.

Cox, R. 1987. *Power, Production and World Order: Social Forces in the Making of History*. New York: Columbia University Press.

Dahl, G. 1979. "Ecology and Equality: The Boran Case." In L'Equipe Ecologieet Anthropologie des Societies Pastorales (ed.) *Pastoral Production and Society*. Cambridge: Cambridge University Press, pp. 261–280.

Dashniam, I. 1974. "The Origin of MPR Revolutionary-Democratic Law." *SKE* 4: 30–34. Republished in Butler, W. E. and Nathanson, A. J. 1982. *The Mongolian Legal System, Contemporary Legislation and Documentation*. The Hague: Martinus Nijhoff, pp. 163–170.

Di Cosmo, N. 1994. "Ancient Inner Asian Nomads: Their Economic Basis and Its Significance in Chinese History." *The Journal of Asian Studies* 53(4): 1092–1126.

Dupuy, T. N. and Blanchard, W. 1970. *Area Handbook for Mongolia.* Washington, DC: U.S. Government Printing Office.

Ebner, A. 2011. "Transnational Markets and the Polanyi Problem." In C. Joerges and J. Falke (eds.) *Karl Polanyi, Globalisation and the Potential of Law in Transnational Markets.* Oxford/Portland, OR: Hart Publishing, pp. 19–40.

Endicott, E. 2012. *A History of Land Use in Mongolia: The Thirteenth Century to the Present.* New York: Palgrave Macmillan.

Fenwick. S. 2007. "Legal Education Reform – the Forgotten Intervention? Assessing the Legal Retraining Model in Transitional Economies." In Lindsey, T. (ed.) *Law Reform in Developing and Transitional States.* Abingdon: Routledge, pp. 180–195.

Fernandez-Gimenez. 1999. "Sustaining the Steppes: A Geographical History of Pastoral Land Use in Mongolia." *Geographical Review* 89(3): 315–342.

———. 2000. "The Role of Mongolian Nomadic Pastoralists' Ecological Knowledge in Rangeland Management." *Ecological Applications* 10(5): 1318–1326.

Fish, M. S. 1998. "Mongolia: Democracy without Prerequisites." *Journal of Democracy* 9(3): 127–141.

———. 2001. "The Inner Asian Anomaly: Mongolia's Democratisation in Comparative Perspective." *Communist and Post-Communist Studies* 34: 323–338.

Fratkin, E. and Mearns, R. 2003. 'Sustainability and Pastoral Livelihoods: Lessons from East African Maasai and Mongolia.' *Human Organisation* 62(2): 112–122.

Fritz, V. 2008. "Mongolia: The Rise and Travails of a Deviant Democracy." *Democratization* 15(4): 766–788.

Gill, S. and Cutler, C. 2014. *New Constitutionalism and World Order.* Cambridge: Cambridge University Press.

Goyal, H. D. 1999. "A Development Perspective on Mongolia." *Asian Survey* 39: 633–655.

Harvey, D. 2005. "Neoliberalism as Creative Destruction." *The Annals of the American Academy of Political and Social Science* 610(21): 21–44.

Hazard, J. N. 1948. "The Constitution of the Mongol People's Republic and Soviet Influences." *Pacific Affairs* 21(2): 162–170.

Heaton, W. R. 1992. "Mongolia in 1991: The Uneasy Transition." A Survey of Asia in 1991: Part One *Asian Survey* 32(1): 50–55.

Honeychurch, W. 2010. "Pastoral Nomadic Voices: A Mongolian Archaeology for the Future." *World Archaeology* 42(3): 405–417.

Humphrey, C. 1978. "Pastoral Nomadism in Mongolia: The Role of Herdsmen's Collectives in the National Economy." *Development and Change* 9: 133–160.

IMF. 2003. 'Mongolia: Poverty Reduction Strategy Paper.' Washington, D.C.: International Monetary Fund. http://www.imf.org/external/pubs/ft/scr/2003/cr03277.pdf Accessed 1st January 2019.

Jayasuriya, K. 2001. "Globalisation, Sovereignty, and the Rule of Law: From Political to Economic Constitutionalism?" *Constellations* 8(4): 442–460.

Jessop, B. 1990. *State Theory: Putting Capitalist States in Their Place.* Cambridge: Polity Press.

Joerges, C. and Falke, J. 2011. "Introduction: The Social Embeddedness of Transnational Markets: Introducing and Structuring the Project." In C. Joerges and J. Falke (eds.) *Karl Polanyi, Globalisation and the Potential of Law in Transnational Markets.* Oxford/Portland, OR: Hart Publishing, pp. 1–15.

Kaplonski, C. 2010. "Introduction: The Qing Period." In D. Sneath and C. Kaplonski (eds.) *The History of Mongolia Volume III.* Boston, MA: Brill, pp. 637–646.

———. 2011. "Archived Relations: Repression, Rehabilitation and the Secret Life of Documents in Mongolia." *History and Anthropology* 22(4): 431–444.

———. 2012. "Resorting to Violence: Technologies of Exception, Contingent States and the Repression of Buddhist Lamas in 1930s Mongolia." *Ethnos: Journal of Anthropology* 77(1): 72–92.

Klein, N. 2007. *The Shock Doctrine: The Rise of Disaster Capitalism.* New York: Henry Holt and Company.

Korsun, G. and Murrell, P. 1995. "The Politics and Economics of Mongolia's Privatisation Programme." *Asian Survey* 35(5): 472–486.

Kotkin, S. 1999. "Introduction. In Search of the Mongols and Mongolia: A Multinational Odyssey." In Kotkin, S. and Elleman, B. (eds.) *Mongolia in the Twentieth Century: Landlocked Cosmopolitan.* Abingdon: Routledge, pp. 3–26.

Kotkin, S. and Elleman, B. (eds.) *Mongolia in the Twentieth Century: Landlocked Cosmopolitan.* Abingdon: Routledge.

Lan, M-H. 1999. "China's 'New Administration' in Mongolia. In Search of the Mongols and Mongolia: A Multinational Odyssey." In Kotkin, S. and Elleman, B. (eds.) *Mongolia in the Twentieth Century: Landlocked Cosmopolitan.* Abingdon: Routledge, pp. 39–58.

Lattimore, O. 1934. *The Mongols of Manchuria.* New York: The John Day Company.

———. 1949. "Introduction: Mongolia's Place in the World." In Friters, G. M. (ed.) *Outer Mongolia and Its International Position.* Baltimore, MD: The Johns Hopkins Press, pp. ix–xliv.

May, C. 2014a. "The Rule of Law as the *Grundnorm* of the New Constitutionalism." In S. Gill and C. Cutler (eds.) *New Constitutionalism and World Order.* Cambridge: Cambridge University Press, pp. 63–79.

———. 2014b. *The Rule of the Law: The Common Sense of Global Politics.* Cheltenham: Edward Elgar.

Mearns, R. 2004. "Sustaining Livelihoods on Mongolia's Pastoral Commons: Insights from a Participatory Poverty Assessment." *Development and Change* 35(1): 107–139.

Mönkhjargal, T. 1977. "Some Questions of the Development of MPR Economic Contracts." *AT* 1: 75–76. Republished in Butler, W. E. and Nathanson, A. J. 1982. *The Mongolian Legal System, Contemporary Legislation and Documentation.* The Hague: Martinus Nijhoff, pp. 498–501.

Munkh-Erdene, L. 2006. "The Mongolian Nationality Lexicon: From the Chinggisid Lineage to Mongolian Nationality." *Inner Asia* 8: 51–98.

———. 2011. "Mongolia's Post-Socialist Transition: A Great Neoliberal Transformation." A Paper Presented at the Conference on *Mongolians after Socialism: Economic Aspiration, Political Development, and Cultural and Spiritual Identity,* Ulaanbaatar, Mongolia, June 27th–29th. www.sarr.emory.edu/MAS/MAS_Chap4_Munkh-Erdene.pdf. Accessed 27th March 2017.

Nisbet, R. 1974. "Citizenship: Two Traditions." *Social Research* 41: 612–637.

Nixson, F. and Walters, B. 2006. "Privatisation, Income Distribution and Poverty: The Mongolian Experience." *World Development* 34(9): 1557–1579.

Orhon, M. 2003. "Post-Soviet Transition: Central Asia and Mongolia." *The Mongolian Journal of International Affairs* 10: 86–101.

———. 2011. Imaginary Nomads: Deconstructing the Representation of Mongolia as a Land of Nomads. *Inner Asia* 13: 335–362.

Polanyi, K. 1944/2001. *The Great Transformation: The Political and Economic Origins of Our Time.* 2nd Edition. Boston, MA: Beacon Press.

———. 1957. "The Economy as Instituted Process." In K. Polanyi, C. M. Arensberg, and H. W. Pearson (eds.) *Trade and Market in the Early Empires.* Chicago: Henry Regnery Company.

Pomfret, R. 2000. "Transition and Democracy in Mongolia." *Europe-Asia Studies* 52(1): 149–160.

Rachewiltz, I. 1973/2010. Some Remarks on the Ideological Foundations of Chingis Khan's Empire. In Sneath, D. and Kaplonski, C. (eds.) *History of Mongolia Vol. I.* Boston, MA: Brill, pp. 165–173.

Reinert, E. S. 2000. "Globalisation in the Periphery as a Morgenthau Plan; The Underdevelopment of Mongolia in the 1990s: Why Globalisation is One Man's Food and Another Man's Poison." In S. Lhagva (ed.) *Mongolian Development Strategy; Capacity Building.* Ulaanbaatar: Mongolian Development Research Centre.

Rossabi, M. 2005. *Mongolia: From Khans to Commissars to Capitalists.* Berkeley: University of California Press.

Sachs, J. 1994. "Understanding Shock Therapy," Occasional Paper No. 7. London: The Social Market Foundation.

Sanders, A. J. K. 1988. "Mongolia in 1988: Year of Renewal." *Asian Survey* 29(1): 46–53.

———. 1992. "Mongolia's New Constitution: Blueprint for Democracy." *Asian Survey* 32(6): 506–520.

Schneiderman, D. 2008. *Constitutionalising Economic Globalisation: Investment Rules and Democracy's Promise.* Cambridge: Cambridge University Press.

———. 2013. *Resisting Economic Globalisation: Critical Theory and International Investment Law.* Basingstoke, Hampshire/New York: Palgrave Macmillan.

———. 2015. "Constitutional Property Rights and the Elision of the Transnational: Foucauldian Misgivings." *Social and Legal Studies* 24(1):65–87.

Skrynnikova, T. 2006. "Relations of Domination and Submission: Political Practice in the Mongol Empire of Chinggis Khan." In D. Sneath (ed.) *Imperial Statecraft: Political Forms and Techniques of Governance in Inner Asia, 6th–20th Centuries.* Bellingham: Western Washington University, Centre for East Asian Studies, pp. 85–115.

Sneath, D. 2001. "Notions of Rights Over Land and the History of Mongolian Pastoralism." *Inner Asia* 3: 41–58.

———. 2003. "Land-use, the Environment and Development in Post-Socialist Mongolia." *Oxford Development Studies* 31(4): 441–459.

———. (ed.) 2006a. *Imperial Statecraft: Political Forms and Techniques of Governance in Inner Asia, Sixth-Twentieth Centuries.* Bellingham: Mongolia and Inner Asia Studies Unit, University of Cambridge/Centre for East Asian Studies, Western Washington University.

———. 2006b. "The Rural and the Urban in Pastoral Mongolia." In O. Bruun and L. Narangoa (eds.) *Mongols from Country to City: Floating Boundaries, Pastoralism and City Life in the Mongol Lands.* Copenhagen: Nordic Institute of Asian Studies, pp. 140–159.

———. 2007. *The Headless State: Aristocratic Orders, Kinship Society, and Misrepresentations of Nomadic Inner Asia.* New York: Columbia University Press.

———. 2010. "Political Mobilisation and the Construction of Collective Identity in Mongolia." *Central Asian Survey* 29(3): 251–267.

Sneath, D. and Boldbaatar, J. 2006. "Ordering Subjects: Mongolian Civil and Military Administration" in D. Sneath (ed.) *Imperial Statecraft: Political forms and techniques of governance in Inner Asia 6th – 20th centuries*. Bellingham: Mongolia and Inner Asia Studies Unit, University of Cambridge/Centre for East Asian Studies, Western Washington University, pp. 293–314.

Sneath, D. and Humphrey, C. 1999. *The End of Nomadism? Society, State and the Environment in Inner Asia*. Durham, NC: Duke University Press.

Sukhbaatar, S. 2012. "Law and Development, FDI, and the Rule of Law in Post-Soviet Central Asia: The Case of Mongolia." In G. P. McAlinn and C. Pejovic (eds.) *Law and Development in Asia*. Abingdon: Routledge, pp. 137–159.

Swyngedouw, E. 2005. "Governance Innovation and the Citizen: The Janus Face of Governance-Beyond-the-State." *Urban Studies* 42(11): 1991–2006.

Tatsuo, N. 1999. "Russian Diplomats and Mongol Independence: 1911–1915." In Kotkin, S. and Elleman, B. (eds.) *Mongolia in the Twentieth Century: Landlocked Cosmopolitan*. Abingdon: Routledge, pp. 69–78.

UNIDO. 2011. 'Strategic Directions on Industrial Policy in Mongolia.' UNIDO: Online https://open.unido.org/api/documents/4811556/download/Strategic%20 directions%20on%20industrial%20policy%20in%20Mongolia. Accessed 1st January 2019.

Upton, C. 2009. "'Custom' and Contestation: Land Reform in Post-Socialist Mongolia." *World Development* 37(8): 1400–1410.

Wachman, A. M. 2010. "Suffering What It Must? Mongolia and the Power of the 'Weak.'" *Orbis* 54(4): 583–602.

Worden, R. L. and Savada, A. M. 1989. "Mongolia: A Country Study: Agriculture." Washington, DC: Library of Congress. http://countrystudies.us/mongolia/53.htm. Accessed 3/08/2013.

World Bank. 1996. "Mongolia: Poverty Assessment in a Transition Economy." Ulaanbaatar: World Bank.

## Mongolian law

1924 Constitution printed in *The China Yearbook 1926–27 Vol. 1*. Shanghai: North China Daily News and Herald.

1940 Constitution of the Mongol People's Republic printed in Friters, G. M. 1949. *Outer Mongolia and Its International Position*. Baltimore, MD: The Johns Hopkins Press, Appendix 2, pp. 325–344.

1960 Constitution of the Mongol People's Republic printed in Butler, W. E. and Nathanson, A. J. 1982. *The Mongolian Legal System, Contemporary Legislation and Documentation*. The Hague: Martinus Nijhoff, pp. 179–193.

# Chapter 4

# See-saws of instability

## Mongolia's mining regime from 1994 to 2014

## Introduction

> "There is no other way: Mongolia was hurt by what we did in the past... There was no predictable investment almost at all." President of the Mongolian National Mining Association[1]
>
> "Now we have a clear policy that says the economy should be based on the private sector and it should be liberalised." Managing Director of Erdenes Mongol LLC (state-owned enterprise managing state shares in mining projects)[2]

This chapter provides a historical overview of transformations in Mongolia's mining regime since the post-socialist transition. Through the lens of chronological legal and policy developments, it attests to the powerful influence of market discipline and transnational legality in transforming the Mongolian state since integrating into the global minerals economy in the late 1990s. I posit that market mechanisms – foreign investment, commodity prices and debt – have forcefully inculcated a new logic and legality *across* and *within* the apparatus of the national state in Mongolia which produces and privileges legal and political stability for the global market in natural resources. These mechanisms have achieved their transformative effect upon the state because of the way they inexorably link national economic conditions with the crisis-prone cycles of global markets in commodities, investment and debt financing, as well as sensitise national legislative and policy institutions to the regulatory preferences and perceptions of transnational institutions and actors.

While the chapter is organised to analyse key periods of change in Mongolia's mineral legislation, the focus on the law is a way of entering its wider political and economic context, as well as the sub-text – or normative basis – of the legislation. Placing the analysis of the legal *text* itself beside its *context* and *sub-text* is the hallmark of a socio-legal approach, as noted in Chapter 1 (Frerichs, 2012, 20133; Perry-Kessaris, 2013).

The chapter is structured chronologically, focusing on major points of legal and policy change in the mining sector from 1997 to 2014 which have shaped the current trajectory of the regime. The chronological approach taken highlights the tensions and challenges of the national state's orientation towards transnational capital and associated legal norms over time. It demonstrates the way that the Mongolian state's policy and legal autonomy to regulate the minerals sector has been systematically challenged and undermined, by narrating the changing terrain of legitimacy for state regulation of the minerals economy in relation to its dependence on mining investment. As this chapter will demonstrate, the transnational legal and political norm of stability and predictability in the national investment environment has been internalised and implemented by successive governments in Mongolia since the crisis of foreign investment in 2012–2013. Notably, the need to resuscitate foreign investment effected not only changes in formal law and policy but also at the level of norms and values within the political ecosystem of the state.

As explained in Chapter 1, the priorities and capacities of national states in general are vulnerable to being reordered and redirected to enable, sustain and protect markets because of their interdependent relationship with capital. Market mechanisms and their enabling legality suture national economies to the global market, so that the global is rather like a quilt of diverse national and regional patches sewn together. When the quilt of the global market gets shaken or shifted by crises – of confidence, of commodity prices, of debt repayment – the "national" sphere has no real protection – or autonomy – from the impacts, although some states are in a stronger position to defend their interests within global markets than others. The extent to which global market integration exerts disciplinary force upon the state's options depends upon its economic and political dependencies and vulnerabilities. States which have limited adaptation options due to the lack of state capital (i.e. dependent on foreign investment) or type of sector (i.e. primary commodity exporter) are particularly vulnerable to structural pressures to use their political and legal resources to stabilise conditions for markets to flourish and expand.

In the Mongolian context, the transformative effects of integrating into the global minerals market are evidenced in the way that national priorities and practices have become increasingly coordinated and unified around the goal of creating a stable investment environment after the crisis of foreign direct investment (FDI) in 2012–2013. Article 5.1 of the 1992 Constitution states that "Mongolia shall have an economy based on different forms of property which takes into account universal trends of world economic development and national specifics." Article 5.4 further establishes the state prerogative to "regulate the economy of the country with a view to ensure the nation's economic security, the development of *all modes of production*, and social development of the population" (Article 5.4, emphasis mine). However, this book shows how the state has allowed these *de jure* rights to be subordinated to a new market principle in practice: legal and political stability in the investment environment. The gap that developed between the legitimate scope for state activity as defined by the written constitution and the increasingly limited scope for state intervention in the minerals economy suggests a deeper *de facto* shift in the constitution of the state.

This chapter narrates the recent history of the subordination of "national specifics" to "universal trends" of economic development in Mongolia. Any attempt to reregulate the mining sector based on national priorities has been fundamentally delegitimised, unless it dovetails with the creation of a stable political and legal environment for foreign and private capital investment. The hierarchy between the national and the global in Mongolia's mineral sector limits the state's constitutional rights to regulate the economy in a way that upholds plural forms of production and protects the public interest of citizens in natural resources vested in the State (Articles 6.1 and 6.2). I argue that the state's impoverishment and growing dependence on FDI 'locks in' (Gill, 1998) reforms that affect state commitments and capacity – in practice – to support diverse modes of production, take responsibility for national economic security (Articles 5.1, 5.2 and 5.4) and assert public ownership rights of natural resource wealth (Articles 6.1 and 6.2). It limits the national expression of the state by institutionalising stability (of the investment environment) as a normative prerequisite for state action in the economy (Schneiderman, 2013; May, 2014). This process can be understood as "destructive" to a national articulation of the state in the minerals sector because the *national* political interests can no longer provide sufficient justification for significant changes to the regulatory environment. However, it also generates a new "global" expression of state power in which its position in the global economy becomes the paramount basis of its legitimacy for its market constituency (e.g. investors and companies operating in its jurisdiction) and even for its public constituents, who increasingly begin to associate economic crisis with state mismanagement rather than question market discipline or the regulatory expectations of foreign investors, multilateral institutions and multinational mining companies.

## 1994–2002: making a minerals market on the "final frontier"

As described in the previous chapter, Mongolia suffered a devastating economic crisis following the collapse of the Soviet Union. Mongolia moved suddenly from the position of a middle-income country with a fairly diversified economy based on national industry (agriculture, manufacturing and mining) to an impoverished "developing" country whose industry base was too small to compete in the global capitalist economy (Reinert, 2000; Rossabi, 2005). Mongolian manufacturing lost its primary export market, the Soviet Union, and could not compete against other regional producers. The only base for Mongolia to develop competitive exports was in the mining and cashmere sectors, and Mongolia's new development financiers and advisors, such as the World Bank, actively promoted foreign-invested mining as a development strategy for the new democracy (Rossabi, 2005; Hatcher, 2014).

Consequently, in 1994, the newly democratised government, led by the Mongolian People's Revolutionary Party (MPRP), initiated the Gold Programme to stimulate investment in the mining sector. This programme was the first of its kind in Mongolia, where private companies had the right to gain access to geological information previously monopolised by the state and to hold mining permits for exploration and exploitation activities (Byambajav, 2012: 17). The Gold Programme was legally enabled by the democratic Constitution's recognition of private property rights, giving the state the option of using private investment to overcome its 'cash deficit' (Byambajav, 2014: 2). The 1994 Minerals Law provided a basic legal framework for prospecting, exploring and exploiting minerals but did not incite serious interest from foreign investors because it maintained a significant degree of potential for state involvement and discretion. Specifically, it introduced three categories of minerals – common, special and strategic (Article 4)[3] – with varying degrees of regulation depending on their importance to the state budget and the national economy. In line with this state-centric emphasis, the law recognised the state as having priority purchasing rights (Article 5.4). It also granted significant discretionary power to Parliament to limit the level of "strategic" minerals mining, 'taking fully into account the interests of future generations to inherit non-renewable natural resources and pursuing the principle of thrifty and rational use' (Article 6.2). The approval of Parliament was mandatory to the granting of strategic mining licences to foreign legal persons (Article 7.5). Furthermore, the 1994 Law only permitted one extension for licences (up to twenty years) (Article 15.5), gave the state the right to participate in joint investment and co-sharing of products and revenues (Article 12.1), and included state costs of exploration in the valuation of deposits (Article 12.4). Licence-holders were prohibited from transferring their licence to third parties without state authorisation (Article 14), which was perceived by investors as a major barrier to competition. As Husband and Songwe (2004: 52) explain in their World Bank report –*Mining in Mongolia: Managing the Future*:

> [T]he right to transfer or pledge licenses to and/or with other parties... is essential for project financing... [it] is one of the fundamental premises that has driven the success of the world's dominant mining jurisdictions – such as the USA, Australia, Canada – from the very beginning of their modern mining histories. It is now an essential "entrepreneurial" component in all successful mining legislation.

Thus, prior to 1997, Mongolia's mining regime was not perceived as attractive or competitive for foreign investors. Mining was still an important economic sector for Mongolia, but the industry was still largely state-owned and operated. A limited amount of mining co-existed with manufacturing and pastoralism, with 12.7% of the total landmass available for minerals exploration (Wu, 1997: 1).

Similar to the 1992 Constitution, the 1994 Minerals Law reflected the tension between the socialist power-holders and the free market reformers in establishing basic juridical frameworks around the role of the state in the economy in the wake of the democratic transition. The 1994 Minerals Law liberalised Mongolia's mineral sector in the sense that it recognised the validity of private property rights to extraction and ownership but within a framework that gave preference to the state. In short, it did not create the framework for *systematic* flows of FDI. However, it seems that Mongolia's status as a transitional market democracy spared the 1994 Law some of the scrutiny that would characterise future mineral legislation. Not only was the Mongolian context struggling to cope with the social change created by the post-socialist transition, but global commodity prices were relatively low, dampening investment interest.

The conditions of economic collapse in the early 1990s and consequent investor uncertainty in both the Mongolian market and the regulatory environment meant that the 1994 Law was not particularly influential in generating investor interest. This did not seem to be a great surprise, or a disappointment, even to the private sector. As the President of the Mongolian National Mining Association (MNMA) reflected in 2015,[4] it was 'very difficult for Mongolia to make a good law… we cannot blame [the government], because that was the situation.' The 1994 Law, however, at least provided a legal framework for the Gold Programme, intended to generate income for the state in a period of crisis. Thus, the 1994 Minerals Law did not make great strides in opening up the minerals sector to investment at the time, but its partially liberalised approach reflected the ambivalence amongst legislators and policy-makers at the time about the extent of marketisation, a conflict that generally characterised political debate in the beginning of the 1990s.

In 1996, the former communist party (MPRP) lost the parliamentary election, allowing the democratic reformers their first opportunity to govern the new democracy. The Democratic Party was partly energised by the presence of young economists eager to integrate Mongolia into the global economy and to further free its market from the lingering constraints of the old command-style economy. 1997 marked a legal and political sea-change in the Mongolian state's approach to both mining and foreign investment with major amendments to the Minerals, Investment and Tax Laws, and significant increase in land made available by the state for mining exploration (from 12.7% to 40%) (Wu, 1997; Lander, 2014). Mongolia also joined the World Trade Organisation in 1997, signalling its commitment to global free trade. The upshot of this dramatic shift was to create the legal infrastructure to attract and enable large-scale FDI in the mining sector and to effectively make the potential of Mongolia's extractive industry globally competitive. The 1997 reforms marked a milestone in terms of Mongolia's openness to private, transnational capital, as well as proof to its transition sponsors – specifically the World Bank, the IMF and the ADB – that the state was serious about finding its comparative advantage both within and on the terms of the global market.

In 1997, a new minerals law was drafted and passed by Parliament. The 1997 Minerals Law was a new piece of legislation, not an amended version of the 1994 Law. The World Bank funded the development of the law, with the support of the new government, and organised a foreign investors conference in the same year to advertise the new framework and stimulate investment into the minerals economy. The 1997 Law provided a comprehensive liberal framework for the mining sector, easing conditions for investment and restricting the role of the state to management and regulation (World Bank, 2006: 2).

The shift towards a 'management and regulation' approach was heralded by the multilateral institutions as a progressive move away from the 'command and control' regulatory approach that characterised the socialist era (ibid.). The role of the state within the new legal framework was to facilitate investment by establishing 'procedures for obtaining mineral licenses [which] are clear, simple, and quick' (Mineral Resources Authority of Mongolia, 2002). A World Bank working paper – *Mongolia Mining Sector: Managing the Future* (Husband and Songwe, 2004: 52) – praised the 1997 Minerals Law:

> The Minerals Law of Mongolia is acknowledged by the international mining community as one of the strongest legal presentations of mineral licensee rights and obligations in the world, and clearly the most investor-friendly and enabling law in Asia. This is due to the clarity of its provisions that establish one-stop "first-come/first served" license application and granting procedures, security of tenure for licensees, regulatory guidance for environmental protection and obligations of licensees, and assignment and transfer of mineral licenses. Nothing should be altered in this law to weaken these important principles.

The following table highlights various ways in which the 1997 Law would ease conditions for investors whilst restricting the role of the state in the mining sector (Table 4.1).

*Table 4.1* Investor-State Rights in the 1997 Minerals Law

| *Easing conditions for investment* | *Restricting role of the state* |
|---|---|
| Eliminated restrictions on number of licences that can be held by one legal person (formerly five under 1994 Law) (Article 13.7) | Removed classification of minerals based on national strategic value (formerly Article 4 of 1994 Minerals Law) |
| Simplified application procedure for exploration and mining licences (Articles 13 and 14) | Parliament restricted from limiting mining activity in general (only on State specially protected land – Article 6.1.4) |
| No longer required feasibility studies | and determining permissions |
| Environmental protection plans and impact assessments made into a secondary procedure, following granting of licence (Article 29) | for foreign investors to mine (Article 6) |
| Licences granted on first-come-first-serve basis (no discrimination between companies) (Article 14.1) | Government restricted from direct participation in exploration and mining – only through a business entity (Article 6.6) |

*(Continued)*

| *Easing conditions for investment* | *Restricting role of the state* |
|---|---|
| Exclusive rights to explore and mine (Article 12) | Significant decentralisation of social and environmental aspects of regulation to local administrations (*aimag, soum, bagh*): |
| No distinction made between domestic and international investors (Article 10.1) | |
| Right to sell mineral products at market prices on domestic or international markets (Article 16.3) | "Ensure and monitor compliance by licence holders of their obligations with respect to environmental protection, health and safety regulations for workers and local residents, and payment of their obligations to the treasuries of local administrative bodies" (Article 6.4.3) |
| Licence extensions for forty years (Article 16.6) (formerly twenty under 1994 Law – Article 15.5) | |
| Right to use water (Article 16.10) | |
| Stability agreement provisions for 10–15 years for investments > two million USD (Article 20) These agreements determine: | |
| Tax rates | Eliminated state priority of purchase of minerals (formerly Article 6 of 1994 Minerals Law) |
| Export and sale of products at international prices | |
| Established universal royalty rate at 2.5% (Article 38.3) | |
| Licensees had the right to transfer or pledge licences to and/or with other parties (Articles 12 and 40; see also Husband and Songwe, 2004: 52) | |

The many proponents and few critics of the 1997 Minerals Law agreed at the time that it inaugurated a major shift in favour of protecting investor rights and shaking off lingering shadows of state control of the sector. The President of the Mongolian Investors' Association would later note that the resurgence of commodity prices in the late 1990s – following the Asian Financial Crisis – complemented the government's efforts to encourage private investment into the mining sector:

> By the 2000s, when commodity prices were rising, our government was also encouraging companies to get involved in mining activities... Whoever had some capital, they started investing into mining activities... Mongolia's market is very small, only three million people, so mining business is the number one chance we can do some big business, you know. So that's why a lot of businesses got involved with mining.[5]

Both domestic and foreign investors – treated equally under the 1997 Minerals Law – leapt at the new opportunity to access this largely untapped frontier minerals market. Many Mongolian entrepreneurs invested newly acquired capital in the mining sector in the late 1990s, particularly those that had benefited from

the privatisation of SOEs. The privatisation of former socialist geological institutions and laboratories in the early 1990s and the lack of new institutions to
control geological information gave companies in the late 1990s a head start on
exploring in the most viable locations. In this "frontier rush" atmosphere, some
of the world's largest and most established companies competed for access to
mineral-rich territories alongside small- and medium-scale enterprises. This initial rush for access to the new market was characterised by diversity in the origins
of companies, from BHP Billiton (Australia), Centerra Gold (Canada), to new
Mongolian companies ready to invest newly acquired capital assets.

The 1997 Minerals Law created a relatively efficient structure for decision-
making about mining licences. An implementation agency was established
within the Ministry of Industry and Trade (now the Ministry of Mining) to
'facilitate the implementation of the new minerals law' (World Bank, 2006: 3):
the Mineral Resources Authority of Mongolia (MRAM). Whilst officially embedded within the Ministry, the agency enjoyed significant decision-making
authority, where licences were issued on a first-come-first-served basis.[6] The concentration of implementation power and discretionary oversight of the minerals
sector within MRAM was remarkable, particularly in light of MRAM's authority to assign 'extensive exploration rights' (World Bank, 2006: 29) through its
Cadastre Division. Stability agreements did not have a review process outside of
the Ministry and MRAM; the signature of one financial minister was sufficient
authorisation (Sukhbaatar, 2012: 225).

The legal environment created by the 1997 Mineral Law not only eased conditions in which to invest, but branded Mongolia as a liberal regulatory environment. According to the former Executive Vice President of Ivanhoe Mines
(Kirwin, 2006), the 1997 Minerals Law was a key catalyst for the development
of the Oyu Tolgoi copper and gold mine in the South Gobi, and highlighted
Mongolia's status as an emerging free market economy. The newly liberalised
framework created by the 1997 Minerals Law enabled Ivanhoe to rapidly extend
the process of exploration beyond the relatively shallow and ad-hoc drilling of its
predecessors.[7] In 2001, an exploration team lead by Robert Friedland of Ivanhoe
Mines discovered unprecedented gold and copper resources 80 kilometres from
the Mongolian–Chinese border.[8] By mid-2003, Oyu Tolgoi was the biggest
mining exploration in the world, with eighteen drill rigs operating twenty-four
hours a day, seven days a week (Turquoise Hill Resources, 2019). In addition
to the 2001 Southern Oyu discovery, three additional deposits were discovered
(2002–2008) which comprise the current Oyu Tolgoi mining complex (ibid.;
Kohn and Humber, 2013). Oyu Tolgoi is now estimated to contain almost 43
million tonnes of copper and 1,850 tonnes of gold, the largest high-grade deposit
of their mineral classification[9] in the world (Porter, 2016: 375–376). The impact
of the investment from the Oyu Tolgoi exploration was swift: the mineral sector's share of GDP grew from 10% in 2002 to 33% in 2007 (Combellick-Bidney,
2012: 273), and also constituted over 70% of total industrial output in 2007 (Tse,
2009), officially putting Mongolia into the category of mineral dependence.[10]

## 2002–2006: re-evaluating the state–market balance

The 1997 Minerals Law fundamentally redefined the state–market relationship in the minerals sector, from a model of relatively strong state control to that of state–market complementarity. Formerly, the command economy and authoritarian political regime of the socialist period had designated the state as not only the owner of the minerals but the main organ of their exploitation. As explained in the previous section, the 1994 Minerals Law was still characterised by the presumption of a strong state. However, the 1997 Minerals Law established a complementary division of regulatory labour, with the central state limiting itself to the technical administration of licences, the collation of geological data and the collection of rents, established at economically rather than politically competitive rates. For example, the tax regime did not reflect the state's ownership of natural resources by establishing substantial, non-negotiable rates. Instead, tax rates were used as leverage to attract investors, established at competitive rates that could be changed, delayed or eliminated in the context of stability agreements. Additionally, the central government delegated significant social and environmental responsibilities to local administrations, thereby dispersing its authority as the central institution of regulation. The growth of investment interest in the Mongolian minerals sector and the ease with which exploration and exploitation licences could be obtained tested this new division of labour in three distinct ways.

Firstly, the increase in mining activity from 1994 onwards produced extraordinary socio-environmental dislocation within a short space of time. The impact of opening Mongolian territory to mining investment had the unanticipated consequence of creating an informal mining economy, characterised by rudimentary extraction techniques and precarious living conditions. By 2001, up to 100,000 illegal gold miners were employed in the informal mining economy that had developed alongside the gold rush in the mid-1990s (World Bank, 2006: 8; Byambajav, 2012). The lack of strong environmental oversight meant that many small- and medium-scale gold-mining operations had failed to rehabilitate the land, leaving it open to artisanal mining. Propelled both by rising poverty levels in the post-transition period as well as the lure of competing, albeit illicitly, in the booming gold market, the phenomenon of illegal "ninja" miners became a sign to many Mongolians of the abdication of effective state regulation of the mining economy.[11]

The sudden appearance of mobile and unregulated illegal miners in rural Mongolia challenged the socio-environmental expectations of a predominantly pastoral population. The administration of pastureland was already under pressure with a rapid increase in the number of herders following the economic collapse of the early 1990s.[12] While these new herders had squeezed available land and water, the presence of illegal miners created a new kind of tension over access to resources because of the conflicting approach to resources by pastoralists and

miners. Illegal miners were often perceived as having no respect for the sustainability of the land, the health of the rivers or respect for the locality, despite many
"ninja" miners being former herders. In particular, the use of mercury by gold
miners in general and the pollution of rivers was a catalyst for growing dissatisfaction with the regulation of mining, as well as the social disruptions associated
with temporary mining camps (i.e. child labour, sexual abuse and various forms
of violence).

Secondly, the introduction of extractive land use created a hierarchy between
the mining and herding economies. The 1997 Minerals Law introduced a new
hierarchy of property rights in the rural economy as pastoral land-use regimes
had to compete for the first time against centrally issued mining licences. Pastoralist property rights were, and still are, uncodified in Mongolia (Tumenbayer,
2002). The presumption of state ownership of property during the socialist
period meant that herders only had access to use-rights, administered initially
through pre-socialist customary systems and gradually institutionalised through
collectivisation. With the disintegration of the *negdels* in the late 1980s, customary norms again became the basis for regulating pastureland. This was a somewhat fraught process, given that "customary norms" had been maintained to
some degree through the socialist period but nonetheless morphed and shifted
significantly. The arrival of "new herders" migrating from the city to the steppe
looking for subsistence during the economic collapse of the early 1990s added
another dimension. However, use-rights were negotiated between old and new
herders in an informal and ad-hoc way. The arrival of mining companies in the
mid- to late 1990s interrupted the informal negotiation of property use-rights
between herders, as companies' codified rights to explore and exploit the minerals under the soil were formally guaranteed by the newly established Mineral Resources Authority and justiciable by national courts and/or international
arbitration.

The issuance of mining licences from the central government created an imbalance of power between herders and mining companies, due to conflicts between centrally issued mining licences and herders' informal entitlements to land
use (Tumenbayer, 2002; Endicott, 2012: 143). By 2004, approximately 26% of
Mongolian land was covered in mining licences for exploration and extraction
(Husband and Songwe, 2004: 7); 50% of these licences were held by only seven
companies, the four largest of which were foreign (ibid.). By 2009, the number
of licences had almost doubled, to cover 45% of Mongolian territory (Suzuki,
2013: 277). The environmental inputs of mining in terms of land and water
not only created an economic conflict of interest with herders, but threatened
to undermine the 'material, environmental and cultural bases of the livelihood
of local communities' (Byambajav, 2012: 13). Small groups of herders suffering
from the pollution and drying up of rivers, displacement from precious cultural
landmarks and customary grazing land began to organise themselves to resist
these changes in the early 2000s. These movements expressed resistance in various ways initially, through short-term direct action protests, such as roadblocks,

hunger strikes and lobbying within the Citizens Councils of local government to block the approval of mining licences (Byambajav, 2012, 2014; Upton, 2012).

Thirdly, the strong presence of foreign companies in the mining sector contributed to negative public sentiment about the use of national wealth for the gain of foreign "others." This "insult" added to the general "injury" expressed in the 'growing public outrage over the country's lack of socio-economic improvements, despite the mining boom' (Hatcher, 2014: 136). Additionally, growing political unrest about environmental degradation, new social ills in rural localities and power imbalances in the distribution of land heightened public concern. It was further heightened in the case of Oyu Tolgoi, once the significance of the deposit was realised. In April 2006, protests erupted in Ulaanbaatar, fuelled by remarks of Robert Friedland, then CEO of Ivanhoe Mines, revelling in the huge profit margins that were to be made by the company out of the resources in the deposit. Friedland's comparison of Oyu Tolgoi to t-shirts being made 'for five bucks and selling them for a hundred dollars' incensed a vocal part of the Mongolian public in 2005, leading to a three-week protest campaign and the burning of an effigy of Robert Friedland and several government ministers (New Internationalist, 2006).

The global context of a commodity boom and the national context of an impending Oyu Tolgoi stability agreement were two important features of this period. The stakes were heightened for the Mongolian government because it had started negotiations with Ivanhoe Mines in 2004 for a stability agreement, the terms of which would likely affect the trajectory of national development for the twenty-first century. The global boom in commodity prices offered an opportunity to gain more control of the Oyu Tolgoi deposit, creating competition between national power-holders as to which party interests would be reflected in the investment agreement. The timely coincidence of a commodity boom with the Oyu Tolgoi stability agreement negotiations engendered political conflicts between political parties at a time when the government was particularly fragile following the 2004 parliamentary election. While the MPRP had been expected to win the election (Schafferer, 2005; Sukhbaatar, 2012), they only received 49% of the vote and half of the seats in Parliament (thirty-six). Without a majority, the MPRP entered into a 'grand coalition government' (Schafferer, 2005: 746) with the Mongolian Democratic Coalition and other major parties.

Despite the rhetoric of unity, the cracks in this "grand coalition" quickly became evident, with the MPRP dissolving the coalition government in January 2006. The political bickering of the parties reinforced citizen anxiety about the close relationship between the government and investors, particularly Ivanhoe Mines, which the opposition parties used to their advantage. For example, in May 2006, twenty-six opposition MPs staged a walk-out to protest government corruption and support 'calls for better terms in negotiations with foreign miners' (Reuters, 2006; White, 2013). This display of nationalism from mainly Democratic Party MPs is somewhat ironic, as that party was the main architect and political force behind liberalising the mining investment framework in the

1997 Minerals Law. The internal conflict between the parties coincided with protest movements urging the state to 'protect the basic interests of the people' and 'provide a legal environment with Mongolia to have an advantage in the minerals sector' (Sukhbaatar, 2012: 223).

To conclude this section, the sudden emergence of illegal mining, the subordination of herders' customary entitlements to miners' property rights and the presence of foreigners in Mongol heartlands – and all the socio-environmental dislocation entailed by these phenomena – provoked a major public concern about the influence of foreign investors on the state, as well as the state's capacity to address the socio-environmental impacts of mining (see Chapter 6). The subsequent push for national law reform reflected a strong sense on the part of voters and their representatives that the government could – and should – regain some regulatory power and political control of the mining sector. The visible disturbance to public life in Mongolia created a fertile political moment for the government to re-evaluate the regulatory balance that had been struck in the 1997 Minerals Law.

## 2006–2009: state-market compromise and the Oyu Tolgoi investment agreement

In May 2006, legislators proposed a new draft Minerals Law. In July, after less than three months of deliberation, a new minerals law was passed by the Parliament. The 2006 Law can be understood as a mixture of the 1994 and 1997 Laws, giving the state wider regulatory powers within an enabling market-based framework that still guaranteed investor access to international markets and a stabilised tax environment. The government framed this decision to "bring the state back in" as a win-win for the public and private sectors, with a government representative stating at an investor conference that:

> The involvement of government will stabilise the project by lowering any risks that may face a project, such as the issue of infrastructure, power and water supplying permission... it [will] not control projects only prevent exploitation and provide a stable business environment.
>
> (Sukhbaatar, 2012: 224 quoting BBC Worldwide Monitoring, September 14, 2006)

However, the 2006 Minerals Law effectively redrew the boundary around the state's involvement in the sector to some extent, giving legal legitimacy to the expression of national interest in the mining economy. The Law reintroduced the concept of mineral classification based on the national strategic value of deposits (Article 6), and expanded the competence of Parliament to 'approve or initiate' the strategic value of a mineral deposit (Article 8.1.4) and determine the state's share in those deposits (Article 8.1.7). It also gave Parliament wider discretion to 'determine' state policy in the mining sector (Article 8.1.1), and 'restrict or prohibit exploration and mining activities' in 'certain territories' at its own initiative or the suggestion of the Government (Article 8.1.5). In terms of the ownership of minerals, the 2006 Law gave rights to the state to hold direct shares in strategic minerals deposits: up to 50% in cases where the State funded exploration and up to 34% where the State did not contribute finance to the exploration (Article 5). The State's right to hold direct shares in the deposit was not unqualified, but dependent upon negotiation of an agreement with other shareholders upon exploitation of the resource.

Reflecting upon the 2006 Law, Sukhbaatar (2012: 225–226) accurately points out the redistribution of decision-making authority in stability agreements in favour of Parliament. While the 1997 Law gave the power to sign a stability agreement to a 'financial minister on behalf of the government' (ibid.: 225), the 2006 Law required 'an investment agreement… to be made jointly by three ministers in charge of finance, mining and environment upon authorisation by the cabinet (Article 29.4)' (ibid.: 226) for investments up to US $100 million. The requirement of parliamentary approval for investment above the "cabinet cap" asserted a strengthened form of representative safeguarding of national "strategic" interests by placing large-scale investment agreement negotiation within an explicitly political state institution, rather than the executive ministries of government. Furthermore, the 2006 Minerals Law concentrated the collection of tax and royalty revenues at the central level, a move that would later frustrate the relationship between the local administrations and the central state. The centralisation of revenue collection reinforced the emphasis on generating *national* wealth through the exploitation of minerals.

Within the contractual framework of investment agreements, the law stipulated a range of additional clauses imposing new duties upon investors and raised the bar of necessary finance to qualify for an investment agreement, from US $2 million to US $50 million (Sukhbaatar, 2012: 225). Introducing investment agreements under Article 29 of the 2006 Law gave the state the opportunity to put more obligations on investors while still incentivising their interest in investing by providing for 'improved recognition to investors making larger, longer term commitments' (Ivanhoe Mines, 2006: 3). In addition to the former rights to a stable tax environment, to sell mineral products at international prices and to discretionary management of income, Article 29 of the Law required the investor to make commitments to 'minimise damage to environment and public health' (29.1.5), protect the environment (29.1.6), leave no negative impacts on other industries (29.1.7) and promote regional development and increase employment (29.1.8).

Furthermore, the 2006 Law gave local governments legal standing in relation to mining companies by requiring them to negotiate agreements 'on issues of environmental protection, mine exploitation, infrastructure development in relation to mine-site development and job creation' (Article 42.1). Articles 42.2 and 42.3 provided pathways for citizen participation in public forums and 'monitoring of the license holder's activities' vis-à-vis an elected representative.

All of these changes clearly responded to demands by new political movements, particularly in rural areas, for the state to make mining companies accountable for environmental damage and to increase the inclusion of citizens in decision-making processes (Byambajav, 2012, 2014). By introducing investment agreements as a stronger form of contract in the international mining sector, the state now had the right to negotiate a specific investment agreement for Oyu Tolgoi but on the basis of improved standing.

Changes in the tax regime in early 2006 evidenced a balancing act by the state in terms of increasing its expected benefits from mining projects while still maintaining investment interest. A few bold new measures were balanced with general ongoing support for investors' rights. For example, the government appeared to champion the national interest by introducing a controversial Windfall Profits Tax in May 2006 and doubling the royalty rate in the Minerals Law from 2.5% to 5%. Combined with the reintroduction of nationally "strategic" deposits and the push for the state to hold direct stakes in mining projects, Mongolia gained a reputation for "resource nationalism" in the international media and amongst investors (Sukhbaatar, 2012; Lander, 2014). Yet at the same time, the 2006 Minerals Law actually reduced corporate income tax (from 30% to 25%) and value-added tax (VAT) (from 15% to 10%) from 1997 levels and instituted a flattened rate of personal income tax (10%) (Ivanhoe Mines, 2006: 3). Furthermore, it provided for an Investment Tax Credit where 10% of the investment amount was deductible from tax duties. The 2006 Law also doubled the time frame of stabilisation to thirty years in the case of investments over 300 million US dollars. This reflected the state's priority on large-scale mining projects, hoping to discourage widespread mining through small- and medium-scale enterprises, which were seen by the government as contributing less to national income and also lacking the "capacity" to follow more stringent socio-environmental regulation.

The imperative to at least appear to respond to citizens' interests, maximise state revenue in a commodity boom and yet sustain investor interest in the Mongolian mining sector generated a complex state-investor dynamic in the post-2006 political-legal environment. The period leading up to the signing of the Oyu Tolgoi Investment Agreement (OTIA) in 2009 was marked initially by anxiety due in large part to the extent to which Oyu Tolgoi offered hope of an accelerated path to economic development. Initially, the move to permit the state to hold direct shareholding stakes in mining projects was met by resistance from investors, particularly from Ivanhoe Mines, but soon became less controversial as investors realised some of the benefits of working closely with the government, particularly in terms of gaining permit approvals (Sukhbaatar, 2012: 224).

In October 2009, after five years of negotiations, the OTIA was signed by the Mongolian government, Rio Tinto and Ivanhoe Mines (now Turquoise Hill Resources). The Mongolian government emerged with a 34% stake,[13] with the right to appoint three members (out of nine) to the Board of Directors. The OTIA determined stabilised tax rates and a zero rate for VAT for specified goods

and services related to Oyu Tolgoi, in addition to the freedom of the foreign
investor to repatriate export earnings (OTIA, Articles 2.1 and 2.18). It also
gave the foreign investor the right to avail itself of lower tax rates if they existed
in applicable international or double-taxation treaties (ibid., Article 2.27). In
turn, the foreign investor committed to a range of initiatives to 'support socio-
economic development policies…to ensure that sustainable benefits from the OT
Project reach Mongolian people, including people in Umnogovi *aimag*' (ibid.,
Article 4.5). The OTIA instituted a division of labour between the parties, with
Rio Tinto responsible for the management of the project as a preferred stakeholder and the Mongolian government responsible to fund its "common" stake
in the project by investing in infrastructure. The context of the global financial
crisis in 2008 hastened the signing of the OTIA as it became clear that 'requiring yet more analysis of the public finance or economic implications of the
project' or 'any further delays in the Oyu Tolgoi Project' would discourage the
investment interest of Ivanhoe Mines and Rio Tinto (World Growth Mongolia,
2009: 4). The Windfall Profits Tax, having sent 'a negative message to foreign
investors' (Ivanhoe Mines, 2006: 4) was also repealed in 2009.

Between 2006 and 2009, the opportunity for the state to regain some influence in the mining sector seemed to provide both an economic and political
solution to the pressing issues of depleted state capital and a discontented public. It could be described as a period of recalibration in the state–market relationship, characterised by outbursts of high emotion and passionate lobbying
by government bureaucrats, legislators, activists and investors as a balance was
struck within the legal framework between claims for the interests of the voting
public, political parties and the private sector. However, as noted, a large degree
of continuity in neoliberal state support for the private sector was maintained
underneath the more vocal aspects of "resistance" to foreign control of Mongolia's mineral wealth (Hatcher, 2014: 108). By 2009, the political volatility
which had characterised earlier years seemed to have settled, with a balance
struck between state and investor interests, with limited state involvement in
strategic mining projects and a more centralised tax framework. Qualified state
participation had been permitted in the minerals market without jeopardising
the unprecedented OTIA.

## 2009–2013: optimism and entanglement

> The government has this idea that these foreign investors are out there. And
> you know, that they're one of the answers to Mongolia's problems, along
> with the NGOs, along with the Asian Development Bank, the EBRD. But
> they're incredible naive about who we are.
>
> Western foreign investor[14]

Initial optimism about the OTIA subsequently gave way to disenchantment,
particularly amongst government officials. One of the members of the OTIA

working group, also a senior policy-maker in the Ministry of Justice, reflected in 2015 that:

> My attitude or my thinking about mining companies has changed... Before 2009 or 2010... my imagination was perfectly positive about the mining companies, especially companies like Rio Tinto, you know, because I was part of the government working group for the [Oyu Tolgoi] Agreement... I was thinking, "This is a multinational company... They will never lie..." But then since 2012 when there was a dispute... Rio Tinto as a global company actually managed all the media... so all the information about investing in Mongolia internationally was very, very negative: "This is one of the worst countries in the world to invest your money!" This was a big attack for Mongolia. No one would risk money, maybe except China or Russia. Why are [Rio Tinto] doing this? It was actually very unbalanced and very unequal.[15]

As explained in the previous section, the Mongolian government had achieved a stronger presence for itself within the minerals economy under the 2006 minerals framework, both in terms of raising expectations on investors, especially in terms of financial commitment and socio-environmental obligations, *and* in terms of generating more substantial revenues for the state. The presumption at the time was that the government could shape the function of the market without interrupting it and by doing so could mitigate its most damaging aspects (i.e. environmental degradation, social dislocation, Dutch Disease, economic inequality).

Institutionally, this optimism had been reflected in the creation of two new funds to (1) redistribute mineral rents to the public and (2) prevent pro-cyclical spending by the government. In November 2009, the Human Development Fund (HDF) replaced the Mongolian Development Fund (est. 2007) 'to counteract rising inequality and distribute the benefits of the mining boom more widely' (Isakova et al., 2012: 10). The state was supposed to allocate a portion of revenue to the HDF each year based on expected earnings from mineral dividends, royalties and taxation (ibid.: 11; Campi, 2012). It was primarily designed as an ongoing 'cash transfer mechanism' (Isakova et al., 2012: 11), in addition to funding education initiatives and social services (ibid.; Moran, 2013; Yeung and Howes, 2015). According to Campi (2012), the HDF was a legal milestone for the Mongolian public, as it enshrined "equal eligibility" for each citizen to share in the country's mineral wealth. To generate savings and prevent reliance on volatile mineral prices, the Parliament passed the Fiscal Stability Law in 2010 and the Integrated Budget Law in 2011. These laws have the combined effect of capping the deficit and public debt at 2% and 40% of GDP, respectively, keeping expenditure in line with the growth rate of Mongolia's non-mineral GDP, and constraining the power of Parliament to influence the state budget. According to the European Bank for Reconstruction and Development (EBRD), the Fiscal Stability Law crucially included the introduction of a 'transparent formula for copper price projections' (Isakova et al., 2012: 15) to help the Mongolian government anticipate the boom and bust cycle of this commodity market. Finally, the Fiscal Stability Law established the Fiscal Stability Fund to accumulate 'excess commodity-related revenues' (ibid.) from boom phases in order to supplement financial losses experienced in bust phases of the cycle.

In 2011, Mongolia recorded the world's highest GDP growth at 17.5% (World Bank, 2013: 3), and was acclaimed internationally as a "Global Growth Generator." The '2010/2011 spike in commodity markets' (World Bank, 2011: 1) created a fever of investor interest. Combined with the initial influx of investment – US $4.6 billion – to develop the surface operation of the Oyu Tolgoi project in 2010, there was a general sense of a "win-win" solution shared by the government and investors in the context of the "global supercycle" of commodity prices. Given that Mongolia's total GDP was only US $4.2 billion in 2009 (Isakova et al., 2012: 2), it is hard to overstate the significance of the Oyu Tolgoi investment for Mongolia's prospects for economic development at the time. As the Director of the Strategic Policy and Planning Department at the Ministry of Mining put it:[16]

> Prices were high, everyone could do business, everyone was satisfied, everyone was too confident.

The influx of natural resource-seeking FDI into the mining sector had a significant effect across the national economy. As expected, support and infrastructure industries also boomed at this time, particularly to service the development of Oyu Tolgoi. The presence of new mining ventures in rural areas created new demand and higher prices for meat, as well as new housing developments in high-income areas on Ulaanbaatar's outskirts to house foreign business people and their families, as well as the rising middle class. Apart from these quite direct effects, the increase in capital flow within the domestic economy caused the *tugrik* to appreciate by 13% against the US dollar in 2010, with record high reserves held by Mongol Bank that year. As citizens' purchasing power increased, so did demand for secondary goods and services, leading to a boom in expensive coffee shops, high-line retail and luxury apartments. However, this new wave of growth had shallow roots, as it was fundamentally linked to the welfare of the mining sector. In hindsight, the President of the Association of Investors in Mongolian Mining reflected on the real risk associated with the boom in mining investment:[17]

> Now everybody's stuck into this. But it's also [a] very big problem because all our capital assets [are] locked in mining business.

The 2006–2009 period had seen the state making strong commitments in two directions: to finance its direct stakes in mining projects and to redistribute tangible benefits from the mining sector to citizens. In 2011, the Mongolian government established the Development Bank of Mongolia through law 'with a mandate to finance development projects' (Isakova et al., 2012: 9) specifically related to mining infrastructure (i.e. transportation) (IMF, 2012: 3). This need for finance was mainly catalysed by the Oyu Tolgoi and Tavan Tolgoi projects in the South Gobi region. The government required finance to fund its 34% stake in the Oyu Tolgoi project through infrastructure development. As the government's stake in Oyu Tolgoi was initially obtained by receiving a loan from Rio Tinto which had to be repaid in order to receive dividends, the government sought to expedite the mine development process by taking on significant debt in the short term. An operating contract with foreign investors for the eastern bloc of Tavan Tolgoi (100% state-owned) was also concluded in October 2011, requiring a renewed level of state investment through its subsidiary company, Erdenes Tavan Tolgoi. To expedite the export of coking coal from Tavan Tolgoi to China and other East Asian markets, infrastructure was required to reduce high product costs associated with freight expenses.

Funding infrastructure development for both of these mega-mining projects required significant capital expenditure from the state. Thus, despite the intention of the fiscal stability framework to prevent "expansionary" spending during boom periods, the creation of the Development Bank enabled the government to technically circumvent the framework and acquire new debt because the Fiscal Stability Law only regulated spending by the central bank. Between 2012 and 2013, the government and the Development Bank 'borrowed over US $2 billion in international debt markets' (Dettoni, 2013), with both public and external debts more than doubling between 2011 and 2012 (World Bank, 2013: 24). In November 2012, the Mongolian government sold its first bond – the "Chinggis Bond" – worth USD 1.5 billion in the international bond market to fund energy and transport infrastructure, such as the Millennium Road project (Frangos and Natarajan, 2012). The Development Bank of Mongolia also sold a bond worth USD 580 million, directly guaranteed by the government (World Bank, 2013: 24). Consequently, the commercial proportion of Mongolia's external debt overtook concessional development loans from IFIs for the first time. The Mongolian government was desperate for loan financing at the time, to fund its infrastructure projects. Consequently, in 2011, Mongolia and China entered into a three-year currency swap agreement to maintain Mongolia's financial liquidity – worth USD 770 million.

In addition to the financial pressure generated by the sudden development of its two mega-mines, the government was also under pressure from its voting constituency to make good on its promises of redistribution (*The Economist*, 2012; Yeung and Howes, 2015). Between February 2010 and June 2012, the government created a universal cash transfer programme through the HDF based on new mineral revenues (Yeung and Howes, 2015). Tangibly, this amounted to a monthly transfer of 10,000 MNT (USD 7.42) to each Mongolian citizen between August and December 2010, and 20,000 MNT (USD 16.57) between January 2011 and June 2012 (ibid.: 14). As the subject of universal cash transfers had been a campaign platform for both the major parties in 2008 – the Mongolian People's Party (MPP)[18] and the Democratic Party – the desire to maintain popular support in preparation for the June 2012 election meant that the programme was continued despite becoming 'increasingly unsustainable' (ibid.). As Yeung and Howes (ibid.) observe, the programme left the state-holding company – Erdenes Tavan Tolgoi – 'technically insolvent' in 2012 when USD 310 million was transferred from the company to the HDF to enable ongoing payments to the public.

The growing financial pressure on the government due to rising debt pushed it towards Mongolia's southern neighbour, China, which consumes the majority of Mongolian coal, effectively controlling the sector. Diminishing reserves in the HDF led to increased dependence on "support" from the state-owned Chinese investor in Tavan Tolgoi – the Aluminium Corporation of China (Chalco). Chalco enabled Erdenes Tavan Tolgoi to remain solvent through an advanced payment of USD 350 million, on the condition that Erdenes would sell coal to Chalco at reduced prices, from an original set price of USD 70 per ton to a quarterly fluctuating rate of USD 53–56 per ton (*InfoMongolia*, 2013). As Chalco was the only buyer at the time from Tavan Tolgoi, a growing sense of Mongolia's seeming inability to dictate favourable export prices created a strong sense of urgency amongst citizens and some politicians. This anxiety was exacerbated by Chalco's almost simultaneous attempt to purchase a majority share in the Ovoot Tolgoi coal deposit, for which Canadian Turquoise Hill held a mining licence through its Mongolian South Gobi Resources mining company (Scharaw, 2018: Chapter 3, Section 2.1.3). Turquoise Hill wanted to sell a 58% equity stake to Chalco for USD 900 million (ibid.). This attempt was blocked by the government, which immediately 'suspended the exploration and mining licenses of South Gobi Resources' (ibid) as 'this merger would have made a single Chinese state-owned company both the owner and the buyer of the mine's resource' (Oxford Business Group, 2013: 115).

The fact that by 2012 China had commandeered 90% of Mongolia's total minerals export market provides a geopolitical explanation for resistance to China's 'growing economic hegemony' (Edwards, 2013) in the Mongolian market. The Strategic Entities Foreign Investment Law (SEFIL) was passed in May 2012, asserting a strong political role for the state in relation to FDI, particularly that coming from foreign, particularly Chinese, SOEs (Scharaw, 2018: Chapter 3, Section 2.1.3). Article 1 of SEFIL stated its primary purpose 'to regulate investment by foreign investors… in the strategic sections and the relations pertaining to the permission with a view to ensuring national security' (cited in ibid.). The Law introduced the concept of "strategic sectors," which included banking, telecommunications and finance in addition to mining (Article 5, ibid.), and introduced a distinction between 'private' and 'State-owned' FDI (Article 4, ibid.). Any business 'partly or fully owned by a foreign State' (ibid) had to be approved explicitly by the government, regardless of sector, whereas private foreign entities were only required to register, unless they were seeking to acquire 'a third or more of the shares of a business entity operating in one of Mongolia's strategic sectors' (ibid.).

SEFIL also introduced more discretionary power for public decision-makers in terms of screening foreign investments. Under Article 7, the Mineral Resources Authority was required to consider the impact on national security, compliance with domestic law and sectoral competition, as well as overall impacts in terms of the State budget, compliance with other policies and activities (ibid.). The more controversial provisions of SEFIL included:

1   The requirement of Cabinet approval to purchase shares above 33% in a company in a strategic sector.
2   The requirement of Parliamentary approval for (a) state-owned investors to purchase a majority share in a strategic entity and (b) state-owned investors planning to invest more than 100 billion *tugriks* (approximately USD 71 million) (Article 4.7).
3   Cabinet approval for any transaction that had the possibility of controlling or diminishing the market price of mineral exports (Article 6).
4   Disclosure of 'ultimate beneficial shareholders' (Hogan Lovells, 2013).
5   Mandatory registration of new equity holdings of more than 5% in "Business Entities of Strategic Importance" had to occur within 30 days, and those already holding more than 5% had to do so within 180 days of the law's entry into force, reflecting a retrospective application of the new law (Article 8).

Most international reflections on SEFIL at the time portrayed this legal development as a blatant overstepping by the state in terms of investment control and an illegitimate exhibition of resource nationalism (Lee, 2012; Manthorpe, 2013; Weafer, 2016).[19] In its 2013 Investment Policy Review, UNCTAD noted that SEFIL had 'generated a feeling of uncertainty among both established and potential investors, even beyond the mining sector' (UNCTAD, 2013: 40), a sentiment that has been echoed in subsequent interviews. As one Western foreign investor put it:

> The problems for Mongolia in terms of foreign investor unhappiness, if you like, started in February 2012 at the end of the last MPP government, when the foreign investment law came in. It seemed to arise because of the attempted takeover by a Chinese entity of South Gobi Sands. There were sections of that [MPP] government that didn't like the idea that there was going to be one of the more prominent mining companies solely owned by the Chinese and they put in that law, and of course, sadly, it brought in all the rest of us. It was actually a major problem for us at the time. So this process, if you like, what I call "the shooting of themselves in both feet," began under the MPP.[20]

In October 2012, following the parliamentary election, the new coalition government led by the Democratic Party attempted to renegotiate the OTIA under the provisions of SEFIL. Importantly for this analysis, a major part of the government's intention at the time was to "unfreeze" the tax and royalty rates that had been stabilised in 2009 (Kosich, 2012) in order to cover a growing fiscal deficit in the 2013 Budget. The proposed changes included a sliding royalty rate on copper, up to 20% depending on the market price, as opposed to the fixed rate of 5%, and removing exemptions from corporate income tax (Macnamara, 2012). This attempt to increase state revenue from the project was rejected by Rio Tinto and Turquoise Hill, and majorly impacted Mongolia's reputation as a stable destination for investment. As Oyu Tolgoi functioned as 'litmus test' (Falconer, 2013) of Mongolia's investment potential, the *perception* amongst investors of Mongolia's stability became a critical factor for capital flows. At the time, a senior U.S. diplomat predicted that:

> If there appears to be an attempt at renegotiating or somehow reneging on the investment agreement, that could have a potentially catastrophic effect on the country. It could stop the flow of foreign capital into Mongolia.
>
> (David Wyche, Economic Section Chief, U.S.
> Embassy quoted in Macnamara, 2012)

In the year that followed, the Mongolian government resolutely continued to challenge Rio Tinto about "missing revenues," with allegations of tax evasion. The government blocked the mine's first shipment of copper in June 2013 on the basis of '77 points of dispute,' including tax evasion, Rio's management fees and cost overruns upwards of USD 2 billion. The government cancelled its double-taxation treaty with the Netherlands, amongst others, claiming that the foreign stakeholders in Oyu Tolgoi were using Turquoise Hill's office in Amsterdam as a tax haven (Deutsch and Edwards, 2013).

Critically, the dispute with Oyu Tolgoi came down to an issue of control over the timing of the project. The USD 2 billion accrued to the project through cost overruns not only increased the government's debt, but increased the "management service fee" –3%–6% – associated with these "investment costs." While Rio Tinto was frustrated by the delays, the national cost was immediate with a virtual walkout of investors, particularly Euro-American companies.[21] As the U.S. Embassy's 2013 Investment Climate Statement (U.S. Department of State, 2013: 3) stated:

> Doubts persist over the [Government of Mongolia's] commitment to honouring the Oyu Tolgoi Investment Agreement and its ability to manage public expectations over mining revenues and related development.

In addition to SEFIL and attempted renegotiation of the OTIA, the cancellation of mining licences due to environmental legislation and corruption allegations further damaged the state's relationship with foreign investors. In 2009, the Law on the Prohibition of Mineral Exploration and Mining Operations at Headwaters of Rivers, Protected Zones of Water Reservoirs and Forested Areas was passed in Parliament, following years of environmental activism to place firm limits on mining activity in these areas. Led by small rural associations of activists known as the River Movements, the appeal to strengthen environmental legislation generated widespread public concern, culminating in letter-writing campaigns across the country and large symbolic demonstrations in Chinggis

Square. The government initially did not implement the legislation because it was perceived as too expensive; not only would the state be responsible to compensate licence-holders, it would significantly impact Mongolia's gold industry by restricting alluvial gold mining. However, in 2011, following public pressure and at the Supreme Court's order, the government cancelled licences for over 200 mining projects that contravened the boundaries set out in the new legislation (U.S. Department of State, 2011: 24). Gold production, which had been contributing up to 20 tonnes of gold per year to the Bank of Mongolia's gold reserve, declined to 4–5 tonnes after the enforcement of the legislation (Fehrbach, 2013).

According to the President of the MNMA, the environmental law 'affected almost 1800 licenses... which should be revoked and compensated.'[22] The enforcement of the law was generally met with enthusiasm from the public at the time, particularly amongst the growing number of environmental activists and citizens concerned about the impact of mining on Mongolian territory. As public debates have shown, the main sources of 'public discontent' (Mendee, 2013) about the regulation of the mining sector were based on environmental damage and corruption in the mining sector. In contrast, the enforcement of this law 'caused intense opposition from miners' (ibid.). The legislation amplified the growing pressure on the state between its voting constituency and the investment sector, as public expectations for stronger regulation of the mining sector conflicted with investor concerns that the state should maintain a stable legal environment.

Investor concerns were further exacerbated when corruption charges brought against senior officials of the Minerals Resources Agency led to the official cancellation of 106 mining licences in November 2013 and a moratorium on granting further licences following the investigation. The illegality of the issuance of the licences did not assuage investors, many of whom openly challenged the cancellation of the licences as a blatant expropriation by the state of their property rights and a failure to honour contracts. Khan Resources, a Canadian mining company, filed arbitration proceedings against the Government of Mongolia in the United Nations Commission on International Trade Law (UNCITRAL) less than a week after the formal revocation of their licence, claiming USD 200 million in damages. The President of Kincora, a foreign-invested copper and gold mining company, stated that 'security of tenure and a transparent legal system are key cornerstones for both domestic and foreign investment' (Reuters, 2013).

## 2014 onwards: facing the crisis of transnational capital and confidence

Well, previously there was a supercycle in the minerals sector everywhere – prices were very high, everyone could do business, everyone was satisfied, everyone was too confident. Too confident, companies [and] government... And there was a strong sentiment of nationalism –"Mongolia should have a bigger stake in everything"– everyone was too confident. The legal changes at that time were too harsh. But recently the boom ended and now we are having difficult times. These hard times they are lessons. The biggest lesson was that we need investment, we need to support business activities, and in order to create a favourable environment to support business, we need to have very close discussions with our industry representatives, investors and other stakeholders including academicians, civil society, international organisations who are big advisors to us... The legal reforms were done not only in [the] minerals sector, but in the general economy as well. We have revised our investment law. Previously we had a law on...foreign investment in strategic sectors [SEFIL] which was a very harsh law that restricted, controlled everything. We changed the investment law, we created a new investment fund law, we created capital markets law, also we have [a] great law on fiscal stabilisation funds and many others. So this is one direction [the] government took to help the industry: legal reform.

(Director-General, Strategic Policy and Planning
Department, Ministry of Mining)[23]

Unfortunately for Mongolia, the increasingly negative perception of instability in the investment environment amongst foreign investors coincided with the downturn in global commodity prices, causing a severe drop in FDI. While some decline in investment was likely in light of global market prices, the plummeting rates of FDI in Mongolia's mining sector between 2012 and 2014 strongly indicate a withdrawal of investor *confidence* in Mongolia's mining economy beyond market cycles. The sudden withdrawal of foreign capital from the economy put Mongolia on the brink of an economic collapse. While Mongolia was hailed as a "growth generator" only the year before, total revenue accumulated in 2012 was 12.1% below the budget projection, with mineral revenue 35.6% below the previous year. Total exports fell by 9% and FDI dropped by 17% (World Bank Group Mongolia, 2013: 4). In 2013, FDI almost halved – dropping 49% – and continued to spiral in the first half of 2014. In May 2014, Mongol Bank reported a 64% year-on-year drop in FDI (U.S. Department of State, 2014: 1). Desperate to maintain capital liquidity, the Mongolian government negotiated another three-year currency swap agreement with China, this time for USD 2.18 billion (Yamada, 2017).[24]

To stem the impending tide of economic crisis, Mongolia legislators passed a new investment law by the end of 2013 with the assistance of the International Finance Corporation of the World Bank Group. The development of this piece of legislation was widely understood as a direct attempt by the government to repair Mongolia's damaged reputation and 'attract fresh capital in the mining sector' (Els, 2013). The stated purpose of the new investment law in Article 1 was to explicitly

protect the legal rights and interests of investors in the territory of Mongolia, to establish a common legislative guarantee for investment, to encourage investment, to stabilise the tax environment, to determine the rights and obligations of investors and the competences of a government body related to investment.

Foreign and domestic investors were given the same treatment under the new law, taxation rates returned to previously low rates, a wider range of tax and non-tax incentives made available to investors and investors gained new rights to avail themselves of international arbitration. The reduction of taxes and reintroduction of stability agreements resembled the liberal provisions of the 1997 Minerals Law. Notably, the new Investment Law significantly restricted the remit of government's involvement in mining projects. Government competence was strictly placed within the remit of a 'central administrative body' (initially the Ministry of Economic Development) with implementation functions centralised in an agency, significantly limiting the previously primary role of Parliament with regard to investors. The new law removed screening and no longer required government approval on private foreign investment, in what were previously considered nationally strategic areas under SEFIL (Scharaw, 2018: Chapter 3, Section 2.1.4). Only foreign companies over 50% state-owned and investing at least 33% into minerals, communication or financial sectors – the former 'strategic' sectors – were obligated to go through a government approval process (ibid.). A new investment promotion agency – the Invest Mongolia Agency – was placed in charge of the approval process (Invest Mongolia Agency, 2014: 60), thus effectively streamlining decision-making into a one-step process at most. Article 6.10 protects the Investment Law from hasty amendment by requiring a two-thirds majority of votes in Parliament, in contrast to the usual prevalence of low quorum rules (Enkhbaatar et al., 2015; Munkhsaikhan, 2016; Scharaw, 2018: Chapter 3, Section 2.6).

The explicit mandate of the Invest Mongolia Agency under the 2013 Investment Law was to resurrect investor confidence in the Mongolian market by providing an in-house government service to 'streamline' decision-making and assist access to preferential financial arrangements for investors: helping 'both foreign and domestic [investors] – in planning their investments and to protect their interests and rights' (IMA, 2014: 62). Its main functions included the international promotion of the investment climate and opportunities in Mongolia, the provision of consultation and 'one-stop online services to foreign investors,' supporting FDI and registering new foreign investments. A significant part of the IMA's promotional activity since 2013 focused on raising awareness about new changes to Mongolia's tax framework that make it "competitive." For example, the IMA's 2014 Investment Guide boasted that 'Mongolia is one of the countries with the lowest tax rate in the Asia Pacific region with 10% and 25% for corporate income tax, 10% for individual income tax and VAT rate of 10%' (IMA, 2014: 28). Further to these standard low rates, the IMA aimed to assist investors to access the numerous options available to relieve both tax and bureaucracy burdens (i.e. 'an alleviated regime of registration and checkpoint' (Investment Law, Article 12.1.2)). It guaranteed the option of an investment agreement to any entity investing above 500 billion tugriks (approximately USD 250 million), within which taxes may be stabilised for periods exceeding those laid out in the Investment Law (Article 16.2.1, see Table 4.2).

*Table 4.2* Tax Stabilisation Periods Based on Region and Investment Amount

| Investment Values (MNT in billions) | | | | | Stabilisation Timeframe | Invest the amount within (years) |
|---|---|---|---|---|---|---|
| Ulaanbaatar | Central Region | Midwest Region | Eastern Region | Western Region | | |
| 10–30 | 5–15 | 4–12 | 3–10 | 2–8 | 5 | 2 |
| 30–100 | 15–50 | 12–40 | 10–30 | 8–25 | 8 | 3 |
| 100–200 | 50–100 | 40–80 | 30–60 | 25–50 | 25–50 | 4 |
| 200 and more | 100 and more | 80 and more | 60 and more | 50 and more | 50 and more | 5 |

Source: IMA (2015a: 31).

Furthermore, the law stipulated that entities operating within economic free zones did not have to pay any tax for the first five years under the terms of the 2013 Investment Law. Notably, Mongolia's main Economic Free Zone – Zamyn-Üüd – is a port on the border with China, a major export route for the mining-intensive South Gobi region. Non-tax benefits included 'longer land lease rights, residential permits for international investors and their families, expedited registration process if the investment involves a free economic zone or industrial complex, and financial guarantees for investment projects involving innovative technology' (Invest Mongolia Agency, 2014: 67).

In addition to the Investment Law and new agency, Mongolia's urgent need for capital led to the swift passing of several significant pieces of legislation to develop its capital markets (Surenjav and Buxbaum, 2015: 323). This included 'managerial and technical reform' to the Mongolian Stock Exchange to comply with 'international standards' through amendments to the Market Security Laws (ibid.). These amendments introduced 'a greater variety of financial instruments, including options, futures, derivatives, and convertible securities' (ibid.: 324), contributing to the development of Mongolia's market 'infrastructure' (ibid.). Additionally, an Investment Fund Law was passed to enable private investment funds, where domestic investors can raise capital on global markets and take advantage of reform to the Mongolian Stock Exchange (ibid). Private investment funds were perceived as 'a positive development in increasing the liquidity of Mongolian capital markets' (Hogan Lovells, 2014a), generating (a) new investment opportunities for shareholders and (b) the hope of making companies more profitable and less vulnerable to bankruptcy.[25] These efforts to deepen access to capital markets and provide domestic frameworks for more complex financial mechanisms made progress towards bringing Mongolia's domestic market environment up to "international standards," the desired basis of global trade being the free movement of capital and predictable rules. Perhaps not surprisingly, foreign investors increasingly took the view that the period of crisis had contributed important market benefits (Oxford Business Group, 2014).

In 2014, the minerals law and policy framework underwent comprehensive reform. A new State Policy on Minerals (2014–2025) was approved by Parliament
in January 2014, with the main stated objective being

> to establish a *stable investment environment*, to improve the quality of min-
> erals exploration, mining and processing by encouraging advanced equip-
> ment, technologies and innovations with low negative impacts on the
> environment, to produce value-added products and to *strengthen competi-
> tiveness in the global market.*
>
> (Article 1.2, emphasis added)

In addition to new institutional mechanisms to protect the investment environment from the destabilising influences of Parliament and local authorities (the
subject of the next chapter), the State Minerals Policy prioritised 'private sector-
led development.' This entailed not only positive support for investors, but an
active reduction for the state's role in relation to the market. As the Director-
General of the Department for Strategic Policy and Planning at the Ministry of
Mining put it in 2015:[26]

> Government should participate only as a tax collector and, of course,
> rules and standards enforcing agency… there is a strong sentiment among
> people – ordinary people – that government officials should not be involved
> in management of business operations of a company. Everything must be
> done by private sector. Private people will be much more rational…

This point of view was affirmed in an interview with a senior legal specialist at
Erdenes Mongol LLC,[27] the state-owned mining company representing the government of Mongolia's interests in its fifteen nationally strategic mineral assets:

> All the stakeholders together worked on this document [State Policy on
> Minerals Sector 2014–2025]. So it is [a] very important document to make
> sure that investment is attracted, and that state-owned companies can work
> effectively, efficiently… The point is that the government is trying to move
> the industry forward because it is a very important industry for the country's
> economy… since Mongolia is a market economy, so also the private sector
> [has a] very important role in the economy and industries, in development.
> So it is quite a liberal policy document, which means that it is open to all
> the partners, all the parties, investors, including all of the investment com-
> munity. So not only the local community but the international community.

The significance of Erdenes Mongol as the SOE representing government interests in the economy put the company under the limelight of reform since
2014. Previously, Erdenes Mongol had been designed to function as a type of
sovereign wealth fund, financing the HDF through dividends. Since 2014,

Erdenes Mongol has been in a process of restructuring, so that it can operate with a 'commercial mandate' (ibid.), to put its daily operation beyond the immediate influence and control of its government shareholders (i.e. the Prime Minister, Ministry of Finance, Mongol Bank, Ministry of Mining). The CEO of Erdenes Mongol at the time, B. Byambasaikhan, placed priority on disentangling the enterprise from the direct influence of the government provided the leadership for this transition, tantamount to a semi-privatisation of Mongolia's most significant SOE. Byambasaikhan stated in a media interview that 'government involvement in business and the negative international perception of this' was the primary issue to be overcome in terms of reforms (News.mn, 17th March 2015).

While the language of privatisation was resisted in the author's interviews with three senior representatives at Erdenes Mongol in 2015,[28] the model upon which the restructuring was guided is explicitly that of Temasek, the Singaporean Holdings company. The Temasek model effectively delinks the operation of SOEs from the government through a Shareholder Representative, who appoints the board of directors, instead of Cabinet and Ministries. This should be understood as a partial privatisation of state property and governance, because it aims to remove the state's direct, political involvement from the operation of the company, rendering a "public" company virtually indistinguishable from private companies in order than it can compete more effectively in the market. According to senior experts at Erdenes Mongol, the bureaucratic checks and balances, and inability to adapt quickly enough to market signals, were the reasons for the shift to a commercial mandate.[29] The emphasis on private sector led the development and the new push to privatise, at least partially, many SOEs more generally reflect an overall trend since 2014 that 'the government should not participate as a shareholder.'[30]

The 2006 Minerals Law was amended in July 2014 to reflect reformed priorities in the minerals economy, favouring the private sector. A summary of changes as they relate the role of the state and investor interests is detailed in the following table (Table 4.3):

*Table 4.3* Investor-State Balance in the 2014 Amendments to the 2006 Minerals Law (see Minter Ellison, 2014; Hogan Lovells, 2014b)

| Investor Benefits | Role of the State |
| --- | --- |
| Scope of mining activity reduced from 8% to 20% of the total territory | Direct stakes in mining projects exchangeable for special royalties, depending on negotiations with the licence-holder |
| Reduced restrictions on licence trading | Formalisation of local development agreements (made mandatory) |
| Newly issued licences may be immediately transferred | |
| Stream-lining procedures for obtaining licences | |

*(Continued)*

| Investor Benefits | Role of the State |
|---|---|
| Replaces former grounds for licence cancellation with fines | Financial burden of limiting mining shifted to local authorities: |
| Introduced a 30–60 day time-limit on government decision-making to reduce bureaucracy | confiscation of licenced areas under the terms of 'specially protected areas' have to be compensated by the local authority |
| Reduction of taxes: | *within a year,* otherwise mining |
| Royalty on gold reduced from 10% to 2.5% | operations may continue |
| Elimination of taxes on imports, equipment, machinery until 2018 | MRAM and Ministry of Mining to pre-determine areas for exploration |
| | Prerogatives of the Ministry of Mining significantly expanded, particularly regarding the approval of regulation related to mine processing, environmental rehabilitation, the collection of geological data, the qualification of official experts and analysts, the classification of resources and public reporting (Article 10.1 and sub-provisions) |

The 2014 changes to the legal framework in the minerals sector also addressed the moratorium on licence issuance, which was 'simultaneously repealed' (Hogan Lovells, 2014b: 1) with the amendment of the minerals law. Mineral licences for exploration and exploitation were available again on a first-come-first-serve basis, reverting to the "competitive" standard of the 1997 Minerals Law. Furthermore, the Law on the Prohibition of Mineral Exploration and Mining Operations at Headwaters of Rivers, Protected Zones of Water Reservoirs and Forested Areas was significantly revised. Operations in headwaters or river basins remained restricted, but limited mining was permitted again along rivers and in forested areas. The amendments to this environmental law have a clear economic explanation: 'there is no money to compensate' the revoked exploration and exploitation licences, as the President of the MNMA frankly put it in 2015.[31]

Apart from legal and policy changes, the Mongolian government made significant efforts to heal its reputational damage in the international investment media. This effort has been particularly prominent since the start of 2015 when Prime Minister Chimed Saikhanbileg assumed the office after his predecessor was ousted for his alleged lack of effort to resurrect investor confidence in the minerals sector (Reuters, 2014). PM C. Saikhanbileg and other senior politicians, including B. Byambasaikhan, CEO of Erdenes Mongol, actively courted the international investment community through demonstrations of contrition for past "mistakes." For example, in April 2015, in the run-up to the Dubai negotiation of the ongoing Oyu Tolgoi dispute, the Prime Minister faulted the Mongolian government for 'lost credibility' in the international market (Reuters, 2015). A striking example of this *mea culpa* discourse was again evidenced in 2015, when Prime Minister Saikhanbileg appeared on national television to explain an SMS referendum in which Mongolian citizens were invited to vote on whether they wanted 'to step up austerity measures or do whatever it takes to get the country's mining sector growing again' (Edwards, 2015; see also Kohn, 2015). This dichotomous frame between austerity and prosperity evidences the growing sense among political leaders of the objective status of the market and the limited options available to the government.

The resolution of the dispute between the government and Rio Tinto over Oyu Tolgoi in 2015 – known as the Dubai Agreement – was a crucial part of the government's effort to restore investor confidence in Mongolia's mining sector. The Dubai Agreement was widely seen by the government and investors as a success, providing a basis of unity amongst private and public stakeholders about the second phase of mine development for Oyu Tolgoi. It was also interpreted as a positive signal for other investors, as Oyu Tolgoi continues to exercise broader influence as a barometer of political for investment in the mining sector in general (Macnamara, 2012; Falconer, 2013).

The "success" of the Mongolian negotiators in Dubai in terms of resolving the dispute between Rio Tinto and the Mongolian government was their ability to demonstrate the "economic facts" that showed the impacts of nationalistic decision-making on investment levels.[32] A business approach – rather than a political approach – was seen as necessary to prevent further reputation damage for the country, according to the Deputy Director of Oyu Tolgoi's Resource Strategy and Innovation Department.[33] USD 30 million was paid to the Mongolian government by Rio Tinto to settle the tax dispute, 10% of the original claim, and a 2% tax that the stakeholders inherited from BHP – a source of dissatisfaction on the Mongolian side – was eliminated. A methodology for the calculation of royalties and income tax was agreed upon, that it should be calculated on the basis of gross rather than net profits.

While many perceived these outcomes as a win for the government against Rio Tinto, others were less convinced. A former advisor to the government in the original Oyu Tolgoi dispute explained that these concessions should not be seen as "big victory" because they are not comparable to other concessions that remain sealed in the investment agreement, such as the Investment Tax Credit and Management Service Fee provisions.[34] However, as low tax barriers and liberal investment conditions are key to Mongolia's competitiveness in the global minerals market, the Dubai Agreement was widely perceived as a necessary step towards regaining credibility amongst investors. As PM Saikhanbileg announced:

> Mongolia is back to business. Oyu Tolgoi is a world-class copper-gold asset and its further development is of great economic significance for Mongolia.

> We have finalised a way forward with our partners which re-establishes the foundations of a new and constructive relationship based on mutual trust and our joint long-term commitment to Mongolia's growth.
>
> (Rio Tinto, 2015, Press Release)

These confident words from the Prime Minister were unfortunately insufficient to stem the tide of the debt crisis which began to grip Mongolia, coming to a head in 2016. The dramatic reduction in mining investment from 2014 had a knock-on effect on budget projections and public debt levels, as well as the government's debt repayment capacity, particularly for the large bonds that had been released in 2012 to fund infrastructure projects. By 2014, investment in the mining sector accounted for only 14% of the country's total investment, having shrunk from 46% and 50% in 2013 and 2012, respectively (Xun, 2014: 17.1). By 2016, economic growth had slowed to a trickle, at approximately 1% of GDP.

With foreign investment having dropped from USD $4.45 billion in 2012 to $508 million in 2014 (Kohn, 2015), a multi-party consensus consolidated across the political spectrum to remove barriers for investors and to make evident Mongolia's commitment to supporting private sector led to the development of its minerals. Consequently, in mid-2016, after the parliamentary election, power changed hands between the Democratic Party and the MPP. Notably, however, the new state policy of promoting a "business-friendly" investment environment did not change. Despite the historical reputation of the MPP as a left-leaning, nationalist party, the MPP vowed to resurrect investment with the same fervour as their predecessor. The MPP demonstrated their commitments to expanding market access for mining companies by increasing the territory available for exploration activities from 9.6% to 20.9%. Under the MPP's leadership, a delegation of Mongolian state officials requested financial assistance from the International Monetary Fund (IMF) in September 2016 to prevent defaulting on imminent debt repayments.

By February 2017, an external financing package of approximately USD 5.5 billion had been negotiated with the IMF and other key supporters,[35] to support the government's "Economic Stabilisation Programme" and to enable the government to meet the March repayment deadline on its US $580 million bond from the Development Bank of Mongolia. This IMF financing package was one of the largest in history, with unprecedented involvement from China, which provided US $2.19 billion in currency swap lines. While it is not within the scope of this book to go into great detail on the wider implications of the 2017 IMF bailout, it has had far-reaching consequences for state spending, particularly on social welfare. The universal child benefit, established in 2006 as part of the government's commitment to increase social welfare spending based on increasing levels of mining revenue, was controversially withdrawn in January 2018, following pressure from the IMF to make it a targeted measure based on income as a condition of loan disbursement.

## Conclusion

Through a chronological schema, this chapter has focused on key legal changes and political dynamics which strongly suggest a changed relationship between the state and the market in Mongolia's minerals sector. Eschewing the paternalistic narrative of "learning from mistakes" that has dominated the international media discourse of the government's action in the mining economy, this chapter has set out to highlight the growing power imbalance between the government and investors since 1997. The initial optimism about free markets quickly led to disillusionment amongst the Mongolian public, as the state's minimal regulatory approach generated a host of new environmental and social issues. The public concern over the benefits that would accrue to citizens through the exploitation of natural resource put pressure on the government to take a stronger hand in the economy.

The assertion of a larger role for the state in the minerals sector in 2006 indicates that re-regulation of the sector was perceived as a viable option at that point. However, the government demonstrated a lack of awareness about the way market liberalisation had created new pressure points on the state through the mechanism of FDI, giving investors economic leverage against the state. This leverage did not operate forcefully until the signing of the OTIA, when the mineral sector's share of GDP and exports pushed Mongolia officially into the category of mineral dependence. After an initial period of optimism following the OTIA in the context of the commodity boom, we can see the ways in which the government has since been incentivised to withdraw or ameliorate its efforts to influence the sector based on geopolitical, environmental or corruption-related concerns. Mongolia's initial entry into the global minerals economy through the 1997 Minerals Law was associated with a liberal investment environment, a key element of the country's comparative advantage. While more powerful countries like China, Australia and Indonesia have been able to raise taxes during the decline in commodity prices since 2011 without reprisal, Mongolia has had to re-liberalise its taxation framework, particularly given the financial vulnerability of domestic companies: 'we don't have the option to increase taxes during hard times.'[36]

The following two chapters engage with the implications of the post-2014 stability commitments of Mongolia's mining regime for the constitution of the national state. The new pro-investment, stability consensus governing the relationship between state and market was not achieved merely with the passing of the new state policy on the mining sector and its associated changes in investment and mineral legislation. To effectively institutionalise – in practical terms – the commitments of the central government to maintaining a stable legal and political environment for capital investment, sources of political risk to the mining regime needed to be systematically addressed. Parliament, local governments and rural environmental NGOs had resisted mining investment in different ways between 1997 and 2014, and were consequently targeted for reform in order to prevent further destabilisation to Mongolia's reputation as a stable destination for foreign investment. The next two chapters analyse the strategic redistribution of power within central state institutions (particularly between the legislative and the executive), the re-interpretation of the principle of self-government (governing the scope of sub-national administration) and the creation of new limits to political contestation (state–society relations) which signify a process of new constitutionalisation of the Mongolian state in a global market environment.

# Notes

1  Author interview, 13th November 2015.
2  Author interview, 15th November 2015.
3  According to Article 4 of the 1994 Minerals Law, 'strategic minerals include gold ore, silver ore, and ores of platinum and other metals of its group...ruby, diamond, emerald, sapphire, uranium ore, oil, and hard coal' (4.3). Additionally, 'special minerals are minerals ores and non-metallic minerals' except those designated as strategic or common (4.4). Finally, 'common minerals include sand, gravel, sandstone, quartzite, clay, argillite, aluerite, chalk, limestone, dolomite, marl, intrusive rock, volcanic rock, altered rock and shale' (4.5).
4  Author interview, 13th November 2015.
5  Author interview, 13th November 2015.
6  Author interview with MRAM Officer, 28th October 2015.
7  While anomalous geological indicators were registered in the 1983 Mongolian Geological Survey, it was not until 1996 when Magma Copper, a large American company, secured exploration rights to the deposit that Oyu Tolgoi generated any serious attention. By the end of that year, Magma Copper had been purchased by BHP Billiton, an Australian company, which took over their exploration rights. BHP Billiton quickly sold their exploration rights to Ivanhoe Mines following the copper bust in 1997.
8  Ivanhoe's 2002 independent research audit states that the initial exploration area contained 10 million ounces of gold and 5.6 billion pounds of copper (Turquoise Hill Resources, 2019).
9  Palaeozoic porphyry deposits (see Porter, 2016).
10 There is a growing literature on the calculation of natural resource dependence. Resource dependence is typically calculated based on the share of natural resources in GDP, national exports and/or government revenue. Over 20% in any category indicates significant mineral dependence (see Hailu and Kipgen, 2017, for an overview of different indices and introduction to the Extractives Dependence Index).
11 The demographic of illegal miners is complex, despite their caricature as polluting criminals (High, 2008). Herders seeking to either supplement or find an alternative livelihood, ex-convicts and unemployed professionals from Ulaanbaatar found their way to the gold fields.
12 The herding population grew from 18% to 50% of the working population in the 1990s (Mearns, 2004: 108; Rossabi, 2005: 121).
13 In the lead up to the 2008 elections, there was an attempt by some leading politicians to renegotiate this level to 50% but Ivanhoe refused.
14 Author interview, 15th July 2019.
15 Author interview with former Deputy Director of the Legal Policy Department, Ministry of Justice, and member of the Oyu Tolgoi Working Group prior to the signing of the Investment Agreement, 13th October 2015.
16 Author interview, 27th October 2015.
17 Author interview, 16th November 2015.

18  In 2010, the Mongolian People's Revolutionary Party (MPRP) changed its name to the Mongolian People's Party (MPP).

19  It is worth noting that in comparison with the investment regulations in many other states, including Western countries, SEFIL was not exceptional (Scharaw, 2018: Chapter 3, Section 2.1). Fourteen of the wealthiest states in Europe as well as the EU itself have investment screening policies designed to scrutinise 'specific' foreign investment (i.e. from China) in strategic sectors (see European Commission, 2019).

20  Author interview, 15th July 2019.

21  Somewhat ironically, SEFIL and other measures intended to give the state greater control of the mining sector (particularly from Chinese state investment) pushed Mongolia into greater dependence on Chinese investment and finance. China provided critical financial support during the investment crisis and commodity price slump (2012–2013) when FDI contracted. While Chinese demand for Mongolian coal had slowed, it did not suddenly withdraw capital following the "resource nationalist" decisions of the Mongolian government. Instead, Chinese SOEs exploited Mongolia's dependence by offering long-term purchase agreements for commodities at 'deeply-discounted' rates, sometimes as low as 11% of 'global benchmark prices' (Wernau, 2017).

22  Author interview, 13th November 2015.

23  Author interview, 27th October 2015.

24  As China is Mongolia's largest trading partner, the *yuan* can be used in relation to Mongolia–China trade settlements, thus protecting other foreign currency reserves (Yamada, 2017). Mongolia's swap agreements with China essentially function as a credit line to finance Mongolia's trade deficit. The Bank of China also set up an office in Mongolia in 2013, which invests in infrastructure, energy and mining companies. By 2014, approximately forty companies had applied for USD\$ 3 billion worth of loans from the Bank, according to a Bank report cited in a national newspaper (Bayarsaikhan, 2016). While the Bank of China has not opened an official branch, there are concerns about the devastating impact such a move could have on Mongolia's financial sector, which would easily be undercut by the lower interest rates of the Bank of China (ibid.).

25  This was arguably most important for Mongolian companies, which have tended to lack 'sufficient financial capability' (Director-General of the Department for Strategic Policy and Planning, Ministry of Mining, author interview, October 2015) in terms of the reliability of their own capital assets.

26  Author interview, 27th October 2015.

27  Author interview, 17th November 2015.

28  Ibid.

29  Ibid.

30  Director-General of the Department for Strategic Policy and Planning, Ministry of Mining, author interview, 27th October 2015. Notably, in 2014, Parliament decided against participation in a 'strategically important deposit' – Tsagaan Suvraga copper mine – reflecting a shifting sense of political will alongside policy reform.

31  Author interview, 13th November 2015.

32  B. Byambasaikhan, CEO of Erdenes Mongol LLC, was particularly influential as the 'internationally experienced' Mongolian negotiator representing the government's interests in Dubai (Institute for National Strategy, 2015). He has a strong reputation as an internationally oriented businessman, with previous experience in banking (Asian Development Bank), investment and advisory services as the Director of NovaTerra LLC, and as the President of the Business Council of Mongolia. In contrast to previous negotiators for the government in relation to Oyu Tolgoi, Byambasaikhan is known for his positive approach to foreign investment and support for

the restructuring and privatisation of SOEs. In August 2015, following the Dubai Agreement, Byambasaikhan was appointed to the Board of Directors for Oyu Tolgoi.
33 Author interview, 18th November 2015
34 Author interview, 13th November 2015.
35 The Asian Development Bank, the World Bank, South Korea, Japan and China supported the deal.
36 Author interview with the Director of Strategic Policy and Planning, Ministry of Mining, 27th October 2015.

# References

Bayarsaikhan, D. 2016. "Could Bank of China Engulf the Mongolian Banking System?" 28th September *UB Post* http://theubpost.mn/2016/09/28/could-bank-of-china-engulf-the-mongolian-banking-system/#comment-822. Accessed 26th February 2017.

Byambajav, D. 2012. "Mobilising Against Dispossession: Gold Mining and a Local Resistance Movement in Mongolia." *Journal of the Centre for Northern Humanities* 5: 13–32.

———. 2014. "The River Movements' Struggle in Mongolia." *Social Movement Studies: Journal of Social, Cultural and Political Protest*, 1–6.

Campi, A. 2012. "Mongolia's Quest to Balance Human Development in its Booming Mineral-Based Economy." *Brookings Northeast Asia Commentary* No. 51 of 65, no page numbers www.brookings.edu/research/opinions/2012/01/10-mongolia-campi Accessed 29/08/2013.

Combellick-Bidney, S. 2012. "Mongolia's Mining Controversies and the Politics of Place." In Julian Dierkes (ed.) *Change in Democratic Mongolia: Social Relations, Health, Mobile Pastoralism and Mining.* Boston, MA: Brill.

Dettoni, J. 2013. "Mongolia: New Samurai Bond Puts Fiscal Rules in Spotlight." 17th December *Financial Times* http://blogs.ft.com/beyond-brics/2013/12/17/mongolia-new-samurai-bond-puts-fiscal-rules-in-spotlight/?Authorised=false&_i_location=http%3A%2F%2Fblogs.ft.com%2Fbeyond-brics%2F2013%2F12%2F17%2Fmongolia-new-samurai-bond-puts-fiscal-rules-in-spotlight%2F&_i_referer=&classification=conditional_registered&iab=barrier-app. Accessed 1st June 2014.

Deutsch, A. and Edwards, T. 2013. "Special Report: In Tax Case, Mongolia Is the Mouse that Roared." 16th July *Reuters* www.reuters.com/article/2013/07/16/us-dutch-mongolia-tax-idUSBRE96F0B620130716 Accessed 1st September 2013.

Edwards, T. 2013. "Mongolia to Ease Conditions on Private Foreign Investors." 23rd April *Reuters* www.reuters.com/article/mongolia-investment-idUSL3N0D6SUQ20130423 3rd April 2014.

Els, F. 2013. "Mongolia Still Has '22 Points of Dispute' with Rio Tinto over Oyu Tolgoi." 17th July *Mining.com* www.mining.com/mongolia-still-has-22-points-of-dispute-with-rio-tinto-over-oyu-tolgoi-48895/. Accessed 3rd August 2013.

Endicott, E. 2012. *A History of Land Use in Mongolia: The Thirteenth Century to the Present.* New York: Palgrave Macmillan.

Enkhbaatar, Ch., Solongo, D., Amarjargal, P. and Ginsburg, T. 2015. "The Role of the Constitution of Mongolia in Consolidating Democracy: An Analysis." UNDP, Ulaanbaatar.www.mn.undp.org/content/mongolia/en/home/library/democratic_governance/RoleoftheConstitutionofMongoliaInConsolidatingDemocracy.html. Accessed 31st March 2017.

European Commission. 2019. "EU Foreign Investment Screening Regulation Enters into Force." Press Release, 10th April 2019. http://europa.eu/rapid/press-release_IP-19-2088_en.htm. Accessed 19th July 2019.

Falconer, R. 2013. "Mongolian Mega-Mine Set to Transform Country," 5th June *Al Jazeera* www.aljazeera.com/indepth/features/2013/06/201364111940133777.html. Accessed 12th October 2014.

Fehrbach, E. 2013. "Law on Prohibiting Mineral Exploration and Extraction Near Water Sources, Protected Areas and Forests." October 23rd *Mongolia Briefing* http://mongolia-briefing.com/news/2013/10/law-on-prohibiting-mineral-exploration-and-extraction-near-water-sources-protected-areas-and-forests.html. Accessed 31st March 2017.

Frangos, A. and Natarajan, P. 2012. "Mongolia Binges on Bond Bonanza," 29th November *The Wall Street Journal* http://online.wsj.com/article/SB10001424127887324020804578147014152179412.html. Accessed 1st June 2013.

Frerichs, S. 2012. "Studying Law, Economy and Society: A Short History of Socio-Legal Thinking." Helsinki Legal Studies Research Paper No. 19 (University of Helsinki). Online. Available at: https://papers.ssrn.com/sol3/papers.cfm?abstract_id=2022891. Accessed 1st June 2019.

———. 2013. "Law, Economy and Society in the Global Age: A Study Guide." In A. Perry-Kessaris (ed.) *Socio-Legal Approaches to International Economic Law: Text, Context, Subtext.* Abingdon: Routledge, pp. 36–49.

Gill, S. 1998. 'New Constitutionalism, Democratisation and Global Political Economy.' *Pacifica Review: Peace, Security and Global Change* 10(1): 23–38.

Hailu, D. and Kipgen, C. 2017. "The Extractives Dependence Index (EDI)." *Resources Policy* 51: 251–264.

Hatcher, P. 2014. *Regimes of Risk: The World Bank and the Transformation of Mining in Asia.* New York/London: Palgrave Macmillan.

High, M. 2008. "Wealth and Envy in the Mongolian Gold Mines." *Cambridge Anthropology.* 27(3): 1–18.

Hogan Lovells. 2013. "Mongolian Strategic Foreign Investment Law Update." Hogan Lovells:www.hoganlovells.com/publications/mongolian-strategic-foreign-investment-law-update. Accessed 2nd February 2014.

———. 2014a. "An Overview of the Law of Mongolia on Investment Funds." Hogan Lovells: www.hoganlovells.com/files/Uploads/Documents/An_Overview_of_the_Law_of_Mongolian_on_Investment_Funds.pdf. Accessed 2nd March 2015.

———. 2014b. "Note on the Amendment to the Law of Mongolia on Minerals." Hogan Lovells: Online www.hoganlovells.com/files/Uploads/Documents/Note_on_the_Amendment_to_the_Law_of_Mongolia_on_Minerals_dated_1_July_2014_HKGLIB01_1158381_F2.pdf Accessed 2nd March 2015.

Husband, C. and Songwe, V. 2004. "Mongolia Mining Sector: Managing the Future." World Bank: http://documents.worldbank.org/curated/en/867261468323101510/pdf/332480ENGLISH01ng1sector1report1ENG.pdf. Accessed 30th March 2017.

Institute for National Strategy, 2015. "Economy is Back to Business." 25th May http://nationalstrategy.mn/?p=3130&lang=en. Accessed 12th April 2017.

IMF. 2012. "Mongolia: Staff Report for the 2012 Article IV Consultation and Third Post-Programme Monitoring – Debt Sustainability Analysis." IMF: pp. 1–16 www.imf.org/external/pubs/ft/dsa/pdf/2012/dsacr12320.pdf. Accessed 3rd April 2013.

Invest Mongolia Agency. 2014. *Investment Guide to Mongolia 2014.* Ulaanbaatar: Invest Mongolia Agency.

InfoMongolia. 2013. "As of today, Erdenes Tavan Tolgoi's debt estimated at 257 million USD, said Mining Minister of Mongolia." 2nd May *InfoMongolia.com* www.infomongolia.com/ct/ci/5940. Accessed 2nd April 2014.

Isakova, A., Plekhanov, A., and Zettelmeyer, J. 2012. "Managing Mongolia's Resource Boom." EBRD Working Paper 138. EBRD, pp. 1–36. www.ebrd.com/downloads/research/economics/workingpapers/wp0138.pdf. Accessed 26th August 2013.

Ivanhoe Mines. 2006. "Revised Taxation and Mineral Laws in Mongolia Set the Stage for Conclusion of an Investment Contract for Ivanhoe's Oyu Tolgoi Project." 10th July. Turquoise Hill www.turquoisehill.com/i/pdf/2006-07-10_NR.pdf. Accessed 1st July 2015.

Kirwin, D. J. 2006. "The Giant Oyu Tolgoi Porphyry Copper Deposit: Discovery History and Implications for Future Exploration in the Gobi." Presentation, SE Europe Geoscience Foundation Conference, Sofia, Bulgaria 10th September 2006. CMI Capital www.cmi-capital.com/Doc_Server/SEEGF_Docs/Kirwin/1-OT%20Discovery%20&%203SEG-Europe-10%20Sep%202006.pdf. Accessed 23rd April 2019.

Kohn, M. 2015. "Mongolia PM Takes to TV and Texting to Win Back Investment." 5th April 2015 *Bloomberg* www.bloomberg.com/news/articles/2015-04-05/mongolia-s-leader-takes-to-tv-and-texting-to-win-back-investment.Accessed 23rd April 2019.

Kohn, M. and Humber, Y. 2013 "Where Raptors Roamed Rio's Dream Stirs Water Worry." 10th July 2013 *Bloomberg* www.bloomberg.com/news/2013-06-20/where-raptors-roamed-rio-tinto-s-copper-dream-stirs-water-worry.html. Accessed 23rd April 2019.

Kosich, D. 2012. "Turquoise Hill, Rio Tinto Refuse Oyu Tolgoi Renegotiation Attempt." 16th October *Mineweb* www.mineweb.com/archive/turquoise-hill-rio-tinto-refuse-oyu-tolgoi-renegotiation-attempt/ Accessed 2nd April 2013.

Lander, J. 2014. "A Critical Reflection on Oyu Tolgoi and the Risk of a Resource Trap in Mongolia: Troubling the "Resource Nationalism" Frame" *Law, Social Justice and Global Development Journal* 2013(2)https://warwick.ac.uk/fac/soc/law/elj/lgd/2013_2/2013_2_lander/lander_lgd_2013_2_pub02_2014-.pdf

Lee, A. 2012. "Mongolia's New Foreign Investment Law Explained." *International Financial Law Review*. London: Euromoney Institutional Investor PLC.

Macnamara, W. 2012. "Tax Proposal in Mongolia Threatens Rio Tinto Project." 15th October *New York Times* http://dealbook.nytimes.com/2012/10/15/tax-proposal-in-mongolia-threatens-rio-tinto-project/?_r=1. Accessed 23rd April 2019.

Manthorpe, J. 2013. "Mongolia Struggles with the Complexity of Resource Development." 29th September *Business in Vancouver* www.biv.com/article/2013/9/mongolia-struggles-with-complexities-of-resource-d/.Accessed 23rd April 2019.

May, C. 2014. "The Rule of Law as the *Grundnorm* of the New Constitutionalism." In S. Gill and C. Cutler (eds.) *New Constitutionalism and World Order*. Cambridge: Cambridge University Press, pp. 63–79.

Mearns, R. 2004. "Sustaining Livelihoods on Mongolia's Pastoral Commons: Insights from a Participatory Poverty Assessment." *Development and Change* 35(1): 107–139.

Mendee, J. 2013. "Major Revision of Mongolian Mining Regulations is Underway." 6th March *Eurasia Daily Monitor* 10(42) www.jamestown.org/single/?tx_ttnews%5Btt_news%5D=40552&no_cache=1#.Vz3o9JErLbl. Accessed 2nd February 2014.

Mineral Resources Authority of Mongolia (MRAM). 2002. "Mining in Mongolia: Presentation." http://www3.gaf.de/mongolia_mining/pages/pub/pdf/mrpam_presentation.pdf. Accessed 10th April 2016.

Moran, T. H. 2013. "Avoiding the "Resource Curse" in Mongolia." Policy Brief 13–18 July 2013. Peterson Institute for International Economics: https://piie.com/publications/policy-briefs/avoiding-resource-curse-mongolia. Accessed 14th May 2014.

Munkhsaikhan, O. 2016. "Mongolia: A Vain Constitutional Attempt to Consolidate Parliamentary Democracy." 12th February *ConstitutionNet*www.constitutionnet.org/news/mongolia-vain-constitutional-attempt-consolidate-parliamentary-democracy Accessed 3rd March 2016.

New Internationalist Magazine. 2006. "Robert Friedland." 1st August 2006 *New Internationalist Magazine* Issue 392 http://newint.org/columns/worldbeaters/2006/08/01/. Accessed 23rd April 2019.

News.mn. 2015. "INS Interview with Byambasaikhan, CEO of Erdenes Mongol." 17th March www.news.mn/r/206963. Accessed 31st March 2017.

Oxford Business Group. 2013. "The Report: Mongolia." London: Oxford Business Group.

———. 2014. "Taking Stock: New Regulations and Guidelines are Aimed at Renewing the Market." www.oxfordbusinessgroup.com/overview/taking-stock-new-regulations-and-guidelines-are-aimed-renewing-market. Accessed 7th April 2017.

Perry-Kessaris, A. (ed.) 2013. *Socio-Legal Approaches to International Economic Law: Text, Context, Subtext.* Abingdon: Routledge.

Porter, T. M. 2016. "The Geology, Structure and Mineralisation of the Oyu Tolgoi Porphyry Copper-Gold-Molybdenum Deposits, Mongolia: A Review," *Geoscience Frontiers* 7: 375–407.

Reinert, E. S. 2000. "Globalisation in the Periphery as a Morgenthau Plan; The Underdevelopment of Mongolia in the 1990s." In S. Lhagva (ed.) *Mongolian Development Strategy: Capacity Building.* Ulaanbaatar: Mongolian Development Research Centre, pp. 157–214.

Reuters. 2006. "Mongolia: Law-Makers Join Protests over Mine." 15th April. *New York Times* www.nytimes.com/2006/04/15/world/15briefs.html?_r=0. Accessed 13 April 2013.

———. 2013. "Foreign Investors Cry Foul as Mongolia Revokes Mine Licenses." 7th November *Reuters* www.reuters.com/article/mongolia-mining-licenses-id USL3N0IS33820131107. Accessed 4th April 2014.

———. 2014. "Mongolia Gets New Prime Minister as Economy Slumps." 21st November *Reuters* www.reuters.com/article/us-mongolia-politics-idUSKCN0J50J020141121. Accessed 31st March 2017.

———. 2015. "Mongolia Must Accept Blame over Rio Tinto Mine Dispute – Prime Minister." 3rd April *Reuters.* www.reuters.com/article/mongolia-oyutolgoi-id USL3N0X01NK20150403.Accessed 31st March 2017.

Rio Tinto. 2015. "Oyu Tolgoi Shareholders Sign Agreement to Progress the Development of Underground Mine." 18th May *Rio Tinto* www.riotinto.com/media/media-releases-237_15020.aspx. Accessed 9th September 2015.

Rossabi, M. 2005. *Mongolia: From Khans to Commissars to Capitalists.* Berkeley: University of California Press.

Schafferer, C. 2005. "The Great State Hural Election in Mongolia, June 2004." Notes on Recent Elections *Electoral Studies* 24: 741–784.

Scharaw, B. 2018. *The Protection of Foreign Investments in Mongolia: Treaties, Domestic Law, and Contracts on Investments in International Comparison and Arbitral Practice.* New York: Springer International Publishing.

Schneiderman, D. 2013. *Resisting Economic Globalisation: Critical Theory and International Investment Law.* Basingstoke, Hampshire/New York: Palgrave Macmillan.

Sukhbaatar, S. 2012. "Law and Development, FDI, and the Rule of Law in Post-Soviet Central Asia: The Case of Mongolia." In G. P. McAlinn and C. Pejovic (eds.) *Law and Development in Asia.* Abingdon: Routledge, pp. 137–159.

Surenjav, O. and Buxbaum, D. C. 2015. "Capital Markets: Mongolia". In La Fleche, E. R. (ed.) *Mining Law Review.* 4th Edition. London: Law Business Research Ltd., pp. 322–334.

Suzuki, Y. 2013. "Conflict between Mining Development and Nomadism in Mongolia." In Yamamura, N., Fujita, N., and Maekawa, A. (eds.) *The Mongolian Eco-System Network: Environmental Issues Under Climate and Social Changes.* Tokyo: Springer, pp. 269–294.

The Economist. 2012. "Mine, All Mine." 21st January 2012 *The Economist* www.economist.com/node/21543113. Accessed 2nd March 2013.

Tse, P. K. 2009. "The Mineral Industries of Mongolia." *Mongolia: 2009 Minerals Yearbook.* U.S. Geological Survey. www.usgs.gov.

Tumenbayer, N. 2002. "Herders' Property Rights vs. Mining in Mongolia." Paper prepared for Conference on Environmental Conflict Resolution, Watson Institute for International Studies, Brown University, Providence, RI, Spring 2002 (University of Vermont: Online): 1–15. www.uvm.edu/~shali/Mining%20Mongolia%20paper.pdf. Accessed 1st June 2013.

Turquoise Hill Resources. 2019. "Oyu Tolgoi Mongolia." www.turquoisehill.com/s/Oyu_Tolgoi.asp. Accessed 23rd April 2019.

UNCTAD. 2013. "Investment Policy Review: Mongolia." Geneva: United Nations https://unctad.org/en/pages/PublicationWebflyer.aspx?publicationid=758

U.S. Department of State. 2011. "US Embassy in Ulaanbaatar: 2011 Investment Climate Statement." U.S. Department of State: Online https://mongolia.usembassy.gov/root/media/pdf/mongolia-ics-2011.pdf Accessed 4th April 2017.

———. 2013. "US Embassy in Ulaanbaatar, Mongolia: 2013 Mongolia Investment Climate Statement." US Department of State: Online http://photos.state.gov/libraries/mongolia/805999/PDFs/mics_2013.pdf. Accessed 1st January 2019.

———. 2014. "2014 Investment Climate Statement: Executive Summary." US Department of State, Washington, DC, pp. 1–51. www.state.gov/documents/organization/231251.pdf. Accessed 9th October 2015.

Upton, C. 2012. "Mining, Resistance and Pastoral Livelihoods in Contemporary Mongolia." In Julian Dierkes (ed.) *Change in Democratic Mongolia: Social Relations, Health, Mobile Pastoralism and Mining.* Boston, MA: Brill, pp. 223–248.

Weafer, C. 2016. "Mongolia: Time to Rethink Your Risk Assessment?" *Financial Times Beyond Brics Forum* http://blogs.ft.com/beyond-brics/2016/02/26/mongolia-time-to-rethink-your-risk-assessment/.Accessed 23rd April 2019.

Wernau, J. 2017. "New China-Mongolia Mining Deal: Economic Windfall or Environmental Threat?" 21st January *Wall Street Journal* www.wsj.com/articles/new-china-mongolia-mining-deal-economic-windfall-or-environmental-threat-1485000058. Accessed 26th March 2017.

White, B. 2013. "In-Depth Analysis: OT Dispute and Expenditure Overruns." 10th March 2013, *The Mongolist.* www.themongolist.com/blog/government/58-in-depth-analysis-ot-dispute-and-expenditure-overruns.html. Accessed 1st August2013.

World Bank. 2006. "Mongolia: A Review of Environmental and Social Impacts in the Mining Sector." Washington, DC: World Bank.

————. 2011. "Global Commodity Markets Annex." *Global Economic Prospects June 2011: Subject Annex*. World Bank, pp. 1–15. http://pubdocs.worldbank.org/en/932501462215865541/CMO-2011-June-GEP.pdf Accessed 31st March 2017.

————. 2013. "Mongolia Economic Update." World Bank, pp. 1–31. http://documents.worldbank.org/curated/en/314181468061495284/pdf/826050WP0Mongo00Box379865B00PUBLIC0.pdf. Accessed 30th August 2016.

World Growth Mongolia. 2009. "The Oyu Tolgoi Investment Agreement: Why It Works for Mongolia." Published online by World Growth International http://worldgrowth.org/site/wp-content/uploads/2012/06/OT-Investment-Agreement_ENG-A4.pdf. Accessed 26th April 2016.

Wu, J. C. 1997. "The Mineral Industries of Mongolia." *Mongolia: 1997 Minerals Yearbook*. U.S. Geological Survey. www.usgs.gov.

Xun, S. 2014. "The Mineral Industries of Mongolia." *Mongolia: 2014 Minerals Yearbook*. U.S. Geological Survey. www.usgs.gov.

Yamada, S. 2017. "China, Mongolia to Extend Currency Swap Agreement." 21st February *Nikkei Asian Review* http://asia.nikkei.com/Markets/Currencies/China-Mongolia-to-extend-currency-swap-agreement.Accessed 26th March 2017.

Yeung, Y. and Howes, S. 2015. "Action Research Report – Resources-to-Cash: A Cautionary Tale from Mongolia." International Mining for Development Centre, Australia National University: http://im4dc.org/wp-content/uploads/2015/09/Combined-Yeung.pdf. Accessed 9th September 2015.

**Mongolian law and policy**

1997 Law of Mongolia on Non-Governmental Organisations. English translation. Published online by the International Labour Organisation (ILO) NATLEXwww.ilo.org/dyn/natlex/natlex4.detail?p_lang=en&p_isn=57969&p_country=MNG&p_count=137. Accessed 31st March 2014.

1994, 1997, 2006 Minerals Laws printed in Ulziibayar, B. and Tsetsenbileg, B. (eds.) 2010. *Minerals Laws of Mongolia 1910–2010*. Ulaanbaatar, Mongolia: MBS Law Firm.

2013 Investment Law. Final Version, English translation published online by the Ministry of Foreign Affairs www.mofa.gov.mn/new/images/banners/regulation/investmentlaw.pdf. Accessed 26th April 2017.

2014 Amendments to the Minerals Law, see Minter Ellison (2014) and Hogan Lovells (2014b).

————. 2014. "State Policy on the Minerals Sector 2014–2025." Appendix to Resolution No. 18, 2014 of the State Great Khural of Mongolia. English translation.

# Chapter 5

# After the crisis

## Strategies for stabilisation within the state

### Introduction

"[Mongolia has been adjusting to] democracy and capitalism in the past twenty years... They're learning a lot so it's a steep learning curve, but they're adjusting and they do things right in many ways, it's just the politics gets in the way. The last twenty years have been an experiment."

CEO, Foreign-Invested Mining Company[1]

"Well, you know, everyone can understand why only 29 years into the free market process that there isn't an understanding about actually how tough the Western markets are. There's this pot of gold, if you like, that Mongolia should be entitled to. And there is a feeling of entitlement amongst the Mongolians, which again one can understand. It's the land of Chinggis Khan... [But], you know, Mongolia is not really a very big country. You know, it's a tiny country in terms of nominal or even the size of grey GDP. The nominal GDP is about 12 billion dollars and let's add in what they call the grey economy, maybe it's 20. But it's not even a rounding error for the global economy... So there is a complete disconnect between where Mongolia sees things... [they] don't quite understand where [they] fit in relative to the world's great financial centres of New York, Hong Kong, London, Tokyo and Singapore."

Western foreign investor[2]

The previous chapter gave a chronological overview of a transformative period in the governance of Mongolia's mining sector, from the genesis of an open investment regime in the late 1990s to an attempt to reassert stronger state interests within it (2006–2012), and the re-liberalisation process which followed after FDI dramatically fell between 2012 and 2014. The stability of the political and legal environments became the object of reform in 2014 following the collapse in foreign direct investment and the global downturn in commodity prices, in the hopes of regaining investor interest and confidence. The collapse of investment flows and investor confidence in the Mongolian case was not the typical risk-aversion that can characterise investor behaviour during commodity busts, although that was surely present. It was characterised by a sense of lost *confidence* amongst investors that the government would respect the boundary between the state and the market.

Having established the broad trajectory of Mongolian mining governance since the post-socialist transition, this chapter takes a closer look at *how* and *why* particular institutional sources of political and legal instability were targeted for reform after the radical decline of investment interest in the Mongolian mining sector in 2012–2013. I argue that these "reforms" constitute a reordering of the state itself and its relationship with Mongolian citizens. While there may be more, three critical axes of reordering have been identified: (1) the redistribution of decision-making power away from representative institutions of government towards the executive within the central state, (2) the redefinition of the boundaries of self-government for provincial authorities and (3) the marginalisation of conflictual social movements from formal governance processes.

These axes are symptomatic of a process of deep change within the state because they relate to fundamental aspects of the national system of government such as the function of the separation of powers, the practice of self-government within the state and the scope of democratic politics (state–citizen relations). I argue that these transformations of the national state were an attempt to insulate the mining economy from political antagonism (i.e. expropriation by the state, protest, etc.) and should be seen as a form of *de facto* constitutionalism, where – in relation to the mining sector – the principles of the national constitution have evidently been reinterpreted, revised or ignored in practice. Notably, this insulation has been effected through legal means and financial incentives, reinforcing the structural nature of this shift within the state itself. Viewing these apparently disparate processes through the lens of stabilisation – to create ideal conditions for FDI – illuminates the way in which distinctly "global" economic processes affect state institutions despite the formal continuity of its nationally constituted structure. In this chapter, I address the first two "axes of reordering" described earlier within the central state itself and between central and sub-national administrations. Specifically, I will discuss the way Parliament and local governments were targeted in the 2014 reforms in the mining regime. The following chapter will address the third state–society axis, regarding the marginalisation of social movements and the institutionalisation of environmental NGOs to prevent overtly "political" activism.

## Unstable institutions at the centre and the periphery: curtailing political risk within the state for foreign investment

In this section, I address two different sources of "instability" within the state that have been targets for reform since the 2012–2013 crisis of investment capital and confidence. Both Parliament and sub-national (provincial and district) governments were problematised by pro-extractive interests for their "nationalist" and "corrupt" behaviour which had contributed an unacceptable level of political risk to the investment environment. The return to an open and competitive investment regime in 2014 under the State Minerals Policy (2014–2025) was accompanied by the transfer of authority from representative to executive spaces of the state or to new institutions to insulate the investment regime from unpredictable political influences. This trajectory was accompanied by the integration of private mining interests into the machinery of national governance, reflecting a shift within the state itself as well as a "cracking open" of its institutions to global market influence.

## Conflict at the core: parliament, politicians and "resource nationalism"

> The Mongolian government finally realised that they really need foreign investors. Before it was more about nationalistic sentiment, overwhelmingly, but I think they realised they need foreign investors to get this economy rolling... Hopefully politicians with a different view on things will start to get elected... [before it was] pretty nationalistic and let's kick out foreigners and what have you, and that starts to be negative politics. I hope it won't happen again. But in the meantime, the tugrik is suffering, their foreign currency reserve is dwindling, all the prices are going up right now, people are complaining... so there's a lot of pressure on the government to do things right.
>
> CEO, Foreign-Invested Mining Company[3]

The question of how to govern the minerals sector has been at the heart of democratic politics in Mongolia since the post-socialist transition. As the previous chapter indicated, the new democratic government was immediately confronted with a crisis of quickly depleting public capital, ballooning debt and the devaluation of the *tugrik* following the collapse of the Soviet Union. The Gold Programme and the speedy adoption of the 1994 Minerals Law both reflect the severity of the imperative to attract private investment in order to stimulate the failing economy. By the late 1990s, a consensus that minerals would be the national economic base had emerged, although this general consensus was characterised by an ongoing conflict about the precise limits of the regulatory role of the state. Following the post-socialist transition, the issue of the role of the state in economic regulation in general had been a major source of contention between the former socialist vanguard and the pro-market reformers (Rossabi, 2005). This conflict was intensified through the 1990s as the stakes of the mining industry, relative to the national economy, became much higher. Consequently, competing claims about which party would maximise national benefit from the mining industry became central to national parliamentary election platforms, especially following the discovery of Oyu Tolgoi.

The authoritarian nature of the state during the socialist period had given the Great Khural more symbolic than actual power, as its representative role was fundamentally compromised by the absence of free elections or institutional accountability. The socialist era of rule can be characterised as a marriage of executive and judicial power (Butler and Nathanson, 1982), a fairly straightforward expression of 'socialist legality' dominated by the institution of the Soviet procuracy (Ginsburg, 1994: 81). Following the Soviet example (Butler and Nathanson, 1982: 83), the MPR established a State Procuracy in 1930 to supervise 'the observance of legality' (ibid.) 'over all ministries, organisations and citizens' (Ginsburg, 1994: 81). As well as 'general supervision' (ibid.), the Procuracy also exercised the power to prosecute, 'maintaining a close link with Party policies' (Butler and Nathanson, 1982: 83).

Democratisation and the constitutional separation of powers in 1992 consequently transformed the Great Khural into an active political institution in its own right (rather than being simply a handmaid of the MPRP), with representative legitimacy and law-making authority. In the democratic constitution, legislation can be proposed by both the executive and legislative arms of government, but representative power, vis-à-vis Parliament, controls the drafting and legislating procedure. Consequently, the Great Khural has become 'the highest organ of state power' (1992 Constitution, Article 20) in the democratic era. The right of single members of Parliament (MPs) to initiate legislation combined with low quorum rules, where as few as twenty MPs out of the seventy-six can pass legislation (Enkhbaatar et al., 2015: 23), has meant that law reform has historically played a key role in national politics.

As we will see in this chapter, one of the key reordering effects of Mongolia's foreign investment dependence since the FDI crisis has been the systematic attempt to insulate the mining regime from "political" forces of law reform. The speed with which legislation can be passed, amended and influenced by individual politicians has been widely portrayed as a major barrier to investment in the mining sector. Parliament has been the main source of risk for investors at the national level; as the legislative organ of the state, it has the most power to directly affect the national political and legal environments. With the hasty introduction of an entirely new piece of minerals legislation in 2006, the politicised negotiation of the Oyu Tolgoi Investment Agreement and, most significantly, the nationalist barriers to investment under the Strategic Entities Foreign Investment Law (SEFIL) of 2012, Parliament quickly gained the status of an unpredictable 'pariah' (Manthorpe, 2013) in the international media.

The close attention paid by investors to the 2012 Parliamentary elections indicated the anxiety felt by the state's new economic constituency about the membership of Parliament. According to an article in Resource Investing News, for example, 'uncertainty concerning just how far politicians are willing to move toward resource nationalism in an effort to win votes is understandably raising Mongolia's political risk factor in the eyes of resource investors' (Pistilli,

2012). Political parties have since been regularly criticised by international investment experts on emerging markets for their 'anti-FDI platforms' (Kohli, 2016), emphasising "domestic politics" as the major "obstruction" for investors rather than 'commodity or China risk' (Weafer, 2016). Resource nationalism has been consistently identified as one of the top five risks facing the major mining investors globally since 2011 in the Ernst and Young "Business Risks Facing Mining and Metals" reports (Ernst and Young, 2011–2016). As Dierkes (2013) commented, 'many non-Mongolians have focused on "resource nationalism" to explain the new laws... generally equated with some evil movement aimed at the nationalisation of resource assets.' The actions of the Mongolian Parliament thus fed into a wider narrative of resource nationalism, shifting the country from its pre-2006 image as the 'darling of international risk-takers' (Manthorpe, 2013) to that of either ineptitude or deviancy from the expectations on states to "play fair" in the market.

Author interviews with foreign and Mongolian investors, pro-mining lobbyists and Ministry of Mining officials in October/November 2015 reinforced the negative image of Parliament. The President of the National Mining Association reflected on the controversy surrounding the Law Protecting Headlands, Water Basins and Forests, that it was MPs and armed activist groups that had been "pushing" the government to implement the law even though 'it cannot be implemented' because the state lacks the means to adequately compensate companies for the revoked licences.[4] Similarly, the President of the Mongolian Investors' Association ultimately blamed MPs for 'wanting to get some name for themselves' and secure electoral votes as the real force behind the environmental legislation:

> Instead of listening to the businesses who were the taxpayers, they started listening to the activists more.[5]

In relation to the State Minerals Policy 2014–2025, a senior official in the Ministry of Mining expressed concern that the strength of Parliament did not bode well for the stability of the policy, given that 'they have a right' not only to propose legislation but also draft it, the implication being that the final product might be quite different from the original proposal.[6] A senior representative from Oyu Tolgoi similarly reflected that:

> We hope it will be stable, but nobody knows... Mongolia has a permanently working Parliament which means they could change any law within four years. The last couple of years made clear that if we will not really support business to be run in a proper market situation, it will badly influence the whole economy.[7]

He concluded that 'for things to move properly and run in commercial ways,' it would necessitate 'less political involvement' (ibid.).

### Conflict at the periphery: local governments, rent-seeking and corruption

Since democratisation in the early 1990s, local governments have become important institutional loci for democratic politics in Mongolia.[8] Previously, under the Soviet-inspired socialist regime, all local authorities were appointed directly from the central government at the provincial (*aimag*), district (*soum*) and sub-district (*bagh*) levels. As discussed in the third chapter, the governance of the pastoral economy was central to socialist economic development requiring a relatively high level of coordination and oversight. The 1992 Constitution ameliorated the system of direct appointment, by establishing a direct election process for local parliaments, which, in turn, nominate a governor. Each level of government comprises a governor's office and a local parliament (*khural*). While representatives in the local *khural* are directly elected, governors gain their positions through nomination by the *khurals* and then approval by the governor at the higher level of government. Thus, the Prime Minister approves provincial (*aimag*) governors, provincial governors approve district (*soum*) governors and district governors approve sub-district (*bagh*) governors. This has been generally considered to be a formalistic process of approval and typically functions as a form of indirect appointment, as the nominee put forward by the elected representatives is usually approved. There have been cases where the governor of a higher order has rejected the nominee and the parliament refuses to nominate a new candidate, although this is rare. In the context of the democratic state, the relationship between the local governments and the central state has consequently been quite ambiguous, because the 1992 Constitution balances both principles of 'self-governance and state management' (Lkhagvadorj, 2010: 79) in sub-national administration. This ambiguity often creates conflict between different levels of government about where the line gets drawn between their authority.

If self-interested nationalism has been the overarching characterisation of central Mongolian politicians and political institutions by pro-FDI reformers, the narrative of local governments in relation to mining has been one of corruption. As the previous chapter outlined, the role of local governments within the mining governance regime shifted considerably over its twenty-year development (1994–2014). Originally in the 1997 Minerals Law, there was a general legal obligation on companies to "cooperate" with local authorities in relation to existing local development priorities. However, the 1997 'consult and coordinate' framework gave local governments considerable room to negotiate the contributions of mining companies to local development without oversight from the central government. The ambiguity of the law and the informality of the arrangements gave governors significant political leverage. This leverage became a major "governance gap" to be addressed in the 2014 reforms to the mining regime. It created space for local governments to express their dissatisfaction with, or make demands upon, mining companies in ways that conflicted with the central state's interests in opening up provincial territories for extraction. The tension between central and local governments in relation to the mining sector was fuelled by two intertwined issues, relating to a lack of sub-national input in the licencing process and a lack of direct local benefits from mining revenue.

Since 1997, in relation to the sense of exclusion from decision-making, there was a mismatch between the centralised licencing process and the "decentralised" approach to addressing the environmental and social impacts of mining. While local governments had significant freedom to negotiate with mining companies without central oversight, the licencing process was deeply centralised. The 1997 Minerals Law established a centralised regulatory regime for the mining sector that concentrated decision-making power in the executive spaces of the central state, particularly the Mineral Resources Authority of Mongolia (MRAM). The 1997 Minerals Law, designed to "regulate relations" in the mining sector, only recognised one primary right local administrative bodies: 'to permit the use of licensed areas for the purposes specified in the licenses, except where exploration or mining is prohibited or restricted by applicable legislation' (Article 6.4.2). Under this law, MRAM was – and still is – expected to receive local government approval in order to issue mining licences. However, an officer at MRAM explained that, formerly, most local governments would "disagree" with the proposed licences,[9] although this allegedly did not always prevent their issuance in practice. A senior policy-maker at the Ministry of Mining put it this way:

> The main problem is the local governor. According to the Mineral Law, the first application – mineral exploration applications – we send to the local government to ask permission. In most cases they said no, no, no. So then how can mineral exploration licenses be issued? If we don't consider their [input], then they complain. So we make an assumption and say 'okay, we will issue the license.' The next day, the mining companies or exploration companies arrive on the land and they start drilling. So again, conflict. Local governors would say, 'We didn't give any permission. We don't want drilling.' This is the main problem... the process starts from the very top. The government has announced that these areas (are available for drilling) but at the bottom level [local government] there is conflict against this.[10]

Secondly, the fiscal structure governing mining revenues was highly centralised in the first decade of the mining boom. Taxes, mining licence fees and royalties were collected centrally and redistributed through the national budget on the basis of Parliamentary decision, advised by the Ministry of Finance (Lhakgvadorj, 2012: 6). This centralised system excluded local governments from both the 'budget planning and approving process' (ibid.).

By the early 2000s, over 40% of Mongolian territory was covered by mining licences (Suzuki, 2013). As noted in the previous chapter, widespread environmental degradation and social dislocation catalysed the formation of the first rural social movements in the early 2000s which contested the preferential access to land and water given to mining companies through MRAM's liberal licencing regime, which had led to the drying and pollution of rivers, a boom in artisanal mining and the subordination of herders' customary use rights to centrally administered mining licences. These social movements were particularly associated with *soum* and *bagh* governors and chairs of local parliaments; their early success and political momentum have been linked to this capacity to forge strong networks with local authorities at all levels of sub-national administration. Many local governments were sympathetic to the groundswell of anti-mining sentiment amongst rural citizens, because they were also largely excluded from central processes of decision-making and accumulation, with mining revenues being redistributed through the central budget.

Without wishing to glorify local governments or deny the presence of personal interests, local authorities at both the provincial and district levels did respond to public concerns in a variety of formal and informal ways. In Mongolian land law, local authorities have the right to set aside land for 'special use' and to grant 'certificates of possession' to customary land users (i.e. herders) (Endicott, 2012: 97). These provisions were used strategically by authorities across the country as a form of indirect intervention to reserve land from mining and to protect herders' land entitlements in the absence of justiciable rights. More informally, governors were widely known to lobby mining companies to contribute to rural projects (i.e. building infrastructure, schools, financing social events) in return for approving various water and land permits for which local authorities' approval is necessary. There have also been instances, particularly in the South Gobi, where local parliaments have banned access to groundwater for mining companies even when they formally have no legal authority to do so. While these decisions were ultimately nullified, they delayed projects in the short term and were a major source of anxiety and frustration for mining companies.

The resistant activities of local governments were typically framed by central policy-makers and mining companies alike as "corruption," based on the personal interests of local authorities trying to squeeze benefits out of mining projects in their regions and manipulate the legal provisions for local agreements. One foreign CEO of a medium-scale mining company stated that 'obviously community relations are about risk management':

> If they see a big mine with hundreds of trucks, obviously generating big revenue, they will say 'where's my piece, where's my cut?' They're not going to be satisfied with government royalty and tax.[11]

The President of the Association of Investors in Mongolian Mining, also the CEO of a Mongolian mining company, similarly framed local governments as putting onerous and superficial demands upon them. He stated that, 'local government or local people want many different things,' characterising local governments' demands as purely self-seeking: 'They want to travel to London... [They say] I'm governor of this village, right, so my wife needs the mink coat, so you bring me the mink coat.'[12] The lack of clarity about which level of government companies should liaise with (i.e. provincial or district) was described as confusing and exhausting for the companies, and as a loophole in the governance regime that facilitated rent-seeking. Similarly, environmental legislation passed in 2009[13] – the "Law with a Long Name" – was perceived by mining companies as creating uncertainty in the legal environment because it gave discretionary privileges to local governments to determine environmental boundaries. The purported vagueness of the legislation and the lack of detailed regulation allegedly created too much room for subjective judgement, particularly by sub-national governors who had the power to determine "upper limits" to mining near rivers, above and beyond the 200-metre boundary established in the law (U.S. Department of State, 2011: 24). This legislation was the subject of revisions by the government following the crisis of foreign investment, as part of the broader effort by policy-makers to increase regulatory certainty for mining companies and to increase gold production, which had dropped significantly following the enforcement of the legislation in 2011 (Fehrbach, 2013).

Senior officials from the Ministry of Mining reinforced and legitimised the negative perspectives about local government held by mining companies. The Director of the Department for Strategic Policy and Planning acknowledged openly that 'there have been cases where local governments demanded too much from mining companies,' describing the needs of rural citizens and authorities as "infinite."[14] These comments were in the context of discussing central state strategies to 'make fences, limitations for local government.'[15] This paradigm of local governments as corrupt and self-interested also dominated policy discussions about company contributions to local development. At a World Bank and Ministry of Mining co-sponsored workshop discussing the draft model of Local Development Agreements (LDAs) in November 2014, for example, local governments and citizens' *khurals* were accused by senior policy-makers of short-term thinking, rent-seeking and misuse of Local Development Funds (LDFs), over-charging mining companies for land, lack of legal knowledge and corruption, and very poor capacity for decision-making, thus requiring the oversight of the central government.[16]

However, the corruption narrative ignores the ways that local governments were actively responding to the concerns of local citizens about foreign access to mineral resources, displacement from customary land and environmental degradation caused by mining. The alleged cases of caricatured corruption (i.e. demanding flights and mink coats) ignore the more substantive and systematic responses that local governments made to limit extraction in their regions in response to pastoral land-use requirements and environmental concerns, or by requiring companies to invest in local infrastructure (i.e. hospitals, roads and schools).

## Stabilisation mechanisms: blurring public–private boundaries and strengthening executive authority in the mining regime

As institutions perceived to have generated instability for mining investment, both Parliament and local governments were targeted for reform under the State Minerals Policy 2014–2025. The primary input into the drafting of the Policy was from the Ministry of Mining, committed to revitalising investment in the minerals sector.[17] While the stabilisation strategy was distinct for each institution in the sense that unique mechanisms were introduced to address specific issues, the Policy's unifying logic hinged on the incorporation of resistant institutions into the extractive order through legal mechanisms and financial incentives. This incorporative intent was manifested by the introduction of private mining interests into the governance regime at both the central and sub-national levels of government (albeit in different ways) and the empowerment of the executive at the expense of representative institutions at each level of government.

### Blurring the public–private divide at the central and sub-national scales

Making concerted and formalised efforts to consult stakeholders and rebuild relationships with investors was a key priority for the Ministry of Mining during the 2014 period of law and policy reform. As the Director-General of the Strategic Policy and Planning Department put it:

> I'd especially like to note that during the legal reform at this time, we were paying special attention to having discussions with our key stakeholders because, to be honest, we have a bad history of changing laws frequently and suddenly... Because the market conditions suddenly changed and the prices went down, we had no choice but to support industry and businesses.[18]

These efforts appear to have been well-received by representatives from the mining community. The President of the Mongolian National Mining Association corroborated the view of the Director-General, stating that 'stakeholder consultation' was a key aspect of the new state policy.[19]

The intention to restore a confident and collaborative working relationship between the government and investors had both an international and a domestic aspect. Internationally, it involved Mongolia being 'very active in terms of foreign relations with our neighbouring countries and other economic partners, according to the Director-General of Strategic Policy and Planning.'[20] In particular, with China, Mongolia has sought 'a very intense and close relationship'[21] since 2014, with currency swaps and the signing of long-term purchase agreements for mineral commodities (i.e. coal). In early 2015, Mongolia signed an Economic Partnership Agreement with Japan and by the end of the year was prepared to sign a Foreign Investment Protection Agreement with Canada. The Director described 'competitive proposals' for financing projects from Germany, Japan and the UK, as well as monthly meetings with the UK and Australian embassies 'exchanging information and discussing about the ways in which we can proceed and cooperate.'[22]

Even more remarkable, however, was the invitation to private stakeholders to participate in mining policy-making at the national level. In terms of stabilising the investment environment, the State Policy provided a policy and legal basis for establishing a multi-stakeholder Minerals Policy Council (MPC) under the supervision of the Ministry of Mining. A 'balanced representation' of government officials, investors, professional associations and civil society organisations was supposed to be included on the MPC. According to a senior official in the Ministry of Mining:

> The Minister of Mining is head of the Mineral Policy Council. One third is government officials related to mineral policy (Ministry of Mining, MRAM, Ministry of Environment, Ministry of Finance), one third is company representatives, big and small; and academicians, researchers, civil society.[23]

The Director of the Mongolian National Mining Association was given the role of Vice Chairman, as the private sector counterpart to the Minister of Mining. The rationale of the council was to professionalise decision-making in the mining sector: 'the main purpose of this Mineral Policy Council is to discuss and assess new legal reform proposals as a professional body' and crucially to prevent legal reform: 'if there is no support from this policy council, no legal reforms can be made in the mineral sector.'[24] When asked what principles will be used to evaluate whether support should be given for legal reform, the Director-General explained that:

> They must act in a professional manner, without politicising issues... The decisions that are made by them must be directed to support industry, because in Mongolia... Any Parliament member can propose, initiate legal reform. But before discussion at Parliament, that initiation must go through this Mineral Policy [Council] and if that proposal gets approval then Parliament will discuss. Without the Mineral Policy [Council's] revision and approval, [nothing] can go to Parliament.[25]

A senior policy-maker, who had played a central role in the drafting of the State Minerals Policy, similarly described the role of the MPC as preventing "election populism":

> We created a special council – policy council – consisting of different stakeholders... The policy council should review any suggested laws. So if they say no, it will be very hard [to get them passed]. In that way, we want to neutralise some election effects.[26]

The MPC thus provides a legislated space for investor representation in government decision-making, in addition to creating a systemic pathway for investors to lobby the government through the Ministry of Mining by including private stakeholders on the council. Prior to the 2014 commitment to the 'consultation of stakeholders,' the state's engagement with the private sector had been ad-hoc and dependent upon the initiator of the law.[27]

In the sub-national context, a similar story unfolded. The new State Policy introduced LDAs within the broader goal of 'supporting local development and protecting local community interests' (Article 3.5). While the phrasing of the article goal suggests that the emphasis was on the "community," LDAs were clearly intended by central policy-makers to function as another institutional mechanism to create a predictable investment environment. A senior policy-maker in the Ministry of Mining stated in an interview that the

> government want[s] to create and approve a long-term model… so the government can say [to local governors] "you [only] have the right to request certain things within a certain framework."[28]

This approach was publicly affirmed at a national policy workshop on LDAs sponsored by the Ministry of Mining, MRAM and the World Bank in November 2014, which the author observed. The workshop was attended by approximately one hundred representatives from major mining companies such as Rio Tinto and Anglo-American, local governments from around the country, the newly formed Anti-Corruption Agency, the Ministry of Mining, MRAM, Hogan Lovells and a few private social consultancy organisations. The then Director of the Department of Strategic Policy and Planning at the Ministry of Mining stated in his introductory presentation that, 'our country has become a mining country,' adding that 'without mining, many countries couldn't have developed' referring to Japan, Russia, Germany and England as examples. He emphasised that the Mongolian government needed to expand and enhance the scope of national geological surveying, and that the public and private sectors needed to work together more because the private sector was apparently bearing the majority of risk for mining projects. In his view, the central government needed to oversee local governments' engagement with corporate stakeholders as local governors and governments occasionally refused geological surveys to be carried out in their jurisdictions and politicised the oversight of the central government to gain election favour with their constituencies. As the then Deputy Minister of Mining, E. Oyun, stated in an interview with Worldfolio (2014):

> There is a problem of miscommunication with local people, from the side of the government and from the side of the private industries… We want more involvement of local governments and we want them to use the mining revenues to benefit their local communities… This is a new approach that will help local people to see and feel the benefits of the mining industry… It is also good for miners, because [there] will be no anti-mining activities.

Despite being framed in terms of community benefits, these private and public comments from senior policy-makers show how LDAs have been designed to effectively discipline local administrations by limiting the scope of their demands within a pro-extractive, pro-FDI framework authorised by the Ministry of Mining. Sub-national administrations at the provincial, district and sub-district levels have been a source of frustration to both mining companies and the pro-extractive agenda advocated by the Ministry of Mining since its formation in 2012 under the Democratic Party-led coalition government. Rural citizens' frustration with the environmental impact of mining and a growing sense of discontent with the centralised distribution of mineral rents established in the 2006 Law had created a situation in which local administrations were often a primary opponent of mining as discussed earlier.[29] As the President of the Mongolian Investors Association put it[30]:

> All of a sudden local people started opposing mining projects in their territory because... they don't benefit from mining. They [had] no benefits, no tax... everything [went] to the central government.

While *aimag* and *soum* governments' approval has been formally required for the approval of mining licences by MRAM, it was their informal power to make financial demands on mining companies that led to significant exasperation on the part of corporate managers and investors. Thus, the investor–local government relationship had become a site of instability and political risk for investors, and tension between the central government and its sub-national administrations. LDAs as construed within the State Minerals Policy and formalised in the amended minerals law (2014) were intended to limit and manage public expectations of mining companies' contribution to local development projects by creating a centralised template for these local contracts.

While a general legal obligation on companies to "cooperate" with local authorities in relation to local development priorities has existed since 1997, the nature of that obligation has shifted from an ad-hoc 'consult and coordinate' model (Article 33.1/1997 Minerals Law), to multiple agreements on specific issues (Article 42.1/2006 Minerals Law) to a single agreement (Amended Article 42.1/2014 Minerals Law). The 1997 'consult and coordinate' model placed local governments at the centre of local development, with extensive leeway to negotiate without oversight from the central government. The 2006 amendment limited the scope of local governments' demands on mining companies to a narrower range of "specific issues," although there was still space for a mining-impacted region to require agreements at different levels of local government depending on the scale of the project. The 2014 amendment, however, limits the scope of local governments' leverage over the social contribution of mining companies by requiring a *single* agreement. It mandates companies to sign a single agreement with local authorities only on 'matters of environmental protection, infrastructure and job creation, *voluntarily* supporting local community development' (Article 42.1, emphasis added), legally placing the corporate part-ner to the agreement in the stronger bargaining position.

The Ministry of Mining, in conjunction with the World Bank, initiated the development of a template for LDAs in 2014, along with model investment agreements, as the negotiation of both of these types of agreements has been fraught by conflict and generative of the kind of political instability so unat-tractive to investors. These models provide authorities and companies with clear formulae for contract negotiation.[31] The template of the Model Community Development Agreement[32] establishes firm parameters for the terms and man-ner of negotiation between local authorities and mining companies, requiring a separate public–private institution to govern the agreement – the "Relationship Committee" – which exists outside the municipal structure of local administra-tions. The Relationship Committee is supposed to be comprising an executive representative of local government (the Governor) and representation from the mining company, with civil associations invited as observers to the agreement (ibid.). Structurally, it is a hybridised agreement, as opposed to a clear public–private arrangement, because it incorporates the public and private sectors into a structure that is decidedly public in its ramifications and yet private in process, with agreement-specific financial and dispute resolution mechanisms. Thus, de-spite their "community" rhetoric and its "public" connotations, LDAs model private contracts that tightly link the executive arm of local governments with that of the mining company.

Within the framework of the agreement, LDA-specific financial and dispute resolution mechanisms are meant to be developed on a case-by-case base, with the basic guidance being that both are "independent." This means that they are ef-fectively insulated from public legal and political power. In financial terms, LDAs are like private development funds, accessible only through the LDA governance structure. While the template allows for different forms of legal review (independ-ent mediation, private arbitration, court settlements), private investors are unlikely to opt for the national court system given the choice. The LDA template model is very long and detailed, resembling a complex contract. In light of their structure and the intentions behind their creation in the Ministry of Mining, LDAs are ev-idently designed to protect company interests and facilitate extraction, rather than encourage a meaningful political process about mining in rural areas.

In terms of the central state's interest in LDAs, the rationale was clear. The Director-General of Strategic Policy and Planning at the Ministry of Mining described the rationale for LDAs in the following terms:

> There were some cases where local governments demanded too much from companies. So, the Cabinet decided that we're going to approve the model contracts of those rural developments, community developments... And [through] that example agreement we are going to make fences, limitations for local governments... Because the previous one was not officially ap-proved by anyone, local governments could follow it, they could not follow.

So the law last year we intentionally included regulation that the model contracts will be approved by Cabinet, local governments should follow that.[33]

The Director-General later emphasised at the National Corporate Social Responsibility (CSR) Forum in Ulaanbaatar that as the law develops in the mining sector, so do the types of contracts available, portraying LDAs as a progressive legal development.[34] In his view, LDAs were part of a legal framework to prevent change in mining policy, by creating clear timelines for decision-making and limited options for local governments and citizens. In an interview with the previous Director, who had played an important role in initiating the model agreement in 2014, he stated that their purpose was to create clarity around the terms and conditions of "social investments" from mining companies:

> It's very hard to distinguish [between] the social license to operate or [if] it's bribery. So we want to make it official. There should be a draft or model agreement, and they can just change the names, locations, maybe size of money or something like this.[35]

This statement was in the context of a discussion about mining companies' frustration with local governments, the emphasis being on the corrupt demands of provincial and district authorities. In a very real sense, LDAs are engaged in political 'boundary work' (Li, 2007: 214), as institutional forms that serve 'the careful management of unruly or disruptive social forces, and the containment of political challenge' (ibid.).

The introduction of LDAs dovetailed with recent changes to the revenue redistribution structure. The 2011 Integrated Budget Law introduced the possibility of a more decentralised model of financial redistribution from the state budget to local administrations to take account of the growing sense of discontent around the terms of sub-national 'revenue sovereignty' in the context of 'rapid economic growth' (ibid.: 26), driven largely by the mining sector in rural areas. Article 59.4 of the 2011 Integrated Budget Law consequently stipulated that LDFs in mining regions would be allocated up to 10% more of the mineral royalties from the central General LDF than non-mining regions (ibid.: 18). The 2011 Budget Law, however, still maintained a significant degree of central control over the redistribution of mining licence fees and royalties. In response to the fact that 'the local government and local citizens don't like to support mining or geological activities',[36] a further incentive of direct revenue sharing of royalties and mining licence fees was introduced in the 2014–2015 mineral sector reform. As of January 2016, 50% of mining licence fees was allocated to *aimag* branches of local government in mining regions (with 25% going to *soum* branches). Formerly, only 5% of mining royalties would be redistributed to local governments through the LDF. While that 5% distributed through the LDF is maintained, additionally provincial governments in mining regions can expect to receive 20% of royalties and district governments to receive 10% through direct transfer.

In conjunction with the introduction of LDAs, the financial incentives for local governments to approve mining licences and work closely with mining companies increased monumentally. Both LDAs and direct revenue sharing mechanisms were portrayed by central state proponents (i.e. Ministry of Mining and MRAM) as positive shifts towards decentralised and participatory governance, where local governments have a greater sense of administrative control around both their budget and local spending priorities. However, as the interviews indicated, these "decentralised" legal mechanisms have been strategically deployed by pro-extractive institutions in the central state to curtail resistance to mining and get local governments "on board" with the national extractive development strategy. Without evidence of "political" coercion, the central government has effectively sought to eliminate cause for resistance by creating incentives for local elites (particularly governors) to support mining companies. This perspective was reinforced by the author's interviews with personnel from local administrations. According to the Director of the Development Policy Department of a mining-intensive *aimag* in northern Mongolia, province, 80% of the *aimag's* income was derived from taxes from the mining sector.[37] A *soum* governor from an *aimag* in Western Mongolia further emphasised the pressure and difficulty he was under to balance local citizens' interests with those of miners, because of the link between supporting mining and receiving development funding from the central government.[38]

### Deepening executive power within central and sub-national administrations

Alongside the strategic insertion of private interests into national and sub-national mining governance institutions, decision-making authority has also been relocated and reinforced in the executive spaces of the state since the 2012–2013 "crisis" in FDI. At the sub-national level, following on from the previous discussion, LDAs have the effect of strengthening executive power, as well as introducing private extractive interests into the fabric of local development planning and policy. Governors have been designated as the "representative" signing party on behalf of local communities, even though they are the least representative office in democratic terms. The incorporation of the executive arm of local governments into the LDA to the exclusion of other bodies like local parliaments insulates mining companies from more "demanding" parties; the structure of the agreements creates a strong incentive for governors to support the agreement. In response to the question, "Is it better to work with the Governor or the local Parliament Chairman in relation to LDAs?" the CEO of a private Mongolian mining company responded:

> The Governor. It's one person. The Chairman, with his cabinet, there are ten people, twelve people... but with just one governor, it's one person, so what the hell, right?[39]

LDAs also structurally encourage vertical stability for mining projects by incorporating governors as the co-signatory, because the appointment of governors is the prerogative of the governor of the higher level. A provincial governor is unlikely to approve a district governor who would challenge the terms of the LDA that they signed, which would interrupt the flow of funding into the local budget. In this way, LDAs are likely to shift the constitutional balance towards state-management at the expense of self-government by incentivising the approval of pro-mining governors in sub-national administrations.

The centralising effect of LDAs is belied by their "decentralising" purpose as articulated in national policy, to provide a stronger institutional mechanism for local community engagement and direct distribution of social investment by companies. The central state appears to be absent from direct oversight of the process of LDA negotiation, apart from setting out a standardised template in accordance with the minerals legislation. However, the power of the central government is expressed through the force of law (i.e. the legislated, compulsory nature of LDAs) and the financial incentives that they offer to the impoverished coffers of local administrations. LDAs do open up space for local administration–company negotiation of direct community benefits, but within a tightened space of self-government. For example, while MRAM still requires local authorities' approval before issuing a mining licence, the basis for a legitimate refusal has been restricted. As the Director of Strategic Policy and Planning at the Ministry of Mining explained:

> Before issuing a license, MRAM sends a letter to the local government to hear their opinion and local governments can agree or they can disagree. But in the case of disagreeing, they must provide legitimate foundations. Reasoning. ... If they have any plans to protect an area for local protection, they must make a decision at the start not afterwards.[40]

The raised bar of legitimacy for refusing of mining licences directly corresponds with the contentious history of local administrations strategically setting aside land for 'special needs' to legally block mining projects in their territories since the early 2000s (Endicott, 2012). This new standard operates in conjunction with the predetermination of land for extractive development by the Ministry of Mining.[41] While the land designated for extractive development was not supposed to 'overlap with any environmental, cultural, [or] historical things that need to be protected,'[42] the territory available for mining and exploration activities doubled in early 2015 to cover just over a fifth of Mongolia's territory (Reuters, 2015).

At the national level, the institutional infrastructure supporting mining within the central government expanded significantly after the investment crisis, strengthening and reinforcing a pro-extractive, executive power bloc within the apparatus of the state. Initially, in 1997, the MRAM was established as an 'autonomous lead agency... to facilitate the implementation of the new minerals law' (World Bank, 2006: 3). MRAM was given a large significant amount

of implementation power and discretionary oversight of the minerals industry, particularly in light of MRAM's authority to assign 'extensive exploration
rights' (ibid.) through its Cadastre Division. The general structure of MRAM
has remained fairly constant since 1997, but the broader institutional context in
which it is located has shifted markedly.

Before 2008, MRAM operated with a substantial degree of autonomy as a
'quasi-independent agency, the acts of which did not require ministerial approval'
(International Business Publications, 2013: 129). However, in 2008, MRAM
was institutionally relocated under the 'direct authority of the Ministry of Mineral Resources and Energy' (ibid.), now the Ministry of Mining. In the context
of the 2006 amendments to the Minerals Law, this restructuring was seen as
contributing a certain level of instability for investors' rights, as MRAM was
under the discretionary oversight of a central government ministry and some of
its prerogatives regarding licencing procedures for 'strategic deposits' had been
transferred to the ministry (ibid.). In the context of the 2014 amendments to the
Minerals Law, MRAM's prerogatives have largely been returned to the original
1997 model, but MRAM has remained under the supervision of the Ministry
of Mining.

The new consensus on promoting the role of the private sector in the mining
sector means that the significant implementation and administrative powers of
MRAM are now concentrated within a very pro-FDI government ministry. Not
only is MRAM the formal source of economic and environmental information
about the mining industry in Mongolia, but MRAM's Cadastre Division has the
sole power to (a) 'receive, register and make decisions with respect to applications
for licenses,' (b) 'collect service and license fees,' (c) 'resolve boundary disputes
between license-holders' and, critically, (d) 'provide the public with access to the
processes of issuing and reissuing licenses...' (MRAM, 2017). While an MRAM
official emphasised in an interview that it is simply an 'implementation agency,'[43]
it has sole decision-making authority regarding licencing, a monopoly on information about the mining sector, and responsibility for the overall economic sustainability of the mining sector, according to the Head of the Mining Division
of MRAM.[44] The empowerment of MRAM within the Ministry of Mining
further centralises decision-making power about the mining sector within a
heavily bureaucratic institutional framework.

This is particularly significant in light of the way that the Ministry of Mining
has gained a position of institutional prominence in relation to the executive
"core" of state institutions. The Ministry of Mining is a line ministry of the
Ministry of Finance, which is one of four core executive ministries, along with
the Ministry of Justice, the Ministry for Environment and Green Development,
and the Ministry of Foreign Affairs. As a product of the deepening relationship
between the Ministry of Mining and the Ministry of Finance, the Ministry of
Mining has also developed a very close relationship with the Central Bank by
extension. This pro-extractive inter-ministerial formation linking the Ministry
of Mining with the Ministry of Finance and the Central Bank helps to explain

the new dominance of economic pragmatism in mining policy. As the Director-General of Strategic Policy and Planning at the Ministry of Mining put it:

> The Minister of Mining is now solely responsible for the development of minerals sector, and we have two agencies underneath of us – the Mineral Resources Authority of Mongolia (MRAM) and Petroleum Authority of Mongolia (PAM). Mongolian legislation requires involvement of Parliament at some levels, but we have a close relationship, basically, with Parliament because Parliament approved the State Policy on Minerals Sector. They were very cooperative in making those legal reforms last year [2014]. Of course, Parliament is a political institution and there are many ongoing debates, but generally we have basic consensus. We work very closed with the Ministry of Finance and especially with the Fiscal Revenue Division, our key counterpart. Previously, the two ministries didn't have unified database, and numbers differed a lot – projections, forecasts, everything differed. Now we have regular meetings with them, and the numbers are now the same.[45]

Furthermore, the elevation of the Invest Mongolia Agency from its former position in the Ministry of Economic Development (now dissolved) to being supervised directly by the Prime Minister's office as of 2014 exemplifies the elevation of the national policy priority to encourage and protect investment through institutional reorganisation.

The close relationship between the financial, investment and extractive ministries has been known to generate conflict with the competing goals of other ministries, such as the Ministry for Environment and Green Development. However, while the purposes of the ministries differ – 'we want to dig, they want to protect'[46] – a sense of pragmatism and the necessity of cooperation following the economic crisis of 2013 helped to stabilise underlying conflicts. This was evidenced in the revisions made to the Law on the Prohibition of Mineral Exploration and Mining Operations at Headwaters of Rivers, Protected Zones of Water Reservoirs and Forested Areas, which had led to the cancellation of licences for over 200 mining projects in 2011 (see Chapter 4, section "2009–2013: Optimism and Entanglement"). This law, pejoratively referred to as "Law with a Long Name," was widely perceived by mining companies and government officials as a "half-baked" law. The lack of clear regulations for the implementation of the law appeared to give local governments and the Ministry of Environment and Green Development (through a working group) too much discretion in the determination of environmental boundaries, according to multiple sources. Consequently, since 2014, the Ministry of Mining worked closely with the Ministry of Environment and Green Development to reduce "discrepancies" in decision-making and to think more realistically about 'compensation and those types of financial issues.'[47]

An important aspect of the pro-extractive consensus has been the effort to consolidate and centralise national geological information under the auspices of the

Ministry of Mining and MRAM through the establishment of a National Geological Survey and designated Office, explicitly mandated by the 2014 amendments to the Minerals Law. In the early 1990s, the socialist-era geological offices and laboratories were privatised along with many other SOEs. Consequently, the state lost a significant degree of control over national geological information. The discovery of Oyu Tolgoi, for example, was based on minerals mapping from the 1980s accessed by BHP Billiton in the early 1990s following the post-socialist privatisation process. National geological information continues to be predominantly based upon socialist-era surveys from the 1970s and 1980s, conducted largely through joint-ventures with Moscow. In the late 1990s and early 2000s, private companies acquired new geological data through exploration activities, which the government has the right to receive upon request.[48] Consequently, the current scope of national geological data is an assortment of rudimentary surveying from the socialist era and exploratory mapping of specific areas by private companies.

Since 2014, consolidating and improving the quality of available geological information has been considered a top policy priority by the Ministry of Mining. In 2014, the Director of the Strategic Policy and Planning Department argued that more consistency was needed, as many mining companies had complained that local governments gave them conflicting geological information.[49] This appears to be partly motivated by a desire to strengthen state control of the mining sector but also to attract investment, indicating mutual interests between the public and the private sectors in the pursuit of FDI-led extractive development. As one senior policy-maker at the Ministry of Mining put it:

> In order to develop or attract foreign or large investments in the mining sector, one of the important things is to manage the exploration and regional geology. The mining companies are coming into the country... based on the information, they have a decision whether to make investment, to do the activity. So one of the most important [items of] information is geological baseline information, [to indicate] the potential of the country where you want to invest... Another thing is, of course, the legal framework: how stable, or how easy to get into. The Mongolian government has decided that attracting foreign investment is important, so therefore we need to promote our potential, our advantages. Therefore, the government has started to issue new exploration licenses [because] the amendment to the Minerals Law (2014) allows us to grant new exploration licenses.[50]

As of 2015, senior policy-makers in the Ministry of Mining favoured a 100% state-owned National Geological Office where the results from the most recent regional survey can be processed, particularly those which have been 'accumulated in different formats and different times' to be 'delivered to different stakeholders.'[51] Private stakeholders, however, apparently favoured a public–private partnership model for the National Geological Office, similar to the Construction Office, to prevent total state control of strategic geological data.[52]

## Conclusion

Following the 2014 reforms, a demonstrable shift occurred within the apparatus of the Mongolian state in relation to the mining sector which insulates investment interests from "political risk" at both the local and central levels of government, and simultaneously attempts to preserve the reputation of the state to encourage further FDI. At both the central and local levels, private actors and direct representation of their interests were inserted within the structure of state governance of the mining sector through the MPC in the Ministry of Mining and LDAs in sub-national administrations. These mechanisms represent a *formalised* encroachment of private interests, actors and norms within the fabric of public government. While this shift towards hybridised governance reflected the lobbying efforts of investors and their private sector groups such as the Mongolian National Mining Association and the Business Council of Mongolia, it also reflects the trajectory of executive strategising within the state. Even at the "local" level, it is the centrally appointed governor that has been elevated as the key actor to negotiate with mining companies. Despite the decentred appearance of LDAs, for example, these "local" public–private "partnerships" are centrally mandated, enforced and structured. Thus, in addition to hybridisation, I have focused on the deepening cooperation and expansion of pro-extractive institutions in the executive arm of the state itself which have significantly increased in terms of scale, degree of ideological consensus and scope of decision-making power.

In this chapter, I have linked the various and innovative means by which "political" actors within the state have been undermined through the pro-extractive, anti-politics of "stability" following the 2014 recommitment to promoting FDI in Mongolia's mineral sector. The process of undermining resistance and redistributing power within the state occurred in different forms, through the introduction of strategic public–private partnerships (i.e. LDAs), the softening of institutional boundaries between the state and corporate representation, and changes to national law and policy (i.e. 2014 reform to the Minerals Law and new State Policy on the Minerals Sector 2014–2025). Although targeting disparate loci of resistance within the central state and between local and central governments, these processes are unified by the way that they smooth and stabilise the path for private sector-led extraction. Within the state itself, private investment interests have become intertwined with strategic bureaucratic institutions, such as the Ministry of Mining and the offices of provincial and district governors. One way in which this has occurred is through the formation of hybridised institutions such as the MPC and LDAs that exist within the municipal structure (i.e. they directly affect public governance) but are structured on the basis of private interests and forms of law (i.e. multi-stakeholder, contractual models). Almost simultaneously, private interests were included within the space of government and representative "political" institutions were marginalised after the FDI crisis, demonstrating the state's renewed commitment – vis-à-vis executive institutions – to enable and promote FDI.

Notably, these dexterous methods of stabilising the investment environment as implemented by the pro-extractive executive lacked an explicitly political character, despite their significant impact in structuring the plane of political legitimacy for critiques of FDI within the state. Executive actors and institutions deployed legal and financial measures rather than relying on overtly coercive means to achieve the goal of ensuring stability for investors conveniently veiling the strategic hand of the central government in constructing a new 'common sense' for mining governance. Since then, it has become increasingly difficult for an alternative paradigm of economic development to be articulated by national actors and institutions, despite electoral turnover.

## Notes

1 Author interview, 8th February 2015.
2 Author interview, 15th July 2019.
3 Ibid.
4 Author interview, 13th November 2015.
5 Author interview, 16th November 2015.
6 Author interview, Senior Policy-Maker, Ministry of Mining, 9th November 2015.
7 Author interview with Deputy Director, Resource Strategy and Innovation, Oyu Tolgoi LLC, 18th November 2015.
8 Mongolia is a unitary state, with 21 provinces (aimags) and 329 districts (*soums*), with a large and indeterminate number of sub-districts (*baghs*). Their precise number is unknown because they often lack a permanent site of government. The sub-districts bear the closest resemblance to pre-socialist customary institutions before nationalist territorialisation occurred in the 1920s.
9 Author interview, MRAM Officer, 28th October 2015.
10 Author interview, 9th November 2015.
11 Author interview, 23rd January 2015.
12 Author interview, 16th November 2015.
13 Law on the Prohibition of Mineral Exploration and Mining Operations at Headwaters of Rivers, Protected Zones of Water Reservoirs and Forested Areas, see Chapter Four.
14 Author interview, 27th October 2015.
15 Ibid.
16 Multi-Stakeholder Workshop on Community Development Agreements, author observation, November 2014.
17 Author interview with Director of the Department for Strategic Policy and Planning, Ministry of Mining, 27th October 2015).
18 Ibid.
19 Author interview, 13th November 2015.
20 Author interview, Director-General of the Strategic Policy and Planning Department, Ministry of Mining, 27th October 2015).
21 Ibid.
22 Ibid.
23 Author interview, Senior Policy-Maker, Ministry of Mining, 9th November 2015.
24 Author interview, Director-General of the Strategic Policy and Planning Department, Ministry of Mining, 28th October 2015).
25 Ibid.

26 Author interview, 20th November 2015.
27 Author interview, President of the Mongolian National Mining Association, 13th November 2015.
28 Author interview, Senior Policy-Maker, Ministry of Mining, 9th November 2015.
29 Author interview, President of the Mongolian National Mining Association, 13th November 2015.
30 Ibid.
31 The models were developed by Hogan Lovells, the international legal firm which won the bid from the World Bank.
32 English translation, official draft.
33 Author interview, 27th October 2015.
34 Author observation, 11th November 2015.
35 Author interview, 20th November 2015.
36 Author interview, MRAM Officer, 28th October 2015.
37 Author interview, 3rd November 2015.
38 Author interview, 25th October 2015.
39 Author interview, 16th November 2015.
40 Author interview, 27th October 2015.
41 The centralised determination of land was part of the 2014 reforms to the minerals law and policy (see Chapter 4, Table 3).
42 Ibid.
43 Author interview, 28th October 2015.
44 Author interview, 17th November 2015.
45 Author Interview, 27th October 2015.
46 Ibid.
47 Ibid.
48 Author interview, Senior Policy-Maker, Ministry of Mining, 9th November 2015.
49 Author observation, Multi-Stakeholder Workshop on Community Development Agreements, author observation, 7th November 2014.
50 Author interview, 9th November 2015.
51 Author interview, Senior Policy-Maker, Ministry of Mining, 9th November 2015.
52 Ibid.

# References

Butler, W. E. and Nathanson, A. J. 1982. *The Mongolian Legal System, Contemporary Legislation and Documentation*. The Hague: Martinus Nijhoff.

Dierkes, J. 2013. "Mongolia's Evolving Foreign Investment Regime." 9th January *East Asia Forum* www.eastasiaforum.org/2013/01/09/mongolias-evolving-foreign-investment-regime/. Accessed 4th April 2017.

Endicott, E. 2012. *A History of Land Use in Mongolia: The Thirteenth Century to the Present*. New York: Palgrave Macmillan.

Enkhbaatar, Ch., Solongo, D., Amarjargal, P., and Ginsburg, T. 2015. "The Role of the Constitution of Mongolia in Consolidating Democracy: An Analysis." UNDP, Ulaanbaatar, www.mn.undp.org/content/mongolia/en/home/library/democratic_governance/RoleoftheConstitutionofMongoliaInConsolidatingDemocracy.html. Accessed 31st March 2017.

Ernst and Young. 2011. "Business Risks Facing Mining and Metals 2011–2012." www.doing-business.gr/wp-content/uploads/2012/09/Metal_Mining_paper_02Aug11_lowres.pdf. Accessed 4th April 2017.

———. 2012. "Business Risks Facing Mining and Metals 2012–2013." www.puertovida. org/docs/Ernst-Young_Business-risk-facing-mining-and-metals-2012-2013.pdf. Accessed 4th April 2017.

———. 2013. "Business Risks Facing Mining and Metals 2013–2014." www. ey.com/Publication/vwLUAssets/Business_risks_facing_mining_and_ metals_2013%E2%80%932014_ER0069/$FILE/Business_risks_facing_mining_ and_metals_2013%E2%80%932014_ER0069.pdf. Accessed 4th April 2017.

———. 2014. "Business Risks Facing Mining and Metals 2014–2015." www. ey.com/Publication/vwLUAssets/EY-Business-risks-facing-mining-and-metals-2014%E2%80%932015/$FILE/EY-Business-risks-facing-mining-and-metals-2014%E2%80%932015.pdf. Accessed 4th April 2017.

———. 2015. "Top 10 Business Risks Facing Mining and Metals 2015–2016." www. ey.com/Publication/vwLUAssets/EY-business-risks-in-mining-and-metals-2015-2016-new/$FILE/EY-business-risks-in-mining-and-metals-2015-2016-new.pdf. Accessed 4th April 2017.

———. 2016. "Top 10 Business Risks Facing Mining and Metals 2016–2017." www. ey.com/gl/en/industries/mining-metals/business-risks-in-mining-and-metals. Accessed 4th April 2017.

Fehrbach, E. 2013. "Law on Prohibiting Mineral Exploration and Extraction near Water Sources, Protected Areas and Forests." October 23rd *Mongolia Briefing* http:// mongolia-briefing.com/news/2013/10/law-on-prohibiting-mineral-exploration-and-extraction-near-water-sources-protected-areas-and-forests.html. Accessed 31st March 2017.

Ginsburg, T. 1994. "The Transformation of Legal Institutions in Mongolia, 1990–1993."*Issues and Studies: A Journal of Chinese and International Affairs* 30(6): 77–113.

International Business Publications. 2013. *Mongolia Mining Laws and Regulations Handbook: Vol. 1 Strategic Information and Regulations.* Washington, DC: Global Investment Centre.

Kohli, P. 2016. "How the Mongolian Elections Will Affect Foreign Investment." 24th March *NASDAQ* www.nasdaq.com/article/how-the-mongolian-elections-will-affect-foreign-investment-cm595590. Accessed 15th July 2016. Republished on MonInfohttp://mongolianviews.blogspot.co.uk/2016/03/how-mongolian-elections-will-affect.html. Accessed 4th April 2017.

Li, T. 2007. *The Will to Improve: Governmentality, Development and the Practice of Politics.* Durham, NC: Duke University Press.

Lkhagvadorj, A. 2010. "Fiscal Federalism and Decentralisation in Mongolia." MPRA Paper 28758, University Library of Munich, Germany. https://mpra.ub.uni-muenchen. de/28758/1/MPRA_paper_28758.pdf. Accessed 4th April 2017.

———. 2012. "An Analysis of the New Budget Law of Mongolia of 2011." MPRA Paper 38681, University Library of Munich, Germany. https://mpra.ub.uni-muenchen. de/38681/. Accessed 4th April 2017.

Manthorpe, J. 2013. "Mongolia Struggles with the Complexity of Resource Development." 29th September. *Business in Vancouver* www.biv.com/article/2013/9/ mongolia-struggles-with-complexities-of-resource-d/.Accessed 5th October 2015.

Mineral Resources Authority of Mongolia (MRAM). 2017. https://mrpam.gov.mn/ article/34/. Accessed 23rd April 2019.

Pistilli, M. 2012. "Resource Investors to Watch Mongolian Parliamentary Elections." 12th March *Resource Investing News* http://investingnews.com/daily/resource-investing/resource-investors-watch-mongolian-parliamentary-elections-resource-nationalism-rio-tinto-ivanhoe-mines-oyu-tolgoi/. Accessed 4th April 2017.

Reuters. 2015. "Cash-Strapped Mongolia Offers More Land for Mining Projects." 16th January *Reuters* www.reuters.com/article/mongolia-mining-idUSL3 N0UV2AH20150116. Accessed 23rd April 2019.

Rossabi, M. 2005. *Mongolia: From Khans to Commissars to Capitalists.* Berkeley: University of California Press.

Suzuki, Y. 2013. "Conflict between Mining Development and Nomadism in Mongolia." In Yamamura, N., Fujita, N., and Maekawa, A. (eds.) *The Mongolian Eco-System Network: Environmental Issues Under Climate and Social Changes.* Tokyo: Springer, pp. 269–294.

U.S. Department of State. 2011. "US Embassy in Ulaanbaatar: 2011 Investment Climate Statement." US Department of State: Online https://mongolia.usembassy.gov/root/media/pdf/mongolia-ics-2011.pdf. Accessed 4th April 2017.

Weafer, C. 2016. "Mongolia: Time to Rethink Your Risk Assessment?" *Financial Times Beyond Brics Forum* http://blogs.ft.com/beyond-brics/2016/02/26/mongolia-time-to-rethink-your-risk-assessment/. Accessed 4th April 2017.

World Bank. 2006. "Mongolia: A Review of Environmental and Social Impacts in the Mining Sector." Washington, DC: World Bank.

Worldfolio. (2014). "Mongolia: Erdenebulgan Oyun, Deputy Minister of Mining." www.worldfolio.co.uk/region/asia/mongolia/erdenebulgan-oyun-deputy-minister-of-mining-mongolia-n2639. Accessed 5th July 2015. Reposted on Cover Mongolia http://covermongolia.blogspot.co.uk/2014/02/mmc-gets-paid-trq-warns-bom-intervenes.html. Accessed 4th April 2017.

## Policy

Government of Mongolia. 2014. "State Policy on the Minerals Sector 2014–2025." Appendix to Resolution No. 18, 2014 of the State Great Khural of Mongolia. English translation.

———. 2015. *Model Community Development Agreements Template.* English Translation, Official Draft.

# Chapter 6

# Redefining resistance

## Strategies for stabilisation in state–society relations

## Introduction

Transformations in law or state institutions necessarily affect the context in which people relate to legal and political authority, and to each other, as subjects of that governance order. In the process of 'conditioning local political economies and societies' (Cutler, 2011: 30), exposure to global markets and transnational legality can produce new 'subjects and objects of legality, localised and delocalised social relations, territorialised and deterritorialised systems of rule, and hard and soft forms of regulation' (ibid.: 31–32). Thus, drawing on Cutler (ibid.: 30), I argue that legal and institutional reordering to enable global economic integration almost inevitably 'defines and regulates the terms of political engagement and contestation,' as transnational norms 'penetrate domestic politico-legal orders.'

This book has already examined in some detail the way that the state–economy relationship in Mongolia has developed and changed over time, from the pre-socialist period up through the current period of global economic integration. Now, I will turn to some of the socio-legal effects of the current extractive "development" strategy on the relationship between the state and civil society. In Mongolia, the idea of an institutional sphere of civil society, formally distinct from the state and commerce, is a relatively new one. The protection of civic space from state interference was introduced through the political and economic liberalisation processes in the early 1990s (Fritz, 2002, 2008; Mendee, 2012) and has appeared to flourish, indicated by the subsequent emergence of a plethora of non-governmental organisations (NGOs) (Byambajav, 2006). I take as my point of departure the institutionalised understanding of civil society as expressed in Mongolian law (and society), which differentiates it as a space of rights and responsibilities along classical liberal lines from the political (state) and economic (commercial) realms, although I hope to demonstrate that these clear conceptual lines between political, economic and social are highly problematic in practice. In this chapter, I examine the ways that civil society organisations have been disciplined by, as well as internalised, the post-2014 "stability consensus," and highlight the way that corporate/development financial institutions exercise an unprecedented degree of authority as "social" actors within mediating public processes of conflict resolution at the sub-national level.

This chapter is an exploration of new boundaries around what potentially may or may not be legitimately contested by civil associations and citizens under the post-2014 mining regime. The nascent nature of this transformation prevents hard-and-fast conclusions, but three distinct shifts are notable. Firstly, strong boundaries have been placed by the judicial arm of the state on organised civic resistance to foreign investment and widespread extraction through the criminalisation of "radical" environmental movements in 2013. Since then, the path of legitimate engagement for civil society organisations has been limited to cooperative participation in governance, incorporated into multi-stakeholder mechanisms of consensus-building, alongside the state and the corporate sector. Secondly, corporate actors and international financial institutions (IFIs) have become powerful authorities in relation to the "social" governance of extractive development, demonstrated by the growth of corporate and multilateral programmes to address disputes between companies and the local "community." This development has been facilitated partly by local government–company collaboration in the framework of Local Development Agreements, and also through new strategies deployed by NGOs and local communities using non-state mechanisms to gain recognition (i.e. vis-à-vis the International Finance Corporation's (IFC) Performance Standards). Thirdly, and relatedly, the "social" governance of extractive development can be characterised by the rising dominance of corporate legal norms of recognition and justice.

Together, all three of these factors work to generate consensus-driven, corporate-dominant power relationships and establish new "rules of the game" for civic engagement with the state beyond the purview of the national constitution. Ultimately, neutralised civil associations and the power of corporate actors and norms in the governance of citizenship enable extractive development by minimising the effects of resistance to it and managing dissent in more "constructive" directions through consensus-based mechanisms, sanctioned and sponsored by the state, the mining sector and its international financiers. This process of neutralisation and dissent management under the aegis of "multi-stakeholder solutions" was a critical piece of the post-2014 "stability consensus" that discursively and institutionally erected and reinforced the 'limits of the possible'[1] (Cox, 2002: 37) in Mongolian law and politics.

## Organised civil society in Mongolia: an overview

The 1992 Constitution expressly recognised the illegitimacy of state repression of collective organisation, guaranteeing the 'right to form a party or other public organisations and unite voluntarily in associations according to social and personal interests and opinion' (Article 16.10). A series of new laws after 1992 guaranteed not only the protection of civic space but recognised civil society organisations – NGOs specifically – as a legitimate partner for the state in creating and implementing legislation, notably in relation to environmental protection (Danaasuren, 2010: 9). Specifically, the 1997 Law on NGOs (hereafter "the Law") authorised legal space for civil society organisations to gain formal recognition as registered NGOs, recognising both Public Benefit Associations and Mutual Benefit Associations (Articles 4.2 and 4.3). The 1997 Law defined NGOs broadly as:

> An organisation which is independent from the state, self-governing, not-for-profit and established voluntarily by citizens or by legal persons other than State bodies (that exercise legislative, executive or judicial powers) on the basis of their individual or social interests and opinions.
>
> (Article 4.1)

The Law still made provision, however, for the state to contribute 'financially and otherwise' (Article 9.3) to the activities of NGOs. The majority of NGOs emerged following the passing of the Law, with 5,077 NGOs registered by September 2005 following a national survey commissioned by the Open Society Forum (Gombodorj and Batsuren, 2005: 3). Approximately, 77% of NGOs in 2005 were based in Ulaanbaatar (ibid.). In 2008, Mongolia's Civil Society Council was established with four sub-councils, covering (1) Environment, (2) Education, Culture and Science, (3) Health and (4) Defence (UNDP, 2012). Based on national statistics, the number of NGOs registered in Mongolia has always been remarkably high relative to the population (2.8 million), growing approximately ten-fold between 1997 and 2007 (Mendee, 2012: 19). However, as Mendee (ibid.: 20) points out, these numbers may be misleading. Since 2005, there has been a lack of national data on the composition of civil society, and the number of registered NGOs is likely to be significantly higher than those that are truly active (ibid.). Furthermore, the Civil Society Council and its sub-councils suffer from a lack of visibility and coherence in relation to 'representative, networking and coordination functions...due to lack of capacity in terms of financial and human resources' (UNDP, 2012: 7).

The limited levels of funding available from the state and the general lack of a culture of organised philanthropy in Mongolian society (Danaasuren, 2012) have given international NGOs and foundations with greater financial backing a high degree of influence within civil society in terms of shaping its norms and organisational mode (Byambajav, 2006). Consequently, Mongolian civil society, particularly in Ulaanbaatar, has tended to reproduce the coherent 'structural pattern of international NGO networks' (Katz and Anheier, 2006: 241) in form and activity (including the hierarchical relationships between international–national–local scales, urban and rural areas). For example, Mongolian NGOs typically have membership links to international NGOs and networks, attend conferences, produce reports, depend on diverse avenues of donor funding (i.e. through transnational organisational memberships, public sector grants and/or corporate contracts) and intervene in society via short-term projects that aim at policy and legal reform or "capacity building" amongst their target groups (ibid.). The transnational NGO network in which Mongolian civil society largely participates is dominated by a specific discourse buoyed by the terms 'participation, empowerment, local, and community' (Fisher, 1997: 442) which connote an organic notion of the "social" without the sinister taint of 'profit or politics' (ibid.).

International NGOs were the first on the scene, so to speak, following Mongolia's impoverishment as a result of the collapse of the Soviet Union and the marketisation of the country's economy (Rossabi, 2005; Byambajav, 2006). Not only this but organisations like the Soros Foundation, the Asia Foundation, World Vision, the Konrad-Adenauer Foundation, to name a few, occupy the unique position of being both directly engaged in civic activities *and* a primary source of funding for domestic civil society organisations. Thus, significant inequalities in power exist between organisations within civil society, with a relatively few number of organisations having privileged access to long-term funding. The concentration of financial resources in Ulaanbaatar-based, foreign-funded civil society organisations creates a serious power disparity, with a few entrenched organisations at the top and a mass of short-term, small-scale associations competing for funding and support. Significantly for this analysis, international NGOs tend to support extractive development (i.e. mining) on the whole, with the caveat that it is carried out in a responsible manner.[2] Despite the presence of a "real" space for civil society, there is a danger of being overly positive about this development in terms of its actual impacts. "Social" actors such as NGOs may very well reinforce and legitimise the dominant pro-mining consensus as they are incorporated into the governing order for extractive development, as will be demonstrated in the following analysis.

## The law and politics of exclusion in the making of a "civil" society: limiting political risk from environmental activists

In this section, I argue that social relations between the state and citizens have been "stabilised" to exclude more radical expressions of resistance from the Mongolian public. Despite constitutional guarantees preventing state repression of collective organisation and freedom of expression, the government has established hard boundaries of legitimacy for those social movements that have openly resisted foreign investment in mining and widespread extraction. Notably, the crackdown on dissident groups has occurred since the crisis of foreign investment in 2012–2013, when Mongolia's reputation as an FDI-friendly country was seriously questioned within the international investment community. New boundaries for collective action have been established through positive measures – financial and political incentives – as well as the increasing threat of criminalisation, as the case of the Fire Nation movement demonstrates. This section will briefly provide the legal and political context for the development of organised action and agitation around mining by resistant groups, and the ways in which the most radical elements have been excluded and "stabilised" for the purposes of diminishing political risk for investors and mining companies and securing renewed FDI flows for the state.

## The emergence of environmental activism around mining in Mongolia

1997 was a momentous year for Mongolia in terms of legal change. It could be termed "the Year of Liberalisation" with the passing of the 1997 Minerals Law *and* the Law on NGOs, as well as World Trade Organisation membership. These measures, respectively, opened up the Mongolian minerals market to investment of unprecedented scale and further legitimised voluntary associations through legislation. Prior to the advent of the mining boom at the end of the 1990s, civil society activism was largely based in Ulaanbaatar. The majority of organisations were either international NGOs responding to the political opportunity for promoting democracy (e.g. the Konrad-Adenauer Foundation and the Asia Foundation) and the social needs created through the transition process (e.g. World Vision, Save the Children), or Western-styled NGOs 'established and led by women' (Byambajav, 2013) in Ulaanbaatar.

In contrast to Ulaanbaatar's centralised NGO-model of civil society organisation, the mining boom catalysed a unique mobilisation of activism (Byambajav, 2014:2), with collective action emerging from rural areas across the country where the impacts of mining and large-scale licencing had been felt most keenly. The input requirements of mining in terms of land and water not only created an economic conflict of interest with herders, but destabilised their entire social environment (Byambajav, 2012: 13). Suffering from the pollution and drying up of rivers, displacement from precious cultural and spiritual landmarks, and customary grazing land, small groups began to organise themselves to resist these changes in the early 2000s. These movements expressed resistance in various ways initially, through direct action protests, such as roadblocks, hunger strikes and lobbying within the Citizens Councils of local government (Byambajav, 2012, 2014; Upton, 2012). Their discourse was explicitly political, drawing on distinctively Mongolian concepts of the *local homeland* (*nutag*) and rivers – 'the people of the one-river' (Byambajav, 2014: 1; Sneath, 2010: 253). The idea of Mongolia as a 'motherland...in which people have their roots' has been described by Sneath (ibid.) as a 'core value in the national political culture.'

Initially at least, the success of rural resistance was dependent on the political support of local authorities and the financial assistance of international NGOs, specifically the Konrad-Adenauer Foundation which supported the first sustained environmental social movement in response to mining in 2002: the Onggi River Movement. In relation to local political backing, the consolidation of collective action to resist mining reflected the support of local institutions for the resistance movement. Byambajav (2012: 21), for example, credits local "elites" and government officials for consolidating the efforts of local citizens in Tsenher *soum* (Arkhangai *aimag*, central Mongolia) into an organised resistance *movement* known as Aruin Suvraga (Sacred Suvraga Mountain). While senior citizens, teachers and a few other motivated citizens had attempted to gain central government attention and catalyse a systematic campaign against the mining company Mongol Gazar ('Mongolian Place') (ibid.), they were unsuccessful. It took the involvement of senior representatives from Tsenher *soum*'s Local Homeland Council and local governmental officials (notably the governor and environmental inspectors) to consolidate collective action strategies (ibid.: 22).

Similarly, in the case of the Onggi River Movement, the support of local authorities greatly aided the initial coalescence of the group as a fully fledged – albeit small-scale – *movement*. This was confirmed in an interview with a key leader of the movement, formerly a *bagh* governor in Uverkhangai *aimag* (province). Governor Sambuu stated that his rationale for getting involved with the Onggi River Movement was on behalf of the local community 'because the whole community was affected by the mining...by joining to the civil movements I could support the local community and its environment.'[3] He attributed the success of the Onggi River Movement in garnering popular support to the fact that the movement's board comprised representatives from each of the eight *soums* (districts) along the Onggi River, who reached out to citizens, mobilising them for direct actions and petitions (around 6,000, sent to central parliament members). He described the support of *aimag* and *soum* governments as "very good," stating that some of the original members of the River Movement board were originally *soum* governors themselves, as well as *bagh* governors like himself. In the early years (2001–2005), apart from soliciting the interest of the Konrad-Adenauer Foundation to provide assistance with resources, the Onggi River Movement and smaller parallel movements maintained institutional distance from Ulaanbaatar-based NGOs. The River Movements were creative strategists, using a combination of informal and formal methods of protest. As Combellick-Bidney (2012: 287) puts it, 'clashes between the River Movements and mining companies took the form of legal battles, rival stories in the media, and physical violence on the ground.'

In early 2006, a loose coalition of River Movements and other rural environmental NGOs was formed through a partnership with the Asia Foundation: The Homeland and Water Protection Coalition of River Movements ("River Coalition"). The Asia Foundation, as 'the first non-profit organisation to be invited into Mongolia' (Asia Foundation, 2016) in 1990, had become an entrenched civil society *institution* of sorts, with a "thick" development programme that ranged from direct service provision to public policy and governance support (ibid.).[4] Its institutionalisation benefitted from its status as a regional NGO with sustained income from a variety of donors (i.e. foreign aid agencies, IFIs, corporations and individuals). The recognition of growing environmental impacts and conflict caused by mining operations opened up *environmental governance* as a new field of engagement for the Asia Foundation.

Different accounts of how the partnership between the River Coalition and the Asia Foundation emerged emphasise varying levels of initiative by the parties. There was a sense, particularly amongst the leadership of the Onggi River Movement, that coordination was needed to effect national-level policy change.

The Onggi River Movement contacted the Asia Foundation, to provide financial and coordination support in creating an umbrella organisation to link these grassroots environmental groups. Seeking support from the Asia Foundation was a strategic step for the River Coalition to sustain nation-wide collective action, widen their influence and develop a central hub to provide resources and administer localised activities. The Asia Foundation, however, was not a neutral actor in this process, but took an active role in selecting the members of the coalition and setting the tone for the mode of engagement that the coalition should seek.

The Coalition, aided by the Asia Foundation, 'began exploring more cooperative, less confrontational approaches to dealing with mining-related issues' (Asia Foundation, 2008), and developed seven principles to inform their legal advocacy:

1   Establish socially and environmentally responsible mining in Mongolia.
2   Require open public access to information related to mining.
3   Promote clear and transparent environmental impact assessment and decision-making on mineral development.
4   Ensure that mining operations meet best international standards for environmental practices.
5   Ensure that public monitoring and public audit compliance with environmental standards becomes a normal practice.
6   Ensure that environmental laws and regulations are adhered to and enforced.
7   Ensure that Mongolia's protected areas remain free from environmental damage (Asia Foundation, 2006).

Notably, this consensus promoted a collaborative – rather than antagonistic – role for civil society in mining governance, focusing on transparency, inclusion and enforcement of the law. Previously, many of the River Movements had engaged in direct action protests and overtly political conflicts against mining companies, emphasising 'the protection of the "local homeland" and its natural landscape' (Byambajav, 2014: 2). The new agenda for the Coalition opened up opportunities for River Movements and other environmental NGOs to engage in legal advocacy and education-based campaigns, but increasingly delegitimised conflictual strategies. These values became the bedrock of the Responsible Mining Initiative (RMI), initiated by the Asia Foundation in 2006 following the formation of the River Coalition. A "grasstops" mechanism – 'a framework for cooperative decision-making' (Asia Foundation, 2008) – the RMI brought different stakeholders together with mutual interest in "responsible mining." As a multi-stakeholder NGO, the board of the RMI was composed of representatives from civil society, industry and government. Similar to the River Coalition, the RMI was founded on seven principles and values of 'responsible mining' (ibid.):

1   Ensure multi-stakeholder engagement.
2   Transparency and openness.
3   Responsibility for the safety of people and the environment.

4    Investment in future development.
5    Ensure fruitful productivity and efficiency.
6    Humane and ethical.
7    Based on advanced and modern technology.

These seven principles assumed that common ground could be found between different interest groups around the values of transparency, responsibility, growth, efficiency, humanity and technological progress. Furthermore, they ascribed inherent value to "multi-stakeholder engagement" and made shared responsibility a goal of the new multi-stakeholder collective, rather than targeting specific duty-bearers (i.e. the government). Leaders from the River Coalition were initially represented in the RMI, as were the Mongolian National Mining Association, Members of Parliament from opposing parties, the head of the trade union and Oyu Tolgoi, amongst others. While on paper the RMI was remarkably impressive, allegedly "uniting" high-level stakeholders together around principles of responsible mining, its functionality as a decision-making forum was fraught with internal conflicts of interest between its members, notably between a faction of the River Movements and the Asia Foundation. Some of the River Movements perceived the Asia Foundation to be too heavy-handed in its facilitation of both the River Coalition and the RMI (Danaasuren, 2012: 258) and the Asia Foundation found that some of its expectations for reciprocity were unmet.[5]

While undoubtedly there were inter-personal tensions that contributed to inter-organisational conflict, the mismatch between an overtly politicised and confrontational approach as expressed by the Onggi River Movement and the consensus-driven ethos of the Asia Foundation became an insurmountable barrier to their continued cooperation. This conflict came to a head in 2008 when a group of the River Movements, led by the Onggi River Movement, publicly stated their 'willingness to organise violent protest, if necessary, against poor mining in local regions' (Danaasuren, 2012: 247). With the Asia Foundation unwilling to support this conflictual approach, the River Coalition splintered, with some movements following the Asia Foundation and others following the Onggi River Movement. The latter formed the United Movement for Mongolian Rivers and Lakes (UMMRL) in 2008. Despite the emergence of fragmentation between different approaches within mining-focused civil society organisations, the River Movements had the political support of large numbers of rural Mongolians, hundreds and even thousands of whom participated in direct action protests across the country (Combellick-Bidney, 2012: 287).

Overall, the first six years (2005–2011) of organised resistance to mining could be understood as a period of optimism for major transformation in the social and environmental regulation of mining.[6] The River Movements had developed from very small, grassroots organisations into a larger coalition based in Ulaanbaatar, with significant donor funding and opportunities to influence policy-making at the national level, not only through the RMI but also through the Mongolian Environmental Civil Council (MECC). Established in 2008, the MECC developed in response to the national groundswell of small-scale environmental movements pioneered mainly through the activism of Ts. Munkhbayar and the Onggi River Movement.[7] According to the Council's Director, the MECC is a national umbrella organisation that functions as a "bridge" between the government, NGOs and mining-impacted citizens.[8] While the MECC does not now solely focus on mining, the public response to the impacts of mining in the early 2000s galvanised its formation as a civic institution. The MECC has since established administrative and regulatory requirements regarding registration, as well as financial reporting duties in order to manage the numerous environment NGOs (700+), the majority of which comprised five to ten people. The MECC has also opened up avenues for smaller NGOs to gain funding from the Ministry of Environment and other donor organisations, and achieve greater visibility for their work at the national level.[9]

In addition to the MECC, the Law on Prohibiting Mineral Exploration and Extraction Near Water Sources, Protected Areas and Forests ("the Law") was passed by the Mongolian Parliament in 2009 following years of advocacy by the UMMRL and the support of a few law-makers. As mentioned in Chapters 4 and 5, this piece of environmental legislation became a critical focus for environmental activism between 2009 and 2013. This Law prohibited 'mineral exploration and mining operations...at headwaters of rivers, protected zones of water reservoirs and forested areas within the territory of Mongolia' (Article 4.1), although 'deposits of strategic importance' (Article 4.2) were excluded from this prohibition. Further, the Law gave the Government the right to delineate these boundaries, without specifying the precise limits or which branch of government had the right to do this (district, provincial or central). The lack of legal precision and openness to political discretion in the determination of environmental boundaries was the main point of contention for mining companies, as well as the requirement that licences operating in these areas be cancelled.[10]

However, the government did not enforce the law, leading to renewed public demonstrations, hunger strikes and the filing of a court case against the Government of Mongolia in a district court in Ulaanbaatar by the UMMRL in 2010. The Law had been unenforced by the government because it would lead to the mass cancellation of mining licences in areas newly protected under the law and grant local governments discretion in the determination of environmental boundaries. The district court ruled that the government was *not* responsible for the environmental damage caused by mining companies, leading to protests from the public led by the UMMRL. In April 2011, one hundred herders on horseback wearing traditional *deels* and armed with bows assembled in a grand symbolic protest in Sukhbaatar Square outside of the Great Khural. With them, hundreds of citizens gathered and called for a national referendum after collecting signatures, which led to the lodging of an appeal of the 2010 judgement in the Supreme Court. The 2010 district court judgement was overruled in October

2011, when the Supreme Court upheld that the government was responsible for environmental damages caused by mining operations, because it had failed to enforce the new environmental law (Global Legal Monitor, 2011). Following the Supreme Court order, the enforcement of the law by the government led to the immediate suspension of over 200 mining licences, apparently affecting up to 1,800 mining projects for exploration and extraction,[11] provoking 'intense opposition from miners' (Mendee, 2013).

In 2013, the radical decline of confidence in the stability of Mongolia's investment environment and downward spiral of foreign direct investment inspired the government to propose amendments to the Law, which would enable the majority of suspended licences to become active again. The prospect of reform and word of 'special sessions of Parliament to weaken the Law' (UMMRL, 2014a) led to the formation of a more radicalised Fire Nation group within the UMMRL. In September 2013, the Fire Nation group and eleven other associations protested again in front of Parliament because of proposed amendments to the Law: their self-proclaimed goal was 'to save our nation' having sworn to give their lives 'for national rights,' arguing that the Government was in breach of the Constitution as the guarantor of environmental protection and citizen's rights (Munkhbayar, 2014).

According to a UMMRL Press Release (UMMRL, 2014a), the government led by the Democratic Party had 'declared that the "Law with a Long Name" was an impediment to economic growth and the Gold Mining Association of Mongolia promised to quadruple gold output in exchange for weakened protection of rivers.' A shot was allegedly fired during the protest and ten members of the movement, including Ts. Munkhbayar, were arrested. On January 21st, 2014, he and four others were sentenced to over twenty-one years in prison on charges of terrorism (Tolson, 2014). The trial of these activists eschewed constitutionally protected rights to fairness and effective representation, highlighted by the fact that the trial was held in a remote detention centre where the activists had been interrogated.

It is important to note the way that the Fire Nation movement perceived themselves as defenders of the national democratic constitution and positioned themselves as *citizen*-activists defending their local homelands (see Sneath, 2010; Byambajav, 2014). According to the formal Appeal to overturn the court's ruling (UMMRL, 2014b), the defendants stated that they were willing to 'resort to their own ways of handling this challenging situation' in circumstances where they deemed that the 'state becomes untrustworthy, when it ignores the [constitutional] rights of citizens to enjoy a healthy environment and turns living conditions and health into continuous suffering, when people are deprived of water, pasture land and wintering places.' In an interview with the author, one of the leaders of the Onggi River Movement, Governor Sambuu, explained the issue in straightforward terms: 'the state has forgotten its reason for being.'[12] The purpose of the UMMRL, particularly under the leadership of Ts. Munkhbayar, ostensibly was to remind the state of its constitutional *raison d'être*.

## Stabilisation mechanism I: excluding dissent through institutional disassociation and state criminalisation

The numbers of arrests were few following the 2013 protests, but symbolic in terms of a seismic shift in the treatment of dissident civic associations by the state. The escalation of the protest movements between 2011 and 2014 coincided, and some would say were partially responsible for, the severe drop in foreign direct investment in 2013 and 2014. Their agitation for the enforcement of the environmental "Law with a Long Name" and the consequent suspension of mining licences following the Supreme Court ruling signalled "state expropriation" to mining companies, a major sign of political risk in the investment environment. The criminalisation of the Fire Nation movement in 2013 was an abrupt reminder of the state's coercive power to re-establish boundaries around legitimate forms and expressions of civil society organisation.

The arrests of UMMRL leaders also led to its marginalisation within the MECC. In November 2014, at the National Forum for Environmental NGOs, some members of the MECC wanted to remain loyal to the charismatic activist Ts. Munkhbayar – 'Munkhbayar remains one of our heroes'[13]– while others pushed to create institutional distance from them to maintain the image of the MECC as a professional and cooperative environmental institution. This latter point was demonstrated pointedly at the Forum to which only MECC-approved NGOs were invited. In the opening panel, a board member of the MECC – also a former State Secretary for the Ministry of Environment and Green Development – argued that there was a need for NGOs that have legitimacy and recognition from the government to take greater responsibility for regulating environmental issues. He argued that NGOs needed to work harder and become more professional, citing the lack of competitiveness amongst domestic NGOs as the reason why international NGOs were given greater roles. Using the River Movements as an example of non-professionalism, he advocated for the development of a professionalised NGO sector – 'almost like a corporation' – to spread specialised NGOs around the country: 'we (MECC) need to produce the professional-level NGOs, giving them skills and capacity.' He added that, 'we all have the same goal concerning the environment and nature, protecting it from harm, but we are making mistakes,' saying that Ts. Munkhbayar's damaged social and legal reputation reflected badly on the environmental NGO sector.[14]

The Director of the MECC explained in an interview with the author that establishing a non-conflictual and cooperative approach with the government was critical in terms of legitimising and expanding the scope of the organisation's remit.

> The majority of the population thinks sometimes that the MECC is kind of the same as the street movement, but it's not. MECC is more about providing the right information based on investigation and strategy and research, so that they can provide knowledge to the citizens, how to protect their rights...how

to amend some laws, how to change the constitution etc... The MECC is not
a political organisation, so our main concern is to run this institute in a classic
way. It is supposed to be separate from political ways, and also try to prepare the
next generation to run the MECC for the future in a very right, independent
way. MECC's main role and hope is how can we pass environmentally healthy
food and environment to our next generation. This is our main concern.[15]

The Director emphasised that the MECC had become involved in environmental management rather than their previously "judgmental" approach because the
government was more willing to listen when they are cooperative. The Director
explained, for example, that

> In my personal opinion, our institution is the biggest NGO that could have
> a [big impact] on our society because our members, our board members, are
> mostly very welcome to advise [government] ministers. For example, the Ministry of Environment, Ministry of Mining and Ministry of Agriculture, all the
> ministers of their advisory meetings invite us to contribute our perspective.[16]

When asked whether cooperation levels have increased or decreased with the
government, the Director was emphatic:

> It has increased enormously... We give advice on how [mining projects] affect the natural environment, not only in the shorter term but also in the
> longer term. So we give input and also require environmental safeguard
> instructions. Not only that, but we also give input relating to the social and
> biological effects [of mining]. We give the advice for major decisions for
> the Ministry of Environment...The only advice or instructions given [from
> NGOs] are from the MECC.[17]

Environmental representatives from the MECC have also been included on the
Minerals Policy Council, which was established in the 2014 amendments to
the Minerals Law to help prevent legislative reform to the mining sector (see
Chapter 5). The Ministry of Mining exclusively included environmental representation from the MECC, reinforcing the status and institutional legitimacy
of MECC-registered organisations.

This approach by "grasstops" civil society organisations like the Asia Foundation and the MECC dovetailed with the state's increasingly hard-line position
on the appropriate boundaries of environmental activism from 2013 onwards.
Environmental activists engaged in *protest* were regularly portrayed as corrupt
trouble-makers by pro-extractive government officials. For example, a director at
Erdenes Mongol LLC and senior policy-maker in the government responded to
the question, 'How has civil society changed in recent years?' by saying,

> We have an Extractive Industries Transparency Initiative Council, headed
> by the Prime Minister, and one third [of the council] is from civil society.

And they are maturing. We had a lot of civil society organisations [in the past] but some of them were very violent, they even took rifles, guns, explosives and tried to attack the government because they believed the government was betrayed by the multinational corporations. They believe that the government is not for the people, just for the multinationals. Some of the so-called civil society organisations...it's kind of like a civilised robbery.[18]

He described the civil society organisations as "rent-seeking" by protesting against mining companies in order to get paid off, reinforcing the negative discourse around activism in the Mongolian media (see also Byambajav, 2015: 6).

## Stabilisation mechanism II: inclusion through multi-stakeholder dialogue, consensus-building and the narrative of "shared responsibility"

The post-2014 climate of civil society engagement can be characterised by the virtual monopoly of a "governance participation"[19] paradigm, which envisions a formal role for civil society in both the production and implementation of governance, crucially in collaboration – rather than confrontation – with industry and government partners. In this paradigm, NGOs and social movements have legitimacy to the extent that they are a *constructive* voice within the mining governance framework itself. This new pattern contrasts with the way that the UMMRL and its allies lobbied for law reform within local and national state institutions, expecting the state to take direct, political responsibility for the negative effects of mining.

While conflictual social movements have been marginalised, the central government has given international organisations and the corporate sector political and legal space to provide consensus-based alternatives to ameliorate social discontent with mining projects, particularly in rural areas. A specific narrative of social responsibility characterises the post-2014 "inclusive governance" paradigm, supposedly shared between "stakeholder" groups and informed by transnational mining governance norms and practices. The following two sections will discuss the influence of transnational norms and practices in relation to participatory decision-making and dispute resolution mechanisms, which have infused the state's governance paradigm for civil society organisations in Mongolia.

### Governing political risk for mining projects through the norms and mechanisms of corporate social responsibility: tracing a transnational normative agenda

In 2002, the International Institute of Environment and Development (IIED) published a report, *Breaking Ground: Mining, Minerals and Sustainable Development,* on the role of the mining industry in relation to 'the global transition to sustainable development' (IIED, 2002). The IIED was commissioned by the

World Business Council at the behest of nine multinational mining companies[20] as part of their Global Mining Initiative (GMI) to conduct research and report on the challenges global mining industries face in contributing to sustainable development. The IIED's *Breaking Ground* report has had a profound shift in affecting the global discourse of mining governance towards a connection with social and environmental sustainability. Dr. John Groom, representing Anglo-American, the mining multinational, in the GMI, reflected in 2012 (Buxton, 2012: 7) that:

> The drivers for the GMI were a clear recognition that mining companies had problems of access to land, and access to markets, and cost of capital. The fundamental underlying reason was the reputation of the industry. To tackle this we would have to work with others and improve the way we worked. This is what drove [Breaking Ground] and started the process of stakeholder engagement. None of the problems have gone away, but the dialogue is much better informed and infinitely more constructive.

While the shift in principles has not always led to changed practice (ibid), it has led to the development of a range of norms in the area of corporate socio-environmental governance, notably an emphasis on gaining a 'social license to operate,' local (vs. national) obligations, transparency/information sharing, gaining community trust and stakeholder participation. These emerging governance norms in the wake of the *Breaking Ground* report have been institutionalised globally in important ways by the international organisations, financial institutions, development agencies and corporate bodies that have played a strategic role in Mongolia's mining governance regime.

The United Nations Global Compact provides an overarching framework for sustainable businesses, with which specific industry bodies collaborate such as the International Council for Mining and Metals, which will be discussed later. The United Nations Global Compact has a General Assembly mandate to promote 'responsible business practices and UN values among the global business community and the UN system' (UN Global Compact, 2017), in line with the Ruggie Principles on Business and Human Rights. In light of the UN Guidelines and Guiding Principles, voluntary frameworks for global finance have been created, such as the Equator Principles. As of 2019, ninety-six financial institutions have adopted the Equator Principles, which is 'a risk management framework, adopted by financial institutions, for determining, assessing and managing environmental and social risk in projects' (Equator Principles, 2019). The Equator Principles are globally applicable in the area of project finance and have 'promoted convergence' amongst multilateral financial institutions such as the European Bank for Reconstruction and Development and export credit agencies (ibid.). The Equator Principles also incorporate IFC standards into its UN-based standard-setting regime, reflecting the intertwined nature of these institutional developments (Equator Principles, 2013).

The World Bank Group has been an active institutional agent in the formation of Mongolia's mining regime (Hatcher, 2014: 140). It has a played a particularly influential role in the promulgation of its 'social development model' in Mongolia, characterised by 'approaches seeking to engage local stakeholder in participatory schemes, new "partnership" initiatives between the private sector and civil society, as well as new monitoring responsibilities assigned to both the state and the private sector' (ibid.: 13). As described in Chapter 3, the World Bank played a pivotal role in the development of Mongolia's 1997 Minerals Law and inaugural investment conference that same year. Since then, the World Bank has provided critical institutional development assistance and foreign direct investment promotion in conjunction with the government of Mongolia, 'targeting the overall policy, fiscal, legal, regulatory and institutional frameworks for the mining and extractive sectors' (ibid.: 111).

Mongolia's interaction with the World Bank Group is not unique. The Group has been widely recognised as 'a site of global norm production' (Szablowski, 2007: 87) for regulating social conflict around extractive and infrastructure projects. As Szablowski (ibid.) argues, the World Bank Group's central role in promoting export-oriented, market-based approaches to the development in the Global South through structural adjustment programmes and 'large-scale infrastructure and energy projects' has given it the function of a transnational legal 'laboratory' for regulating the social conflict attending these "development" initiatives. The World Bank Group comprises financial institutions which offer public and private sector development assistance. The public branches of the World Bank Group – referred to as the World Bank – are the International Bank for Reconstruction and Development (IBRD) and the International Development Association (IDA), which provide direct support to national governments. In addition to the public-sector-focused World Bank institutions, the IFC focuses on 'unlocking private investment' (IFC, 2019a) to support economic development in frontier and emerging economies, with the Multilateral Investment Guarantee Agency (MIGA) providing political risk insurance guarantees for private investors and lenders.

The increased scale of the World Bank Group's private sector investments in extractive and infrastructure sectors in the past twenty years has led to the development of eight investment performance standards in 2006. These performance standards are the private sector equivalent of the public environmental and social safeguard policies adopted by the IBRD and IDA for public sector financing in the 1990s. Since 2018, the World Bank's safeguard policies have been recapitulated as the World Bank's Environment and Social Framework for investment project financing, with ten standards that align closely with the IFC standards. The revision of the public safeguards for investment projects represents the effort of the World Bank to harmonise the standards adopted by multilateral financial institutions through a 'common approach' (World Bank, 2019). The influential role of the World Bank Group as a global standard-setting institution is evidenced in the way that the IFC Performance Standards have informed the development of voluntary standards adopted by private banks (e.g. through the Equator Principles) as well as the performance standards of other IFIs (e.g. the European Bank for Reconstruction and Development).

The IFC is a major financier of the Oyu Tolgoi mining project, which has led to the introduction of its eight Performance Standards on environmental and social sustainability into the Mongolian governance context. The eight Performance Standards cover risk management (1), labour and working conditions (2), resource efficiency and pollution prevention (3), community health, safety and security (4), land acquisition and involuntary resettlement (5), biodiversity conservation and management (6), indigenous peoples (7) and cultural heritage (8). These standards incorporate principles of sustained "community engagement" and "impact assessment" into the terms of investment contracts with private entities and give recourse to a grievance mechanism for populations impacted by development projects to determine whether or not the IFC and MIGA are in compliance with their obligations (i.e. Compliance Advisor/Ombudsman (CAO)). The CAO is the independent accountability mechanism for the World Bank Group's private sector branches, namely the IFC and MIGA, and offers compliance and dispute resolution services. CAO functions like an in-house monitoring and evaluation service, reporting directly to the President of the World Bank Group, giving it the status of a 'specialised interlocuter with IFC, MIGA and the WBG president on private sector environmental and social issues' (Szablowski, 2007: 105).

The Extractive Industries Transparency Initiative (EITI) is another significant global governance initiative to promote the transparent and accountable management of revenues derived from natural resources which has impacted Mongolia's mining governance regime. It developed out of 'the intersection of a number of complementary agendas and overlapping transnational networks, particularly those concerned with corruption, conflict, and corporate social responsibility' (Haufler, 2010: 54). However, it addresses these concerns through a market-based mechanism of 'disclosure' (ibid.), based on the assumption that '[transparency] makes markets work more efficiently; enhances trust and cooperation; strengthens institutions; [and] reduces corruption and mismanagement,' (ibid.: 55) amongst other things.

Based on a correlation between resource wealth and corruption, the EITI creates an international standard whereby participating governments disclose the amount that they receive from companies, and these companies disclose what they have paid (EITI, 2017). It was initiated by former British Prime Minister Tony Blair in 2002, in response to an emerging consensus amongst the global development community of IFIs, NGOs and prominent development economists about the corruption effect of dependency on natural resources, a key element of the 'resource curse' (Aaronsen, 2011: 52–53). Thus, since its inception, the EITI has been intended by its proponents to serve as a global anti-corruption standard. The EITI framework has gradually become more comprehensive over time, with the introduction of the revised EITI Standard in 2013, which has been designed to dovetail with wider reforms in each country. This 'contextual' approach is a hallmark of the revised Standard, which goes beyond original reporting expectations, to include balancing what governments received overall with what companies paid. The revised Standard requires disaggregated reporting, to include details of individual payment type as well as specification of company, government agency involved and the particular project. It also brings SOEs, sub-national transfers to local governments and social spending by companies into its transparency remit. Countries are encouraged to go beyond the minimum reporting duties set out in the standard, to include other critical areas of governance.

The idea of a socially responsible extractive industry has also been adopted by international development agencies as well as global industry and finance bodies. A relevant example of this for the Mongolian context particularly is that of the Deutsche Gesellschaft für Internationale Zusammenarbeit (GIZ), the German 'federal enterprise' that provides 'international cooperation services' in over 130 countries (GIZ, 2019a). Predominantly commissioned by the German Federal Ministry for Economic Cooperation and Development, GIZ also works closely with private partners, 'fostering successful interaction between development policy and trade' (GIZ, 2019b). GIZ's core value is the promotion of sustainable development more generally. In the Mongolian case, this value is expressed through the Integrated Mineral Resource Initiative (IMRI) by supporting the creation of 'platforms to facilitate constructive communication between the local population, local government and businesses' (GIZ, 2019c).

The dominant mechanisms promoted by multilateral, global and international organisations are premised upon a procedural concept of responsibility and justice. Mechanisms which focus on developing information-sharing systems (including transparent impact assessments) and multi-stakeholder platforms for dialogue and collaborative monitoring processes are intended, at least in theory, to include local communities in the process of decision-making to enhance trust and build closer relations between the corporation and the community. Notably, these strategies reflect distinctive corporate modes of negotiation and "due diligence." While most corporate-led initiatives are voluntary, there is a corpus of international standards which can be enforced via private law through investment obligations to financial institutions (e.g. the IFC's Performance Standards). While these standards have an element of "hard" legal power behind them to ensure enforcement (i.e. through investment contracts), the mode of redress is "soft" in nature, focusing on conciliatory measures such as mediation rather than the formal adjudication of disputes.

Thus, despite the diversity of opportunities for corporate social responsibility (CSR) and the various levels of obligation companies can accede to, one is hard-pressed to identify CSR norms and practices in the global governance toolkit that are not basically market instruments, 'strategic tool[s] to achieve economic objectives, and ultimately, wealth creation' (Garrigaand Mele, 2004: 53). As Vogel (2005: 2–3) put it in *The Market for Virtue*:

> There are many reasons why some companies choose to behave more responsibly or virtuously in the absence of legal requirements. Some are strategic,

others are defensive, still others may be altruistic or public-spirited... But in the final analysis, CSR is sustainable only if virtue pays off. The supply of corporate virtue is both made possible and constrained by the market.

In the following section, I will examine the way that global norms and practices have been transmitted into the Mongolian context through prominent multi-stakeholder initiatives and non-state dispute resolution mechanisms available through project financing by IFIs. In particular, I will discuss the way that the norms of community engagement and collaboration inform the practice of "multi-stakeholder management" in the context of these projects, noting the powerful role of norm transmission played by the international institutions and organisations behind them. These projects have been chosen as case studies because they evidence the power of international institutions (e.g. IFC) and organisations (e.g. GIZ, EITI) in setting standards and introducing new "socially responsible" governance practices in the mining sector that have the sanction of the state, in contrast to some sections of "politicised" civil society (i.e. the River Movements) which have been delegitimised.

## Institutionalising multi-stakeholder norms and practices in Mongolia's mining regime:[21] the extractive industries transparency initiative and the integrated mineral resource initiative

> What is the [EITI's] theory of change, as it were? The constitution of a multi-stakeholder dialogue and group...to increase accountability and development for the country. There are a number of key tangible benefits, really. The first is to support evidence-based debate. One must agree on the facts and get all three stakeholder groups to agree on the basic facts of the sector. This makes for good debate and good policy. On the other hand, by having these three stakeholder groups on these national commissions – multi-stakeholder groups – one sees a process of trust-building...We also see a process of improved community relations, and perhaps our friends from Mongolia can tell us a bit more about this through their process of sub-national implementation. By collecting information that is relevant to communities, one increases the understanding of these communities and creates links between national and sub-national communities, government and companies.
>
>        Alex Gordy, EITI Country Manager for East Asia, speaking at
>            the G7 Fast Track Partnership Conference on the EITI[22]

For long-term sustainable development, it is of utmost importance that all Mongolians can benefit from their country's resource wealth. Therefore, it is crucial to have in place a reliable business environment and to ensure good governance. Let me repeat. It is crucial to have in place a reliable business environment and to ensure good governance...The German EITI partnership fits well into our bilateral cooperation with Mongolia to support sustainable development [for] almost 25 years.

H. E. Gerard Thiedemann, Ambassador of the Federal
Republic of Germany to Mongolia, speaking at the G7
Fast Track Partnership Conference on the EITI[23]

The EITI has been increasingly recognised as a 'founding principle' (Sh. Tsend-Ayush, Ministry of Mining quoted in Carter and Davaanyum, 2015b) to shape accountable state–society relations in the development of Mongolia's mining policy. The EITI promotes a multi-stakeholder model of accountability through an anti-corruption framework. It creates opportunities for some form of accountability within a market-based paradigm, through the production of transparent information about revenue payments and receipts in resource-rich economies (Haufler, 2010). However, a significant underlying motive of this transparency drive is to remove political risk from the business environment, by targeting state corruption. As Aaronsen explains in relation to the 'limited partnership' of the EITI (2011: 51), 'corporate executives are increasingly aware that corruption not only affects profits, but also increases business risk.'

The EITI's multi-stakeholder approach creates institutional space for the expression of interests related to mining, representing different sectors – economic, political and civil – and also the specific agendas of powerful organisations from that triad. The emphasis on equality of standing and responsibility appears to offer a significant political opportunity for civil organisations to address political and economic actors from a position of strength. At one level, this is true: the EITI is a helpful institutional development in the sense of tracing revenue flows and mitigating bare-faced corruption on the part of the state or mining companies. However, apart from counting numbers within the agreed framework, the EITI does not offer a platform to contest the way in which accumulation or redistribution of mineral rents occurs in the first place. It functions as an oversight mechanism and a data generator, which arguably also contributes to the stability of the investment environment by giving other investors indicators of the state's corruption performance.

The national EITI in Mongolia comprises two multi-stakeholder organisations – the National Council and the Working Group – and a national office of the EITI Secretariat based in Ulaanbaatar. Sub-national Working Groups are in the process of being established within mining regions, to expand the EITI to inform 'dialogue between mining companies, mine-affected communities and local government' (Adam Smith International, 2014). The National Council functions as the coordinating and monitoring body of the EITI, chaired by the Prime Minister and his deputy, the Minister of Mining, with a mandate to meet at least once a year. Civil society, industry and governmental stakeholders are equally represented on the Council with ten seats, respectively. The Working Group functions as the main site of EITI governance implementation, meeting at least four times a year. Similar to the National Council, each group of stakeholders – civil, corporate and governmental – is equally represented in a body of thirty-three members. In a recent Asia Pacific Memo (Carter and Davaanyam, 2015a), the Stakeholder Superintendent at Oyu Tolgoi LLC described the EITI as a 'platform where government, civil society and extractive company sit together in equal level, with equal rights, with equal responsibility.'

EITI multi-stakeholder councils have also been recently introduced at the *aimag* level across Mongolia to supervise sub-national transfers from the central government and mining companies (Shagdarsuren, 2018). These sub-national EITI councils have become key institutional loci to facilitate Local Development Agreements 'by organising consultative meetings and negotiations' (ibid.: 6), in addition to monitoring transfers. The EITI model has thus achieved a degree of institutional primacy at both national and sub-national levels, complemented by other international development organisation's initiatives, such as the IMRI led by the Deutsche GIZ.

The GIZ has played a key role in supporting the EITI in Mongolia since 2014 under the auspices of its IMRI. Initially, in 2010, the GIZ's work in Mongolia was mainly focused on supporting the Mongolian government through its Investment Policy Advisory Service programme, as well as working with mining companies on their CSR efforts. This programme was expanded in terms of its remit and financing following a visit from the German Minister for Development and Economic Cooperation, Dirk Niebel. Minister Niebel advocated that an additional three million euros be committed 'for advisory services and training in connection with development-oriented use of Mongolia's mineral deposits' (BMZ, 2010). In a meeting with the Mongolian Minister for Mineral Resources and Energy, he stated that:

> The best poverty reduction tool is endogenous economic development. The mineral resources sector is the key to this. We want to support Mongolian efforts to exploit the country's resources in an environmentally responsible way so that there are lasting benefits for the population. At the same time it is important to note that the rule of law and good governance constitute essential conditions that are vitally necessary when trying to woo foreign investors, particularly medium-sized enterprises.
>
> (ibid.)

While Germany itself has no mining companies in Mongolia, the IMRI supports broad-based social and economic development through 'capacity building' in public institutions and provides expertise on the sustainable management of mineral revenues (GIZ, 2019c). Prior to the elections in 2012, the IMRI worked primarily with a partner agency in the government – the National Development Innovation Committee – which was directed by the Prime Minister's office. Following the disbanding of this committee in 2012 after the election, the IMRI shifted focus from national-level governance to supporting sub-national administrations in Mongolia's *aimags* to engage with mining companies, local businesses and civil society organisations in their jurisdictions. However, the IMRI is still supported institutionally by the Ministry of Industry and the Ministry of Mining.

The IMRI provides training and support for each of four stakeholder groups in sub-national jurisdictions (mining companies, local businesses, civil society organisations and government) to enable a relatively even plane of negotiation, which was the initial focus of the programme (2011–2014). The purpose of this training and support is ultimately to enable the formation of 'multi-stakeholder platforms' (GIZ, 2015) and to facilitate 'public-private dialogue' under the rubric of the Integrated Community Development Partnership (ICDP) concept (GIZ, 2015: 3–7). The *aimag* administrations are supposed to hold the "public" position in the dialogue, and the three other stakeholders are treated as "private." In the ICDP concept, each stakeholder group is supposed to constitute itself organisationally and choose representatives who will engage in the facilitated negotiation of an "Inclusive Sustainability Agreement," as a basis for negotiating LDAs as required by national law.

The ICDP concept and platform has a unique place amongst other multi-stakeholder initiatives led by donor organisations in Mongolia, which tend to focus on specific issues or groups, such as revenue transparency, environmental civil society and herders' rights. In contrast, the ICDP concept extends multi-stakeholder dialogue to a new level by trying to institutionalise its organisation and practice in a way that includes most local issues related to the mining sector: effective public governance, the functionality of the local economy, sustainability of the environment and local social priorities. The rationale of the "inclusive" aspect of the ICDP maintains that the solution to the economic, environmental and social problems that arise with mining must be collective and collaborative. According to a senior representative from the IMRI, this collaborative approach can be a challenge to develop in practice, given the reality of power disparities between different stakeholder groups:

> It's not possible to solve [all these problems] as an individual stakeholder group. "One against the other" clearly doesn't work. No matter how loud they shout and how radical their activities are, people understand that it needs a kind of inclusive approach... The problem is that their relationships are clearly asymmetrical. Asymmetrical when it comes to knowledge, when it comes to power, when it comes to money, when it comes to other resources.[24]

Consequently, the express purpose of the first phase of the ICDP project was to develop the negotiating power of each stakeholder group prior to a multi-stakeholder dialogue so that its outcomes could be as fair as possible:

> We find it necessary to create some sort of fundamental basic principle knowledge of the topics [to be negotiated] before we send them into the

arena, so that they have a reasonable chance to meet on a level playing field and understand each other and speak the same language...[25]

In this way, the IMRI 'aims at a harmonisation of interests between these interdependent actors in the public and private sectors' (GIZ, 2015: 5). Similar to the EITI, the aim of the IMRI is to create a sense of mutual interest between civic, state and corporate actors. However, the model of "public-private dialogue" resembles a private negotiation of a contract, where each actor is responsible to negotiate their position and the outcome is a just one, as long as each party has sufficient resources and knowledge. Similar to Local Development Agreements (see Chapter 5), the ICDP concept that underpins the IMRI rests on the ambiguous notion of "stakeholding." While the IMRI has made a laudable effort to 'level the playing field,' it contains social conflict in mining-impacted regions within a distinctly *business-like* mode of deliberation, representation and decision-making, vis-à-vis the interaction of "stakeholders." As Crane et al. (2008: 90) put it:

> The notion of a "stakeholder" is, on the surface, very simple, but at heart, deceptively complex.

Despite being ubiquitous in corporate governance and management discourses, the process of determining 'what constitutes a legitimate stake, and how different stakes should be evaluated' (ibid.) is far from straightforward. As White (1996: 7) argues, there are two questions related to *who* participates and what *level* of participation a stake gives to its holder. This process-related complexity is particularly exacerbated when the concept is deployed beyond the boundaries of a corporate organisation, to include diverse groups of actors with *non-economic* stakes in the future of a mining project. Particularly when the coordinator or initiator of "multi-stakeholder negotiations" is not local to the "community," there are serious risks that local complexities and hierarchies (e.g. gender, livelihood base, political affiliations, age) will not be recognised in the formulation of stakeholder groupings (see also, Li, 2007: 192–229).

In this sense, the stakeholder concept is an *imposed* concept: it is not indigenous to local social or political institutions but derives its value from its "business-friendly" association with corporate governance and international standards. While the stakeholder framework may be appropriate for intra-organisational conflict in companies where employees are already *participants* in the organisation, it poses significant normative and practical problems when laid over pre-existing socio-political governance arrangements. For example, employee stakes in an organisation are mediated clearly by employment status and contractual relations with the employer. In contrast, the determination of stakeholder status for a particular project within a representative democratic system of national governance is a deeply ambivalent process. It is difficult to draw boundaries around the sphere of impact, particularly for large mining projects, and even when boundaries are decided upon, it is yet another ethical and practical question of how to engage stakeholders in a participatory process. Who is engaged? On what terms? Participation, as White (1996: 7) argues, 'can take on multiple forms and serve many different interests.' This dilemma is particularly exacerbated in light of the fact that, in the case of the IMRI, it is an influential Western development organisation doing the "engaging" with rural populations.

Not only does the concept of stakeholder participation obscure the very *political* process of "multi-stakeholder negotiations" in general, but more specifically displaces "community" relations from their social context and into a new market-friendly arrangement. Despite the "social" and "community" discourse, these arrangements are a unique technique of governance for the purposes of protecting the mining economy from political risks. As Li (2007: 234) puts it, the emphasis on community in the governance of development projects belies a deeply political motivation, that of making 'collective existence intelligible and calculable' for the purposes of political risk assessment.

### Non-state dispute resolution and conflict mediation: the role of the International Finance Corporation in the South Gobi[26]

'If you have the social license to operate, all the [mining] activities will go better, right?'

(IFC Consultant B)[27]

Semi-nomadic pastoralists in Umnogov *aimag* (South Gobi) have faced the most intensive impacts from extractive and infrastructure development activities, given the volumes and range of minerals – coal, copper and gold – that lie in this large region of the Gobi desert. This desert steppe environment hosts the lion's share of large-scale mining activity in Mongolia, even though it is probably the least suited to such intensive natural resource extraction given the fragility of its eco-system. Water scarcity, dust pollution and displacement from customary grazing land have consequently become lightning rod issues between local pastoralists and extractive industries. At least thirteen mining companies are currently operating in the province, which is home to two of the largest mining projects in the world: Oyu Tolgoi (copper and gold) and Tavan Tolgoi (coking coal). As both mega-mines receive significant levels of financing from the IFC and the EBRD, multilateral investment performance standards and dispute resolution mechanisms have become a central reference point for corporate–community conflicts in the region. For Oyu Tolgoi alone, the IFC and MIGA have collectively facilitated US $2.2 billion in loan financing and insurance guarantees (IFC, 2019b). Notably, as Bhatt (2017: 5) points out, these mechanisms are becoming increasingly important in the context of 'weak domestic legal protection' to safeguard pastoralists' rights when it comes to displacement, environmental impacts and safeguarding cultural heritage (see also Bhatt, forthcoming).

In October 2012, a group of pastoralists from Khanbogd *soum* in Umnogov submitted a claim to the CAO of the World Bank Group, which oversees compliance and dispute resolutions associated with IFC and MIGA-supported projects. These complaints were submitted with the help of a local NGO (Gobi Soil) and a national NGO (Oyu Tolgoi Watch), supported by an extensive transnational advocacy network.[28] The local pastoralists' claim was made on the basis of IFC Social and Environmental Performance Standards (PS), as well as the contractual provisions of the Oyu Tolgoi investment agreement regarding socio-environmental protection. Their concerns specifically focused on the 'impacts [of the mine] to land and water (PS 6), indigenous culture and livelihoods (PS 7), compensation and relocation (PS 5), [and] project due diligence' (CAO, 2019). The 2012 claim was shortly followed by a second complaint from the same group in February 2013, which focused on community concerns over the proposed diversion of the Undai River to supply Oyu Tolgoi and other mining projects. These claims were accepted for further assessment by the CAO dispute resolution mechanism. Consequently, local pastoralists elected a group to represent their interests in a "collaborative" dispute resolution process supervised by CAO, between herders, local government and Oyu Tolgoi LLC (CAO, 2019). Notably, this is the first time that Mongolian pastoralists have been formally engaged as a distinctive social group on the basis of their livelihood, cultural identity and connection to the land.[29]

The CAO facilitated a series of 'interim agreements' between the parties, leading to comprehensive agreements and action plans. In 2015, a Tripartite Council (TPC) was established to provide an institutional framework for joint fact-finding studies about the cumulative impacts of river diversion projects, the socio-economic impacts of mining on herder households and the environmental impacts on vegetation and water, as well as evaluate the adequacy of compensation packages. The TPC is comprised of representatives from Oyu Tolgoi, the *soum* government (Khanbogd) and local herders to facilitate ongoing dispute resolution and oversee the implementation of new agreements on collaborative water monitoring, compensation and local economic investment to support herder livelihoods. The complaints of the local community were assessed by a multi-disciplinary team of independent evaluators which carried out a series of impact assessments of the mine on areas of socio-environmental concern. The 'multi-disciplinary team and independent expert panel' produced in-depth reports covering

> issues related to pasture and herd water; changes in, and sustainability of, traditional herding; the adequacy of compensation of herders by Oyu Tolgoi; impacts on the Undai and Haliv Dugat rivers and consequences for herders, and the integrity of the tailing storage facility and the impacts of any leakage in the Haliv Dugat river.
>
> (Shankleman and Sternberg, 2017: 1)

While the details of the lengthy mediation are available elsewhere (CAO, 2019), the CAO dispute resolution process introduced a new adjudicative model as well as a soft legal basis to address company–community conflict in Mongolia. CAO's dispute resolution approach uses constructive 'assisted negotiation methods' (CAO, 2009) to assist 'parties identify alternatives for resolving the issues of concern' (ibid.). Through 'mediation...consensus-building...multi-stakeholder problem-solving, and interest-based facilitation and negotiation,' the ombudsman process is modelled as an alternative dispute resolution system. It provides a consensus-based alternative to traditional modes of dispute resolution (i.e. courts), with a focus on finding a collaborative procedure to resolve grievances through knowledge sharing and negotiation, a feature shared generally by the independent accountability mechanisms increasingly available through development project financing (Bhatt, forthcoming).

At the same time, it also shares features with formal judicial mechanisms. As Szablowki (ibid.: 98) observes, the 'particular juridical character' of this safeguard system does selectively reflect formalised features of administrative law in common law jurisdictions, 'involving mandatory policies and procedures, mechanisms for transparency and accountability, stakeholder engagement in policymaking, and even a form of judicial review.' In terms of its judicial review-like component, the CAO uses independent evaluations to determine whether or not the IFC and MIGA are acting "lawfully" (i.e. in compliance with the performance standards). In order for a complaint to be accepted for assessment by the CAO dispute resolution process, the claimants should have direct or representational "standing" (i.e. to have suffered a direct impact, or be directly representative of those who are immediately impacted):

> If the party lodging the complaint is doing so on behalf of an affected person or community, it must identify on whose behalf the complaint is made. It must also present evidence that it has been requested to present the complaint on behalf of the project-affected people/person.

These rules for eligibility are remarkably similar to the test of sufficient interest which determines the standing of claimants seeking a judicial review of an administrative or judicial decision in common law jurisdictions. Furthermore, the CAO, like the judicial review jurisdiction of the courts in common law systems, expressly affirms that it is a supervisory function rather than an appellate role in the sense that 'CAO's assessment of the complaint does not entail any judgment on the merits of the complaint' (CAO, 2013: 13). Thus, despite the explicit claim that 'CAO has no authority with respect to judicial processes... [it] is not an appeals court or a legal enforcement mechanism' (ibid.: 4), there are remarkable parallels between this allegedly non-judicial mechanism and the structure of judicial review proceedings in common law courts. Furthermore, as Jokubauskaite (2019) argues, accountability mechanisms like the CAO give international financial institutions authority to determine the boundaries of who is "affected" by the project and, consequently, which claims have legitimacy.

The distinctions and similarities between this non-state "global governance" grievance mechanism and state-based judicial mechanisms (i.e. courts) are significant. The CAO is self-styled as a "soft" dispute resolution mechanism focused on building consensus and providing an opportunity for impacted communities to co-create solutions with extractive industries. Notably, these mechanisms often only become available to communities once an extractive project is underway and has attracted project financing support from an international development financial institution (see Bhatt, forthcoming: Chapter Four). Furthermore, as a soft-law mechanism, there are limitations as to what a collaborative dispute resolution process can achieve. For instance, the independent expert report highlighted the effect of 'gaps in initial monitoring' (ibid.) by the company as well as 'a range of changes in herding in Khanbogd *soum* not related to Oyu Tolgoi' which meant that 'some critical concerns of herders, particularly relating to the impacts of Oyu Tolgoi on herder water, cannot be definitively resolved' (ibid.). The report offered recommendations for the company to rebuild trust, but no sanctions could be authorised by the independent panel or by CAO to address corporate mismanagement. This is a significant point, given that anxiety over water was a primary impetus for local pastoralists to submit their original claims to CAO in 2012 and 2013.

However, the CAO dispute resolution process does exceed mere "mediation" by assuming a distinctive quasi-judicial structure, as noted earlier, which involves recognition of standing (based on impact and identity), creating systems of community representation, evidence gathering and the negotiation and acceptance of new terms for the relationship. While it is impossible to determine the long-term implications of this new institutional arrangement at this early stage, the CAO dispute resolution process has been instrumental in introducing new procedures, parameters and platforms which channel social conflict in "constructive" directions. Not discounting the significant benefits associated with access to independent impact assessments as well as a new dispute resolution platform, the absence of effective national alternatives to mediate local concerns suggests that these non-state dispute resolution mechanisms have a more important judicial and political effect than CAO claims (CAO, 2013)..

Furthermore, as Bhatt (2017: 9; forthcoming) powerfully argues, these new methodologies of non-state dispute resolution in a context of weak domestic legal protections exemplify the power of private investors 'to plug the gap with informal norms implemented through complex financial mechanisms.' The 'layered nature of private finance' (ibid), characterised by relations of complex subsidiarity in the investment structure of a project like Oyu Tolgoi, 'obfuscates the legal relations such that affected communities remain unaware of the ultimate identity of the developers... restricting their ability to access land' (ibid). Bhatt's argument highlights the way in which the dispute resolution processes facilitated by IFIs create a mirage of corporate-community accountability managed by Rio Tinto and the CAO, while the actual investors and shareholders maintain their anonymity. The opacity of these processes belies the involvement of these actors in shaping the extent and manner in which pastoralists' claims are to be addressed. For example, with regard to the 2012 and 2013 submissions to the CAO, both the IFC and Rio Tinto exploited the alleged 'legal ambiguity' (ibid: 14) regarding indigenous recognition in international law to effectively disregard pastoralist claims under IFC PS 7. While pastoralists have been recognised as a distinctive economic and cultural "group" through the CAO process and represented as such on the TPC, they have effectively been prevented from realising rights to free, prior and informed consent which have been widely affirmed in international case law as applicable to 'persons claiming a special socio-economic, cultural and communal relationship to traditional land' (ibid: 8). The role of the IFC's formal accountability mechanism in shaping the realisability of rights, remedial measures and redistributive benefits available to impacted communities – particularly through processes of 'factual identity demarcation' (ibid: 17) – evidences the increasingly authoritative influence that transnational agents and norms are having over legal issues traditionally considered to be the domain of the state (see also, Jokubauskaite, 2019).

Formal dispute resolution processes have been accompanied by more informal influencing strategies by the IFC. As the CAO dispute resolution was in process, the IFC also initiated a voluntary CSR initiative in the South Gobi targeting social conflict over water. The South Gobi Water and Mining Industry Roundtable (SGWMIR) project was established by the IFC after consultation with its client, Oyu Tolgoi LLC, in 2012. The SGWMIR project set up two roundtables for mining companies in the South Gobi region, one for company 'decision-makers' and another for 'boots on the ground' (ibid.) staff who work in areas like community relations. The goal of both roundtables was 'three-dimensional': to (1) develop 'short- and medium-term action plans to improve internal alignment' (2) 'use multidirectional communications on water management' and (3) 'co-managing knowledge and other resources with other decision-makers' (ibid.: 8) which correspond with shared risks, shared realities and shared responsibilities. 'Internal alignment' refers to 'raising awareness of the responsibilities, realities, and risks of water management across business functions' (ibid.). Amongst other things, internal alignment entailed a process of information sharing between mining companies about water management techniques and engaging in what is called 'peer-to-peer learning' (ibid.: 34). The aim of this process was to standardise mining companies' approach to water management by developing 'symmetric standards and policies' (ibid.). This process culminated in February 2016 with the signing of a Voluntary Code of Practice (VCP) by eight mining companies operating in the South Gobi.

Amongst the signatories of the VCP are significant operators in the Gobi, including Oyu Tolgoi, Erdenet Tavan Tolgoi and Energy Resources. These three major mining companies are all in receipt of financing from either the IFC or the European Bank of Reconstruction and Development. The VCP includes nineteen obligations which cover participatory monitoring programmes, grievance mechanisms for residents, the impact of mining on water for pastureland, the transparent measurement and publication of water data 'in a format accessible to local communities' (Elbegsaikhan, 2016). Notably, these nineteen obligations are framed in almost identical terms to the IFC's performance standards. The Government of Canada, the EBRD and the International Council on Mining and Metals provided external support for the development of the VCP, again highlighting the role of international institutions and organisations in providing the institutional foundation for "socially responsible mining" in the South Gobi.

The implications of this development are significant in the sense that it evidences the normative standard-setting power of global governance actors like the IFC and the institutional consolidation of corporate power in a strategic extractive region. Rather than having mining companies at odds with each other, the SGWMIR sought to enable collaboration between companies over their shared "risk" as water-dependent companies. The project also sought to standardise their approach to operate as a semi-cohesive bloc in relation to regional water governance. More specifically, in the case of Mongolia, the development of corporate roundtables through the SGWMIR directly enhances their lobbying power on the multi-stakeholder councils for the newly formed River Basin Administrations (RBAs) which allocate permits for medium- to large-scale water use (i.e. for mining projects). One of the hoped-for outcomes of the SGWMIR was to institutionalise the representation of the companies involved in the consultative councils for the RBAs, according to an IFC consultant.[30] Notably, the World Bank has also supplied the development funding for the creation of three strategic RBAs in the South Gobi through its Mining Infrastructure Investment Support Project (P118109). These are the most controversial RBAs, given the extent of power local governments have to lose through the delegation of decision-making authority to these new administrations which are supposedly determined by hydrological as opposed to political boundaries.[31] The second dimension of the SGWMIR focused on mining companies' communication strategies with the local population and *soum/aimag* authorities. The amelioration of anxiety about water through dialogue with local residents was seen by the IFC as crucial to the stability of mining projects. According to the IFC's 2014 *Water, Mining and Communities* report (Darling et al., 2014: 15), gaining 'tacit community approval of a project, specifically around water and a company's stewardship of it, can play a direct role in a government's decision to grant additional exploration or mining licenses and necessary water use permits.' The IFC puts this 'social and political license' forward as an important 'value driver' for companies to engage (ibid.). One of the core-stated objectives of using 'multidirectional communication' is to use 'communication and engagement as a form of risk management' (ibid.: 25). In this framework, companies produce objective and scientific knowledge about water, whilst still engaging with 'trust and empathy' (ibid.) to 'assuage fears, suspicions and anxieties' (ibid.: 17).

Thirdly, not only must the local pastoralists' perceptions be adjusted to face "the facts," but they are also offered the opportunity to become co-managers with mining companies through participatory monitoring. The logic of 'co-managing knowledge and other resources' (ibid.: 8) is evidently supposed to develop a sense of *shared responsibility* for the future of water. For example, in addition to participatory monitoring in the South Gobi as part of the SGWMIR project, an Integrated Water Resource Management training module (ibid.: 35) was offered by the companies to 'broader stakeholder groups – government, civil society, communities, academia and media' for the purpose of 'building knowledge for informed and increased co-management of water.' The Report (ibid.: 17) puts it this way:

> Educating the community about technical aspects of mining and water, understanding traditional beliefs and the community's use of water, incorporating those values and uses into water management, and providing opportunities for stakeholders to participate in the development and monitoring of water plans can reduce misconceptions.

The SGWMIR is thus imbued with the global discourse of CSR, particularly through the distinctively "social" – as opposed to political – language of "community," "social license" and "participation." The inherent hierarchy of the relationship created by the imbalance in economic and discursive power between the large-scale mining companies and the predominantly pastoralist residents of the South Gobi is not overtly addressed within this conception of their "social" relationship. The SGWMIR is framed by the IFC as a "win-win" solution for companies and communities, without an evaluation of how such an initiative could expand and consolidate the influence of the private sector on critical aspects of water governance and the terms of its contestation.

Drawing on the earlier discussion of the IMRI case study, there is good reason to be wary of the language of community and participation in the SGWMIR project. It obscures the reality of 'boundary work' (Li, 2007) in these "collaborations," where conflicted relations are re-translated into collaborative terms without first transforming the 'material roots' (Li, 2007: 263) of the conflict. Even though the IFC and corporate facilitators of a participatory process like the SWGMIR may put the community at centre stage in the name of autonomy, participation and empowerment, the deeper function of such initiatives is evidenced in the motivations of the project initiators. As the quotes from the IFC Report (Darling et al., 2014) indicate, the driving purpose of the SWGMIR, like many participatory programmes initiated by the World Bank (see Li, 2007: 230–269), is to "help" local communities learn 'how to conduct themselves in competitive arenas, and [make] appropriate choices' (ibid.: 263) in the context of a market economy.

### Summary of case studies

In the Mongolian context, the emerging global framework of norms and practices around what is considered socially responsible corporate behaviour has been influential in shaping the way that mining companies engage with Mongolian citizens. In the absence of a national legislative framework for the impacts of mining on critical aspects of rural social life (i.e. herding livelihoods, the cultural and spiritual value of land and water) (Erdenebolor and Baigal, 2012),[32] international institutions and organisations have introduced global governance norms and mechanisms in conjunction with mining companies to ameliorate conflict around extractive projects. The localisation of the social impacts of mining implicates the state because of its 'strategy of selective absence' (Szablowski, 2007: 27) in limiting these conflicts to provincial and regional spaces of negotiation. In turn, the localisation of social conflict has enabled the entry of global governance norms into rural political environments. Without discounting the ethical intentions of individuals working to enhance the social responsibility of mining companies, global CSR norms and mechanisms materially enhance the security of corporate access to "natural resources" in the long term and insulate the process of extraction from political risks, both in mineral and surplus value terms, for the benefit of state, corporate and shareholder interests.

The amelioration of local social conflict by IFIs and international organisations has introduced a new "social" frame to corporate–citizen relations that still operates along (political) lines of exclusion-inclusion. For example, groups of residents impacted by mining projects become the "affected community," but the boundaries about who is included in "the community" are determined on a case-by-case basis in the context of negotiations between companies and local representatives (Erdenebolor and Baigal, 2012). This process naturally depends upon political decisions about which level of local government to engage, which civil society organisations to include and which "other" community groups to recognise as legitimate representatives of the "community" (ibid.: x). Fundamentally, the substance of Mongolian citizenship for rural communities is in the balance, as corporate and state institutions and actors try to find collaborative solutions to the problem of local "political risk" to mining projects. The reality is that the ideal of multi-stakeholder negotiations is, in fact, riven by local hierarchies around 'community' representation, and not helped by the local perception of inequality in their treatment by different mining companies (ibid.: vi).

The coercive quality of projects like the SWGMIR and the IMRI is subtle, as they contrast with the top-down mode of state bureaucratic planning backed by military power, characteristic of the socialist period of state transformation. However, in the new era of the extractive market economy, these social governance schemes have their own coercive power, seeking influence over local knowledge, consent and cooperation, exercised through *economic* forms of material and normative power. 'Empowerment is still a relationship of power' (Li, 2007: 275), just as participation is an inherently political issue: 'there are always questions to be asked about who is involved, how, and on whose terms' (White, 1996: 14). The fairly ubiquitous notion of "community capacity building" – i.e. 'that communities need to be enabled to actively present and protect their interests' (Erdenebolor and Baigal, 2012: vii) – uncritically accepts the governing power in that "empowerment." Furthermore, "community" access to corporate processes of recognition and redress is usually determined by whether or not they have experienced "direct" or "indirect" impacts by the project or by having a special status. Again, this depends upon the recognition by the company and the strategic representation of impacted populations by their political represent-atives and NGOs, as a 2012 research study of 'social impacts and stakeholder interactions' in mining-impacted areas attested (ibid.).

For example, as evidenced in the discussion of the CAO dispute resolution pro-cess, herders impacted by a mining project have the opportunity to be given a special group status by international financiers even in the absence of state recogni-tion.[33] In this way, mining companies and banks can become politically authorita-tive in the governance of sub-national claims, depending on the orientation of the particular company to the global governance milieu of norms and mechanisms. Notably, the independent evaluators' summary report for the Joint Fact-Finding mission in the CAO dispute resolution process highlights the way in which pas-toralists in Khanbogd *soum* ascribe roles and expectations 'commonly ascribed to government' regarding environmental governance to Oyu Tolgoi LLC.

## Conclusion

In this chapter, I have analysed the process by which parameters for civic en-gagement in the governance of the mining sector following the crisis of foreign investment in 2012–2013 have been established through state action and cor-porate initiatives. The crackdown on confrontational protest and resistance to widespread mining coincided neatly with the government's renewed commit-ment to stabilising the investment environment from the unstable influence of "nationalist" politicians in Parliament and "corrupt" local governments under the 2014 State Policy on the Minerals Sector. This stabilisation impetus also extended to non-state institutions, particularly dissident NGOs and social move-ments that had engaged in and encouraged direct action protests against the government and specific mining projects. Major donor organisations withdrew financial and political supports to these associations, which were ultimately side-lined within the MECC following the arrest and imprisonment of five River Movement leaders under charges of environmental terrorism.

This violent closure of political space for dissident civic mobilisation has left consensus-based alternatives, primarily informed by global norms and mecha-nisms, as the dominant modus operandi. While utilising multi-stakeholder chan-nels may have a strategic value for local residents and civil society organisations in the short to medium term, there are deeper questions about how these new stakeholder-based modes of participation, recognition and dispute resolution construct new constitutional realities at the local level. Through these collabora-tive alternatives, social conflict has been effectively co-opted into the apparatus of pro-extractive governance, despite the rhetoric of inclusion and "community engagement." These consensual frameworks, exemplified in the case studies ex-amined in the second half of this chapter, may have some immediate utility for mining-affected populations, but are fundamentally part of an enabling constitutional framework for extractive development. The implications of the state's stabilisation agenda in the extractive sector for the overall democratic constitution of the Mongolian state will be analysed further in the next chapter.

## Notes

1 Cox's often-quoted term 'the limits of the possible' refers to 'the strong bonds that hold the existing order together, and the influences that orient its direction of development' (Cox, 2002: 37).

2 For example, the Asia Foundation promotes "responsible mining" in line with global good governance standards, as will be discussed in relation to its Responsible Mining Initiative and Engaging Stakeholders in Environmental Conservation Projects.

3 Author interview, 19th November 2014.

4 In Mongolia, specifically, its programmes range from helping 'to strengthen anti-corruption efforts and improve administrative reform; improve governance of cities and citizen engagement; increase gender equality; advance responsible resource use and environmental conservation; and support Mongolia's multilateral foreign policy engagement' (Asia Foundation, 2016).

5 Author interview, former Asia Foundation Consultant on the RMI, 26th September 2014.

6 Notably, this period of activist optimism was a critical factor in "destabilising" the investment environment because the state revised mining and environmental legislation partly in response to its increasingly vocal public about the negative impacts and lack of benefits from mining (see Byambajav, 2014: 5–6). For more details of the 'destabilising' effects of legislative change between 2009 and 2013, see Chapter 4.

7 Author Interview, Director of the Mongolian Environmental Civil Council, 11th November 2014.

8 Ibid.

9 Ibid.

10 Author Interview, President of the Mongolian National Mining Association, 13th November 2015.

11 Ibid.

12 Author interview, 19th November 2014.

13 Author observation, President of the MECC, Speech at the 4th National Forum for Environmental NGOs, 24th November 2014)

14 Author observation, 24th November 2014.

15 Author interview, 11th November 2014.

16 Ibid.

17 Ibid.

18 Author interview, 20th November 2015.

19 I specifically use the term "governance participation" rather than participatory governance, as the latter suggests that governance is *constituted* by its participants, rather than the Mongolian case where the governance system appears to be pre-constituted in a pro-mining direction, regardless of the participation of civil society organisations.

20 The nine companies involved were Anglo-American, BHP Billiton, Rio Tinto, Codelco, Newmont, Noranda, Phelps Dodge, Placer Dome and WMC Limited. Of these nine companies, six (Anglo-American, BHP Billiton, Rio Tinto, Phelps Dodge, Placer Dome and WMC Limited) have invested in Mongolia's mineral sector.

21 The data for this section was acquired through attendance at the GIZ-sponsored 'G7 Fast-Track Partnership Conference on the EITI,' 10–11th November 2015, analysis

of GIZ promotional publications for the Integrated Mineral Resources Initiative (IMRI), and an interview with a senior representative from the IMRI project.

22 Author observation, 20th November 2015.

23 Ibid.

24 Author interview, 19th January 2016.

25 Ibid.

26 The data for this section has been acquired through cited IFC publications and in-depth interviews with IFC consultants on this project (20th September 2014 and 5th November 2015).

27 Author interview, 5th November 2015.

28 For example, Gobi Soil, Tsetsii Nutag and Steps without Borders, which are all local herder NGOs from Khanbogd Soum (area most affected by Oyu Tolgoi) have connected with Oyu Tolgoi Watch, a national NGO who is partnering with other national NGOs such as Citizens Alliance Centre, the Centre for Human Rights and Development, the Federation of Trade Unions and Eco-Asia Institute. OT Watch has linked up with numerous NGOs and mining watch groups at the international and global levels, such as the London Mining Network, Sierra Club, the Accountability Counsel and the Environmental Law Alliance Worldwide. Sukhgerel Dugersuren, the Executive Director of OT Watch, has accompanied leaders of the local NGOs, such as Bayarsaikhan Namsrai of Steps Without Borders to Washington DC to lobby the US government and other funders (i.e. Export-Import Bank) to stop funding Oyu Tolgoi until herders' claims have been recognised and acted upon relating to the mine's devastating environmental and social impacts.

29 Apart from the reindeer herders in northern Mongolia who are part of an internationally recognised indigenous group - the *Dukha* - Mongolian pastoralists have no specific legal status or protection under domestic law.

30 Ibid.

31 Author interview, IFC Consultant A, 20th September 2014.

32 Apart from the provision for local development agreements in the Minerals Law (see Chapter 5) and the new template for LDAs, there is no specific legislation to address or assess the social impacts of mining.

33 This is especially the case where companies are financed by institutions such as the IFC or the European Bank for Reconstruction and Development, which have specific protocols for dealing with impacts on people with 'land-based' livelihoods (i.e. IFC Performance Standard 1).

## References

Aaronsen, S. A. 2011. "Limited Partnership: Business, Government, Civil Society and the Public in the Extractive Industries Transparency Initiative (EITI)." *Public Administration and Development* 31: 50–63.

Adam Smith International. 2014. "Show Me the Money! Strengthening EITI Implementation in Mongolia." Republished by the Invest Mongolia Agency http://investmongolia.gov.mn/en/?p=867. Accessed 6th April 2017.

Asia Foundation. 2006. "Mongolia Highlight: Homeland and Water Protection Coalition of River Movements Targets Mining Law Changes." https://asiafoundation.org/resources/pdfs/MGenvironment.pdf. Accessed 6th April 2017.

———. 2008. "Mongolia Highlights: 51 Signatories Agree to a Definition of Responsible Mining that will Advance National Objectives for the Benefit of All Mongolians." https://asiafoundation.org/resources/pdfs/MGMultistakeholderIV.pdf. Accessed 6th April 2017.

————. 2016. "Mongolia: Country Overview." http://asiafoundation.org/wp-content/uploads/2016/10/Mongolia2016.pdf. Accessed 6th April 2017.

BMZ (German Federal Ministry for Economic Cooperation and Development). 2010. "German Development Minister Dirk Niebel Ends Visit to Mongolia." 23rd August Press Release. www.bmz.de/en/press/aktuelleMeldungen/archive/2010/august/20100823_pm_136_mongolei/index.html. Accessed 7th April 2017.

Bhatt, K. 2017. 'New "Legal" Actors, Norms and Processes: Formal and Informal Indigenous Land Rights Norms in the Oyu Tolgoi Project, Mongolia.' TLI Think! Paper 63/2017; King's College London Dickson Poon School of Law Legal Studies Research Paper. Available at SSRN: https://ssrn.com/abstract=2995505.

————. Forthcoming. *Concessionaires, Financiers and Communities: Implementing Indigenous Peoples' Rights to Land in Transnational Development Projects.* Cambridge: Cambridge University Press.

Buxton, A. 2012. "MMSD+10: Reflecting on a Decade of Mining and Sustainable Development." Sustainable Markets Discussion Paper (June). IIED: London. http://pubs.iied.org/pdfs/16041IIED.pdf. Accessed 6th April 2017.

Byambajav, D. 2006. "NGOs in Mongolia: A Crucial Factor in Mongolian Society and Politics." *The Mongolian Journal of International Affairs* 13: 132–146.

————. 2012. "Mobilising Against Dispossession: Gold Mining and a Local Resistance Movement in Mongolia." *Journal of the Centre for Northern Humanities* 5:13–32.

————. 2013. "A Network Approach to NGO Development: Women's NGOs in Mongolia." *The International Journal of Not-For-Profit Law* 15(1). http://www.icnl.org/research/journal/vol15iss1/art_4.htm. Accessed 28th September 2019.

————. 2014. "The River Movements' Struggle in Mongolia." *Social Movement Studies: Journal of Social, Cultural and Political Protest*: 2014: 1–6. DOI: 10.1080/14742837.2013.877387

————. 2015. "Mining, "Social License" and Local Level Agreements in Mongolia." Proceedings from the International Conference on Perspectives on the Development of Energy and Mineral Resources Hawai'i, Mongolia and Germany. February 11th–13th 2015 http://socialsciences.hawaii.edu/conference/demr2015/_papers/byambajav-dalaibuyan.pdf. Accessed 6th August 2016.

CAO (Compliance Advisor Ombudsmen). 2009. "CAO Dispute Resolution: Ombudsman." www.cao-ombudsman.org/howwework/ombudsman/. Accessed 23rd April 2019.

————. 2013. "CAO Operational Guidelines." IFC, www.cao-ombudsman.org/howwework/documents/CAOOperationalGuidelines2013_ENGLISH.pdf. Accessed 23rd April 2019.

————. 2019. "Mongolia/OyuTolgoi-01/Southern Gobi." www.cao-ombudsman.org/cases/case_detail.aspx?id=191. Accessed 23rd April 2019.

Carter, C. and Davaanyam, D. 2015a. "How the EITI May Become Mongolian: Part 1 of 2." 11th May *Asia Pacific Memo* https://apm.iar.ubc.ca/eiti-become-mongolian-part-1/ Accessed 6th April 2019.

————. 2015b. "How the EITI May Become Mongolian: Part 2 of 2." 14th May *Asia Pacific Memo* https://apm.iar.ubc.ca/eiti-become-mongolian-part-2/. Accessed 23rd April 2019.

Combellick-Bidney, S. 2012. "Mongolia's Mining Controversies and the Politics of Place." In Julian Dierkes (ed.) *Change in Democratic Mongolia: Social Relations, Health, Mobile Pastoralism and Mining.* Boston, MA: Brill.

Cox, R. 2002. *The Political Economy of a Plural World: Critical Reflections on Power, Morals and Civilisation.* London/New York: Routledge.

Crane, A., Matten, D., and Moon, J. 2008. *Corporations and Citizenship.* Cambridge: Cambridge University Press.

Cutler, C. 2011. "The Globalisation of International Law, Indigenous Identity, and the New Constitutionalism." In W. D. Coleman (ed.) *Property, Territory, Globalisation: Struggles Over Autonomy.* Vancouver, BC: UBC Press, pp. 29–55.

Danaasuren, V. 2010. "NGOs as Accountability Promoters: In the Mongolian Case." Paper Presented at the Sixth Asia Pacific Interdisciplinary Research in Accounting Conference, University of Sydney (AUS), 12th and 13th of July 2010. http://apira2010.econ.usyd.edu.au/conference_proceedings/APIRA-2010-166-van DanGombo-NGOS-as-accountability-promoters-Mongolia.pdf. Accessed 6th April 2017.

———. 2012. "Account(ing)/(Ability): Democratising the Environmental Impact Assessment in Mongolian Mining." PhD Thesis, Victoria University of Wellington of New Zealand, Research Archive.

Darling, R., Jones, V. N., Lukic, J., and Read, L. 2014. "Water, Mining and Communities: Creating Shared Value Through Sustainable Water Management." IFC Discussion Paper. Washington, DC: World Bank. www.commdev.org/water-mining-and-communities/. Accessed 23rd April 2019.

Elbegsaikhan, Ts. 2016. "Voluntary Code of Practice for Mining Companies." *Mongolian Economy Journal.* 2nd March http://mongolianeconomy.mn/en/i/8750. Accessed 7th April 2017.

Equator Principles. 2013. "The Equator Principles III." http://equator-principles.com/resources/equator_principles_III.pdf. Accessed 25th March 2017.

———. 2019. "Equator Principles." http://equator-principles.com/. Accessed 25th March 2019.

Erdenebolor, B. and Baigal, L. 2012. "Mining and Communities: Social Impacts and Stakeholder Interactions in Mining Areas of Mongolia." Ulaanbaatar: Responsible Mining Initiative for Sustainable Development.

Extractive Industries Transparency Initiative (EITI). 2017. "EITI Standard: Overview." https://eiti.org/standard/overview. Accessed 6th April 2017.

Fisher, W. F. 1997. "Doing Good? The Politics and Anti-Politics of NGO Practices." *Annual Review of Anthropology* 26: 439–464.

Fritz, V. 2002. "Mongolia: Dependent Democratisation." *Journal of Communist Studies and Transition Politics* 18(4): 75–100.

———. 2008. "Mongolia: The Rise and Travails of a Deviant Democracy." *Democratization* 15(4): 766–788.

Garriga, E. and Melé, D. 2004. "Corporate Social Responsibility Theories: Mapping the Territory." *Journal of Business Ethics* 53: 51–71.

GIZ (Deutsche Gesellschaft für Internationale Zusammenarbeit). 2015. "GIZ's Integrated Mineral Resource Initiative." Pamphlet distributed at the 5th National Corporate Social Responsibility Forum 2015.

———. 2019a. "About GIZ: Identity." www.giz.de/en/aboutgiz/identity.html. Accessed 6th April 2019.

———. 2019b. "About GIZ: Profile." www.giz.de/en/aboutgiz/profile.html. Accessed 6th April 2019.

———. 2019c. "Integrated Mineral Resource Initiative." www.giz.de/en/worldwide/17750.html. Accessed 6th April 2017.

Global Legal Monitor. 2011. "Mongolia: Supreme Court Orders Government to Enforce Law." www.loc.gov/law/foreign-news/article/mongolia-supreme-court-orders-
government-to-enforce-law/. Accessed 6th April 2017.

Gombodorj, U. and Batsuren, O. 2005. "NGOs in Mongolia: Mapping Results." Research Commissioned by the Open Society Forum. Ulaanbaatar: Democracy Education Centre.

Hatcher, P. 2014. *Regimes of Risk: The World Bank and the Transformation of Mining in
Asia*. New York/London: Palgrave Macmillan.

Haufler, V. 2010. "Disclosure as Governance: The Extractive Industries Transparency
Initiative and Resource Management in the Developing World." *Global Environmental
Politics* 10(3): 53–73.

International Finance Corporation (IFC). 2019. "Partner with Us." (IFC Website Homepage)
www.ifc.org/wps/wcm/connect/corp_ext_content/ifc_external_corporate_site/
home. Accessed 23rd April 2019.

———. 2019b. "IFC Support for Oyu Tolgoi." www.ifc.org/wps/wcm/connect/
industry_ext_content/ifc_external_corporate_site/ogm+home/priorities/mining/
oyutolgoi2c. Accessed 23rd April 2019.

International Institute for Environment and Development (IIED). 2002. "Breaking
Ground: Mining, Minerals and Sustainable Development." IIED: London. http://
pubs.iied.org/9084IIED/. Accessed 6th April 2017.

Jokubauskaite, G. 2019. "Tied Affectedness? Grassroots Resistance and the World Bank."
*Third World Thematics: A TWQ Journal* 3(5–6): 703–724.

Katz, H. and Anheier, H. 2006. "Global Connectedness: The Structure of Transnational
NGO Networks." In M. Glasius, M. Kaldor, and H. Anheier (eds.) *Global Civil Society
2005/2006*. Thousand Oaks, CA: SAGE Publications, pp. 240–265.

Li, T. 2007. *The Will to Improve: Governmentality, Development and the Practice of Politics*. Durham, NC: Duke University Press.

Mendee, J. 2012. *Civil Society in a Non-Western Setting*. Saarbrücken, Germany: Lambert
Academic Publishing.

———. 2013. "Mongolia Takes Longer View of Resource Wealth." *Asia Times Online*
www.atimes.com/atimes/China_Business/CBIZ-01-070313.html.    Accessed    6th
April 2017.

Munkhbayar, Ts. 2014. "Complaint to the City Criminal Court of Appeals, No. 10."
February 24th. Written petition submitted to court. Source: UMMRL.

Rossabi, M. 2005. *Mongolia: From Khans to Commissars to Capitalists*. Berkeley: University of California Press.

Shagdarsuren, O. 2018. "Experience of Mongolia in Managing Joint International Projects through Cooperation between Government, Civil Society, Local Communities
and Industry on the Issue of Local Development." Conference Paper, International
Baikal Forum "Eurasian Integration Project: Civilisational Identity and Global Posi-
tioning", Irkutsk, Russia, September 2018.

Shankleman, J. and Sternberg, J. 2017. "Multi-Disciplinary Team and Independent
Expert Panel Joint Fact Finding: Summary of the Experts' Reports." Oxford: JSL
Consulting.

Sneath, D. 2010. "Political Mobilisation and the Construction of Collective Identity in
Mongolia." *Central Asian Survey* 29(3): 251–267.

Szablowski, D. 2007. *Transnational Law and Local Struggles: Mining, Communities and
the World Bank*. Hart Publishing.

Tolson, M. 2014 (January 28th). Eco-Warrior or Eco-Terrorist? Mongolia Jails Environmentalist for 21 Years. *The Asian Correspondent* http://asiancorrespondent. com/118997/mongolia-tsetsegee-munkhbayar-jail/. Accessed 1st April 2018.

UNDP. 2012. "Situation Analysis and Recommendations on Promoting Volunteerism in Mongolia." Ulaanbaatar: UNDP. www.mn.undp.org/content/dam/mongolia/ Publications/UNV/VWG-VolSAR-Publlication-Eng-12Dec5.pdf. Accessed 6th April 2018.

United Movement for Mongolian Rivers and Lakes (UMMRL). 2014. "Press Release" 16th February 2014 *Ulaanbaatar Post.*

———. 2014b. "Appeal to Dismiss Ruling 126 Criminalising the Fire Nation Movement." Source: UMMRL. English translation.

United Nations Global Compact. 2017. "Our Governance." www.unglobalcompact.org/ about/governance. Accessed 25th March 2017.

Upton, C. 2012. "Mining, Resistance and Pastoral Livelihoods in Contemporary Mongolia." In Julian Dierkes (ed.) *Change in Democratic Mongolia: Social Relations, Health, Mobile Pastoralism and Mining.* Boston, MA: Brill, pp. 223–248.

Vogel, D. 2005. *The Market for Virtue: The Potential and Limits of Corporate Social Responsibility.* Washington, DC: The Brookings Institute.

White, S. 1996. "Depoliticising Development: The Uses and Abuses of Participation." *Development in Practice* 6(1): 6–15.

World Bank, 2019. "Environmental and Social Framework." www.worldbank.org/en/ projects-operations/environmental-and-social-framework. Accessed 23rd April 2019.

# Part III

# Theoretical reflections

Chapter 7

# Transnational legal ordering and state transformation in Mongolia

## Summarising the case study

## Introduction

"Mongolian politicians have now learnt the lesson that they can damage the economy with too much resource nationalism." O. Chuluunbat, Former Vice-Minister of Economic Development
(quoted in Oxford Business Group, 2015)

"Investment comes when the market is open, policies are supportive, government is stable, roadmaps are clear and opportunities are available. We have them."
National Development Agency Investment Guidebook (2019: 4)

The previous four chapters provided an empirical overview of Mongolia's integration into the global minerals economy through the lens of state transformation and transnational legal ordering (TLO). In the Mongolian context, I have examined the way that the stability of the national legal and political environment has become a normative prerequisite for law and policy-making in the mining regime following the FDI crisis in 2012–2013. The primacy of stability, not only as a guiding principle for law and policy development but also as a catalyst for structural reform, indicates that a more profound transformation has occurred within the institutions of the state in relation to the market. The overarching theme running through all four chapters is the negotiation of the state's relationship with capital over time: (1) through the transition to industrial capitalism and alignment with the Soviet Union (1921–1990); (2) in the post-socialist context of democratisation and dependency upon multilateral financial institutions; (3) through dependency on foreign direct investment and mineral exports; and (4) by consolidating Mongolia's reputation as a competitive and stable destination for foreign investment in the mining sector.

Chapter 3 set out the historical complementarity between state formation, production and accumulation in the Mongolian context, noting that the creation of an economic sphere as separate to the political was a gradual process achieved during the socialist period. The post-socialist transition process institutionalised and deepened this separation through the marketisation of Mongolia's economy in the early 1990s. Chapter 4 provided a chronological overview of the main legal and political dimensions of investor–state conflict between 1994 and 2014, specifically the way that the revisions of the mining regime reflected a form of constitutional bargaining between the state, its national political constituency (voters) and its new transnational economic constituency (foreign investors and mining corporations). In 2012–2013, Mongolia suffered a major crisis of foreign direct investment in its mining sector as a result of investor backlash against the alleged "resource nationalism" of the state, which was compounded by the downturn in global commodity prices for minerals and Mongolia's huge debt burden. I argue that the "economic" crisis of FDI functioned as a constitutional crucible to strongly shape the conflicted sense of national and global priorities within the state, firmly establishing the primacy of protecting the flow of transnational capital, along with investors' rights and preferences, over other sociopolitical interests and economic possibilities. The state's primary dependency on foreign capital consolidated the ordering process that had begun following Mongolia's integration into the global minerals market as an exporter of primary commodities in the late 1990s.

In Chapters 5 and 6, I analysed institutional and normative reordering processes along three different axes of state power: within the central state itself (intra-institutional); between national and sub-national levels of government (inter-institutional) and between the state and civil society (state–society relations). Some might argue that these three axes of reordering could be analysed as separate phenomena, but I argue that they make a comprehensive sense in relation to an underlying reorientation of the state to transnational capital in the context of global economic integration. The Mongolian navigation of its "global" position in relation to transnational capital investment is the underlying social context in which these three distinct but interrelated programmes of reform took place.

This chapter concludes the book by examining the overall processes and implications of the current "global capitalist" phase of state transformation in Mongolia. The 2014 legal and policy reforms in the mining sector, where the state reverted to a liberal model of economic regulation, should be understood as a process of TLO (Shaffer, 2014), with significant constitutional implications for the democratic state of Mongolia. Despite the ongoing inter-dependency of capitalist accumulation and the legal-political frameworks provided by the state, there are losses for national democratic forms of the state as it reorients towards accumulation strategies based on harnessing transnational capital flows. I will firstly argue that the 2014 reforms to Mongolia's mining regime should be conceptualised as a TLO process, and then outline the democratic losses and risks at stake in such a transformation.

## Transnational legal ordering

In this book, I have traced the way in which transnational legal norms related to political risk mitigation have effectively penetrated Mongolian law, policy-making and state–society relations. In this sense, the book adopts a socio-legal approach to the study of TLO, which focuses on transnational norms as a 'source of legal change within a national legal system' (Shaffer, 2014: 5). Shaffer (ibid.: 12) argues that the transformative effect of a transnational legal order in relation to the state may become apparent through both symbolic and practical aspects of legal change. *Symbolic* legal change refers to change 'on the books in terms of constitutional, statutory or administrative law revisions, or the creation or restructuring of agencies and courts' (ibid.). Transnational legal orders may also impact 'legal and organisational *practice*' (ibid., emphasis added). As previously mentioned in Chapter 1, Shaffer's analytic framework for the state transformative effects of TLO processes has five dimensions, which can be expressed in "symbolic" and/or "practical" modes. These are:

1 Changes in substantive law and practice.
2 Changes in the boundary between the state, the market and other forms of social ordering.
3 Changes in the institutional architecture of the state.
4 Changes in professional expertise and expertise's role in governance.
5 Changes in associational patterns, institutionalised through transnational accountability mechanisms with their accompanying normative frames (ibid.: 23).

The following section will briefly situate the empirical findings of the previous three chapters within Shaffer's analytical framework in order to indicate the extent of an overall reordering process within the Mongolian state, before assessing its implications and concluding the book. As I explained in Chapter 1, the notion of TLO offers a way to move beyond the binaries (i.e. national/international, local/global, public/private, political/economic) which have shaped the majority of our language for law, capital and the state.

## Stabilising Mongolia's investment environment as a process of transnational legal ordering

In the context of Mongolia's mining regime, I argue that a significant reordering shift is demonstrable within the apparatus of the state since the 2012–2013 crisis of investment/investor confidence. Since this crisis, the regulatory preferences of investors have become institutionally embedded across the governance regime. This embedding process has occurred partly as a result of the deep dependence of the state upon foreign capital investment in the mining sector (i.e. making it economically almost impossible to resist) as well as the strategic promotion of competitive globalism by an elite network of national policy-makers and decision-takers. Consequently, institutions within the state that provide the necessary architecture for a favourable investment environment have been strengthened, while those that are seen to threaten investor interests (e.g. through the politi-cisation of mining investment) have been neutralised. Intra-state neutralisation was the subject of Chapter 5, in which the influence of various institutional loci of resistance, particularly legislative and deliberative organs of national and sub-national governments, was curtailed. Additionally, a major consequence of the new stability consensus within the state was the targeting of conflictual civil society organisations, which were increasingly perceived as agents of political risk and instability between 2004 and 2013. The criminalisation of a few environ-mental activists and the "mainstreaming" of NGO engagement in "governance participation" have served to further neutralise the destabilising effects of civil society on state–investor relations, as analysed in Chapter 6.

All five dimensions of a transnationally induced process of state transformation can be evidenced in the 2014 reforms to Mongolia's mining regime. The overall change in the direction of protecting investor rights and interests from national and local sources of political-legal instability was effected through (a) substantive legal reform affecting the balance of state–investor rights and responsibilities; (b) the redefinition of the appropriate boundary of state action in the market; (c) the strengthening of executive power at the expense of legislative/deliberate power within the state; (d) the privileging of technical expertise and "objective" decision-making in the governance of the mining sector and (e) an institution-alised shift from conflictual to collaborative forms of association between the state, mining companies and civil society through tri-partite multi-stakeholder models of accountability. These five indicators of change correspond with each of the five dimensions of TLO outlined earlier. The following discussion will be structured upon each of these five dimensions, in turn, for clarity, although naturally they reinforce each other in practice as will be noted when relevant. It makes sense to analyse these elements separately in order to show the way that state transformation cuts across the three relational axes of reordering that were analysed in Chapters 4–6, connected to the reconfiguration of central state power, central–local state relations and state–society relations vis-à-vis environ-mental NGOs.

### Substantive legal reform

One of the clearest conduits of the "stability norm" following the 2012–2013 crisis was substantive law reform. At the end of 2013, a new investment law was passed, and the 2006 Minerals Law was amended in 2014 to reflect the norma-tive and regulatory goals of the 2014–2025 State Policy on the Minerals Sector. The new investment law replaced the Foreign Investment Law and the Strategic Entities Foreign Investment Law (SEFIL). As set out in Chapter 4, these laws had given Cabinet and Parliament fairly far-reaching rights of review regarding the purchase of shares, state-owned investments, large-scale transactions and board appointments for 'strategic business entities.' Similarly, under SEFIL, investors in strategic sectors had unprecedented obligations to disclose shareholders and equity holdings (Scharaw, 2018: Chapter 3, Section 2.1.3).

In contrast, the 2013 Investment Law had the explicit purpose to

> protect the legal rights and interests of investors in the territory of Mongolia, to establish a common legislative guarantee for investment, to encourage investment, to stabilise the tax environment, to determine the rights and obligations of investors and the competences of a government body related to investment.
>
> (Article 1)

Under the new investment law, anti-discrimination measures were introduced that guaranteed the equal treatment of foreign and domestic investors, and reduced restrictions on licence trading. Crucially, it removed approval processes for foreign private investment (Hogan Lovells, 2013: 1). Furthermore, the 2013 Investment Law introduced general rights to tax stabilisation and international arbitration. Previously, access to tax stabilisation and alternative dispute resolution were accessible only on a case-by-case basis, through the framework of investment agreement negotiations. Specific quorum measures also protect the new investment law to prevent legal change, particularly during election cycles; a two-thirds Parliamentary majority is required to amend it.

Since 2013, other laws have been adopted to reduce legislative "instability" in general. In September 2013, the U.S. and Mongolia signed an Agreement on Transparency in Matters Related to International Trade and Investment ("Transparency Agreement") which has been in force since January 2017, with full implementation required by 2023. The Transparency Agreement 'applies to any measures adopted or maintained by a Party affecting trade in goods or cross-border trade in services (other than financial services) or relating to bilateral investment, trade in financial services, or intellectual property rights' (Article One). It specifically focuses on setting out 'clear processes for drafting and commenting on new legislation and regulations,' requiring 'strict transparency related to laws involving trade and investment' (U.S. State Department, 2019). As part of implementing the Transparency Agreement, the government introduced a Law on Legislation in 2016 which specifies four key requirements for legislative change:

> (1) provide a clear process for both developing and justifying the need for the draft legislation; (2) set out methodologies for estimating costs to the government related to the draft law's implementation; (3) evaluate the impact of the legislation on the public once implemented; and (4) conduct public outreach before submitting legislation to the public.

In early 2014, the government introduced the State Policy on the Minerals Sector (2014–2025), with the explicit goal of limiting the state's role in the mining sector to that of regulation and management, instead of pursuing direct shares in mining projects as it had done since 2006. Substantive amendments to the 2006 Minerals Law to enhance 'private sector-led development' and to reduce the role of the state can be seen in the introduction of provisions for the state to trade its direct shares in mining projects for special royalties, depending on the outcome of negotiations with the licence-holder. The state formalised its 2014 policy commitment to stabilising the investment environment by offering general tax and non-tax incentives, and by reducing bureaucratic steps in gaining investment permissions and mining licences. The 2014 amendments to the Minerals Law also clarify compensation duties for government authorities which use their powers to interrupt or delay mining licences, particularly addressing the timing of compensation to licence-holders. According to revised Article 14.4, compensation from any government authority must be paid within one year, even when land has been set aside as a specially protected area by local authorities. In the latter case, if compensation has not been paid, exploration and exploitation may continue.

Several substantive changes to minerals legislation affect the rights and duties of local governments in relation to mining companies. For example, the 2014 amendments to the Minerals Law legislated *mandatory* Local Development Agreements between local governments and mining companies at the sub-national level, specifying a limited number of issues that could be addressed (environmental protection, infrastructure development and employment). As discussed in Chapter 4, the balance of negotiating power was addressed in the amendments, in favour of the investing party. For example, regarding Local Development Agreements, the investor cannot be compelled to contribute above a 'voluntary' level (Article 42.1). Furthermore, revisions to Article 15.1 increased the scope for reconnaissance for minerals exploration on land set aside for special purposes/protection by local governments (Minter Ellison, 2014). While local authorities still have the right – vis-à-vis the Land Law – to set land aside for local needs, the substance of this right is arguably undermined by the new provision in the Minerals Law that local governments compensate mining companies within one year should their decision conflict with a mining licence. These new provisions and amendments provide a substantive legal basis for the protection of investment and investors' rights in Mongolian law, shifting the balance away from the kind of "nationalist" prerogatives that undermined investor confidence between 2006 and 2012.

## Changes in the boundary between the state and the market, and other forms of social ordering

The 2014 law and policy reform process introduced a host of new rights for investors, providing a legal foundation for policies that articulated a reduced role for the state in relation to the market. The substantive changes to mining and investment legislation described in the aforementioned section were part of a broader political and policy shift to reorient the state towards investment as a stable regulator. As outlined in Chapter 4, the stated goals of the State Policy on the Minerals Sector (2014–2025) (hereafter "the Policy") are to 'strengthen private sector development,' 'establish a stable investment environment' and 'strengthen the international competitiveness of the Mongolian mining industry' (Otgochuluu, 2016: 68). As the Oxford Business Group put it, 'the policy frames the state's role as one of support and encouragement for the private sector, with its role limited to regulation and supervision' (Oxford Business Group, 2015). The Policy encourages a shift to a governance culture that emphasises the importance of 'human capital, corporate governance, business ethics and rule of law' (Otgochuluu, 2016: 74). In this way, the Policy sets out a symbolic normative boundary of appropriate state behaviour in relation to the market.

Creating a market-friendly approach to mining governance was not simply a normative project; it underpinned wider market reform. In order to practically strengthen the marketisation of the economy and to limit state intervention – in the name of economic stability and competitiveness (Articles 3.7.4 and 3.7.5) – the Policy proposed the establishment of a 'special purpose fund for mining sector income generated to the state budget,' meaning that the state's access to mining income would be institutionally limited, as opposed to ordinary state income. The World Bank has played a key role in advising the Ministry of Finance regarding the establishment of a sovereign wealth fund, as part of its broader agenda 'to build government and public support for more disciplined fiscal policy' (Robbins and Smith, 2014: 3). The Policy also discouraged direct state involvement in mining projects, recommending instead that SOEs be converted into public companies that run as commercial entities, guided by principles of corporate governance in the selection of management (Articles 3.7.2 and 3.7.3). In particular, this can be seen in the partial privatisation and commercialisation of Erdenes Mongol LLC, which represents state interests in mining projects.

In 2015, a new state energy policy (2015–2016) was passed, with the core pillar being the privatisation and restructuring of state property (Woolley, 2015). One of the key principles for the reform was 'efficiency and productivity,' expressed as 'privatisation, market regulation and technological innovation' (ibid.). In late 2015, the State Property Committee in charge of regulating SOEs in Mongolia was dissolved, in order that SOEs could operate with a commercial mandate. Notably, in August 2016, an Investor Protection Committee was established 'to protect investors' rights and interests, promote cooperation within the legal framework of Mongolia, minimise foreseeable risks and facilitate settlement of disputes swiftly' (Amartuvshin, 2016). According to a statement published by Lehman Law, an international law firm, this move was perceived as 'another positive step for Mongolia and for potential foreign investors… If the committee works as planned it could significantly reduce costs and mitigate risks for foreign investors in major projects in the country' (ibid.).

Furthermore, the '100 Days of Reform' led by Cabinet that followed the promulgation of the new State Policy on the Minerals Sector included a range of market reforms not only related specifically to the minerals sector, but also enhanced Mongolia's overall reputation as a supportive destination for foreign investment (Hogan Lovells, 2014). The liberalisation of capital markets, including securities, transfer of pledges and registration reforms, affirmed the priority of protecting foreign capital interests, stimulating trade and expanding financing options for investors. For example, Mongolia's capital markets were made more competitive internationally through the adoption of international standards related to financial markets and securities. In June 2014, the Financial Regulatory Commission signed the International Organization of Securities Commissions' Multilateral Memorandum of Understanding Concerning Consultation and Cooperation and the Exchange of Information. This significantly increased the competitiveness of Mongolia's capital markets internationally through standardisation (Surenjav and Buxbaum, 2015: 325).

Moreover, it is important to recall that the steep investment decline in 2012–2013 prompted a major debt crisis, culminating in a structural adjustment for the state, facilitated by the IMF and China. In late 2016, Mongolia's overall debt burden was estimated at approximately USD 23.5 billion (200% of GDP), with government debt at USD 8.4 billion (70% of GDP) (Hornby, 2016). While commodity prices increased (as in the case of coal) or at least stabilised (as in the case of copper) in 2016 (Benard, 2016), it was not enough to balance the trade deficit in addition to debt repayments. Facing the first major debt repayments on its bonds and swap agreements in 2017, the Mongolian government was on the brink of default. In January 2017, after a brief negotiation, the IMF coordinated approximately USD 5.5 billion worth of debt financing for the Mongolian government to prevent default, which included an extension for Mongolia's currency swap agreement with China, which had been set to expire in August 2017 (Edwards, 2017).[1]

A key consequence of this structural adjustment, which has its origins in the investment crisis of 2012–2013, has been the strengthening of fiscal and monetary institutions (i.e. the Central Bank) and the creation of new limits on government spending. The introduction of ceilings in government spending, which exists *prior* to the approval of the national budget by Parliament (e.g. Fiscal Stability Law), is an important 'shift of functions' (Anderson, 2005: 21) from the political to the economic, as the Central Bank gains institutional primacy in relation to the budget. While Parliament still approves the budget, its decision-making is structured by 'market principles' (ibid.), eschewing redistributionist or otherwise "political" approaches to resource allocation (ibid.).

### Changes in the institutional architecture of the state

One of the major aspects of change in the state following the 2012–2013 investment crisis was the strengthening of executive power in relation to the mining sector. As analysed in Chapters 4 and 5, Parliament had played a major role in "destabilising" the investment environment by regularly amending the minerals law or passing new legislation, such as the Strategic Entities Foreign Investment Law (2012) and the Law on the Prohibition of Mineral Exploration and Mining Operations at Headwaters of Rivers, Protected Zones of Water Reservoirs and Forested Areas (2009). Members of Parliament had also initiated the renegotiation of the Oyu Tolgoi Investment Agreement (OTIA), signalling insecurity of contract and tenure for investors. The 2014 stability reforms recalibrated the balance of power between different institutions in relation to the mining sector, by limiting Parliament's power to revise new pro-investment legislation (i.e. the 2013 Investment Law) and introduce new bills that could affect the minerals sector. In the case of the Investment Law, it was as straightforward as introducing a higher quorum (two-thirds majority) for that particular law.

However, with a view to more generally prevent swift legal change, the 2014 amendments to the Minerals Law legislated the formation of the Minerals Policy Council (MPC), a multi-stakeholder body working under the auspices of the Ministry of Mining. The MPC was supposed to review any legal or policy changes to the minerals sector prior to parliamentary debate, allowing investor and mining association representatives to have advisory input in the mining governance regime. Follow-up communications with the original Vice President of the MPC (President of the National Mongolian Mining Association) confirmed that the council has been convened thrice since it was officially instituted in 2015, to review draft amendments. While he noted that the new government (as of June 2016) had not been paying much attention to the MPC, the Prime Minister's cabinet has established a new Investment Protection Council (IPC) to deal with the claims and appeals of investors: 'in general, the government is trying its best to improve the relationship with foreign investors'.[2]

The IPC was established through a government resolution, in recognition that 'one of the leading priorities of the government is to protect the needs and rights of investors [and] to provide foreign investors with stable legal policies and cooperation as well as a comfortable environment' (IPC, 2018). The IPC was established with a view to 'further work hand in hand with the investors and to maintain a steady relationship with them' (ibid.). Since 2017, the IPC has resolved approximately 150 grievances (National Development Agency, 2019: 30), with 40% of the total number of cases arising from the mining sector (IPC, 2018). The creation of the IPC under the Cabinet in addition to the MPC (attached to the Ministry of Mining) indicates the ongoing priority of successive governments to protect and promote the interests of foreign investors, despite the change in political power resulting from the Parliamentary election in June 2016 where the Mongolian People's Party ousted the Democratic Party.

In a similar way, Local Development Agreements were designed to function as hybridised governing spaces where investors and local authorities can negotiate and find common ground about the role of mining companies in local development. While there is a public–private element to these new forms of deliberation at the central and sub-national levels of government, they represent an architectural transformation within the state, whereby investors and mining companies have a formalised role in governance as "partners" and "collaborators" with the executive office of local governments in relation to specific issues. At the sub-national level, the nomination of district and provincial governors as the signatories of local development agreements further consolidates the proactive relationship between executive authority and mining.

Additionally, pro-investment spaces of executive power have been strengthened in the central government, specifically the Ministry of Mining, the Ministry of Finance and the Mineral Resources Authority (MRAM). The decision-making powers of the Ministry of Mining and the Mineral Resources Authority were expanded, and two new agencies were formed: the Invest Mongolia Agency (IMA) and the National Geological Office. The IMA, as the implementation agency of the Investment Law, was set up as a one-stop-shop for investments (IMA, 2014: 60) to be directly supervised by the Prime Minister's cabinet. Since 2016, the IMA has been replaced by the National Development Agency (NDA), with a broader mandate to facilitate foreign investment in the wider context of national development policy (IFC, 2018: 61). Buoyed by the new discourse associated with 'bold actions to reform the investment environment' (National Development Agency, 2017: 1) in the 2013 Investment Law and the new State Policy on the Minerals Sector 2014–2025, the NDA has consistently addressed FDI as its 'core priority' (ibid.).

While the IFC has framed this institutional shift as a return to 'a traditional, central planning body' that does not keep 'market-economics and the private sector' as its 'guiding principles' (ibid.), these strong claims are belied by the fact that investment protection and promotion services are still supported by a dedicated department within the NDA. Thus, it is still the case that designated executive agencies are being institutionalised to directly facilitate foreign investment. The IFC's desire to see more "pure" forms of market-led policy-making and regulation may be frustrated at some level, but it is fair to say that the Mongolian bureaucracy has shifted into definitive institutional patterns – despite turnover in political parties – which support private-sector-led development. Despite its criticisms of shortcomings in investment promotion implementation by the Mongolian government, the IFC has played an official role in supporting ongoing reforms to foreign investment protection and promotion. On July 19th 2017, the IFC and the Cabinet Secretariat signed a memorandum of understanding 'to improve investment policies, promote economic diversification, enhance investor protection – thus inspiring investors' confidence – and further attract and retain private investments' (Press Release, IPC, July 19th 2017). As a result of this partnership with the IFC, the NDA opened the '"Invest in Mongolia" one stop service centre' in February 2019 which offers a virtually identical set of services to foreign investors as those provided formerly by the IMA (see National Development Agency, 2019: 32; Xinhua, 2019).

### Enhancement of professional expertise and its role in governance

In line with the new emphasis on easing investment restrictions and separating mining governance from nationalist politics, the 2014 reforms promoted a stronger role for technical and professional expertise in governance. For example, Article 2.1.1 of the State Policy on the Minerals Sector (2014–2025) stipulated that one of its principles with regard to the minerals sector is objective decision-making:

> to base any decision with respect to the legal and tax environment on the results of research and analysis, to ensure long term sustainability of the policy in minerals sector and to ensure that the legal interests of participants are not negatively affected.

In line with this principle and 'within the framework of improving the legal environment for the minerals sector' (Article 3.1), the State Policy commits to promoting 'international initiatives for transparent and responsible mining and social and economic impact assessment' (3.1.7). As discussed in Chapter 6, the pursuit of an audit-based model of social and economic impact assessment, as well as stakeholder-based mechanisms of participation, has opened the gateway for a new tide of international consultants, independent experts and facilitators of alternative dispute resolution mechanisms to influence Mongolia's mining regime. Multilateral financial institutions and international development organisations have taken a lead role in creating "independent" mechanisms and forums for dispute resolution, as well as directly mediating disputes between communities, companies and local governments. Furthermore, at both the national and local levels, international experts exert strong influence in defining standards of transparency, responsibility and justice.

The State Policy also supports the professionalisation of research in the minerals sector (i.e. through teams of qualified engineers) (3.1.8), and a 'shift to international standards for the evaluation of minerals deposits.' The link between gathering geological data and attracting foreign investment has been pursued as a top priority by the Ministry of Mining to facilitate investment interest in Mongolia's mineral sector, as discussed in Chapter 5. In October 2014, Mongolia became a member of the Committee for Mineral Reserves International Reporting Standards (CRIRSCO). The purpose of this international standard-setting body is to strengthen and develop communication of the 'risks associated with investment effectively and transparently in order to earn the level of trust necessary to underpin its activities' (CRIRSCO, 2017). CRIRSCO reports are based on mineral reserve estimates and exploration progress, in order to enhance 'market-related and financial investment' (ibid.) through standardisation. Consequently, CRIRSCO membership enhances Mongolia's international reputation as well as strengthens market promotion of Mongolian minerals through geological data collection. In line with these developments, the State Policy also calls for the professionalisation of a minerals board – which comprised 'qualified experts' (3.1.11) – to facilitate and enforce international reporting standards. In January 2014, the Mongolian Professional Institute of Geosciences and Mining was established as a non-governmental organisation.

### Change in associational patterns instituted through transnational mechanisms of accountability with accompanying normative frames

The 2014 stabilisation reforms effectively repositioned political issues as "economic," "legal" or "social" within the governance regime to prevent politicised discourse or activities from disrupting the stability of the investment environment. The institutionalisation of distance between spaces of representative democracy and mining governance on the one hand, and the legitimation of multi-stakeholder politics as a collaborative alternative to politically risky social conflict on the other are both symptomatic of a deeper process of political neutralisation to protect the market. For example, formerly political aspects of mining investment, which involved democratic processes of deliberation and review, have been re-determined as issues of economic administration, and institutionally relocated in executive agencies and ministries, outside formal political control. The strengthening of executive power in relation to investment and the creation of hybridised spaces of governance *within* the Ministry of Mining and local governments reinforce the deepening alignment between state and capital investment interests. Furthermore, national political conflict – characterised by systematic processes of election and representation, debates around the boundaries of the public interest and infused with the language of national political community – has been transferred to alternative stakeholder-based forums which are issue-, identity- and interest-based in their orientation. These "governance participation" alternatives are based on direct negotiating power, akin to a commercial transaction of stakeholders, in which all parties have nominally equal value based on their private interests.

The depoliticising impetus behind the 2014 reform effort, and the emphasis on technical, objective and professional decision-making, has also affected the relationship between civil society organisations, mining companies and the state. As analysed in Chapter 6, one of the targets of the 2014 "stability consensus" was to place stronger limits on the role of environmental NGOs and rural activism in relation to the mining sector. In part, the state has aided the institutionalisation of NGOs through criminalising "radical" movements on the one hand, and through offering a legitimate place for NGOs to have influence upon the mining governance regime vis-à-vis the Mongolian Environmental Civil Council on the other. The shift in role from activism to expertise for environmental civil society is important, as it signals the relative strengthening of NGOs as governance *partners* with the state and the private sector within a pro-extractive framework.

Furthermore, the legitimation of transparency-based, multi-stakeholder models of accountability at the national and sub-national levels, as part of a "responsible mining" discourse, breaks new ground not only in terms of *who* represents public interests but in terms of *how* those interested are represented. The emphasis on stakeholding, negotiation and collaboration for mutual benefits has shifted the antagonistic encounters between competing interest groups to new "multi-stakeholder" fora, ushering in market-friendly representation and rule-making around company-"community" conflicts.

## Summary

The brief recapitulation described earlier highlights key aspects of the 2014 reform process to regain investment and investor confidence in Mongolia's minerals sector. The relationship between state and capital grounds the five aspects of TLO, indicated along three axes of institutional reordering studied in this book. Within this broader context, a boundary-shifting and redrawing process has occurred that enables the Mongolian state to suppress and even evade the social conflict which had destabilised the political and legal conditions for investment particularly in the period between 2006 and 2013. By closing avenues of risk and establishing a new hierarchy of priorities, while still permitting limited outlets for contestation through institutionalised forms of civil society, the Mongolian state has consolidated a positive overall orientation towards transnational capital. Fundamentally, this positive orientation has been made relatively secure through legal and financial mechanisms that either incentivise or enforce the cooperation of national and civil institutional actors which could otherwise present a challenge. When situated within Shaffer's framework of TLO, the diverse ways in which the norm of legal and political stability (for investors) has infused law, state institutions, state–market relations and civil society become apparent.

In the previous three chapters, I analysed the stabilisation process along three key axes (within the central state, between central and local governments, and state–society relations). In the next section, I will focus on the overall effects of this case study of material constitutional change within the national democratic state of Mongolia. Prior to doing this, though, it is timely to ask the counterfactual question. A sceptical reader might be unconvinced that a process of deep transformation was catalysed by the crisis of investment/investor confidence in 2012 and 2013. Conceivably, a sceptic might not see the underlying connection between the legal and political reforms targeting diverse actors and institutions undertaken since 2014. My response to the sceptic would be to ask the following: if there had been no decline in foreign direct investment and a "crisis" of investor confidence associated with it in 2012 and 2013, would the post-2014 governance configuration be present? While there are certainly domestic factors at play in affecting the responsiveness of the government to investor interests, removing the 'transnational story' (Shaffer, 2014: 2) would arguably produce a very different outcome for Mongolia's mining regime. Without an externally imposed crisis, there would have been no incentive for such stringent reform of national law and politics. Why would political elites such as members of Parliament voluntarily support legislation that reduces parliamentary powers in relation to the mining sector? Why would a cross-party consensus have emerged so suddenly (in the wake of falling investment), when many politicians and parties were previously known for their anti-FDI platforms?[3] The sudden recognition that 'we are the cause of the economic crisis' (Prime Minister Saikhanbileg quoted in *Mongolian Economic Journal*, 2014) does not reflect an organic process of change, but rather a pragmatic response to a new reality: 'These hard times are lessons. The biggest lesson [is that] we need investment, we need to support business activities.'[4]

## The legal and political costs of transnational legal ordering in Mongolia's mining regime

It would be inaccurate to suggest a "hollowing out" of the state or even an over-all weakening in the Mongolian case, given the evident *expansion* of pro-market legality, bureaucracy and the increase of executive authority in relation to the minerals sector, alongside efforts to re-engage foreign investment interest. How-ever, the cost of insulating the mining sector from political and legal risk is also borne by certain components of the state, in this case, democratic institutions and norms. In this section, I will examine the redrawing of the boundary be-tween the "political" and the "economic" within Mongolia's mining regime and examine the risks that such a redrawing poses for the future of national demo-cratic politics and law-making.

### "Who cares about politics?" The significance of transnational legal ordering for democratic politics in Mongolia

The crisis of investment (confidence) led to the deepening separation between the political and the economic spheres within Mongolia's market democracy. In general, the liberal democratic model can be said to be premised upon the dis-tinction between two spheres of power: the economic and the political (Wood, 1995: 234). The former is distinguished from the latter in the mode of its power relations as 'not dependent on juridical or political privilege' (ibid.) but rather dependent on 'the power of appropriation, exploitation and distribution.' In Po-lanyi's words (1944/2001: 71), 'a market economy is an economic system con-trolled, regulated, and directed by market prices.' Economic power in a market democracy is distinguished by its relative *freedom from* the direct control of the state. Although the state may attempt to shape market activities through regu-lation, this is not the same as state control. Wood (1995: 235) puts it this way:

> As with most kinds of freedom, there may have to be certain restrictions or regulations on it to maintain social order; but it is still a kind of freedom.

Consistent with this observation, investors in Mongolia's mining sector were largely not contesting the state's right to regulate the sector per se, but rather its substance and manner in which regulation was imposed. It was the state's interference in the market – by assuming direct stakes in mining projects (designating them as "nationally strategic" as opposed to simply "valuable") and imposition of some controls – which was the root cause of investor–state conflict. These political behaviours within the market were deemed inappropriate in the economic sphere, particularly the nationalist use of law to legally legitimise the state's actions. Consequently, the 2014 reforms were devised to rebuild investor confidence. Not surprisingly, the way to achieve this goal in a market economy is to demarcate the boundary of appropriate state behaviour in relation to the economic sphere in general. This demarcation effort has two key implications for democracy, in practice and as a normative ideal.

Practically speaking, the new consensus to protect the minerals market from national "instability" means that fewer legal and policy issues are available for national contestation or review, either by transferring decision-making power to different institutions or by creating strong financial incentives and/or legal barriers to keep them from becoming "politicised." These practical measures have already been explored in some depth in previous chapters, for instance, the "locking in" of local governments' support for mining projects through financial incentives and new legal institutions (i.e. LDAs). Limiting local budgets, whilst providing the opportunity for local governments to receive more from the state through national budgetary allocation if they support mining licences in their jurisdictions, constitutes another incentive structure. The new possibility to generate capital independently of the central state through LDAs and local fee payments from mining companies reinforces this incentive structure. Regarding negative incentives, local governments are now burdened with new time pressure to compensate mining companies *within a year* should their decision to protect land conflict with mining licences, localising financial pressure to effectively prevent such measures. As a senior official from the MRAM put it, local governments need to have "a good reason" to reject mining licences, based on objective factors.[5] In this way, the more fundamental question of 'do we want mining in our districts and regions?' shifts to the more instrumental issue of 'how can we benefit the most from mining in our districts and regions?' By raising the requirements for legitimate restrictions on mining, the baseline moves from questions of "if" to questions of "how," constituting a closure of political space as well as the possibilities of alternative development pathways (Schneiderman, 2013; Anderson, 2005: 147).

While I have used the case of local governments here, similar examples abound in the central state regarding the use of a combination of incentives and negative pressure to limit the state's "political" involvement in the mining sector. In a sense, it no longer seems that popular to be a populist. The legitimacy of executive power in the state has grown since the FDI crisis, as public frustration mounted over the state's seeming inability to effectively manage and administer the economy. As a prominent NGO advocate explained, people seem to be 'moving away from the essential things that we chose [after communism], such as democracy and human rights.'[6] In particular, he warned that 'young people are forgetting the danger of authoritarianism,' citing new studies that give evidence of this worrying trend. For example, the Asian Barometer conducted a survey to measure the extent of 'detachment from authoritarianism' between 2001 and 2016 (Asian Barometer, 2016), discovering that more than 64% of Mongolian citizens now support the removal of Parliament 'in favour of rule by a strong leader' (ibid.), as opposed to 40% in 2001.

The growing public cynicism about politics thus dovetailed with criticism from investors and the mining industry about the government's "unprofessional decision-making." This domestic legitimacy crisis reinforced the necessity of redistributing the state's power in the mining sector towards investment promotion, legal implementation and regulation, licencing procedures and administrative management, as opposed to the state playing a direct role as an owner or shareholder in mining projects. Significantly for democracy, parliamentary power has been constrained by the shift of most decision-making capacities to pro-extractive ministries and agencies, which have opened advisory and consultation spaces to investors in order to provide input on general policy-making trajectories.

The shift of state power in relation to the country's most strategic economic sector has normative significance, apart from the practical implications of making the legal environment more investor-friendly. Decision-making and norm-generating power has generally shifted from legislative, representative and deliberative spaces in the state, on the one hand, to executive, appointed and technocratic spaces on the other. By targeting representative and legislative spaces as being too "political" with regard to the country's most significant economic sector, the 2014 reforms communicate an implicit message about the legitimacy and value of politics in democracy. The preservation of investor confidence as a new baseline for legitimate politics homogenises the scope of policy options and interventions available for the state, privileging the freedom of the market as opposed to the freedom of the national *demos*. As Polanyi (1944/2011: 60) warned, the creation of an economic sphere regulated by export competition and price mechanisms relegates society to the position of "adjunct" to the market, where the security and stability of market relations take primary position. To put it simply, the scope of national democracy has been limited in Mongolia in relation to the market-protecting preferences of transnational capitalists, as a result of the state's dependence on capital investment.

As Schneiderman (2013: 165) argues, the loss of openness has significant negative implications for democratic political life, because it signals the closure of alternatives. While it is possible and even necessary for closure to occur within democratic polities as a sign of self-rule – 'not everything can be contested all of the time' (ibid.) – the insulating impetus of transnational legality seeks to *permanently* exclude political processes from influencing the global market. Schneiderman argues convincingly that the inherent value of democracy, with its ideals of 'collective self-revisability' (ibid.), is its systemic openness to change (ibid.: 165, 15). In this sense, the underlying undemocratic issue with the transnational legality associated with economic globalisation is that it seeks to (permanently) place itself beyond the reach of the democratic domain.

The affirmation of pluralism (i.e. diverse conceptions of "the good"), particularly when it comes to significant areas of public law and policy-making, can be understood as a core norm of democracy; political processes provide a *unified* system to express the *diverse* interests and needs of "the people." This unity–diversity dynamic is a critical part of democratised collective life; the elements of unity (e.g. through universal categories such as citizenship) which create a "we" can then be nuanced by the reality that "we" do not all share the same interests, perspectives or values. While not wishing to 'romanticise politics' (Spicer, 2010: 51), the value of values-pluralism contained in democracy at its most basic is precisely that the reality of social complexity acts as an antidote to coercive attempts by states to *totalise* their subjects into one objective unit. Furthermore, Spicer (2010: 62) makes the argument that an instrumental approach to public administration which seeks to 'downplay if not actually deny' the political character of governance can 'erode our sense of moral responsibility' (ibid.) to the "demos" (i.e. the people). As Spicer (ibid.: 64) puts it:

> The rhetoric of instrumental rationalism in public administration... hides moral choices from the view of administrators by focusing their attention single-mindedly on technical questions about how to best accomplish some pre-defined set of measurable goals, missions, or ends... it can foster the idea that those whom the administrator must deal with – citizens, politicians, and other administrators – are not human beings as such but are mere objects to be manipulated at will.

Returning to the Mongolian case, the idea that citizens and their representatives were incapable of contributing to effective policy because they lacked sufficient knowledge was a common theme amongst "stability" reformers. As one of the main contributors to the State Policy on the Minerals Sector (2014–2025) put it in a recent policy brief (2016: 2):

> Ultimately, only educated voters can assist in creating a political environment that enables the formulation of government policy geared towards effective regulation and sustainable development. To do this, policy-makers must acknowledge the degree to which the country's socialist past and semi-nomadic traditions shape policy debates, and adopt a communication strategy that allows for a constructive national discussion of the role of mining in Mongolia's new economy.

In my interviews with senior government personnel, semi-nomadic culture was regularly associated with a lack of discipline and consistency, not helped by Mongolia's socialist heritage; citizens allegedly have high expectations from the state to provide welfare, services and generally redistribute mineral rents on a universal basis. As the aforementioned quote suggests, the perceived benefit of an educated mass was that the public will consequently not make *unreasonable* economic demands of the state (i.e. by agitating for direct redistribution), having appropriate understanding of the challenges of navigating the boom and bust cycles of commodity markets. This expert emphasis on the making of a "reasonable" (i.e. market-friendly) public reinforces the dominance of economic values in mining governance, such as avoiding government overspending during "boom" cycles in commodity markets and preventing legislative change to support foreign investment flows. The instrumental, rationalistic thinking at work in state administration denies its very political nature, augmented by the fact that its proponents work mainly in the opacity of executive institutions. Consequently, this technocratic, anti-political discourse remains institutionally protected from being challenged by other perspectives and rationalities. Thus, there is a strong reason to be wary of the lure of 'anti-politics; it originates in a 'technological "style of thought" that promises to "rescue mankind from the lack of certainty and the glut of compromises in politics"' (Spicer, 2010: 68, citing Crick, 1962/1993: 92).

Thus, when the political sphere experiences closure of any significant degree (e.g. in relation to mining and resource distribution in Mongolia's case), we can logically argue that this amounts to a substantive 'undoing' (Brown, 2015) or, at the very least, a *de facto* reconstitution of the scope of democratic politics. This point was expressed cogently in an interview with a prominent NGO advocate as the cost of preferring expertise and professionalism over politics in decision-making.[7] While careful not to idealise politicians in Mongolia, this interviewee highlighted the distinction between a critique of political leadership and the exclusion of *politics* and *political institutions* (e.g. Parliament) in relation to the mining sector. By excluding politics, pro-stability lobbyists and reformers did not adequately recognise the democratic values at risk, apart from national control over strategic resources. In the advocate's terms, Mongolian politicians now take pride in describing themselves as "so pragmatic" but he noted the lack of political *principles*: 'they [political parties] are divided in terms of business groups, without ideology.'

This observation has some merit when one looks at the policy platforms of the two major political parties following the FDI crisis; they both supported, and continue to support, private-sector-led development and the promotion of foreign investment in the mining sector. The contraction of the political spectrum across political parties reinforces the stability of mining law and policy across election cycles, which were formerly a source of anxiety for investors. This can be clearly seen in the way that the 2016 elections did not lead to the reform of the 2014 "stability consensus," even though the Mongolian People's

Party, opposition to the Democratic Party (the main political force behind the 2014 reforms), won the election. Rather than complementing the system of representative democracy by incorporating additional avenues of public participation into the heart of the mining regime, the "stability consensus" embodied in the 2014 reforms shifted the balance of state power in the opposite direction, strengthening its 'bureaucratic, administrative and coercive apparatuses' (Held, 2006: 196). Under the new regime, it is no longer legitimate to contest an export-oriented, foreign-investor-friendly mining sector, or to encourage direct state intervention in the minerals market beyond the facilitation of extraction by providing a "reasonable" jurisdiction for investment to occur. This shift marks a normative closure for democratic politics, by homogenising a formerly more heterogeneous political debate, and by limiting the scope of redistributive intervention by the state.

Before concluding this section, it is important to mention the extent to which the strategies of organised civil society might ameliorate the new anti-politics of the mining regime. Unfortunately, so far, the increasingly institutionalised nature of NGOs, as examined in Chapter 6, has left the new political-economic boundary relatively uncontested. Civic actors and institutions, like the MECC, structured as they are by the boundaries of foreign donor and state funding, largely concentrate on aspects of the *process* of extractive development, such as revenue transparency, environmental impact assessments, monitoring mining projects and representing "community" interests in LDAs. While these are important issues, NGO advocacy in general does not challenge the pro-investment orientation of the state or the anti-political direction of state mining policy. In this sense, mainstream civil society does not fundamentally require 'accountability of power' (Anderson, 2005: 147) but may rather contribute to making the new order hegemonic.

NGOs can inadvertently reproduce distrust of national politics by presenting themselves as a more trustworthy alternative to national political representation through multi-stakeholder politics. Despite the subtlety of its introduction in Mongolia's mining regime, stakeholding offers a new orientation to political representation and participation. On the one hand, it opens up the possibility of wider participation and inclusion of different interest groups in the negotiation of a particular issue based on the idea of having a "stake" in it. On the other hand, stakeholder politics is yet another example of arena-shifting in Mongolia's mining regime, where conflict gets relegated to specifically "non-political" forums designed to contain and resolve it. Particularly at the sub-national level, NGOs have gained prominence as governing institutions for "participatory" initiatives, like local development agreements and environmental co-monitoring with mining companies. However, it is difficult to assess the benefit(s) of participation, particularly when the initiatives are offered by the private sector or by international financial institutions, who have their own "business case" reasons to engage and their own modalities of intervention which often serve to limit rather than open up meaningful pathways to remedy and justice (see Jokubauskaite,

2019; Bhatt, forthcoming). Rather than reflecting the organic, grassroots politics that participatory governance is supposed to generate, NGOs can be complicit in furthering 'governance participation,' a 'perverted' (Santos and Avritzer, 2007: lxix) form of popular engagement wherein participation is bureaucratised and professionalised, without a genuine democratic scope (i.e. which offers the possibility of systemic change) (Schneiderman, 2013: 165; Jokubauskaite, 2019).

For example, there is a great deal of opacity about the actual *process* by which NGOs receive a community mandate for representation in local development agreements. NGO activists can also become governance technicians, as 'a matter of instructing people in the proper practice of politics' (Li, 2007: 25), even under the seemingly progressive framework of participation which connotes a 'people-centred' approach (White, 1996: 6). The role of NGOs as agents of participation is particularly ambivalent when they are institutionally circumscribed by the state to pursue a limited range of activities in *partnership* with state organisations and mining companies. Participation can become a way to mobilise and organise citizens in "constructive" directions, rather than reflecting a genuine democratic process that is attentive and open to local perspectives. As White (ibid.) incisively puts it, 'sharing through participation does not necessarily mean sharing in power.' Thus, to conclude, the programmatic, project-based and stakeholder-oriented approach of current civil society efforts in relation to mining renders them largely ineffective against the structural reorientation of the state towards foreign capital in Mongolia. Furthermore, NGOs can also act as a potential force for deepening the anti-political trajectory of mining governance. Of course, the hegemony of the stability order is not immune to challenge, but a strong disciplinary incentive structure protects the mining regime legally, politically and socially.

### A new rule of law? Stability as the new grundnorm for mining law and policy

The new anti-politics described in the previous section, alongside the expansion of what is now considered as an "economic" issue (as opposed to political) has occurred through legal development. Legal solutions to investor confidence have also been the focus of central policy-making for the mining sector. The centrality of law to the 2014 "stability" reforms reflects an assumption about the law's relationship with politics, namely that it is a relationship of constraint. Using law to constrain politics and to enable 'an economic sphere with its own power relations not dependent on juridical or political privilege' (Wood, 1995: 234) remains the function *par excellence* of legal liberalism, the legal ideology that accompanies liberal democracy and economics. In this ideology, the rule of law mediates the boundary between the political and the economic, as the juridical guarantor for the existence of an economic sphere, based on the supposedly rational exchange of price value, against the political sphere, based on irrational power and interest (May, 2014a: 68).

While we know that the division between the political and the economic is not so clear in practice, the idea of the rule of law as securing space for the market to operate has major ideological purchase in the governance of the global economy generally (May, 2014a: 63). As Wood (1995: 30) puts it:

> Absolute private property, the contractual relation that binds producer to appropriator, the process of commodity exchange – all these require the legal forms, the coercive apparatus, the policing functions of the state... the differentiation of the economic sphere means simply that the economy has its own juridical and political forms whose purpose is purely 'economic.'

Thus, from a market perspective, the rule of law has a distinctly economic purpose even though it is enforced by the state. In fact, as noted in Chapter 1, markets have historically depended upon a certain variety of the rule of law for their very existence. As Ebner (2011: 22) puts it:

> The rise of the market as a set of hegemonic institutions which shape the modern exchange economy coincides with the rule of law, which implies a reduction of social relations to the regulation of property and contract.

The rule of law, in this view, is supposed to protect the market from any political and legal influences that are not economic in purpose. Thus, the rule of law is not actually about protecting the market from the state *per se*, but from particular forms of "illegitimate" state behaviour in relation to the market; the market would not actually exist if it were not juridically protected and enabled by the state (Polanyi, 1944/2001). As Wood (ibid.: 31) astutely concludes, 'the differentiation of the economic and the political in capitalism is, more precisely, a differentiation of political functions themselves and their separate allocation to the private economic sphere and the public sphere of the state.'

In Mongolia, we can see the influence of a distinctively *global* rule of law discourse in shaping expectations of state behaviour, promoted by both internal policy elites and external actors. Historically, the "rule of law" referred to the basic idea that law applied to everyone in the polity (including the Monarch), that it should be made properly (i.e. prospective, open and clear) and that legal disputes should be adjudicated by an independent court. As Schneiderman (2008: 206) argues, 'the broadest understanding of the rule of law is that of government limited by law: that government must play by the rules it lays down.' The well-known corollary concepts of the rule of law include 'publicity, equality, generality, nonretroactivity and access to judicial review' (ibid.). This formal approach to the rule of law was bound up with the concept of the territorial state (Jayasuriya, 2001: 448), designed to protect the legal rights of citizens from arbitrary exercises of power. In that sense, as pointed out in Chapter 1, the rule of law was critical for the establishment of market economies in Europe by establishing legal boundaries over the scope of the state's political power to expropriate.

However, on the basis of this more minimalist definition of the rule of law, the state would be under no obligation to formulate investment-*enabling* laws and policies, particularly for foreign investors. In fact, the law could be changed to permit direct state involvement in the economy and, as long as the conditions are met regarding universal application, due process and non-arbitrariness, this type of state action would still fit within the rule of law criteria.

However, in a context where states participate in a *global* market, the rule of law concept has become denationalised and takes on a new emphasis. Rather than a minimum standard, the concept of the rule of law has acquired a particular substantive content, in addition to general procedural principles. Through international investment and trade regimes, states are obligated to remove systems of national preference by adopting "non-discriminatory" rules that apply equally to domestic and foreign investment (Schneiderman, 2008: 206). Furthermore, these regimes 'prohibit expropriation or measures "tantamount" to expropriation' (ibid.). Consequently, any expression of national strategic interest in the economy can be rendered as discriminatory or heightening the risk of expropriation. Even *discussing* the possibility of renegotiation in Parliamentary debates or in national newspaper flags issues of political risk. As one foreign investor put it:

> There's this lack of awareness that if you get up in the Diet and you make comments about Oyu Tolgoi or you make comments in any of the better quality dailies here about the fact that the structure of the deal is not correct and has to be renegotiated, and you're not aware that people who are looking at Mongolia in the financial markets are aware of this... every time you do that it basically ratchets up the amount of money you're going to have to pay to access foreign capital.[8]

Rather than functioning as a minimum standard, states will be held in contempt of the rule of law by an international "jury" of transnational investors, financial institutions and corporations unless states *actively* protect and promote private property rights as well as regulatory interests. Within this neoliberal ideological framework, the rule of law becomes a code for certainty and stability. The conflation of issues of legal rights protection, on the one hand, and regulatory and policy preferences on the other risk producing a "chilling" effect on the legitimacy of national policy-making.

A major implication of the "stability consensus" in Mongolia is that it has imposed a particular definition of legitimate legal action by the state in relation to the market. Not only were investor rights and preferences protected and promoted in the 2014 reforms to the mining regime but the public rights of the state to legislate in its own interest were also curtailed, ironically, by state institutions themselves. 'Thresholds of legitimate behaviour' (Schneiderman, 2013: 35) based on the stability of the legal environment and principles of non-intervention in the minerals market were actually well above the minimum criteria for the recognition of the rule of law by a *national* state. However, as I have been arguing throughout this book, Mongolia's dependence on foreign capital has made the state vulnerable to processes of state transformation on the basis of transnational legal norms which privilege private-sector-led development, marketisation and political risk mitigation.

The legal dimension of Mongolia's extractive reordering is a fundamental part of what renders it "constitution-like":

> It holds separate the political and economic to ensure that the economic remains uncontaminated by the political, and the rule of law stands between them: markets are facilitated by the legal structures of property, contract and other laws… In this sense, the pre-commitment to the rule of law limits and shapes any subsequent reformist dynamic (May, 2014b: 153).

Where previously the Mongolian government promoted legal change in relation to the mining sector whilst maintaining a national conception of the rule of law, the post-2014 reforms implicitly presume the *stability* of the legal environment as a new criterion for the rule of law. In this sense, a version of the rule of law that privileges the stability of the investment environment functions as the new basic norm upon which the new extractive order rests. Citing Kelsen (1923/1998: 13), May (2014a: 65) argues that the sign of a basic norm, or *grundnorm,* is that it exists as "'the highest rule of law creation, establishing the unity of the entire system, [and] is indeed on hand for the issuance of other legal norms, but it must itself be assumed to be *presupposed* as a legal norm and not *issued* in accordance with other legal norms."' The stability of the investment environment has never been legislated explicitly, but it is the *a priori* intent, purpose and normative rationale for mining governance post-2014. This is a remarkable 'hidden' (ibid.: 69) constitutional development; this shift in the basic governing norm reflects a fundamental change in the legal normativity of state organisation and action. As May (ibid.) argues, citing Gill (1998: 25, 30), what is actually 'hidden' is not simply the emergence of a new normative basis for governance, but 'the manner in which powerful (class) interests shape the forms of political economic relations that *can* be established.'

## "It is our destiny to work with our neighbours": from geo-politics to geo-economics

The previous two dimensions of state transformation discussed were related to aspects of democratic 'undoing' (Brown, 2015) of the national state to prioritise foreign investment. The anti-political and anti-nationalist effects on law and politics are the more obvious implications of Mongolia's integration into the global minerals economy, but there is a third implication that I will briefly unpack that has been a more implicit theme in the book: how does the said integration reposition the Mongolian state in relation to other states? As the historical narrative of the Mongolian state (see Chapter 3) indicates, the formation of nation-states as distinct political entities is intrinsically linked with their international context: the state does not exist 'analytically prior' (Dunn, 2014: 24) to its relations with other states and societies. The 'coeval' (ibid.) development of societal and inter-societal formations means that major transformations "within" a state also entail a re-articulation of the state's social position "outside" of its national borders. When states are integrated into the global economy, the foundation of their "national" political economies becomes distinctly non-national in character (Dunn 2014: 23; Sassen, 2007), even though transnational capital is grounded by national institutions and jurisdiction. Thus, while there are distinct implications for Mongolia's democratic constitution on the one hand and its relative sovereignty within the inter-state system on the other, these are effects of the same *global* process of demarcating new boundaries for the state in relation to capital.

One of the main goals of Mongolian foreign policy since the post-socialist transition was to steer a path clear of its two neighbours – Russia and China – through alignment with Western powers. Mongolia's "Third Neighbour Policy" struck a delicate 'balance between its two neighbours... by declaring itself neutral as between Moscow and Beijing' (Wachman, 2010: 589), while reaching out to new allies. The negotiation of this balancing and distancing strategy was to 'avoid being subordinated to either of the two, whilst benefiting from the munificence and commercial opportunities each might provide' (ibid.). While not *overcoming* its asymmetrical position in relation to its neighbours, Mongolia carefully achieved relative autonomy in the 1990s and early 2000s. During this time, Mongolia was primarily indebted to international financial institutions, such as the World Bank, the IMF and the Asian Development Bank (Rossabi, 2005), and was a beneficiary of significant Euro-American aid, particularly from the U.S. and Germany.

However, dependence on minerals has inevitably led to a new *economic* imbalance in Mongolia's relationship with its neighbours, particularly China. Since 2012, China has commanded over 90% of Mongolia's mineral exports – up from 20% in the early 2000s (World Bank, 2019: 11) – and provided critical financial support during the investment crisis and commodity price slump (2012–2013) when FDI contracted. As examined in Chapter 4, the Mongolian government had taken on significant debt to expand energy and transport infrastructure, selling its first bonds on competitive debt markets in 2012 and 2013, the Chinggis and Samurai bonds. The Mongolian government was desperate for loan financing at the time, and had few other options. In 2011 and 2014, Mongolia and China entered into three-year currency swap agreements to maintain Mongolia's financial liquidity – worth USD 770 million and 2.18 billion, respectively – as its foreign currency reserves were dwindling, particularly after the FDI crisis in 2012–2013. As China is Mongolia's largest trading partner, the *yuan* can be used in relation to Mongolia–China trade settlements, thus protecting other foreign currency reserves. The swap agreements essentially function as a credit line to finance Mongolia's trade deficit. The Bank of China also set up an office in

Mongolia in 2013, which invests infrastructure, energy and mining companies. While the Bank of China has not opened an official branch, there are concerns about the devastating impact such a move could have on Mongolia's financial sector, which would easily be undercut by the lower interest rates of the Bank of China.

The increasing role of China in relation to Mongolia's debt burden and currency stability is part of the development of a "comprehensive strategic partnership" between the two states. Mongolia has strategic importance for China's Silk Road Economic Belt and Maritime Silk Road ("One Belt, One Road") project, which aims to expand and integrate economic regionalism in Eastern, Southeastern and Central Asia, as well as Eurasia through development finance and infrastructural expansion for regional trade networks. In 2013, the Central Committee of the Communist Party of China published a noteworthy decision, which explicitly highlights China's intention to deepen trade and financial ties with other countries in the region. In Article 26, Section VII of the Decision (cited in Tao, 2015), the Central Committee stated their intentions as follows:

> We will set up development-oriented financial institutions, accelerate the construction of infrastructure connecting China with neighbouring countries and regions, and work hard to build a Silk Road Economic Belt and a Maritime Silk Road, so as to form a new pattern of all round opening.

The plan 'to form a new pattern of all-round opening' dovetails with President Xi Jinping's promotion of Chinese development finance through the Asian Infrastructure Investment Bank. Mongolia's role in relation to the One Belt, One Road project lies in its central location between Russia and China. A proposed trilateral economic corridor linking Russia, Mongolia and China was the wider context for the 2016 Mongolia–China export agreement, as well as the creation of Free Trade Areas on the Mongolian–Chinese border to boost trade volumes up to USD 10 billion by 2020. In 2014, President Elbegdorj invited Xi Jinping and Vladimir Putin to Ulaanbaatar to engage in the first trilateral consultations. Only months later, a second consultation was held in Beijing to 'carry out comprehensive cooperation in fields of politics, economy, local governments, science and technology, people to people cultural exchanges, and international affairs' (Ministry of Foreign Affairs of the People's Republic of China, 2015). The Chinese Ministry of Foreign Affairs stated in their press release (ibid.) that these consultations were premised on the recognition of the 'necessity of formulating a trilateral cooperation road map and establishing an economic corridor among China, Russia and Mongolia.' On June 23rd 2016, a trilateral economic partnership agreement (EPA) was signed, which includes thirty-two proposed infrastructure, energy and mining projects as well as a joint investment centre to assess finance and feasibility issues.

Mongolia's relationship with China has been accelerated through pressing debt obligations as well as new commitments to non-discriminatory investment promotion under the 2014 reforms. While the 2012 Strategic Entities Foreign Investment Law sought to limit investment in strategic sectors (i.e. mining, energy and infrastructure) from Chinese state-owned enterprises, the new investment framework prevents the state from acting defensively against particular kinds of investment, such as from Chinese state-owned enterprises. While non-Chinese foreign investment was initially slow to respond to Mongolia's improved investment framework, China capitalised on Mongolia's debt crisis and its position as the only "game in town."

In my interviews with senior officials from the Ministry of Mining, a close relationship with China was seen as inevitable; in the terms of one senior policy-maker, 'it is our destiny to work with our neighbours.'[9] Mongolia was seen as gaining benefits from regional integration through access to expanded trade and investment networks. When asked about the potentially negative impact of Chinese economic influence for Mongolia in terms of its political effects on state sovereignty, the officials were reluctant to conflate the political and the economic dimensions of the burgeoning relationship between China and Mongolia: 'it's important to keep the political and the economic separate. They are different issues and Mongolia has a lot to benefit from its relationship with China.'[10]

Arguably, however, Mongolia actually has the most to lose from intensified "cooperation" with very little leverage. While there may be immediate economic benefits through regional economic integration, the cost is the state's relative *control* of its economy. The conceptual separation of the economic and the political begins to break down very quickly when the state concedes aspects of its *power* to govern a national economy and instead contributes its authority to a regional economic project. While Mongolia's participation in the One Belt, One Road project has not been coerced through violence, it has been "facilitated" by profound financial need. While Mongolia's borders are not at stake in a "political" sense (i.e. China is not "invading" Mongolian territory), a new territorial integration *is* emerging alongside deepening economic ties with China. Linking back to the discussion in the previous section about the false dualism between the political and the economic, the new geo-*economics* pursued by China and Mongolia really represents a reorganisation of inter-state power. While Mongolia retains its political independence, the state's economic power has become intertwined in a new way with its southern neighbour which has already begun to corrode the relative sovereignty that Mongolia had established in relation to its two neighbours following the post-socialist transition.

## The law of unintended consequences: perils in new patterns of state transformation

One might expect that the inculcation of a new market-friendly institutional framework within the apparatus of the state would lead to a new equanimity between the Mongolian state and foreign investors. That was, after all, the intention behind the reforms to the mining investment regime traced in this book.

At least some measure of renewed confidence can be evidenced by the sheer fact that levels of foreign investment have begun to resuscitate alongside the increase in global commodity prices. From the heights of USD 4.5 billion in 2011 to 100 million in 2015 and negative figures in 2016 as a result of the debt crisis (IFC, 2018: 15), the resurgence of FDI inflows in 2017 and 2018 – USD 1.4 billion and 2.1 billion, respectively – indicates a renewal of foreign investment interest (UNCTAD, 2019). It is not possible to say definitively if this is *actually* in response to the perception of legal stability or a product of global market trends,[11] or a combination of both, but it is safe to say that Mongolia's economy is regaining some buoyancy at the time of writing.

However, follow-up interviews and correspondence with foreign investors and former policy-makers, as well as analysis of investment climate reports by the IFC (2018) and the U.S. Department of State (2019) suggest that concerns remain, despite the fact that 'cosmetically, Mongolia seems to have the right laws in place.'[12] These concerns are largely focused upon the effects of patronage and elite corruption in influencing the alleged (dys)function of Mongolian capitalism and effective marketisation of the economy. As one foreign investor put it:

> The way that the [Mongolian] government– whether it's the politicians or the bureaucrats – and the way in which [Mongolian] company owners think about the process of ownership and capitalism is not one which respects those rules of the market.

One of the key concerns documented in the 2019 U.S. Department of State's Investment Climate Statement on Mongolia was the expropriation of 'domestic investor assets without compensation' (U.S. Department of State, 2019). While the statement acknowledged that Mongolia's market is 'largely free of access barriers' and that 'investors also face few meaningful investment restrictions in Mongolia, enjoying mostly unfettered access to the market' (ibid.), concerns were raised about two particular signals of investment instability. These relate to ongoing government flirtations with renegotiating the OTIA and a recent expropriation – without compensation – of one private domestic investor's shares in the Erdenet copper mine (ibid.), historically a joint venture operation between Russian and Mongolian state-owned mining companies. The 49% shares of Russia's Rostechnology company in the Erdenet copper mine were sold through an international tender to an unknown private Mongolian company – the Mongolian Copper Corporation (MCC) – in June 2016 (Boldsukh, 2018). These shares were consequently nationalised without compensation in March 2017, following heated political debates about the partial privatisation of one of Mongolia's key mineral assets. The administrative court ruled in April 2017 that this expropriation was illegal, a ruling that was consequently appealed by the government but upheld by the Supreme Court in December 2017 (ibid.).[13]

The murmurs about the potential renegotiation of the OTIA within domestic politics as well as expropriation of the private shares of the MCC have led to strong concerns that Mongolia has not really learned its lesson about respecting foreign investor perceptions of political risk. These concerns are well summarised in a quote from a subsequent interview with a foreign investor in Mongolia:

> And there's this whole issue of Erdenet… It suggests that there is no rule of law. It's basically a free for all in terms of taking control of these entities. I think a lot of people like me previously would have said, if we have 51% or more of whatever entity we're involved in, we have legal protection. But following the Erdenet thing, and it revolves around Oyu Tolgoi as well, that's not even clear… I'm not going to use the word pantomime but I am going to throw it out there… You can identify the networks which control this place.[14]

Concerns have become magnified in recent months with the adoption of emergency amendments to the Laws on the Legal Status of Judges, Public Prosecutor's Office and Anti-Corruption Agency on March 27th 2019. According to Transparency International (2019a), these amendments give new powers to the National Security Council (i.e., the Prime Minister, President and the Speaker of Parliament) to remove senior members of the judiciary, prosecutor's office and anti-corruption agency on recommendation from the Judicial Council (led by the President). The U.S. Department of State's 2019 Investment Climate Statement stated that this change 'effectively simplifies the President's ability to remove judges and prosecutors' (U.S. Department of State, 2019). In June 2019, seventeen judges were dismissed, following the removal of the two directors of the anti-corruption agency in May (Transparency International, 2019b).

It could be argued that these signals of ongoing unpredictability in the investment environment suggest that there is a gap between paper and practice when it comes to the process of TLO analysed in this book. There appear to be aspects of investment ease and stability which have not been delivered in practice, according to the IFC's Investment Reform Roadmap (2018). These narratives about Mongolia's ongoing "underperformance" when it comes to mitigating political risk (IFC, 2018: 48) frame domestic corruption and elite politics as the sole cause. Foreign investors and some policy actors would argue that the post-2013 reform process has essentially been stalled since 2016 by renewed populism and politicisation under the MPP,[15] as well as ongoing matters of elite corruption which cuts across both political parties, leading to continued frustration on the part of foreign investors.[16] However, the MPP has largely continued the DP's commitment to investment attraction through the establishment of the IPC and the passing of a Law on Legislation in 2016 following the ratification of a Transparency Agreement with the United States. Furthermore, in May 2019, Parliament also passed a decree following extensive lobbying efforts by Cameron McRae – former CEO-President of Oyu Tolgoi LLC – and the Business Council of Mongolia to establish a consultation committee of foreign investors that the government is legally obliged to consult before changing the investment regime.

Of notable concern to civil society organisations, this decree explicitly states that civil society organisations which contribute to destabilising the investment environment will be shut down.

Similarly, academic publications also emphasise elite behaviour, patterns of oligarchy and kinship networks in influencing the shape of Mongolian market practices (Sneath, 2018) as well as specific cultural attributes of Mongolian capitalism (Wheeler, 2004). Notably, these academic analyses of Mongolian capitalism – while very engaging in the terms of their focus on local specificities[17] – do not engage systematically with the way in which these specifics have emerged in a *transnational* context. While inevitably different academic disciplines and analytical lenses will tend to focus on one part of the transnational "string" (local, national, international, global), there is a risk of skewing the analysis of corruption as a "local" problem rather than understanding how it is produced in the context of global capitalism.

Consequently, the reason I have treated the corruption and political culture arguments which drive the "dysfunction narrative" with some caution is twofold. Firstly, such arguments tend to ignore the internationalisation of the state (Jayasuriya, 2001) and reinforce a bifurcated division between domestic and international. The production of a discourse of fault in the "domestic" state absolves the "international" market of its involvement in producing extrinsic legal and economic conditions for state transformation. Secondly, and relatedly, such an emphasis undermines analysis of the *interaction* between foreign and domestic capital dynamics which may have unintended consequences. Foreign investors and international financial institutions may want to get some credit for the reforms they view as positive following the crisis of investment (confidence), but will always lay the blame for the shadow side of the capitalist state at the door of "culture." The steps of transformation towards the regulatory state are applauded, but the more insidious flip-side of this coin is still framed as a purely domestic matter, scrutinised in order to further inculcate a deeper process of reform.

For example, the corruption narrative ignores the vociferous appetite of the investment climate discourse promulgated by the World Bank Group to continually identify an ever-widening set of market indicators which national governments should incorporate. Across these narratives of failure to "truly" reform, the (dys)function of the government is again under the microscope and the "fact" of the market – its rules, norms and values – implicitly treated as neutral, inevitable and mechanistic. The reforms taken since the investment crisis may be praised to a certain extent – 'Mongolia is among the most open economies for foreign investment in the East Asia Pacific Region' (IFC, 2018: 40) but there is (always) more work to be done. The more recent reform effort driven by the World Bank Group and key foreign investors is less focused on reform to the substantive laws of the mining and investment regime, but instead targets 'other constraints' which suggest that 'statutory (or de jure) openness is not sufficient' (IFC, 2018: 2). For example, the IFC's most recent 'investment reform map for Mongolia' (2018) emphasising 'a more conducive and friendly environment for private investment' through 'political stability and policy continuity,' 'transparency,' 'governance effectiveness' and 'accountability and regulatory quality' (ibid.: 6, 12, 47) reflects the elasticity of the World Bank's investment climate discourse (see Perry-Kessaris, 2008: 19–31). Now that the investment law, commercial code and mining law have been reformed quite satisfactorily, a new range of regulatory targets – previously on the margins of the reform drive – are being brought into centre stage.

Thus, another way of understanding the reform trajectory since foreign direct investment began to seriously decline in 2013 is not that it has stalled, but that a deep process of change is occurring to which there is inevitably some resistance by the state, as it continues to be constituted by the legitimacy perceptions of its domestic constituents. The echoes of resource nationalism at the national level are arguably a product of the current moment in the commodity price and debt repayment cycles, when such articulation does not existentially threaten the state with imminent contractions of financial crisis (given the resuscitation of FDI inflows). As another election cycle looms (June 2020), the government may very well be hedging its bets that the domestic constituency's preferences should take relative priority and relatively small risks may be taken with its international reputation. While the foreign investor's aforementioned quote highlights frustration with a government that seems to speak "double-tongue," the reality is that this is precisely the kind of political speech that global economic integration requires of states as governments must balance the perceptions of the public and foreign investors.

The bigger reality underpinning all of this domestic "pantomime" is that Mongolia's debt repayment schedule to the IMF will begin to bite in 2020, further inhibiting "populist" tendency of prospective governments to 'sway voters' through 'high public spending' (IFC, 2018: 12). Political *rhetoric* – rather than actual policy and legislative changes – and isolated incidences of "instability" do not form a sufficient evidence base to suggest that Mongolia is indeed recapitulating to "resource nationalism" or seeking to reverse the marketisation of the economy. What is far more telling is the distinctive lack of concrete variation between the policies supported by two main political parties. Whilst having the reputation as the more "nationalist" party, since 2016 the MPP has overall maintained the commitments and virtually identical institutional frameworks of its predecessor in power (the Democratic Party) to support private-sector-led economic development. The claims about rising nationalism need to be moderated by an analysis of the specific instances where expropriation without compensation has allegedly occurred: in relation to one *domestic* private investment (Mongolian Copper Company) and *Chinese* investment in the Tumurtei iron ore mine. Both of these instances of expropriation since 2016 are directly linked with domestic perceptions about the privatisation of state-owned assets and Chinese investment in Mongolian minerals, both highly contentious practices in the Mongolian (geo)political climate (notably given far less international legitimacy than the investment climate). Equally, it could sensibly be argued that the rumours of renegotiation of the OTIA are just that: political grandstanding to maintain a perception of control over Mongolia's most important mineral deposit to the public. Consequently, I have not taken the same view as many other international commentators about the "failure" of the reform process to produce meaningful change in the state. There has been a significant change on paper and in practice to create a more conducive environment for FDI, even if foreign investors and international financial institutions see the glass half full.

However, further research could meaningfully explore the subtle and not-so-subtle shifts to authoritarianism that have continued to grow under the MPP in the context of increasing state impoverishment and scrutiny from foreign investors and Mongolia's international debt financiers. Political elites within the state are increasingly acting outside of the legal frameworks created to facilitate FDI inflows and private capital formation. While the dominant international perspective is that this is a product of "kinship culture" and systems of patronage in Mongolia, I am more curious about the more nefarious effects of such a political culture's *interaction* with the effects of TLO associated with global economic integration. The systematic privatisation of national wealth since the 1990s combined with the erosion of national controls over the mining economy since the early 2000s has created a situation where the public power of the state has declined, in addition to becoming increasingly illegitimate in terms of taking a direct role in the economy. Consequently, it may well be the case that state institutions are increasingly becoming a vehicle for the interests of *private* power-holders, who increasingly use nefarious and illicit means to access capital in the context of the state's public impoverishment. Crucially, the mainstream discourse ignores the role of privatisation, marketisation and TLO in delegitimising the public power of the state and contributing to new opportunities for elite capture.

The limited scope of this particular study has not been able to fully address the entanglements between marketisation of the economy, internationalisation of the state and elite corruption. I hope that a spark curiosity will be lit in the mind of a critical corruption studies scholar to take Mongolia as a case study in order to explore these relationships in more detail. Against the grain of focusing on elite corruption in narrow domestic terms, I have sought to focus on the transnational context of state transformation and the introduction of competing legitimacy variables for the state in a way that might explain the simultaneous rise of authoritarianism alongside the embrace of pro-market reforms.

## Conclusion

In this chapter, I have attempted to deliver a more concise account of the broad-based processes of state change and transnational legal influence detailed in the book. The purpose of this chapter has been to summarise and weave together the analytical threads of the whole book and to develop some of the implications for democratic politics and law that are at stake in Mongolia's integration into the global minerals economy. Of course, only a limited amount of time has passed since the "crisis" of investor confidence, but already significant "symbolic" shifts are evident in Mongolian law and politics, alongside a demonstrable level of "practical" change within Mongolia's mining regime (Shaffer, 2014: 12). I will not belabour the point about the inter-connections between the different 'axes of reordering' described in this book, as the first half of this chapter and the earlier portions of the book have already gone to considerable lengths to make these connections self-evident to the reader.

All five dimensions of a TLO process (Shaffer, 2014) are evident in the Mongolian case as a result of the pro-investment "stability" consensus. These include: substantive legal reform in minerals and investment legislation; new scope for the market in relation to the state; the redistribution of institutional power to executive and administrative state institutions; an increase in the state's value of professional expertise and international standards; and new patterns of "multistakeholder" modes of association, between the state, investors/mining companies and civil society. These dimensions of reordering reflect the shift in power along the three key institutional axes analysed in the previous three chapters: within the central state; between the central state and local governments; and between the state and organised civil society. Designed to resurrect investor confidence after the collapse of FDI and beginnings of a debt crisis in 2012, these diverse mechanisms promote and guarantee the stability of the investment environment to varying degrees. Some aspects, such as national legal reform, have an immediate impact on the investment environment, while others, such as the promotion of tri-partite collaboration between state, corporate and civic actors, have more long-term normative implications. In either case, the combination of legislative and policy reform, a shifting discourse of state responsibility and the recalibration of strategic governance relations around the premise of depoliticising the mining sector suggest that a fairly holistic process of state transformation is underway in Mongolia.

## Notes

1 The increasing role of China in relation to Mongolia's debt burden and currency stability is part of the development of a 'comprehensive strategic partnership' between the two states (Turmunkh, 2016). Mongolia has strategic importance for China's Silk Road Economic Belt and Maritime Silk Road ("One Belt, One Road") project, which aims to expand and integrate economic regionalism in Eastern, Southeastern and Central Asia, as well as Eurasia through development of finance and infrastructural expansion for regional trade networks 'connecting China with neighbouring countries and regions' (Decision of the Central Committee of the Communist Party of China on Some Major Issues Concerning Comprehensively Deepening the Reform, Article 26, Section VII, cited in Tao 2015).
2 Personal communication, President of the Mongolian National Mining Association, February 2017).
3 After foreign investment continued to spiral downwards in 2014, Prime Minister N. Altankhuyag was ousted by a parliamentary vote of no-confidence on 5th of November. By the end of November, a new Prime Minister, C. Saikhanbileg, had been

appointed from the ranks of the Democratic Party and formed a 'super coalition' (Hornby, 2014) with the opposition (the Mongolian People's Party), the Justice Coalition and the Civil-Will Green Party to regain foreign investment and prevent further economic crisis. With foreign investment having dropped from USD 4.45 billion in 2012 to $508 million in 2014 (Kohn, 2015), a multi-party consensus emerged across the political spectrum to remove barriers for investors and to make evident Mongolia's commitment to supporting private-sector-led development of its minerals.

4  Author Interview, Director-General, Strategic Policy and Planning Department, Ministry of Mining, 27th October 2015.
5  Author interview, Head of Mining Division, Mineral Resources Authority of Mongolia, author interview, 17th November 2015.
6  Author interview, prominent NGO advocate, 13th November 2015.
7  Ibid.
8  Author interview, 15th July 2019.
9  Author interview, 9th November 2015.
10  Ibid.
11  See Perry-Kessaris, 2001 for a relevant analysis of the challenges of determining the actual drivers of foreign investor behaviour.
12  Author interview, 15th July 2019.
13  The ongoing legal dispute between the government and the courts over the legality of this nationalisation remains unresolved at the time of writing.
14  Ibid.
15  Author interview (follow-up), former mining policy-maker under the Democratic Party government (2013–2016), 13th June 2019.
16  Author interview, Foreign Investor, 15th July 2019.
17  See also Issue 3, Volume 37 (2018) on Capitalism in Mongolia in the Central Asian Survey journal for more academic contributions in this vein of analysis.

# References

Amartuvshin, A. 2016. "Mongolia Moves to Protect Foreign Investors." Lehman Law Blog. http://lehmanlaw.mn/blog/mongolia-moves-to-protect-foreign-investors/. Accessed 7th April 2017.
Anderson, G. 2005. *Constitutional Rights after Globalisation*. Oxford and Portland/OR: Hart Publishing.
Asian Barometer. 2016. "Survey Results by Topic: Detachment from Authoritarianism." Findings published online by the Centre for East Asia Democratic Studies. www.eastasiabarometer.org/survey/detachment-from-authoritarianism. Accessed 7th April 2017.
Benard, A. 2016. "Why Chinese Money is Not the Answer to Mongolia's Economic Woes." 20th October *The Diplomat* http://thediplomat.com/2016/10/why-chinese-money-is-not-the-answer-to-mongolias-economic-woes/. Accessed 7th April 2017.
Bhatt, K. Forthcoming. *Transnational Development Projects, Private Mechanisms and the Rule of Law: Implementing and Alienating Indigenous Peoples' Land Rights.* Cambridge: Cambridge University Press.
Boldsukh, D. 2018. "Supreme Court Says Cabinet Broke the Law in Seizing Minority Shares in Erdenet." 21st September *UB Post*. www.pressreader.com/mongolia/the-ub-post/20180921/281496457198706. Accessed 19th July 2019.
Brown, W. 2015. *Undoing the Demos: Neoliberalism's Stealth Revolution*. Boston, MA: MIT Press.

CRIRSCO (Committee for Mineral Reserves International Reporting Standards) 2017. "Welcome to CRIRSCO." www.crirsco.com/welcome.asp Accessed 7th April 2017.

Crick, B. 1962/1993. *In Defense of Politics 4th Edition*. Chicago, IL: University of Chicago Press.

Dunn, B. 2014. *The Political Economy of Global Capitalism and Crisis*. Abingdon: Routledge.

Ebner, A. 2011. "Transnational Markets and the Polanyi Problem". In C. Joerges and J. Falke (eds.) *Karl Polanyi, Globalisation and the Potential of Law in Transnational Markets*. Oxford/Portland, OR: Hart Publishing, pp. 19–40.

Edwards, T. 2017. "Mongolia Agrees $5.5 Billion Economic Bailout Plan with IMF, Others." 19th February *Reuters* www.reuters.com/article/us-mongolia-imf-idUSKBN15Y02S. Accessed 7th April 2017.

Gill, S. 1998. "New Constitutionalism, Democratisation and Global Political Economy." *Pacifica Review: Peace, Security and Global Change* 10(1): 23–38.

Held, D. 2006. *Models of Democracy*. 3rd Edition. Cambridge, UK: Polity Press.

Hogan Lovells.. 2013. "Mongolia Revises its Regulatory Framework for Foreign and Domestic Investment." www.hoganlovells.com/files/Uploads/Documents/13.11.01_F_Mongolia_revises_its_regulatory_framework_for_foreign_and_domestic_investment_October_2013.pdf. Accessed 7th April 2017.

Hogan Lovells. 2014. "Mongolia's 100-Day Plan: Legal Developments." www.lexology.com/library/detail.aspx?g=53d66f03-3561-418e-9652-78886c6b09eb. Accessed 7th April 2017.

Hornby, L. 2014. "Mongolia Politicians Form Super Coalition." 3rd December *Financial Times* www.ft.com/content/685e9f8a-7a8b-11e4-a8e1-00144feabdc0. Accessed 7th April 2017.

———. 2016. "Mongolia: Living from Loan to Loan." 9th December *Financial Times* www.ft.com/content/4055d944-78cd-11e6-a0c6-39e2633162d5. Accessed 2nd March 2017.

IFC. 2018. "Investment Reform Map for Mongolia." Washington, DC: World Bank Group.

IMA. 2014. *Investment Guide to Mongolia 2014*. Ulaanbaatar: Invest Mongolia Agency.

IPC. 2017. "IFC Helps Mongolia Strengthen Investment-Climate Reform and Restore Investor Confidence." Press Release 17th July www.ipc.gov.mn/news.php?n=18. Accessed 11th July 2019.

———. 2018. "Introduction: Investment Protection Council." www.ipc.gov.mn/news.php?n=10. Accessed 11th July 2019.

Jayasuriya, K. 2001. "Globalisation, Sovereignty, and the Rule of Law: From Political to Economic Constitutionalism?" *Constellations* 8(4): 442–460.

Kelsen, H. 1923/1998. "'Forward' to the Second Print of *Main Problems in the Theory of Public Law*.' In S. Paulson and B. Paulson (eds.) *Normativity and Norms: Critical Perspectives on Kelsenian Themes*. Oxford: Clarendon Press, pp. 3–22.

Kohn, M. 2015. "Mongolia PM Takes to TV and Texting to Win Back Investment." 5th April *Bloomberg* www.bloomberg.com/news/articles/2015-04-05/mongolia-s-leader-takes-to-tv-and-texting-to-win-back-investment. Accessed 7th April 2017.

Li, T. 2007. *The Will to Improve: Governmentality, Development and the Practice of Politics*. Durham, NC: Duke University Press.

May, C. 2014a. "The Rule of Law as the *Grundnorm* of the New Constitutionalism." In S. Gill and C. Cutler (eds.) *New Constitutionalism and World Order.* Cambridge: Cambridge University Press, pp. 63–79.

———. 2014b. *The Rule of the Law: The Common Sense of Global Politics.* Cheltenham, UK: Edward Elgar.

Ministry of Foreign Affairs of the People's Republic of China. 2015. "Vice Foreign Ministers of China, Russia and Mongolia Hold Second Consultation." 24th March 2015 www.fmprc.gov.cn/mfa_eng/wjbxw/t1248724.shtml. Accessed 27th May 2019.

Minter Ellison, LLC. 2014. "High Level Overview: Amendments to the 2006 Minerals Law." www.minterellison.com/files/uploads/documents/publications/articles/Pub_A_20142107_UB_Minteral_Law(2).pdf. Accessed 31st March 2017.

*Mongolian Economic Journal.* 2014. "The Newly Elected Prime Minister's Economic Policy." 26th November *Mongolian Economic Journal* http://mongolianeconomy.mn/en/i/7019. Accessed 7th April 2017.

National Development Agency. 2017. "Your Guide to Invest in Mongolia 2017." Ulaanbaatar: National Development Agency/Bank of Mongolia. http://nda.gov.mn/backend/f/LlR2IRPVYj.pdf?id=14. Accessed 31st May 2019.

———. 2019. "Your Guide to Invest in Mongolia 2019." Ulaanbaatar: National Development Agency/Invest in Mongolia.

Otgochuluu, Ch. 2016. "Mongolia's State Policy on the Minerals Sector and Its Application in the Promotion of Sustainable Development." *Law in Transition Journal* 2016: 66–75.

Oxford Business Group. 2015. "Mongolia's Mining Sector Awaits Key Rules for Implementation of Legal Reform." www.oxfordbusinessgroup.com/analysis/legal-reform-industry-awaiting-number-key-implementing-rules Accessed 7th April 2017.

Perry-Kessaris, A. 2001. *Legal Systems as a Determinant of Foreign Direct Investment: Lessons from Sri Lanka.* The Hague: Kluwer Law International.

Polanyi, K. 1944/2001. *The Great Transformation: The Political and Economic Origins of Our Time.* 2nd Edition. Boston, MA: Beacon Press.

Robbins, A. B. and Smith, G. 2014. "Case Study: World Bank Engagement with Mongolia's Sovereign Wealth Fund." World Bank Brief. http://documents.worldbank.org/curated/en/450721468060545662/pdf/858180BRI0REPL00Box382147B00PUBLIC0.pdf Accessed 7th April 2017.

Rossabi, M. 2005. *Mongolia: From Khans to Commissars to Capitalists.* Berkeley, CA: University of California Press.

Santos, B. de S., and Avritzer, L. 2007. "Introduction: Opening Up the Canon of Democracy." In B. de S. Santos (ed.) *Democratising Democracy: Beyond the Liberal Democratic Canon.* London/New York: Verso.

Sassen, S. 2007. *The Sociology of Globalisation.* London/New York: W. W. Norton & Co.

Scharaw, B. 2018. *The Protection of Foreign Investments in Mongolia: Treaties, Domestic Law, and Contracts on Investments in International Comparison and Arbitral Practice.* New York: Springer International Publishing.

Schneiderman, D. 2008. *Constitutionalising Economic Globalisation: Investment Rules and Democracy's Promise.* Cambridge: Cambridge University Press.

———. 2013. *Resisting Economic Globalisation: Critical Theory and International Investment Law.* Basingstoke, Hampshire/New York: Palgrave Macmillan.

Shaffer, G. 2014. *Transnational Legal Ordering and State Change.* Cambridge: Cambridge University Press.

Sneath, D. 2018. "Afterword: Mongolian-made Capitalism." *Central Asian Survey* 37(3): 475–483.

Spicer, M. W. 2010. *In Defense of Politics in Public Administration: A Value Pluralist Perspective.* Tuscaloosa: University of Alabama Press.

Surenjav, O. and Buxbaum, D. C. 2015. "Mongolia." In La Fléche, R. A. (ed.) *The Mining Law Review.* 4th Edition. London: Law Business Research Ltd, pp. 322–334.

Tao, X. 2015. "Is China's 'Belt and Road' a Strategy?" 16th December *The Diplomat* http://thediplomat.com/2015/12/is-chinas-belt-and-road-a-strategy/ Accessed 26th February 2017.

Transparency International. 2019a. "Parliament of Mongolia Should Uphold the Independence of the Judiciary and the Anti-Corruption Agency." www.transparency.org/ news/pressrelease/parliament_of_mongolia_should_uphold_the_independence_of_ the_judiciary. Accessed 19th July 2019.

———. 2019b. "Rule of Law and Independence of the Judiciary under Threat in Mongolia." www.transparency.org/news/pressrelease/rule_of_law_and_independence_ of_judiciary_under_threat_in_mongolia. Accessed 19th July 2019.

Turmunkh, B. 2016. "China Seeks Fruitful Cooperation with Mongolia." 3rd October *UB Post* http://theubpost.mn/2016/10/03/china-seeks-fruitful-cooperation-with-mongolia/. Accessed 5th February 2017.

UNCTAD. 2019. "World Investment Report: Mongolia." https://unctad.org/sections/ dite_dir/docs/wir2019/wir19_fs_mn_en.pdf. Accessed 19th July 2019.

U.S. State Department. 2019. "2019 Investment Climate Statements: Mongolia." www. state.gov/reports/2019-investment-climate-statements/mongolia/. Accessed 19th July 2019.

Wachman, A. M. 2010. "Suffering What It Must? Mongolia and the Power of the Weak.'" *Orbis* 54(4): 583–602.

Wheeler, A. 2004. *Moralities of the Mongolian 'Market': A Genealogy of Trade Relations and Zah Zeel.* Cambridge: Cambridge University Press.

White, S. 1996. "Depoliticising Development: The Uses and Abuses of Participation." *Development in Practice* 6(1): 6–15.

Wood, E. M. 1995. *Democracy against Capitalism: Renewing Historical Materialism.* London/New York: Verso Books.

Woolley, A. 2015. "Legal Developments and Upcoming Legislative Agenda." Hogan Lovells presentation prepared for 9th Annual Frontier Conference 8th–9th September 2015, Ulaanbaatar www.frontier-conference.com/tokyo/index.php/download/ category/19-presentations?download=63:1120-presentation-general-legal-update-in-mongolia-hogan-lovells. Accessed 7th April 2017.

World Bank. 2019. "Mongolia: Systematic Country Diagnostic." Washington, DC: World Bank Group. http://documents.worldbank.org/curated/en/576101543874150141/ Mongolia-Systematic-Country-Diagnostic. Accessed 1st July 2019.

Xinhua. 2019. "Mongolia Launches One-Stop Service Centre for Foreign Investors." 22nd February *Xinhua* www.xinhuanet.com/english/2019-02/22/c_137842846. htm. Accessed 11th July 2019.

# Chapter 8

# Reflecting on material constitutional change in Mongolia

## Seeing the forest for the trees

The twin purposes of the book have been (a) to narrate the political and legal ripple effects of global economic integration across national and local scales, and (b) to demonstrate how seemingly disparate changes in governance are, in fact, connected and constitutional in nature. The Mongolian experience provides an empirically informed example of state transformation in a global era based on a tangible encounter between the national state and transnational processes of investment, highlighting the critical role of the state in securing broad-based constitutional conditions for the expansion of global markets. The fundamental inter-dependency between state, market and law in capitalist political economy is particularly revealed in contexts where the state *imports* capital; the limited room for manoeuvre for the role of the state in Mongolia's mining economy highlights the relationship between the centrality of capital-access and the range of policy options available. For those in the Mongolian context, I hope that the theoretical framework offered in this book helps in some way to explain the real significance of "tedious," "random" or "political" reforms to the mining regime over the past twenty years. For those interested in studying other jurisdictions, the analytical framework of relational "axes" both within and beyond the state provides a novel conceptual basis to connect policy and legislative change with the material constitution of state power.

In this sense, the Mongolian case study is not unique. Virtually, every other "frontier economy" in the Global South has experienced the vicissitudes of global economic crisis, as well as the effects of the 'investment climate discourse' (Perry-Kessaris, 2008: 3) which marshal and mobilise the global governance technologies of regulatory indicators, technical assistance projects, credit ratings and debt financing legitimised and localised by the regular suspects of 'meta-regulation' (ibid.: 21–22; Morgan, 2003; Perry-Kessaris, 2011: 406; see also Hatcher, 2014). Meta-regulation broadly refers to the embedding of national policy and legislation within a governance framework committed to a particular regulatory goal with its own reflexive mechanisms for enforcement (see Morgan, 2003: 2), which bears strong resemblance to liberal constitutionalisation:

> Just as constitutions place extra-political constraints on the lawmaking process, so too meta-regulation places a different kind of extra-political constraint on law-making.
>
> (ibid.: 35)

Notably, when it comes to institutionalising market economies in the Global South, market "meta-regulation" has been routinely facilitated by the World Bank Group, amongst other international financial institutions, which promote a 'culture of rule-making' where national policy and legislative 'outputs' (ibid.: 23) are assessed in terms of 'economic values, such as efficiency, competition and cost-benefit analysis' (ibid.: 37 cited in Perry-Kessaris, 2008: 21). However, these are only a limited sub-set of possible values that one could attach to a national legal system (ibid.: 12), and the preferences of a relatively small number of foreign investors should, by no means, dominate the mining regime, given that the state is, at least in theory, constitutionally obligated to attend to and balance an array of political demands and regulatory goals. As Perry-Kessaris (ibid.: 29) notes, 'little thought is spared for the idea that the interests of investment actors – local or foreign – might be seen as wholly or partly incompatible with those of others.'

The influence of these meta-regulating processes, as well as the meso and micro aspects of their domestication, are more visible in a place where (a) there is a simultaneously deep process of 'market-building' (Carroll, 2012) occurring in a legal and political system that has, until the 1990s, been relatively insulated from the vagaries of the global economy, *and* (b) a relatively effective democratisation of state institutions has taken place. While many countries in the Global South could be said to be in category A, the opacity of many institutional systems makes concrete constitutional effects difficult to identify. The extremity of the economic crisis combined with the relative openness of the political system in Mongolia offers 'a clarification, just as the addition by a computer of "extreme" colours to a remote scanning image does not distort but "enhances" the photograph by improving the visibility of the phenomena we are interested in' (Ferguson, 1990: 257–258).

The Mongolian case study thus offers a unique insight into the constitutional stakes of global economic integration, as well as the power of investor perceptions in terms of constructing a legitimacy crisis which drives law reform in states that are FDI-dependent. Each major shift in the organisation of economic production in the territory of Mongolia has enabled and been enabled by a reorganisation of state power, reinforcing the co-constitutive pattern of relations of production and state. The 'instituted' nature of economic systems in general (Polanyi, 1957: 248) makes a historical analysis of power and production not only interesting, but a vital component to understanding the meaning and implications of any current development. There is a clear historical relationship between Mongolia's pursuit of extractive development on global terms, the selective restructuring of national and local governance, and the introduction of legal norms and forms which enhance regulatory security for capital investment.

The impact of these shifting economic, political and legal relations can be seen at formal constitutional intersections in the national state, notably between the legislature and the executive branches, and between central and local administrations. The claim in Mongolia's 1992 Constitution that the state will promote diverse modes of economic development based on different conceptions of property rings hollow, in light of recent historical reality. State institutions and actors appear to have accepted global market terms to exploit Mongolia's natural resources. In the attempt to purge nationalist, "risky" politics from Mongolia's mining regime, the promotion of a neoliberal ideology of the rule of law and the internalisation of a discourse of stability and certainty amongst policy elites, we can certainly deduce a "constitution-like" demarcation of the economic from the political, *constraining* state power in certain directions.

In this sense, the book contributes to the literature on new constitutionalism, which identifies a globally operative structure for the global market, cutting across regional, national and local scales (Cutler, 2015: 89). Extrinsic governance actors and institutions (i.e. multinational corporations, multilateral financial institutions and transnational civil society) have exercised a tremendous degree of influence in bringing norms derived from the lexicon of international investment and commercial law related to stability, predictability and certainty to bear on Mongolia's mining governance regime. In the process of negotiating its relationship with the owners and enablers of foreign capital investment, the state has internalised market-enabling regulatory preferences. There is a clear historical relationship between the discursive construction of "resource nationalism" by transnational proponents of FDI and the tangible production of crisis in Mongolia's financial system coinciding with the quelling of openly nationalist or "politicised" sources of resistance to the global terms of extractive development.

This phenomenon clearly demonstrates the way in which the uneven outcomes of economic globalisation depend upon the capacity of the state to negotiate the discursive and psychological dimensions of capital investment (i.e. to maintain confidence) as well as its mechanisms (i.e. to maintain actual capital flows) (Schneiderman, 2013: 35; Streeck, 2014: 23). The value of the case study in relation to the new constitutionalism literature is its demonstration in quite stark terms of the *extrinsic* disciplinary power of global economic mechanisms and associated legal structures of foreign direct investment against states when they do not cooperate with the expectations of foreign investors and multilateral financial institutions (Streeck, 2014: 23). New constitutionalists would likely argue that the value of the Mongolian case study lies in its capacity to explicate 'how transnational legal norms effectively institutionalise pathologies associated with neoliberalism, thereby legally constraining alternative paths to development'

(Schneiderman, 2013: 6). From an extrinsic perspective, focusing on the role of international norms and actors we can see the limiting and constraining effects of transnational legal ordering in relation to public government.

However, overemphasis on the extrinsic story risks reinforcing a clearer distinction between national and global economic processes than what exists in reality (Jayasuriya, 2001). In order to actually 'illuminate precisely the circumstances and the means by which transnational legality operates' (Schneiderman, 2013: 6), the book has offered a detailed account of the creative responses by policy elites to resolve the conflict between economic nationalism and globalism. Not only are these agents largely responsible for internalising and interpreting the regulatory preferences of external market actors through institutional change, but in the process of doing so, they shift the practices of state governance in new directions. The adoption of new modalities of governance within the state to enhance market-based accumulation, ease access to natural resources and engender new collaborative relations between public institutions, corporations and NGOs suggests material constitutional change. Recalling the approach to material constitutionalism put forward in Chapter 1 of this book, the material constitution refers to the coupling of legal ordering and political authority which produces the grain against, around and through 'want satisfying material means' (Polanyi, 1957: 248) are produced and accumulated (i.e. the economy). The material constitution is the lynchpin of the political, economic and legal order that is privileged within the jurisdiction of the state.

The reconfiguration of relations between state, market and civil society into a new rubric fundamentally oriented around producing stable conditions for market-based resource extraction crucially institutionalises a new degree of "reciprocity" between systems of national state power and market-based production in Mongolia (Cox, 1987:1). As evidenced towards the end of Chapter 3 and in Chapter 4, the collapse of the Soviet Union and the transition to "market democracy" dramatically shifted the terms of socialist constitutionalism. The rapid disembedding of the economy from political controls in the early 1990s, particularly signified by the deregulation of the pastoral economy, evidenced a constitutional upheaval in both *de jure* and *de facto* terms. The 1992 democratic constitution reflected the ideological and political tensions at the time regarding the state's role in the pursuit of economic development. While the state swallowed the terms of structural adjustment "hook, line and sinker" by adopting the political, legal and economic institutions associated with market democracy, there was still – in practice – a disjuncture between the new market economy and state governance. If the 1990s can be characterised by a period of constitutional upheaval, with a direction of travel but many unresolved questions regarding the shape of the new social order, the race for Mongolia's minerals in the early 2000s brought these issues to the fore.

As discussed in Chapter 4, the relationship between the state and foreign capital was tested by a series of legal developments between 2006 and 2012. While the text of these legal developments is interesting in itself, as discussed, the wider political and economic context in Mongolia as well as the global commodities market explains why the revisions to the minerals, investment and environmental laws were so controversial. The democratisation of the state and the marketisation of the economy in the early 1990s had introduced two potentially competing dimensions of legitimation for the state to contend with. State government depended in a new way upon the direct electoral support of the Mongolian public. The democratic overhaul of the national constitution not only instituted representative systems of government, but freed the media as well as civil society to openly criticise the state. While one could argue that even authoritarian governments still depend on public legitimation to some degree, the Mongolian state no longer could use open tactics of repression and control to address legitimation gaps.

In addition to the national public, the opening up of Mongolia's economy to the influence of *global* market forces introduced a new dimension of legitimation. The impoverishment of the state through the collapse of the Soviet Union and consequent privatisation of national assets meant that the state became heavily dependent on foreign capital to effectively embark on its new development strategy in natural resource extraction. Consequently, elected governments not only had to manage the Mongolian public's expectations, but also those investing foreign capital into the sector. The Mongolian public could withdraw political support for the governance regime through voting, activism and public-opinion forming strategies (i.e. media campaigns), and foreign investors could withdraw their capital and target government policies through international media campaigns, reinforced by the activities of IFIs and international financial markets.

From 2006 to 2012, we can see the tension building as governments prioritised national interests within the mining regime, while rapidly losing legitimacy amongst foreign investors. In particular, investors' ire was provoked by measures which (a) designated some mineral deposits as "nationally strategic" (thereby permitting direct state participation as a shareholder), (b) introduced new screening requirements for investment, (c) limited further mining licences and (d) increased taxation and royalty levies. The attempted renegotiation of a major investment agreement over the Oyu Tolgoi deposit, and the cancellation or freezing of many mining licences under new anti-corruption and environmental measures in 2011 further frustrated the mining sector as signs of 'creeping expropriation' (Schneiderman, 2005: 847) and nationalism. By 2013, almost every international business or financial analysis of Mongolia's mining economy was saturated with predictions of economic failure and investment withdrawal unless the state curbed its "nationalist" legal reforms and policy-making.

The coincidence of declining global commodity prices with declining investor confidence produced a financial crisis that reverberated across the Mongolian economy, as discussed in Chapter 4. This economic crisis, and the crisis of public confidence in the government which followed, provided an opportunity to bring the political and legal regimes governing the extractive sector into line with the global market system of production and accumulation. Both the Mongolian public and transnational investors blamed the state for mismanaging the economy, giving a degree of alignment between previously opposing forces of legitimation, and policy elites and political leaders used the narrative of crisis to restructure the mining regime so that it would support and expand the marketisation of Mongolia's natural resources.

It is no small matter that the interests and rights of a transnational *economic* constituency have been inscribed into national law in Mongolia. The inordinate influence of investor preferences, powerfully reinforced by the very real prospect of economic crisis, on the trajectory of law reform in Mongolia's mining regime reflects a new hierarchy between the state's national and 'supraterritorial' (Scholte, 1997: 430) constituencies. In the political and economic fall-out of the crisis of investment, debt and confidence in Mongolia's mining regime, we can see the state functioning as a 'site of strategic action' (Jessop, 1990: 10), clearly privileging 'some strategies over others... the access of some forces over others, some interests over others, some time horizons over others, some coalition possibilities over others.' The way in which investor *perceptions* about the stability and legitimacy of Mongolia's mining regime have become inculcated within the symbolic and practical dimensions of national governance suggests the triumph of a particular set of normative values associated with "economics imperialism," those which glorify markets and prioritise the reduction of transaction costs (see Perry-Kessaris, 2011: 403–410). The reductive assessment of Mongolia's legal system in terms of the benefits and stability which it offers for foreign investors signifies not only the marketisation of the economy but of the legal system itself. Perry-Kessaris (ibid.: 408) reflects on one of the key "marks" of such marketisation thus:

> The first mark is left on our understanding of what law is for. When we think of legal systems as commodities, and investors as their main audience, we devalue, or even forget about, the other "sacred" social functions of law.

This is not to say that the relationship between the state and investors is not a relevant consideration, but it is, by no means, the only or most important one from a national perspective. When it comes to natural resource extraction, the state has a variety of considerations that *should* arguably feature in the legal frameworks produced at the national level. The law mediates the relationship not only between the investor and the state, but also between the Mongolian public and the state, in addition to the multiple interests and institutions within the domestic milieu (e.g. civil society organisations, sub-national governments). In this sense, national law should be understood as a 'communal resource' (Perry-Kessaris, 2008: 13, citing Cotterrell, 2002: 643). Making the investor–state relationship the primary reference point for legal developments in the national mining regime overextends the legitimate influence of this particular group, particularly because its influence clearly comes at the expense of the values and priorities of others with a serious "stake" in the matter.

The theoretical framework of material constitutionalism captures the significance of such "marks" of change within the legal and political architectures of the state wrought by market-building processes. The constitutional implications of making a global market-friendly mining regime in Mongolia – in both normative and empirical terms – are significant. Fundamentally, the trajectory of governance conflicts with the formal constitution's normative commitments relating to state sovereignty (Article 1), the vesting of state power in citizens alone (Article 3) and support for pluralistic modes of property and strategies of economic development (Article 5). It also establishes – without formal constitutional deliberation – a new practical balance between the principles of central and sub-national government. The disjuncture between the formal and material constitutions is reinforced by observations of the significant shift in modalities of governance, as executive power has been institutionally strengthened at both the central and local levels of national governance, and civil society engagement has been channelled into collaborative, market-enhancing mechanisms of governance, as discussed in Chapters 5 and 6. Beyond any "limit" or "constraint" on state power, transnational processes of legal and economic ordering have given internal agents of state change the opportunity to increase the scope of executive power within the state, as well as provide opportunities for the private sector to directly influence governance.

In addition to increasing the responsibilities of executive institutions and agencies within the state in relation to the extractive sector and changing the terms of engagement between the state and mining-critical civil society, the introduction of new means and modes of recognition for Mongolian citizens impacted by natural resource extraction is constitutionally significant. It speaks to a new era in the relationship of governance, between the governing and the governed, as the national state facilitates new transnational modes of dispute resolution, benefit negotiation and recognition in sub-national sites of extractive activity. While stakeholder-based models of participation and benefit sharing may open up new degrees of voice and access to resources in some cases, these new modalities of socio-environmental governance displace citizenship as the key trigger for recognition. Participation in new corporate-driven governance mechanisms relies upon the capability of individuals and groups to make an argument that they hold a distinctive and sufficient stake in decision-making processes about the socio-environmental impacts of mining. These individuals and groups are often facilitated to participate in multi-stakeholder mechanisms by donor agencies as well as NGOs, which mediate access to participatory platforms.

The marked change in the basis of Mongolia's economy away from national industrialisation towards a globalised mode of production based on FDI and exports, the attendant shifts in the state's political and legal coordinating apparatus for a new mode economic governance, and the recalibration of state–society relations points to the construction of a new constitutional settlement. Beyond the demarcation of a public–private divide or limits on state power, the Mongolian state is evidently securing, through its regulatory apparatus, a new configuration of global market-supporting legal, political and economic relations. The active construction of a new overarching foundation and frame for governance relations, based on global competitiveness and certainty for markets, suggests not only a process of state transformation but a corresponding shift in the material constitution secured by the state. While the material constitution is shaped by processes that exceed the scale of the national state (i.e. global economic patterns and transnational legality), the state plays the crucial function of securing 'the cohesion of the social formation of which it is merely a part' (Jessop, 2008: 7). Consequently, the book offers a detailed empirical case study about the tangible constitutional effects of participation in the contemporary paradigm of development premised upon deeply neoliberal social projects of state transformation and market-building. Thus, in addition to addressing the growing debates about global constitutionalism, the book speaks to critical examinations of what may lie "beyond" the post-Washington Consensus in development studies (see Carroll, 2012).

The creation of a legal and institutional framework which enables foreign capital flows by removing national barriers to investment involves a substantial 'denationalisation' of state functions and the 'internationalisation' or 'globalisation' of mining law and policy (Jessop, 1999: 7, 10), as the Mongolian state consolidates an overall positive orientation with global market capitalism. 'Denationalisation,' in Jessop's (ibid.: 7) terms, 'involves the active re-articulation of the various functions of the national state' (ibid.), such as 'shifts in the relative power of the executive, legislature, and judiciary... [and] the reordering of relations among different political tiers' (ibid.). In addition to the 'structural' (ibid.: 6) aspects of denationalisation, 'internationalisation' (ibid.: 10) concerns the 'strategic orientation [of the state] and the changing nature of policy-making.' More specifically, it refers

> to the increased strategic significance of the international context of domestic state action and the latter's extension to a wide range of extraterritorial and transnational factors and processes. It involves both a change in the balance of the state's strategic orientations to different scales of political action and a change in the relative importance of national and international sources of policy. This shift blurs the distinction between domestic and foreign policy, and widens the territorial bases of actors who are either directly involved in decision-making and/or whose opinions and likely reactions are taken into account.
>
> (ibid.: 10)

However, the "economic" frame of Mongolia's mining transformation disguises its profound constitutional dimensions, making it all too easy for the deeper implications of Mongolia's globalised mining economy to be ignored or not even recognised. While no formal constitutional reform has been officially made, the substance of law and politics, as well as the scope of national autonomy in relation to foreign capital, have been significantly altered by the FDI crisis and its denouement. Notably, the transformation of governance norms and relations has been largely implemented by state actors and institutions, reinforcing the point that 'as institutions, national states are becoming deeply involved in the implementation of the global economic system' (Sassen, 2007: 33). Importantly, however, Sassen notes that, depending on the outcome of the 'negotiations between the global and the national' (ibid.: 22), there is a change in 'the meaning of the state's exclusive authority over that territory' (ibid.: 33). While Sassen does not use the term, the idea of a change in the 'meaning' (ibid.) of the political and legal authority of the state relates precisely to *constitutional* change. Whether the constitutional is construed in terms of practical limits to particular types of state power, the legitimation of new modes and expressions of social ordering or even the gap between the material constitution and the formal legal constitution, the concept of material constitutionalism opens our eyes to perceive the wider forest of governance patterns through the trees.

Finally, the Mongolian experience is an important lesson for other jurisdictions about the contradictory messages about democracy that accompany so-called natural resource-based "development." On paper, democracy, participation and the political voice of local communities are seen in mainstream development policy as good and essential elements of governance. But in practice, political engagement at both the national and local levels is consistently castigated by foreign investors, corporations and development financial institutions for generating instability and risk for the market. The international delegitimisation of national politics and democracy in the name of development gives rising authoritarianism a further foothold within the state. Two of the key consequences of transnational legal ordering described in this book have been the deepening centralisation of control over the mining sector and the privileging of bureaucratic, executive power. In order to systematically access a new resource frontier in Mongolia, foreign investors have consistently pushed for depoliticised (i.e. insulated from the vagaries of democratic influence) central institutions to administrate the mining regime and for sub-national and civic influence to be curtailed. Consequently, it should be no surprise that alongside the deeper inculcation of neoliberal governance that supports FDI and global exposure of Mongolia's mining economy, we can see the rise of more authoritarian forms of rule that undermine political opposition and even judicial independence. Mongolia's 'vibrant democracy' (U.S. State Department, 2019) has been so routinely problematised as a source of instability by investment climate activists that I cannot help but wonder at the irony now that Mongolia's democracy does appear to be pulling apart at the seams (see Chapter 7).

While the 'ideal paradigm' of market-based regulation (Perry-Kessaris, 2001) animates processes of transnational legal ordering to make the state into an effective facilitator and enabler of markets, the long-term effects may be much more insidious than anticipated, and *almost* impossible to untangle. Despite the rhetoric of freedom and prosperity, the pressure to continually expand markets and mitigate investment risk invites new forms of unchecked, authoritarian power as state institutions adapt to and seek competitiveness within our global capitalist environment. One should be careful what one wishes for when it comes to transforming the state in the image of the market.

## References

Carroll, T. 2012. "Introduction: Neo-Liberal Development Policy in Asia beyond the Post-Washington Consensus." *Journal of Contemporary Asia* 42(3): 350–358.

Cotterrell, R. 2002. "Subverting Orthodoxy, Making Law Central: A View of Socio-Legal Studies." *Journal of Law and Society* 29(4): 632–644.

Cox, R. 1987. *Power, Production and World Order: Social Forces in the Making of History.* New York: Columbia University Press.

Cutler, C. 2015. "New Constitutionalism, Democracy and the Future of Global Governance". In S. Gill (ed.) *Critical Perspectives on the Crisis of Global Governance.* Basingstoke, Hampshire/New York: Palgrave Macmillan, pp. 89–104.

Ferguson, J. 1990. *The Anti-Politics Machine: Development, Depoliticisation and Bureaucratic Power in Lesotho.* Minneapolis: University of Minnesota Press.

Hatcher, P. 2014. *Regimes of Risk: The World Bank and the Transformation of Mining in Asia.* New York/London: Palgrave Macmillan.

Jayasuriya, K. 2001. "Globalisation, Sovereignty, and the Rule of Law: From Political to Economic Constitutionalism?" *Constellations* 8(4): 442–460.

Jessop, B. 1990. *State Theory: Putting Capitalist States in Their Place.* Cambridge: Polity Press.

———. 1999. "Narrating the Future of the National Economy and the National State? Remarking on Remapping Regulation and Reinventing Governance." Working Paper, Department of Sociology, Lancaster University. www.comp.lancs.ac.uk/sociology/papers/Jessop-Narrating-the-Future.pdf. Accessed 8th July 2019.

———. 2008. *State Power: A Strategic-Relational Approach.* Cambridge: Polity Press.

Morgan, B. 2003. *Social Citizenship in the Shadow of Competition: The Bureaucratic Politics of Regulatory Justification.* Dartmouth: Ashgate.

Perry-Kessaris, A. 2001. *Legal Systems as a Determinant of Foreign Direct Investment: Lessons from Sri Lanka.* The Hague: Kluwer Law International.

———. 2008. *Global Business, Local Law: The Indian Legal System as a Communal Resource in Foreign Investment Relations.* Aldershot, Hampshire and Burlington, VT: Ashgate Publishing Company.

———. 2011. "Prepare Your Indicators: Economics Imperialism on the Shores of Law and Development." *International Journal of Law in Context* 7(4): 401–421.

Polanyi, K. 1944/2001. *The Great Transformation: The Political and Economic Origins of Our Time.* 2nd Edition. Boston, MA: Beacon Press.

———. 1957. "The Economy as Instituted Process." In K. Polanyi, C. M. Arensberg, and H. W. Pearson (eds.) *Trade and Market in the Early Empires.* Chicago, IL: Henry Regnery Company.

Sassen, S. 2007. *The Sociology of Globalisation.* London/New York: W. W. Norton & Co.

Schneiderman, D. 2005. "Banging Constitutional Bibles: Observing Constitutional Culture in Transition." *University of Toronto Law Journal* 55: 833–852.

———. 2013. *Resisting Economic Globalisation: Critical Theory and International Investment Law.* Basingstoke, Hampshire/New York: Palgrave Macmillan.

Scholte, J. A. 1997. "Global Capitalism and the State." *International Affairs* 73(3): 427–452.

Streeck, W. 2014. *Buying Time: The Delayed Crisis of Democratic Capitalism.* London/New York: Verso Books.

U.S. State Department. 2019. "2019 Investment Climate Statements: Mongolia." www.state.gov/reports/2019-investment-climate-statements/mongolia/ Accessed 19th July 2019.

# Index

Note: Bold page numbers refer to tables

Printed in the United States
by Baker & Taylor Publisher Services